Java Transaction Processing

Design and Implementation

Hewlett-Packard® Professional Books

HP-UX

Cooper/Moore	HP-UX 11i Internals
Fernandez	Configuring CDE
Madell	Disk and File Management Tasks on HP-UX
Olker	Optimizing NFS Performance
Poniatowski	HP-UX 11i Virtual Partitions
Poniatowski	HP-UX 11i System Administration Handbook and Toolkit, Second Edition
Poniatowski	The HP-UX 11.x System Administration Handbook and Toolkit
Poniatowski	HP-UX 11.x System Administration "How To" Book
Poniatowski	HP-UX 10.x System Administration "How To" Book
Poniatowski	HP-UX System Administration Handbook and Toolkit
Poniatowski	Learning the HP-UX Operating System
Rehman	HP-UX CSA: Official Study Guide and Desk Reference
Sauers/Ruemmler/Weygant	HP-UX 11i Tuning and Performance
Weygant	Clusters for High Availability, Second Edition
Wong	HP-UX 11i Security

UNIX, LINUX, WINDOWS, AND MPE I/X

Mosberger/Eranian	IA-64 Linux Kernel
Poniatowski	UNIX User's Handbook, Second Edition
Stone/Symons	UNIX Fault Management

COMPUTER ARCHITECTURE

Evans/Trimper	Itanium Architecture for Programmers
Kane	PA-RISC 2.0 Architecture
Markstein	IA-64 and Elementary Functions

NETWORKING/COMMUNICATIONS

Blommers	Architecting Enterprise Solutions with UNIX Networking
Blommers	OpenView Network Node Manager
Blommers	Practical Planning for Network Growth
Brans	Mobilize Your Enterprise
Cook	Building Enterprise Information Architecture
Lee/Schneider/Schell	Mobile Applications: Architecture, Design, and Development
Lucke	Designing and Implementing Computer Workgroups
Lund	Integrating UNIX and PC Network Operating Systems

SECURITY

Bruce	Security in Distributed Computing
Mao	Modern Cryptography: Theory and Practice
Pearson et al.	Trusted Computing Platforms
Pipkin	Halting the Hacker, Second Edition
Pipkin	Information Security

WEB/INTERNET CONCEPTS AND PROGRAMMING

Amor	E-business (R)evolution, Second Edition
Apte/Mehta	UDDI
Chatterjee/Webber	Developing Enterprise Web Services: An Architect's Guide
Kumar	J2EE Security for Servlets, EJBs, and Web Services
Mowbrey/Werry	Online Communities
Tapadiya	.NET Programming

OTHER PROGRAMMING

Blinn	Portable Shell Programming
Caruso	Power Programming in HP OpenView
Chaudhri	Object Databases in Practice
Chew	The Java/C++ Cross Reference Handbook
Grady	Practical Software Metrics for Project Management and Process Improvement
Grady	Software Metrics
Grady	Successful Software Process Improvement
Lewis	The Art and Science of Smalltalk
Lichtenbelt	Introduction to Volume Rendering
Little/Maron/Pavlik	Java Transaction Processing: Design and Implementation
Mellquist	SNMP++
Mikkelsen	Practical Software Configuration Management
Norton	Thread Time
Tapadiya	COM+ Programming
Yuan	Windows 2000 GDI Programming

STORAGE

Thornburgh	Fibre Channel for Mass Storage
Thornburgh/Schoenborn	Storage Area Networks
Todman	Designing Data Warehouses

IT/IS

Anderson	mySAP Toolbag for Performance Tuning and Stress Testing
Missbach/Hoffman	SAP Hardware Solutions

IMAGE PROCESSING

Crane	A Simplified Approach to Image Processing
Gann	Desktop Scanners

Java Transaction Processing

Design and Implementation

Mark Little

Jonathan Maron

Greg Pavlik

PRENTICE
HALL
PTR

Prentice Hall PTR
Upper Saddle River, New Jersey 07458
www.phptr.com

Library of Congress Cataloging-in-Publication Data

A CIP catalog record for this book can be obtained from the Library of Congress.

Editorial/production supervision: *Mary Sudul*
Cover design director: *Jerry Votta*
Cover design: *DesignSource*
Manufacturing manager: *Maura Zaldivar*
Acquisitions editor: *Jill Harry*
Editorial assistant: *Brenda Mulligan*
Marketing manager: *Dan DePasquale*
Publisher, Hewlett-Packard: *William Carver*

© 2004 Hewlett-Packard Corp.
Published by Prentice Hall PTR
Pearson Education, Inc.
Upper Saddle River, New Jersey 07458

Prentice Hall books are widely used by corporations and government agencies for training, marketing, and resale.

The publisher offers discounts on this book when ordered in bulk quantities. For more information, contact Corporate Sales Department, Phone: 800-382-3419; FAX: 201-236-7141;
E-mail: corpsales@prenhall.com

Or write: Prentice Hall PTR, Corporate Sales Dept., One Lake Street, Upper Saddle River, NJ 07458.

Printed in the United States of America
1st Printing

ISBN 0-13-035290-X

Pearson Education LTD.
Pearson Education Australia PTY, Limited
Pearson Education Singapore, Pte. Ltd.
Pearson Education North Asia Ltd.
Pearson Education Canada, Ltd.
Pearson Educación de Mexico, S.A. de C.V.
Pearson Education — Japan
Pearson Education Malaysia, Pte. Ltd.

We'd like to dedicate this book to Ed Felt from BEA.
Ed was a friend and colleague with whom one of us
collaborated in the development of the OASIS
Business Transactions Protocol specification.
He was killed in the crash of the hijacked United Airlines
Flight 93 near Pittsburgh on September 11, 2001.

CONTENTS

Chapter 3 The Java Transaction Service 95

Part 2 Transactions in J2EE

Chapter 4 JDBC and Transactions 153

Appendix A Resources 361

Appendix B Experiences Gained and Lessons Learned 367

Foreword

It seems oddly appropriate that the authors of this book entered into my world through a complex business transaction. As various exceptions occurred during the transaction, compensating actions left Greg Pavlik and Jon Maron in my team at Oracle, and we had the great opportunity to continue collaboration with Mark Little and the world-class group at Arjuna Technologies. It's really a pleasure to see this important book emerge as a result.

In the end, transactions are all that business is about. Much of the software industry centers around making those transactions happen faster and more reliably than the next guy. Eight years ago, few people would have thought Java would ever emerge as a viable platform for supporting reliable, performant transactional applications. I remember seeing a cartoon once showing a frazzled soldier pushing a button labeled "LAUNCH," with a message on the computer screen: "Please wait. Collecting garbage." That cartoon captured succinctly, if not very fairly, the barrier that Java has overcome. Today, people don't hesitate to bet their business on Java's ability to process their transactions.

Java's success as the premier language for developing server applications has to rest squarely on the shoulders of the transaction processing technologies that come with it. Duke (the Java applet equivalent of Microsoft's annoying talking paperclip) had his fifteen minutes of fame, but the stuff that has fueled Java adoption has been in the server. The low-level Java Transaction Architecture and the larger pieces built on top of it, such as Enterprise JavaBeans, Java Message Service and Java Connector Architecture, have made transactions as much a part of everyday Java programming as strings. Understanding how those pieces work is probably one of the most important things you can do as a Java programmer.

One of the great values this book provides is the detailed technical context behind the APIs. Java may have provided the Renaissance for transactional programming, but it was built on a huge technology investment in industry and academia over many years. We're seeing that same investment applied today in service oriented architecture and web services. It would not be right to characterize these newer areas as simply reinvention, particularly in the realm of transactions. As the world moves more toward loosely coupled, large grained services as opposed to monolithic applications, we have to apply the lessons of the past to solve a different class of problems. What kind of infrastructure do we need to build transactional applications across businesses in a loosely coupled, mostly connected world? These are the kinds of problems that aren't solved by simply understanding APIs. They're the kinds of problems that people like Mark, Jon, and Greg work on every day. It's terrific to have them share that kind of insight in this book.

Steven G. Harris
Vice President, Java Platform Group, Oracle Corporation

Foreword

Waves of software technology come and go. Some manage to become mature enough to be used in the most demanding types of business applications—often called mission critical or more simply *transaction processing* applications.

And once they do, you can usually be sure of two things: they have the features, functionality, performance, and stability to handle the types of applications that reserve travel, trade stock, and enter orders; and that they are by that point no longer the coolest new technology on the planet.

J2EE has established itself as such a technology, extending its useful sphere from the original Web-facing presentation layer for back end systems into a back end technology in its own right. From their first appearance about 15 years ago, application servers included some kind of transaction management features. However, early implementations such as Kiva and Tengah (which grew up to be WebLogic) included only the most rudimentary level of support for what the back-end transaction processing technologies provided. Their main job was to integrate Web servers with those back end systems, typically TP monitors, and basically just kept track of the fact that a transaction was being executed by one or more of them. If everything succeeded, there was no problem. But if a back end execution failed for any reason, the early application server could do nothing more than record the fact.

As anyone familiar with the nearly 40-year old field of transaction processing knows, recovery from failure is the hard part, and the good news is that the J2EE application environment now includes everything necessary to develop and run the kinds of mission-critical applications that were once only the province of the proprietary TP monitors.

This book does a great job of describing each of the major technologies involved in the full J2EE solution for transaction processing applications, despite the fact that the technologies are derived from a variety of sources, including X/Open (now the Open Group), CORBA, message queuing systems, and the Java Community Process itself.

Although for obvious personal reasons, I might have wished that the authors gave more space in their review of TP history to the technologies I contributed to – Digital's ACMS TP monitor and the Open Group's Structured Transaction Definition Language, since they pioneered many RPC-oriented TP concepts – they are right to focus on the more relevant developments in the object-oriented world such as the Object Management Group's Object Transaction Service and Additional Structuring Mechanisms specifications, since they represent the core of modern TP innovation.

In general, the authors have drawn the appropriate parallels between the modern J2EE environment and the historical TP monitor technologies in which the essential TP concepts and principles were established, and have provided important perspectives on the similarities and important differences between those older technologies and the world of J2EE. The J2EE architecture is in fact based on the classic three-tier TP monitor architecture, with its separation of the presentation layer (servlets), the workflow or business logic layer (session beans), and the transaction server or data layer (entity beans), but the authors do a good job of describing when this is the right architecture for modern applications, and when it is not.

The book provides an excellent description of best practices information based on general TP principles as applied within the J2EE development environment. Ironically, to me at least, the authors seem to feel there's a need to add some technology specific focus to TP literature rather than writing a book that adds to the number of theoretical works available. When I started on TP about 25 years ago, all we had were the products – there was no theoretical or general literature about TP at all. I suppose that's one measure of how far the field has come.

In any case, in those days, TP systems were very closely aligned with their underlying operating systems and hardware platforms, and TP monitors were typically adapted to work with a specific database management system such as IMS or a specific networking technology such as DECnet (since in those days there were no real standards for either). Because it's such a difficult problem to ensure transactional consistency with automatic recovery and good performance, TP programs often used system-level APIs for device and network drivers as well as operating system specific locking, memory management, and logging techniques.

Now that J2EE is maturing as a kind of cross-operating system TP platform, which on the one hand presents new challenges for Java (i.e. how does the VM handle the requisite low level operating system interactions), but on the other hand presents new opportunities for joining disparate systems more easily into the recoverable units of work that are so important for operational business systems, simplifying development and deployment and reducing the need for low-level programming. The need for understanding how the technologies work has not changed, however, since good design remains essential to obtain the benefits of TP technologies, and this book delivers the goods for J2EE.

The book also deals effectively with the mixture of cross-platform standards that enables J2EE, which is important since most of them were not originally developed within the JCP effort itself but were adapted from other sources such as the Open Group and OMG. It also highlights the transactional interfaces, or interactions, between the various application-level components such as JDBC, JMS, JCA, and EJBs.

Web services can and should be treated separately, as they are in this book, since they are a language-independent mapping technology, not an execution environment in and of themselves. As of J2EE 1.3 the transactional capabilities of the platform are largely complete. Web services, the primary focus for J2EE 1.4, represent another layer of abstraction and don't change the core of J2EE TP. But the book does include an overview of the emerging direction around Web services transactions, and summaries of the major candidate technologies.

This book is being offered at the right time in the J2EE adoption cycle for programmers starting to use J2EE to implement such TP production applications. The technology foundation is there; this book provides the overall architectural view, best practices information, excellent perspectives on technical trade off decisions, and an overview of future directions toward extended transaction models and Web services.

The team of authors provides a good mix of experience with hands-on development of core technologies, their application in real-world solutions, and participation within industry activities such as standards committees and consortia. They provide information in the context of the various stages of evolution of TP, from what's historically there in existing applications to what's made it from those systems into J2EE (which is now pretty stable), to what's likely to evolve or emerge in Web services. Helpful tips, suggestions, and perspectives are provided throughout the chapters.

The book includes clear motivations of why TP is important, the cost/benefits of using it within the J2EE environment, and where things need to evolve in the future. Significantly, the book includes an overview of the so-called Activity Service from OMG and how it has influenced both the WS-Transactions family of specifications from Microsoft and IBM and the WS-Composite Application Framework family of specifications from OASIS.

Overall, the authors have done a great job of explaining what makes J2EE a good fit for transaction processing applications, and why, and of highlighting the important technologies and how to use them alone or in combination to support a wide range of TP application requirements. I'm not sure anyone would have thought in the early days of application servers that they would one day include such richness of capability to be used in these heavy-duty production environments as a replacement for those old tried and true TP monitors, but I remember saying the same thing once about CORBA...

Eric Newcomer
CTO, IONA Systems

Preface

As the title suggests, this book provides a technological survey of current transaction processing technologies available to system architects who are using the Java platform to develop mission-critical applications and solutions. That first sentence is a mouthful, so in the following sections we break it down and provide some background context. This introduction will give you a feel for what's coming in the remainder of the book, as well as a basic understanding of the concepts that will be explored. While we recommend that the book be read in order of presentation, this introduction provides enough information to allow readers to jump from chapter to chapter to explore topics that are of specific interest.

The target audience for this book is software architects, senior application developers, e-commerce developers, system architects, system integrators and enterprise architects. Typically, these are experienced technical decision makers that are responsible for implementation decisions on critical projects. The book is a practical guide for practicing professionals who need to implement real, reliable systems.

Many architects for Java systems are not deeply experienced with transaction monitors. In addition, many experts in transaction processing have limited experience with Java.

The book contains enough depth to illustrate what options are available and viable today, yet it is not intended to be a theoretical text for graduate studies. We've made some effort to avoid discussions that are of purely theoretical interests—one of the liabilities of immersing yourself in the literature of transaction processing—in order to focus on issues that are of real concern to working engineers who require a depth of knowledge that is directly applicable to their job. In that sense, the book is not intended for Web developers, junior programmers, or technical managers, though all should benefit from a better understanding of transactions and their use.

Additionally, it is important to note that this book is not a cut-and-paste cookbook of programming examples. Instead, it will provide the critical level of understanding that is required, but too often absent, when decisions are made about leveraging transactions. We try to provide useful insights into problems that are present in real solutions, but often glossed over in books that regurgitate technical specifications or promote particular products.

About this Book

This book is structured into three major parts.

Part I—Introduction to Transactions and Java

The first part, consisting of the first three chapters, is an introduction to transactioning models and their representation in Java. Chapter 1 presents a thorough examination of distributed transaction fundamentals. We highly recommend reading this chapter since it presents concepts and principles that recur throughout the book.

Chapter 2 presents an explanation of the Open Group Distributed Transaction Processing (DTP) Model and its representation in Java. This examination of the Java Transaction API (JTA) is important for anyone working with transactional J2EE components.

Finally, Chapter 3 examines the Object Transaction Service and its associated Java mapping, the Java Transaction Service (JTS). It is important to understand this specification and its implications since it extends the DTP model to the object domain.

These chapters relate the fundamental principles and themes that are repeated throughout the book as we examine various technologies and APIs. We therefore recommend that you take the time to read these chapters and understand them before reading the rest of the book.

Let's examine some of the key concepts explored in this first section.

Transaction Processing

The term "transactions" can have different meanings in different domains, many of which overlap with the professional experience of software developers. For example, Web developers will talk about the number of transactions per second handled by a Web server; this corresponds to a throughput count for simple HTTP request handling. E-commerce architects will refer to purchase orders as transactions. However, when we talk about transactions in this book we are focusing on something altogether different: constructs that scope work done on behalf of applications that allow us to provide correctness guarantees. We focus, in particular, on technologies that allow us to provide these guarantees in the distributed environments that are typical of IT application topologies today. Transaction processing in this sense is a critical technology that can be applied across multiple problem domains—enterprise architectures, e-commerce solutions, financial systems, and many other areas. That's not to say that there's a one-size-fits-all solution for providing correctness guarantees. Rather, each application has its unique reliability requirements. Understanding those requirements and how they map into available technology options is a complex and difficult programming task.

It has been our experience that transaction processing is both widely recognized as a critical technology for modern applications and at the same time very poorly understood by practicing engineers. We've heard experienced architects repeatedly make incorrect pronouncements about different aspects of transaction processing. The goal of this book is to provide up-to-date information about what transaction processing really is, the guarantees it provides, and how to exploit this technology in a modern programming environment. We also explain some of the practical limitations and complicating factors inherent in these options

History

Modern transaction processing technologies developed in the context of mainframe computing starting in the 1960s, and in many respects, the technologies that we use today are refinements and adaptations of those models. Many systems required high-volume, reliable transaction processing as data centers were called on to automate business functions.

For example, early transaction processing systems included the well-known SABRE airline reservation system. Companies such as IBM were quick to realize that this same kind of technology could be applied across other industries. From that epiphany came CICS, which originally was written entirely in assembler with rudimentary database capabilities. By 1979, it was rewritten in a modern programming language and developed into a full-blown transaction monitor—a managed environment for writing application logic that requires consistent and reliable outcomes. This mainframe technology was client/server based. The servers were called "application servers," the continuity of which sometimes comes as a surprise to programmers reared on a diet of "Internet" applications. Other, similar products were developed by software system vendors, including BEA's Tuxedo, HP's (formerly Tandem's) Pathway, and NCR's TOP END.

Transaction monitors provided a complete runtime for executing business logic in the middle tier, allowing secure and transactional access to backend systems, including databases. Transaction monitors were very much procedural analogues to the contemporary object transaction monitors that began to appear in the 1990s, the most successful and popular of which were based on the Enterprise JavaBeans specification spearheaded by Sun Microsystems. Many transaction monitors are built on queued communication bus architectures, such as that developed in IMS. This is a bit different than the standard Java architectures, though most of these systems can be accessed from within a programming environment with the appropriate client libraries. There is a fairly rich literature on these legacy TPMs, so we do not cover those systems in any detail in this book.

ACID Properties

Many people consider correctness guarantees provided by transaction processing systems to be intricately linked to ACID properties. We explain what this means in depth in Chapter 2, but this boils down to a guarantee that actions on multiple components within a system can be executed atomically, in isolation from other actions, and recorded permanently as a result of the completion of the activity. A familiar ACID transaction is a simple database transaction that scopes several SQL queries as a single unit of work. Since we live in a world of many databases and many kinds of systems, most of the chapters of this book focus on global and distributed transaction processing technologies that allow us to extend these concepts across system boundaries.

Two Phase Commit

In order to preserve ACID properties in a distributed system, we need to ensure all of the participants in a distributed unit of work reach a consensus before any of them can make permanent and visible the results of the work they are responsible for managing. This is most commonly accomplished by using the two-phase commit protocol. Typically the two-phase commit protocol is described in terms of a voting process where a transaction coordinator asks all participants if they are prepared to commit. If the coordinator determines that a consensus to commit has been agreed upon, the coordinator tells all participants to commit their transactions.

While this explanation is accurate as far as it goes, it neglects other key requirements of the protocol. For the protocol to guarantee an all-or-nothing outcome in the face of any number of potential failures, there are explicit requirements for managing checkpoints of completed work in the resource managers and state information about the transaction in the coordinator. The combination of logging requirements and distributed communication between participants leads to a solution that is often less efficient than may be desirable. There are optimizations that can be employed, but they may not be applicable in all circumstances.

To add to the complexity, two-phase commit by itself doesn't guarantee that the ACID properties of a transaction are maintained. Resource managers are responsible for acquiring and releasing locks following the well-known two-phase locking rule. We explore how these two protocols work in detail and how they fit together in Chapter 2. We also provide answers to some related questions throughout the book: How is two phase commit supported in Java? How do components interoperate within the protocol? How do we know if a system can tolerate limitations of the protocol?

ACID transactions are only a class of transaction technologies, but also represent the approach most widely supported by transaction managers and resource managers today. Maintaining ACID properties means that resources must be locked for the duration of a transaction. This may be acceptable for the classic example of a bank account transfer done within the context of a single unit of work, but it is not acceptable for long-running business processes that may last for many hours, days, or even years.

An example of such a process might be opening a mortgage, which may take several weeks to complete. We may desire not only that certain resources remain unlocked for the duration of the process, but also that parts of the work may be rolled back independent of others. These models are often seen in workflow literature and they are slowly making their way into the mainstream of commercial software products.

In addition, Chapter 2 focuses in more depth on transactions in theory and practice. It is a good starting point for getting a conceptual handle on how transactions work and what they do.

Part II—Java 2, Enterprise Edition

This book focuses primarily on the Java platform. We've made this decision for three reasons. Java is the standard language for new enterprise applications and integration projects. We don't regard this as hype or vendor preference; at the present time this is a simple fact. The core of the Java programming platform is the Standard Edition. At the time of this writing, the fourth revision of the platform is available. The Standard Edition includes an implementation of the platform APIs and a virtual machine that provides a runtime engine for applications. Built on top of the base runtime environment is the Java 2 Enterprise Edition (J2EE).

This section of the book, made up of Chapters 4 through 8, focuses on particular J2EE APIs and their utilization or implementation of distributed and local transactioning. Each chapter focuses on a particular component of the J2EE platform and can be read separately.

Chapter 4 details Java's transactional connectivity to relational databases through the JDBC API. This is the fundamental API that Java provides for communicating with databases while utilizing transactions.

Chapter 5 extends the review of the Java platform's support for transactions to messaging resources by examining the Java Message Service (JMS) facilities for local and distributed transactions. Asynchronous messaging is increasingly a key component of system architectures and leveraging transactions appropriately is critical to successful application deployments.

Chapter 6 provides a thorough examination of the transactional support provided by Enterprise JavaBeans (EJB). This distributed component architecture is the core of the J2EE platform and as such provides the richest support for transactions.

Chapter 7 details the transactional interactions with Enterprise Information Systems (EIS) afforded by the Java Connector Architecture (JCA). This is an evolving standard that has the potential for allowing transactions to be scoped across databases, legacy systems, messaging systems and multiple applications servers.

Finally, Chapter 8 details some key architectural considerations that should be contemplated when leveraging the J2EE platform to create mission critical applications. Moreover, it provides the rationale for leveraging the platform for mission-critical, high-volume, transactional applications.

At this point a quick overview of the J2EE platform is probably in order.

J2EE

Over the last two years, J2EE has become synonymous with server-side Java development. J2EE is a formal standard defined through the Java Community Process. Sun Microsystems maintains oversight and control over the Java standards definitions, especially as they relate to J2EE. Sun defines J2EE as an application model, a platform, a test suite and a reference implementation. Other vendors can license J2EE and provide implementations of the standards that are certified as compliant.

The current market-leading platform providers are IBM, Oracle and BEA. In some cases, open source implementations of some of the standards have been provided by non-licensed organizations like the Apache Foundation, but these implementations until recently could be neither branded nor marketed as being either J2EE compliant or compatible. The process has had great success in forcing licensed vendors to be compliant with the relevant standards, something that open standards bodies have had a notoriously difficult time achieving. This has led to relatively portable programming models and some level of interoperability among different implementations.

Sun provides a set of BluePrints for building applications based on J2EE. These Blue-Prints are typically written before the newest pieces of technology are put into widespread use. As such, they are interesting proposals, but rarely a model that should be followed. In fact, Sun and most of the industry have recently backpedaled on the appropriateness of the "Java Petstore" reference application as a best-practices model.

As programmers have begun to use and apply the technologies, "patterns" literature explaining best practices have emerged from end-user feedback, two notable examples being *EJB Design Patterns* by Floyd Marinesceu and *Core J2EE Patterns* from the Sun series by Prentice Hall. This literature is a far better guide for using J2EE. A relevant case in point: the J2EE programming model suggests a deployment scheme for Web applications where multiple tiers are used for the Java Web container and the EJB component containers, the so-called n-tier architecture.

Although there are times when this model is appropriate, in practice it is somewhat dated. Most application servers allow Web content to be served from a front end Web server farm that delegates requests for dynamic content or interaction with data systems and applications to be load balanced to a cluster of application servers. Application servers typically handle the Web request and subsequent Enterprise JavaBeans requests within the same application server instance. This is an important reference model to bear in mind when building transactional systems, since it tends to minimize the latency associated with transaction processing and the two phase commit protocol; it's also the easiest way to configure and use most application servers.

J2EE is composed of a number of technologies, including Servlets, JavaServer Pages, security APIs, and directory and naming facilities. In this book we devote chapters that look at the transactional aspects of JDBC for database access, the Java Connector Architecture for integration, JTA, which maps to the industry standard X/Open Distributed Transaction Processing model, the Java Message Service for asynchronous messaging, the CORBA Object Transaction Service and the Enterprise JavaBeans transactional component model. All of these standards either enable or support distributed transactions in ways that are often required to implement real enterprise solutions.

J2EE itself defines a set of independent technologies and it is often common for a vendor to specialize in a single technology area. For example, there are a number of vendors that offer standalone JMS implementations. However, the major J2EE vendors tend to offer complete, integrated platforms. This can be particularly important when it comes to transactional capabilities, since the interfaces for transaction management between components can be poorly defined (as we shall see is the case with JMS 1.0.1 and EJB 2.0). The platform vendors tend to have an embedded transaction manager within the application server JVM, which means that integrated containers can coordinate smoothly with a single transaction manager. Combining containers with independent transaction managers can be difficult, though vendor partnerships may resolve this problem in some cases.

To be certified as J2EE compliant, the infrastructure provider must license the technology from Sun Microsystems and pass a suite of Compatibility Tests. The Compatibility Test Suite for J2EE 1.4 contains about 22,000 individual tests. In the CTS implementation, each test often verifies a battery of functionality. Infrastructure vendors whose products are certified J2EE compliant can be treated as reasonably portable, although a combination of vendor extensions, omissions in the specifications, and implementation decisions can conspire to make porting complicated J2EE applications reasonably involved. As an aside, the CTS is not an absolute guarantee of correctness within the application server itself since it does not attempt to verify behavior under load or in particularly complicated interactions. Vendors that only offer a piece of the J2EE puzzle can run the CTS by using the reference implementation to pass sections in which they don't provide technology.

The reference implementation (RI) provides a proof-point that the technologies can be implemented and work together. When J2EE first arrived on the scene, it was common for application developers to work on the RI and deploy to commercial servers. The RI is not a deployment platform for real applications and is of limited utility for developers now that many robust application servers are available at little or no cost. We generally recommend that you implement your work on the platform on which you intend to deploy your application.

It is clear that J2EE is the de facto standard for dynamic Web application development. For our purposes, J2EE is also the primary platform for writing transactional applications in Java. We discuss each of the technologies that have transactional semantics in some detail, starting with EJB, the component model for J2EE. Readers are most likely familiar with J2EE on some level. We suggest you take the time to investigate the platform at more than a superficial level. Our discussion of J2EE and its constituent elements is focused on how they enable and interact with distributed transaction technology. We won't try to explain every facet of these technologies; there are a lot of overview books on each standard within the J2EE umbrella available and many are longer than this book. We assume some working familiarity with the constituent components that make up J2EE.

J2EE 1.3 was the current version of the enterprise Java platform while we wrote this book. As far as implementations go, it is the version of the platform you should count on using through 2004. Extensions to most of the specifications have been completed in the new J2EE 1.4 release. Where the specifications appear mature enough to ensure a high degree of stability, we touch on those aspects that relate to new transactional capabilities within the platform. For example, the

Java Connector Specification 1.5 has been enhanced to support inbound transaction context flow originating from an external coordinator. This coordinator, potentially associated with a legacy Enterprise Information System, will infect the thread of control handling a particular invocation in the application server.

Other specifications are being developed with the Java Community Process that relate to transactional technologies, such as JSR 156 (JAXTX), that provide a bridge into a Web services environment. Currently these specifications are immature and it remains to be seen whether these new technologies will become a part of the J2EE platform in a future revision. If that happens, they will become ubiquitous. While we provide an overview of some of the new developments in the last chapter, this material focuses on our possibilities for the future and should not be the basis for technology choices that are made today.

Part III—Beyond J2EE

Despite the economic slowdown of the last several years, the tidal waves of new technologies continue to crest the walls of the enterprise. And the latest tsunami is undoubtedly Web services. While we don't think that Web services are going to be the panacea for all the problems of IT, they will play an important role in the coming years for integration and B2B solutions.

A lot of the hype with respect to Web services is that they will be interoperable across vendor platforms. Basic SOAP interoperability seems likely to be a reality, but things are less well defined in the transaction space. This deficiency must be addressed in order to utilize Web services across organizations; support for transactions that maintain the integrity of an organization's resources is of paramount concern to system architects.

Chapter 9 provides an overview of the macro trends that are occurring in this rapidly evolving space. This chapter examines in detail some of the evolving standards for transactional support across Web services. In addition, we examine the modifications to the J2EE platform that are planned to support this new distributed application paradigm.

About the Authors

The authors have worked for years on and with transaction processing infrastructure and in combination bring more than 30 years of experience to the table.

Mark Little was a part of the core research team at the University of Newcastle where one of the first distributed object transaction systems was developed. He worked on the definition of the OMG Object Transaction Service and led the development of the first available implementation of that specification. He co-founded Arjuna Solutions, a company specializing in transactional Java products, which was acquired by Bluestone Software. He later led the transactions team in the Arjuna labs at Hewlett Packard Corporation, where he was also a Distinguished Engineer. He has remained engaged with standards in the Java Community Process, OASIS, W3C and the OMG, and is the chief architect for Arjuna Technologies, a recent Hewlett Packard spin-off.

Jon Maron has worked with middleware and application server technology for the last decade, both as a professional consultant and as a product architect. He has implemented multiple subsystems in J2EE, including EJB and JDBC. He has served on multiple standards bodies in the Java Community Process including J2EE and EJB. Jon is currently on the technical staff of Oracle Corporation focused on J2EE.

Greg Pavlik has been working with distributed systems since the early 1990s. He got started with Java-based application servers while working as Senior Architect at Bluestone Software; there he specialized in object transaction technology, with a focus on EJB container design and development. He was architect for the application server division of Hewlett Packard during the development and release of the highly regarded HP Application Server. While at Hewlett Packard, Greg was promoted to Distinguished Engineer. Greg has served on multiple standards in the Java Community Process, including the Expert Group that defined the Enterprise JavaBeans specification, and the OASIS consortium. He is now Consultant Member of Technical Staff for Oracle Corporation, where he is focused on the intersection of J2EE, Web services, and transactions.

We have a great deal of hands-on experience defining, working with and implementing the technologies we discuss and hope to bring our experience to bear to provide a practical understanding of the state of transaction processing capabilities available to solution architects working in Java.

Acknowledgments

First of all we'd like to thank the reviewers of this book for helping us to better formulate on paper what we'd muddled over in our minds for more than a year. Without them this book wouldn't read as well as it does. We'd also like to thank the people at Prentice Hall for steering us through this long process. Also thanks to Steve Harris and Eric Newcomer for their kind words.

We'd like to thank the various companies that we've worked for in the past, in particular Arjuna Solutions Limited, Bluestone Software, Hewlett-Packard, and Oracle. Over the years they've provided us with wonderful working environments and many smart people to interact with. To all of the ex-Bluestonians, in particular those we worked with on the excellent Hewlett-Packard Application Server, we'd just like to say an extra word of thanks.

Mark Little

I'd like to thank my family for putting up with yet another spell on the book-writing carousel. In particular my thanks and love go to my wife Paula, who's had to live with my ghost for so many months. My two sons, Daniel and Adam, are too young to understand what any of this is about, but their combined love has helped me through some long and arduous writing spells. To my parents, Peter and Elizabeth, I'd also like to say thanks for the love and support throughout the years.

The individuals I'd like to thank would fill another book, but I must single out Professor Santosh Shrivastava who dragged me into the field of transaction processing back in the 1980s, and Bob Bickel who helped turn the academic into a commercial reality. I'd also like to say thanks to my co-authors Greg and Jon for helping to make this project a success and for being good friends throughout.

Finally I'd like to thank all of my friends and colleagues at Arjuna Technologies Limited who have kept the faith and stayed together despite the uncertainties in our industry. Thanks especially to Stuart, Dave, Steve, and Barry.

Jonathan Maron

First and foremost, I'd like to thank my beloved wife and children: Laura, Josh, and Jason. Without your understanding, encouragement, and love I would never have been able to complete this project. Laura, you have been an extraordinary "book widow."

I'd also like to thank my father and mother, Irving and Lena, for providing me with the disposition, attitude, and courage required to undertake writing this book; your love and support have always been unwavering.

In addition, I'd like to express my gratitude to Bob Bickel, Al Smith, Bruce Kratz, Erik Bergenholtz, JJ Snyder, and Richard Friedman—you provided me with friendship, steadfast guidance, and inspiration.

Finally, I can not say enough about my co-authors—their dedication and knowledge have been truly inspiring. Thank you for allowing me to participate in this endeavour.

Greg Pavlik

I'd like to give my deepest appreciation to the following persons for their support and patience: my loves, Ruth and Kylie; my parents, George and Cindy; the professionals that made this project possible, Al Smith and Bob Bickel; and my co-authors, Mark Little and Jon Maron who stuck with this through corporate takeovers, two new company launches, another new job, and my inability to stop writing code into the night when I should have been writing this book. Mark was the technical lead, so to speak, in all of this, and Jon was as usual the most tenacious guy I know. They deserve the credit. Thanks also to all of the reviewers—their feedback was indispensable—and to my colleagues at Bluestone, Hewlett-Packard, MediaGroks and Oracle for their patience and for all they've taught me.

The authors wish to thank the following colleagues and reviewers for their invaluable feedback, comments, and assistance: Mark Hansen, Michael Keith, Judith M. Meyerson, Debabrata Panda, Vijay Phagura, Madhu Siddalingaiah, Rajkumar Irudayaraj, Anthony Lai, Jyotsna Laxminarayanan, Tom Beerbower, John Speidel, Sugu Venkatasamy, J.J. Snyder, Paul Parkinson, and Mike Spille.

PART 1

Java Transactions Fundamentals

Our first three chapters delve into the underpinnings of transaction processing in the Java environment. This material provides a practical framework not only for the rest of the book, but also for your day-to-day experiences in development, deployment and operation of transactional systems. Much of what we present in these chapters is broadly applicable to existing systems and environments other than the Java platform. At the same time, we try to make sure that the Java platform remains the main focus in order to make the material as practical and relevant as possible to working J2EE and Java developers.

Chapter 1 focuses on transaction theory: what is a transaction, how transactions work to provide correctness guarantees, what practical limitations exist with transactions, and what developments are happening to extend the transactions to address new problem domains. This is an accessible and practical explanation of ideas that are generally only explained in difficult academic texts. Using transactions blindly is a mistake and this chapter helps lift the veil of mystery from what has often been an inaccessible and seemingly arcane subject. The chapter also looks at examples of how transactions are used in practice. We recommend you read this chapter before you dive into the rest of the book and revisit it frequently. This is the only chapter that is not focused on the Java platform. You may find it a useful guide for many programming environments.

From there, we begin to examine the technologies that are used to build the transaction infrastructure of Java. Chapter 2 provides a detailed examination of the Open Group Distributed Transaction Model (DTP) as it is applied to the Java platform. The DTP model is the basis for a number of Open Group specifications that define how applications, transaction managers, and resource managers work together to preserve ACID properties for a unit of work that spans many transaction participants. We examine how these specifications are mapped into Java and how to use them effectively both with the J2EE platform and in Java in general via the Java Transaction API. The Java Transaction API began as a model for layering object models on top of existing transaction monitors, but its use has evolved into the implementation of new transaction managers written in Java and typically embedded in application servers. Understanding the ins and outs of JTA is becoming increasingly important for two reasons: the J2EE platform has begun to define new models that allow developers to build proxies to resource managers that are based on JTA and more complicated solutions may require functionality beyond what is traditionally exposed in J2EE.

The last area we look at is the Object Transaction Service (OTS), a CORBA specification that defines a transaction processing model for distributed systems. Because it is based on the OMG/CORBA standards, it is intended to be broadly interoperable, including across transaction systems and programming languages and platforms. OTS may be used as a standalone technology. This is an advanced and somewhat error-prone use case, but using the OTS by can be a powerful way to tie together heterogeneous environments and one way the mechanism for RPC interactions with J2EE components to support transaction inflow: the OTS is the basis for interoperability between different EJB environments.

CHAPTER 1

Transactions Fundamentals

In order to fully understand the issues involved in designing transaction systems and using transactions in applications that will be covered in subsequent chapters, it's necessary to have some understanding of the fundamental principles behind transactions. For example, to understand the effect that distributed transactions have on your EJB application it's obviously necessary to know what a "distributed transaction" is and how it is likely to be implemented.

Transaction processing systems and the theoretical and implementation principles behind them have been around in one form or another for nearly five decades. Describing all of these various principles in detail would require a book in its own right and unfortunately we don't have the space. Fortunately we don't need to cover all of these principles in great detail. However, we attempt to provide enough information that you won't have to go elsewhere for answers to questions this book might raise.

> What this chapter does is lay the groundwork for all of the other chapters, providing readers with little or no transaction knowledge with enough information to place the rest of the book in context. If you are an experienced transaction user then you may be able to skim through this chapter, although you may still find some interesting new facts. For a more detailed treatment of many of these topics we would recommend other texts such as *Transaction Processing: Concepts and Techniques* by Jim Gray and Andreas Reuter and *Principles of Transaction Processing* by Philip Bernstein and Eric Newcomer.

What Are Transactions and Why Do I Need Them?

Imagine that you are implementing a centralized (single machine) bank application, where the information about each bank account is stored in a persistent database. Let's also assume that each account is managed separately within the database. Now, your users won't be very happy if their money gets lost because of failures. For example, your bank has to allow the transfer of money from one account to another, but obviously a failure after the money has left the original account and before it has been placed into the new account could mean that the money is lost in the system! What you would like is an all-or-nothing operation: the money either moves between the two accounts or it stays in the first account. This would be referred to as an *atomic operation*: such an operation is indivisible, i.e., it is not possible to decompose it into smaller operations.

It's obviously difficult enough to consider how to provide this functionality in a centralized system, so you can imagine the additional problems that are presented when we add multiple machines or components to the application. Distributed systems pose reliability problems not frequently encountered in more traditional centralized systems. A distributed system consisting of a number of computers connected by some communication network is subject to independent failure modes of its components, such as nodes, links and operating systems. What this means is that the lack of any centralized control can mean that part of the system can fail (e.g., a machine may crash or a network connection cease to work) while other parts are still functioning, thus leading to the possibility of abnormal behavior of application programs in execution. This explains why one definition of a distributed system is "any system where the failure of a machine you have never heard of prevents you from doing work."

If you had to consider all possible failure scenarios when designing and building a distributed application, it is unlikely that you'd ever finish. Imagine all of the "what if?" conditions that might arise; for example, "what if the client crashes in the middle of making a request to a server?" or "what if the server crashes while updating the back-end database?" and "if the system recovers, how do I restart the application and ensure those invocations in progress when the failure occurred continue or are undone?" Asking all programmers to have to consider such scenarios whenever they build applications is impractical and that's why there has been a lot of work over the years involved in building tools to assist in the construction of fault-tolerant distributed systems.

One of those tools is the *atomic transaction*. As we see in the following sections, an atomic transaction (often abbreviated to *transaction*) provides an "all-or-nothing" property to work that is conducted within its scope, also ensuring that shared resources are protected from multiple users. Importantly, application programmers typically only have to start and end a transaction; all of the complex work necessary to provide the transaction's properties is hidden by the transaction system, leaving the programmer free to concentrate on the more functional aspects of the application at hand.

Let's take a look at just how a transaction system could help in a real-world application environment. Consider the case of a distributed system (shown in Figure 1-1) where each machine provides various services (e.g., data storage, printing, bank account) that can be invoked by an application program. It is natural for an application that uses a collection of these services to require that they behave consistently in the presence of failures. In the figure the bank offers two kinds of accounts to users: a CurrentAccount and a SavingsAccount. Both of these accounts are maintained on persistent (durable) storage, in this case represented by a database, with suitable front ends (represented as services in the figure). Finally there is a transaction manager service that will be used to manage any transactions that the bank may require in order to process the user's requests. We see later why the transaction manager requires a log, but in brief it's to ensure that transactions can tolerate failures.

Let's consider a simple example: imagine an online bank that allows customers to transfer funds between accounts (CurrentAccount and SavingsAccount), and let's further assume that Mr. Smith has both of these accounts whose balances are $500 and $1,400, respectively. As shown, the bank is responsible for communicating with the transaction service to start and end the transaction Mr. Smith will use to manage transferring his funds.

Mr. Smith wants to transfer $400 from the CurrentAccount to the SavingsAccount and because of bank processes, this will occur in the following steps:

1. Read the amount of money in the CurrentAccount to determine that there are enough funds to transfer.
2. Debit $400 from the CurrentAccount.
3. Credit $400 to the SavingsAccount.
4. The bank checks that the CurrentAccount is still in credit and if not, charges Mr. Smith for an overdraft. This last step is just in case there are concurrent accesses to the Smith account. As we see later, the use of atomic transactions can make this step redundant, but without them something along these lines will obviously be required.

The transfer process may be affected by failures of software or hardware that could affect the overall consistency of the system in a number of ways. For example, if a failure occurs between step 2 and 3 then it is entirely possible for the $400 to be removed from the CurrentAccount and to vanish into the ether rather than be credited to the SavingsAccount. This loss of data integrity would have dire consequences for the user and ultimately the bank.

Now let's assume that Mrs. Smith wants to withdraw $200 from the CurrentAccount to go shopping. The steps her withdrawal goes through are:

1. Check the CurrentAccount has sufficient funds.
2. Withdraw $200.
3. The bank checks that the CurrentAccount is still in credit and if not, charges Mr. Smith for an overdraft.

If Mrs. Smith withdraws at the same time her husband is transferring funds, then it is entirely possible for both operations to see sufficient funds in the CurrentAccount for their own

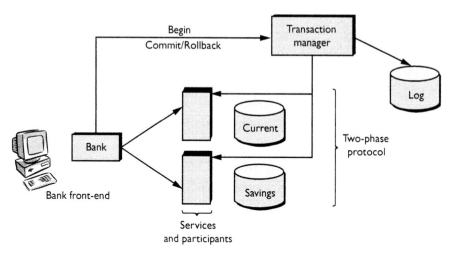

Figure 1-1   Bank account transfers.

requirements, when in fact there are insufficient funds for both. The result is that the CurrentAccount ends up $100 overdrawn and Mr. Smith gets an overdraft charge he didn't expect.

What Mr. Smith would like is that accesses to the account are handled in such a manner that consistency of both accounts is maintained despite failures or concurrent access. And this is in fact a more general statement of desirability for distributed applications that manipulate data or shared resources. Fortunately, atomic transactions (transactions) have the following properties that make them ideal for solving this kind of problem (these are often referred to as ACID properties):

- *Atomicity*: The transaction completes successfully (commits) or if it fails (aborts) *all* of its effects are undone (rolled back). In the bank example, Mr. Smith wants his money to move between the two accounts or for it to remain in the CurrentAccount; the atomic property would guarantee this.
- *Consistency*: Transactions produce consistent results and preserve application-specific invariants (preserves the internal consistency of the data it acts on). The consistency of Mr. Smith's account data is maintained.
- *Isolation*: Intermediate states produced while a transaction is executing are not visible to others. Furthermore, transactions appear to execute *serially*, even if they are actually executed concurrently. This property would ensure that Mr. Smith and Mrs. Smith's bank operations don't conflict.
- *Durability*: The effects of a committed transaction are never lost (except by a catastrophic failure). As we saw earlier, the bank account information is maintained on some external database and the transaction ensures that it is updated correctly.

A transaction can be terminated in two ways: *committed* or *aborted* (rolled back). When a transaction is committed, all changes made within it are made durable (forced onto stable storage, e.g., disk). When a transaction is aborted, all of the changes are undone. As we shall see later, atomic transactions can also be nested; the effects of a nested action are provisional upon the commit/abort of the outermost (*top-level*) atomic transaction.

Associated with every transaction is a *coordinator*, which is responsible for governing the outcome of the transaction. The coordinator may be implemented as a separate service or may be co-located with the user for improved performance. It communicates with enlisted participants to inform them of the desired termination requirements, i.e., whether they should accept (*commit*) or reject (*rollback*) the work done within the scope of the given transaction. For example, it communicates whether to purchase the (provisionally reserved) flight tickets for the user or to release them. A *transaction manager factory* is typically responsible for managing coordinators for many transactions. The initiator of the transaction (e.g., the client) communicates with a transaction manager and asks it to start a new transaction and associate a coordinator with the transaction.

In the following sections, we examine each of these properties in more detail.

Atomicity

In order to ensure that a transaction has an atomic outcome, a multi-phase commit protocol is required. The industry standard transaction protocols use *two-phase commit*. (Some transaction protocols support a three-phase termination protocol, which tries to reduce the chances of blocking due to the failure of the coordinator, but two-phase is the most popular protocol in practice.) This protocol is used to guarantee consensus between participating members of the transaction. Figure 1-2 illustrates the main aspects of this protocol: during phase 1, the transaction coordinator, C, attempts to communicate with all of the action participants, A and B, to determine whether they will commit or abort. An abort reply, or no reply, from any participant acts as a veto, causing the entire action to abort.

> **N O T E**   The failure to deliver the initial prepare request may also cause the coordinator to roll back (possibly after retrying to deliver the message some number of times).

Based upon these (lack of) responses, the coordinator arrives at the decision of whether to commit or abort the transaction. If the transaction will commit, the coordinator records this decision on stable storage, and the protocol enters phase 2, where the coordinator forces the participants to carry out the decision. The coordinator also informs the participants if the transaction aborts.

> **N O T E**   Failure to write the intention should also cause the transaction to roll back.

When each participant receives the coordinator's phase 1 message, they record sufficient information on stable storage to either commit or abort changes made during the action. After returning the phase 1 response, each participant that returned a commit response *must* remain blocked until it has received the coordinator's phase 2 message. Until they receive this message, these resources are unavailable for use by other actions. If the coordinator fails before delivery of this message, these resources remain blocked. However, if crashed machines eventually recover, crash recovery mechanisms can be employed to unblock the protocol and terminate the transaction.

If the client decides to roll back the transaction then the coordinator won't run a two-phase protocol: the participants will simply be told to roll back.

> **N O T E**   The two-phase commit protocol is not client-server based. It simply talks about a coordinator and participants, and makes no assumption about where they are located. Different implementations of the protocol may impose certain restrictions about locality, but these are purely implementation choices.

You might wonder what happens if during the second phase A or B decide that they cannot commit. In the strict two-phase protocol, this is not allowed: once participants have agreed to a decision during the first phase, this is considered a *guarantee* and they cannot deviate from this promise. However, in practice this doesn't always happen and the two-phase protocol on which most transaction systems are based allows participants to make different choices during phase 2 than were made during phase 1 *in exceptional circumstances* (e.g., a critical failure occurs which means that the participant simply cannot ever commit). As we see later, this can result in non-atomic behavior and gives what are commonly known as *heuristic outcomes.*

When running the first phase of the commit protocol, it's not strictly necessary for each participant to be sent the prepare message sequentially: the coordinator could invoke each participant in parallel to improve performance and collate all responses to then decide whether to commit or roll back the transaction. In fact, some commercial transaction systems support this option (e.g., the Arjuna Transaction Service).

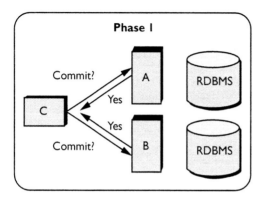
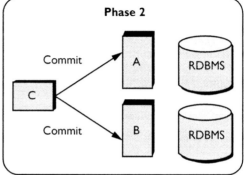

Figure 1-2   Two-phase commit protocol.

Consistency

A transactional application should maintain the consistency of the resources (e.g., databases, file-systems, and so on) that it uses. In essence, transactional applications should move from one consistent state to another. However, unlike the other transactional properties (A, I and D), this is something that the transaction system cannot achieve by itself since it does not possess any semantic information about the resources it manipulates: it would be impossible for a transaction processing system to assert that the resources are moving to (or from) consistent states. Take our previous example of Mr. Smith's bank accounts: how would a transaction system know that the accounts should never go into the red? All a transaction system can ensure is that any state changes that do occur are performed in a manner that is guaranteed despite failures. It is the application programmers' responsibility to ensure consistency (in whatever way makes sense for the application concerned).

Isolation (Serializability)

If we assume that objects and services can be shared between various programs, it is necessary to ensure that concurrent executions of programs are free from interference, i.e., concurrent executions should be equivalent to some serial order of execution. We have already seen a fairly trivial example of this through the online bank account, where Mr. and Mrs. Smith conflict over their bank accounts, but it is worth formalizing this requirement.

Let's try to illustrate what we mean by a serializable execution. Consider the following two programs (where w, x, y and z are distinct state variables) and P1 and P2 are programs that perform the specified operations on those variables:

$$P1 : z := 10; x := x+1; y := y+1$$

$$P2 : w := 7; x := x * 2; y := y * 2$$

If we assume that $x=y=2$ initially, then a serial execution of P1 followed by P2 (P1;P2) will produce the result z=10, w=7, x=y=6, and execution P2;P1 will produce the results z=10, w=7, x=y=5.

However, if you look at P1 and P2 you can see that z and w are variables that are not shared between the two programs. So it should be possible to execute some aspects of P1 and P2 concurrently. The partly concurrent execution order given below (indicated by the ||, which means that the operations on z and w execute in parallel) will be termed *interference free* or *serializable*, since it is equivalent to the serial order P1;P2, i.e., it produces the same results:

$$(z := 10 \parallel w := 7); x := x+1; y := y+1; x := x * 2; y := y * 2$$

However, an execution order such as the one below is not free from interference since it cannot be shown to be equivalent to any serial order.

$$(z := 10 \parallel w := 7); x := x+1; x := x * 2; y := y * 2; y := y+1$$

Programs that possess the above-mentioned serializable property are said to be *atomic with respect to concurrency*. What this means is that the execution of a transaction is serializable from the perspective of an external user if it appears to that user as though that transaction runs by itself (exclusively). Even though multiple transactions may be executing concurrently, it is not possible for the external user to see this, if those transactions are serializable.

Combined with the consistency property we've already mentioned, any serial execution of these transactions will continue to preserve consistency of the data that is manipulated by the transactions. If we only had the consistency attribute, then executing transactions in parallel would not result in a globally consistent system.

Obviously this says nothing about durability (persistence) of these computations or the effect of failures on them, e.g., a failure may occur part way through a computation or in such a manner that all data is lost (remember the bank account?). However, the serializability property is extremely important, especially in an environment where multiple concurrent users may be attempting to use the same resources consistently. With this property, Mr. and Mrs. Smith can at least rest assured that neither will be able to push the account into the red (at least not unintentionally).

One obvious way of maintaining serializability would be to execute all transactions serially. However, that's obviously a very inefficient approach, especially if some operations within transactions can logically occur in parallel, as we saw above. So, to ensure serializability, transactional systems like relational databases typically make use of concurrency control mechanisms.

Two-Phase Concurrency Control

In this section we briefly discuss the topic of concurrency control for transactions. A very simple and widely used approach is to regard all operations on objects to be of type "read" or "write," which follow the synchronization rule permitting concurrent "reads" but exclusive "writes." This rule is imposed by requiring that any computation intending to perform an operation that is of type read (write) on an object, first acquire a "read lock" ("write lock") associated with that object. A read lock on an object can be held concurrently by many computations provided no computation is holding a write lock on that object. A write lock on an object, on the other hand, can only be held by a computation provided no other computation is holding a read or a write lock.

N O T E Although we talk in terms of locks, this should not be used to infer a specific implementation. Timestamp-based concurrency control could just as easily be used, for example.

In order to ensure the atomicity property, all computations must follow a "two–phase" locking policy, as illustrated in Figure 1-3. During the first phase, termed the growing phase, a computation can acquire locks, but not release them. The tail end of the computation constitutes the shrinking phase, during which time held locks can be released but no locks can be acquired. Now suppose that a computation in its shrinking phase is to be rolled back, and that some objects with write locks have already been released. If some of these objects have been locked by other computations, then abortion of the computation will require these computations to be aborted as well. To avoid this *cascade roll back* problem, it is necessary to make the shrinking phase "instantaneous," as shown by the dotted lines. In effect this means that all the held locks are released simultaneously.

Optimistic Versus Pessimistic Concurrency Control

Most transaction systems utilize what is commonly referred to as *pessimistic concurrency control* mechanisms: in essence, whenever a data structure or other transactional resource is accessed, a lock (for example) is obtained on it as described earlier. This lock will remain held on that resource for the duration of the transaction. The benefit of this is that other users will not be able to modify (and possibly not even observe) the resource until the holding transaction has

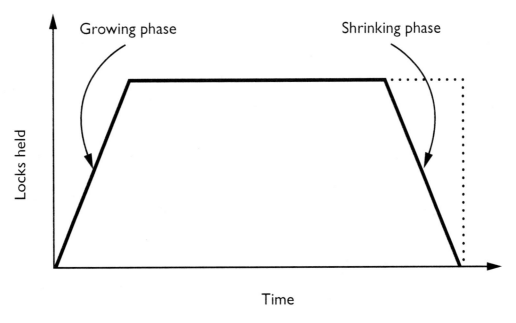

Figure 1-3 Two-phase locking.

terminated. There are a number of disadvantages of this style: (1) the overhead of acquiring and maintaining concurrency control information in an environment where conflict or data sharing is not high; (2) deadlocks may occur, where one user waits for another to release a lock not realizing that that user is waiting for the release of a lock held by the first (we talk about deadlocks in more detail later); (3) concurrency may be limited by the granularity of the locks; for example, page-level locking sometimes occurs in systems where multiple objects reside within the same page, and obtaining a lock on one object means locking them all, even if the objects are really independent.

Therefore, *optimistic concurrency control* assumes that conflicts are not high and tries to ensure locks are held only for brief periods of time: essentially locks are only acquired at the end of the transaction when it is about to terminate. This kind of concurrency control requires a means to detect if an update to a resource does conflict with any updates that may have occurred in the interim and how to recover from such conflicts. Typically, detection will happen using timestamps, whereby the system takes a snapshot of the timestamps associated with resources it is about to use or modify and compares them with the timestamps available when the transaction commits.

Resolution of conflicts is a different problem entirely, since in order to do so requires semantic information about the resources concerned (exactly what does it mean to find that the state of Mr. Smith's CurrentAccount has changed because Mrs. Smith got her transaction in first?). Therefore, most transaction systems that offer optimistic schemes will typically cause the detecting transaction to roll back and the application must retry, this time with a fresh copy of the data. Obviously this may result in a lot of work being lost, especially if the transaction that rolls back has been running for some time.

Assuming both optimistic and pessimistic concurrency control are available to you (and they may not be), then which one to use is up to you. A close examination of the environment in which the application and transactional resources reside is necessary to determine whether (a) shared access to resources occurs, and (b) the relative probability that sharing will cause a transaction to roll back. This might very well not be a black or white choice and may change over the lifetime of your objects or application. Certainly the use of different concurrency control schemes can be important when trying to improve the throughput of user requests and committed transactions, so it's well worth considering and understanding the issues involved. Optimistic and pessimistic locking strategies are often available in both database systems and middleware application servers, as we discuss in more detail later.

Type-Specific Concurrency Control

Another possible enhancement is to introduce *type-specific concurrency control*, which is a particularly attractive means of increasing the concurrency in a system by reducing the granularity of the locks used to achieve isolation. Concurrent read/write or write/write operations are permitted on an object from different transactions provided these operations can be shown to be non-interfering (for example, for a directory object, reading and deleting different entries can be permitted to take place simultaneously). Object-oriented systems are well suited to this approach, since semantic knowledge about the operations of objects can be exploited to control permissible concurrency within objects. Additional work may be needed when working with procedural systems.

Deadlock Detection and Prevention

When multiple transactions compete for the same resources in conflicting modes (locks), it is likely that some of them will fail to acquire those resources. If a transaction that cannot acquire a lock on a resource waits for it to be released, then that transaction is *blocked*—no forward progress can be made until the lock has been acquired. In some environments, it is possible for some transactions to be waiting for each other, where each of them is blocked and is also blocking another transaction. In this situation, none of the transactions can proceed and the system is *deadlocked*.

For example, let's consider two transactions T_1 and T_2 that operate on two resources X and Y. Let's assume that the execution of the operations involved in these transactions is:

- T_1: read(X); write(Y)
- T_2: read(Y); write(X)

If the serial execution of these transactions were to result in:

- readT$_1$(X); readT$_2$(Y); writeT$_2$(X); readT$_1$(Y)

N O T E   readT$_1$ means the read operation performed by T$_1$, etc.

Assume that T_1 obtained a read lock on X and then T_2 gets a read lock on Y—possible because these operations aren't conflicting and can thus occur in parallel. However, when T_2 comes to write to X its attempt to get a write lock on X will be blocked because T_1 still holds its read lock. Likewise, T_1's attempt to get a write lock on Y will block because of the read lock that T_2 holds. Each transaction is blocked waiting for the release of the other's read lock before they can progress: they are *deadlocked*.

The only way for the deadlock to be resolved is for at least one of the transactions to release its locks that are blocking another transaction. Obviously such a transaction cannot commit (it has not been able to perform all of its work since it was blocked); therefore, it must roll back.

Deadlock detection and prevention is complicated enough in a non-distributed environment without then including the extra complexity of distribution. In general, most transaction systems allow deadlocks to occur, simply because to do otherwise can be too restrictive for applications. There are several techniques for deadlock detection, but the two most popular are:

- *Timeout-based*: If a transaction has been waiting longer than a specified period of time, the transaction system will automatically roll back the transaction on the assumption it is deadlocked. The main advantage of this approach is that it is easy to implement in a distributed environment; the main disadvantage is that some transactions may execute for longer than expected and be rolled back when they are not in fact deadlocked.

• *Graph-based*: This explicitly tracks waiting transaction dependencies by constructing a waits-for graph: nodes are waiting transactions and edges are waiting situations. The main advantage of this approach is that it is guaranteed to detect all deadlocks, whereas the main disadvantage is that in a distributed environment it can be costly to execute.

A slight variation on the timeout-based approach exists in some transaction systems, where timeouts can be associated with lock acquisition, such that the system will only block for the specified period of time. If the lock has not been acquired by the time this period elapses, it returns control to the application indicating that the lock has not been acquired. It is then up to the application to determine what to do; for example, it may be possible to obtain the required data elsewhere or to ask for a lock in a different mode. The advantage of this approach is that a transaction is not automatically rolled back if it cannot acquire a lock, possibly saving the application lots of valuable time; the disadvantage is that it requires additional effort on behalf of the application to resolve lock acquisition failures. However, for many objects and applications, this is precisely the best place to resolve lock conflicts because this is the only place where the semantic information exists to know what (if anything) can be done to resolve such conflicts.

Durability

The durability (or persistence) property means that any state changes that occur during the transaction must be saved in such a manner that a subsequent failure will not cause them to be lost. How these state changes are made persistent is typically dependent on the implementation of the transaction system and the resources that are ultimately used to commit the work done by the transactional objects. For example, the database will typically maintain its state on disk in order to ensure that a machine failure (e.g., loss of power) does not result in loss of data.

> **N O T E** The durability property can never be an absolute guarantee, since a catastrophic failure (e.g., corruption of hard disk) could ultimately result in total loss of information.

Services and Participants

Up to this point we've been fairly general with the terms "participant" and "service." However, most transaction processing systems make a clear distinction between a service (also known as a transactional object) and the participants that are controlled by the transaction coordinator. This distinction is important because it shows where the responsibilities lie for the ACID properties:

- *Transactional object/service*: This is the object or application entity that encapsulates the business logic or work that is required to be conducted within the scope of a transaction. This work cannot be committed by the application unless the transaction also commits; control is ultimately removed from the application and placed into the transaction's domain. An example (shown in Figure 1-4) of such an object would be an object (e.g., EJB) that is responsible for buying a seat on a flight given user input; only if the user commits the transaction does the ticket for the flight actually get purchased. This means that the EJB cannot by itself make the work it is asked to do happen: that is down to the transaction and the associated transactional participant. However, it is the service that is ultimately responsible for *consistency* and *isolation*. It may do this with help from the resources it uses to accomplish the business work (e.g., databases typically provide concurrency control) or through an explicit concurrency control service.
- *Transactional participant/resource*: This is the entity that takes part in the two-phase commit protocol and controls the outcome of the work performed by the service. In the example above, and shown in Figure 1-5, if the flight purchasing EJB uses a database to store information on seat availability, it will typically access this information via a JDBC driver; SQL statements will be sent to the database for processing (e.g., how to reserve seat 12E) via the driver, but these statements will be tentative and only commit when (and if) the transaction does so. In order to do this, the driver/database will associate a two-phase commit participant (an `XAResource`, as we see in Chapter 2) with the transaction. When the transaction terminates (either commits or rolls back), it informs the `XAResource`, which will in turn inform the database of the transaction outcome, by committing or rolling back the state changes. Obviously the participant, working with the database in this case, must be able to identify the work that the transactional object did within the scope of a specific transaction and either commit the work or roll it back. The participant takes part in the two-phase commit protocol to ensure atomicity and is also responsible for durability (it must make state changes on behalf of the service provisionally durable during the prepare phase, for example).

So far, we've looked at the basics of ACID transactions and the protocols that go to make up the various guarantees. In the following section we extend our investigations into the two-phase commit protocol and illustrate various optimizations that may be available in certain implementations.

N O T E   You should be aware that it is not necessary for a transaction system to implement any of these optimizations.

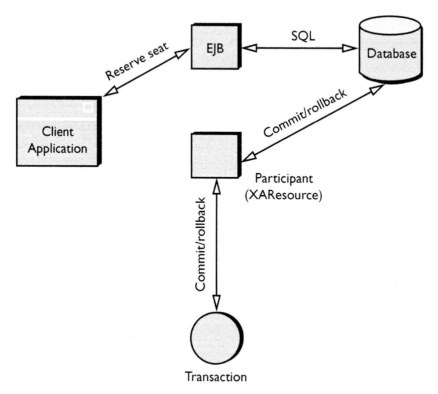

Figure 1-4   Transactional object and participant.

Two-Phase Commit Optimizations

As we've seen, the two-phase commit protocol is the standard mechanism for achieving atomic outcomes for transactions. When you use a transaction service, it is almost certain that it will use two-phase commit. To support high volume and performance applications, most transaction services will support optimizations to the protocol. There are several variants to the standard two-phase commit protocol that can have significant impact on performance and failure recovery. We shall briefly describe the three most common variants on the protocol that are found in most modern transaction processing systems:

- *Presumed abort*: If a transaction is going to roll back then it may simply record this information locally and tell all enlisted participants (even this record is actually optional). Failure to contact a participant has no affect on the transaction outcome; the coordinator is informing participants as a courtesy. Once all participants have been contacted (or as many as can be) the information about the transaction can be removed.

If a subsequent request for the transaction's status occurs, there will be no information available and the requestor can assume that the transaction has aborted (rolled back). In some situations, the courtesy message from the transaction could be omitted entirely, requiring participants to eventually call back to the transaction to determine the outcome. (Although this can lead to an increased chance of heuristic outcomes, as we see later.) This optimization has the added benefit that no information about participants need be made persistent until the transaction has decided to commit (i.e., progressed to the end of the prepare phase), since any failure prior to this point will be assumed to be an abort of the transaction.

- *One-phase*: If there is only a single participant involved in the transaction, the coordinator need not drive it through the prepare phase—there is implicit consensus among participants in this case. Thus, the participant will simply be told to commit and (in some variants) the transaction coordinator need not record information about the decision since the outcome of the transaction is solely down to the participant.

- *Read-only:* When a participant is asked to prepare, it can indicate to the coordinator that it is responsible for an object/service that did not do any work during the course of the transaction, or at least did not do any work that modified any state. This is known as a read-only participant and it does not need to be informed about the outcome of the transaction since the fate of the participant has no affect on the transaction. As such, a read-only participant can be omitted from the second phase of the commit protocol.

- *Last resource commit:* In some cases it may be necessary to enlist participants that aren't two-phase commit aware into a two-phase commit transaction. As we've already seen with the one-phase optimization, if there is only a single resource then there is no need for two-phase commit. However, what if there are multiple resources in the transaction? In this case, the Last Resource Commit optimization comes into play. It is possible for a *single* resource that is one-phase aware (i.e., can only commit or roll back, with no prepare), to be enlisted in a transaction with two-phase commit aware resources. The coordinator treats the one-phase aware resource slightly differently, in that it executes the prepare phase on all other resource first, and if it then intends to commit the transaction it passes control to the one-phase aware resource. If it commits, then the coordinator logs the decision to commit and attempts to commit the other resources as well. As you can imagine, there are failure scenarios where loss of atomicity is possible here, but we go into more details in Chapter 2.

If we look at Figure 1-5, we see how the transaction coordinator interacts with the transaction log and the various transaction participants. In the figure, we assume an implementation of the presumed abort protocol and for simplicity we ignore the read-only optimization. As we can see, prior to the prepare phase, there is no need for the coordinator to interact with the log, since any failures of the application or transaction will simply cause the transaction to roll back. Then the coordinator enters the prepare phase and sends the prepare message to the participants. If any

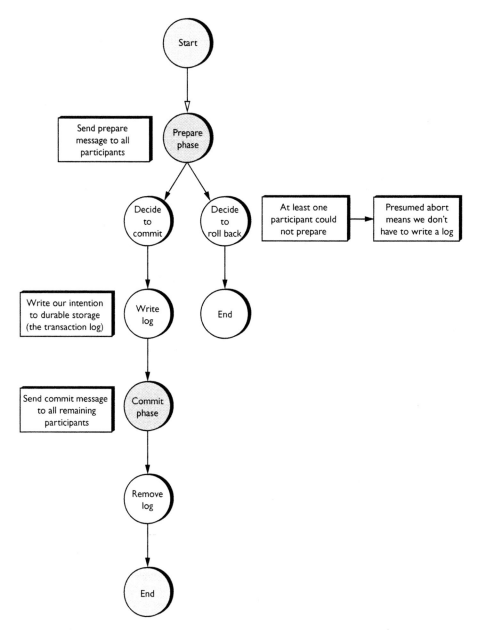

Figure 1-5   The coordinator, participant and transaction log interactions.

of the participants votes to roll back or fails to respond, the coordinator decides to roll back the entire transaction. As we saw earlier, there is no requirement in the presumed abort protocol for the coordinator implementation to write a log stipulating its intention to roll back.

However, if the prepare phase completes successfully and the coordinator decides to commit, then it must record this fact in the transaction log. (If the entire transaction used read-only participants, then no log updates will be required and the transaction can end.) Additional information such as references to the participants will also typically be recorded. At this point the coordinator can enter the commit phase and inform all participants that they should commit. Assuming this phase completes successfully, the transaction log can be removed.

If the commit phase does not complete in its entirety, the log will remain in existence, usually for failure recovery mechanisms to use later to try to finish the transaction. As we see later, it is possible for the second phase to fail in a number of ways. For example, the coordinator could crash, participants could find that they are unable to commit, network connections could fail, and so on. Luckily in most cases mature transaction systems have solutions to these problems that don't lead to data inconsistencies. Probably the worst type of failure during the second phase is that which leads to *heuristic outcomes*, but we deal with that in the next section.

So why is this important? Despite the fact that hardware gets faster year after year, it's still a fact that most durable store implementations (raw operating system file systems, databases, etc.) are the performance bottleneck for transaction services. Although durable storage media such as hard disks are faster than they were years ago, the performance gains of your typical processor have been much greater. What this means is that any attempt to reduce the number of disk accesses can also help to improve performance. Therefore, the fact that in a presumed abort protocol, the transaction coordinator need not access the durable log until it has decided to commit means that any potential bottleneck only occurs when required: when the transaction commits.

Earlier in this chapter we described the two-phase commit protocol that is used between coordinator and participants when terminating a transaction. In the following section we discuss another protocol that may also be used during termination and is yet another possible optimization available to transaction users.

Synchronizations

You may think that two-phase commit is sufficient for your transactional needs. However, if you want your applications to perform, you'll quickly be looking for ways to reduce the amount of time your application interacts with the persistence store. Caching of an object's state (e.g., an entire database table) in the local memory and operating on that cached state for the duration of a transaction can significantly improve performance over the alternative: continually going back and forth to the database. However, what happens if you update that cached state? You'll then need some way of forcing that state back to the original persistence store *prior* to the transaction committing.

In many transaction systems this is accomplished through *Synchronization participants*. Synchronizations are informed that a transaction is *about* to commit, so they can, for example, flush volatile (cached) state, which may have been used to improve performance of an application, to a recoverable object or database prior to the transaction committing. They are then informed when the transaction has completed and in what state it completed.

Let's take a look again at our banking example and try to show how Synchronizations could be used there. If you remember, the bank maintains the information on its accounts on a durable store, such as a database or disk. Now let's suppose that along with the amount of money held in each account, the bank maintains contact information on behalf of each client (name, address, home phone number, work phone number, and so on.) As part of its service to its clients, the bank supports the online update of this information by its clients, but this has to happen within a transaction.

Now, if Mr. Smith wants to update his contact details, a straightforward way of doing this would be for the bank to give direct access to the database on which the information resides. So, if he changes his address, that translates to a provisional update at the database; it has to be provisional, because Mr. Smith isn't done yet and so the transaction hasn't committed. If Mr. Smith wants to update a lot of information, this may take a while because each update (and even each read) requires access to the database.

Because of criticism of the poor performance of this service from its clients, the bank decides to re-implement slightly and use Synchronizations. When Mr. Smith first accesses his personal details, a cached copy of all of the information is (transparently) taken into the bank servers' memory and managed on behalf of the transaction by a Synchronization. Mr. Smith doesn't see any difference in terms of what he can do, but he will see a noticeable performance improvement. When Mr. Smith is eventually finished, the transaction terminates and this will cause (via the Synchronization) the cache to be flushed to disk before the two-phase commit protocol executes on the database.

Synchronizations essentially turn the two-phase commit protocol into a four-phase protocol:

- Before the transaction starts the two-phase commit, all registered Synchronizations are informed. What they do will obviously depend upon the specific implementation, but as we've seen, typically an implementation will flush a cached copy of some transactional object state to a database or other repository where its ultimate fate will be controlled by a participant in the two-phase commit protocol. Any failure at this point (the Synchronization fails to flush the state, for example) will cause the transaction to roll back. Note that synchronizations do not need to flush their state if the termination command for the transaction is abort: the changes would be rolled back.
- The coordinator then conducts the normal two-phase commit protocol. This protocol does not involve the Synchronizations.
- Once the transaction coordinator has finished the two-phase commit protocol, all registered Synchronizations are informed. However, this is a courtesy invocation because any failures at this stage are ignored: the transaction has terminated so there's nothing to affect.

Now that we've looked at possible optimizations to the traditional transaction protocols, let's consider how failures are tolerated and recovered from by transaction implementations.

We've already hinted at one of the most significant types of failure that can occur in a transaction system, so let's now take a detailed look at heuristic transactions. It's very important that we describe what heuristic transactions are, because they can mean a lot of work for you or a system administrator to resolve. Unfortunately, as we're about to see, they can be almost impossible to avoid entirely, especially in a distributed environment. Heuristic transactions are an inevitable fact of life.

Heuristic Transactions

In order to guarantee atomicity, the two-phase commit protocol is necessarily blocking. If the coordinator fails, for example, any prepared participants must remain in their prepared state until they hear the transaction outcome from the coordinator. When discussing failure recovery, we saw how recovery may be driven from both the top-down (coordinator to participant) and the bottom-up (participant to coordinator). However, in order for recovery to occur, machines and processes obviously need to recover! In addition, even if recovery does happen, the time it takes can be arbitrarily long.

What this means is that as a result of failures, participants may remain blocked for an indefinite period of time even if failure recovery mechanisms exist. Some applications and participants simply cannot tolerate this blocking (for similar reasons as deadlock). Imagine poor Mr. Smith having to wait days to be able to access his bank account again. As such, relatively early on in the development of transaction processing systems there was work on how to address this issue in a controlled manner.

To break the blocking nature of two-phase commit, participants that have gotten past the prepare phase are allowed to make autonomous decisions as to whether they commit or rollback: such a participant *must* durably record this decision in case it is eventually contacted to complete the original transaction. If the coordinator (or failure recovery mechanisms) eventually informs the participant of the transaction outcome and it is the same as the choice the participant made, there is no problem. However, if it is contrary, then a possibly non-atomic outcome has happened: a *heuristic outcome*, with a corresponding *heuristic decision*.

Just because a participant makes a heuristic choice does not automatically mean that the transaction outcome will be a heuristic. There are two levels of heuristic interaction:

- Participant-to-coordinator: If the participant makes an autonomous decision, it must assume that it has caused a heuristic and remember the choice it made so that eventually (and somehow) this could be resolved. At this point the participant is in a *heuristic state*.
- Coordinator-to-application: If the participant(s) really did make a choice contrary to the coordinator, then a heuristic outcome must be reported to the application. The transaction will still be marked as either committed or rolled back, but it will also be in a heuristic state, which will reflect the heuristic state(s) of the participant(s).

Some transaction service implementations will strive very hard to prevent heuristic outcomes from occurring. For example, let's assume the first phase of the termination protocol completes successfully and the coordinator decides to commit; if the very first participant the coordinator communicates with during the second phase tells the coordinator that it has rolled back, despite previously telling the coordinator it could commit, then obviously a heuristic could result. However, if the coordinator then changes its mind to match the participant's rollback decision and tells all other participants to roll back, no heuristic has actually happened: the state of all participants matches the coordinators (despite the fact that the coordinator actually changed its mind part way through the process!).

How a heuristic outcome is reported to the application and resolved is usually the domain of complex, manually driven system administration tools, since in order to attempt an automatic resolution requires semantic information about the nature of participants involved in the transaction, which is normally not available to most transaction processing systems. In Chapter 3, The Object Transaction Service, we see how the CORBA OTS specification maps heuristics to language-level exceptions that can be thrown by the transaction API. However, heuristics could occur after the transaction has officially terminated: for example, if not all participants can be contacted during the second phase of the commit protocol, the failure recovery system may be responsible for completing the transaction later. If that happens, any heuristic outcomes cannot be reported directly to the application, which may have long since terminated. It is for this reason that versions of the OTS allow heuristic reporting to be made through an external event-notification service.

Remember that participants in a heuristic state must remember the decision they took. Once the transaction has been resolved, these participants can be informed about the resolution and may then safely remove the information from durable storage.

Let's look the a specific example shown in Figure 1-6, where a transaction (shown by the Coordinator) is committing updates performed on two databases (shown by RDBMS). The two RDBMS participants confirm their ability to commit the transaction and obviously store this decision in a durable storage system. The resources used within the transaction (e.g., database tables) then remained blocked until they receive the final transaction outcome (are unavailable for other transactions/users).

The transaction moves to the second phase of the commit protocol and sends both participants the commit decision. Unfortunately, between the two calls the network connection between the coordinator and the second database fails. The first database has already committed (correctly), while the second does not receive the second phase message and hence keeps the resources blocked, pending the decision of the transaction manager. After some implementation specific period of time the second RDBMS (or the system's administrator) takes the autonomous decision to roll back the transaction in order to free these resources.

In this particular case, data integrity is compromised, as the entire transaction is no longer atomic. When the network connection is eventually restored and the coordinator's second phase message is eventually retransmitted (probably by the failure recovery system), the transaction

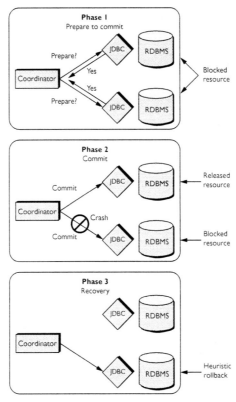

Figure 1-6 Example of heuristic outcomes.

system will determine that the second database took a decision that resulted in non-atomic behavior.

If the network failure had been between the coordinator and the *first* database, then the coordinator could have decided to roll back the transaction to try to ensure consistency. This would be based on the assumption that since no second phase message has been seen by any participant, the decision to commit hasn't been seen outside of the coordinator. In general this is probably the safest option to take in this situation, but it can't guarantee not to lead to heuristic outcomes. In this example, the first database may decide to autonomously commit if it doesn't receive the coordinator's second phase message.

When a participant makes a heuristic decision is obviously up to the participant: some may decide never to make an autonomous choice for fear of causing a non-atomic outcome. Others may choose when they have not heard from the coordinator within a long period of time after being asked to prepare, since most transaction commits take seconds or minutes to complete.

Obviously the choice the participant makes (to commit or to roll back) will depend upon the participant implementation and possibly the application/environment in which it finds itself.

The possible heuristic outcomes are:

- Heuristic rollback: the commit operation failed because the participants unilaterally rolled back the transaction.
- Heuristic commit: an attempted rollback operation failed because all of the participants unilaterally committed. This may happen if, for example, the coordinator was able to successfully prepare the transaction but then decided to roll it back (e.g., it could not update its log) but in the meantime the participants decided to commit.
- Heuristic mixed: some updates (participants) were committed while others were rolled back.
- Heuristic hazard: the disposition of some of the updates is unknown. For those which are known, they have either all been committed or all rolled back.

As we saw in the example, heuristic decisions should be used with care and only in exceptional circumstances since there is the possibility that the decision will differ from that determined by the transaction service and will thus lead to a loss of integrity in the system.

Heuristic outcomes are perhaps the worst type of failure that can befall an application using transactions. However, as we've seen, any good transaction system will provide support to help alleviate the problems that may arise from them. This support is usually part of a much larger subsystem component of the transaction system: the failure recovery system, which we discuss in more detail in the next section.

N O T E In some cases an application may not want to be informed of heuristic outcomes at all. (We would caution against this, for fairly obvious reasons.) In this case, when the application instructs the coordinator to terminate the transaction, it is possible for a transaction service implementation to return control to the application as soon as the first phase of the commit protocol has completed, spawning a separate (asynchronous) thread to perform the second phase (commit or rollback). This has obvious performance benefits, but failures in the second phase may not be made available directly to the application. Some commercial transaction services provide this option (e.g., the Arjuna Transaction Service), but it should be used with caution.

The Transaction Log

Although most users of transactions will see durability from their application's point of view, there is also an aspect of durability within the transaction system implementation itself. In order to guarantee atomicity in the presence of failures (for both the transaction coordinator and resources), it is necessary for the transaction service itself to maintain state. For example, in some implementations the coordinator must remember the point in the protocol it has reached (i.e., whether it is committing or aborting), the identity of all participants that are registered with the transaction and where they have reached in the protocol (e.g., whether they have received the prepare message). This is typically referred to as the *transaction log*, though this should not be interpreted as implying a specific implementation. Some implementations may maintain a sepa-rate log (file) per transaction, with this information recorded within it and removed when it is no longer needed. Another possible implementation has a single log for all transactions and the transaction information is appended to the end of the log and pruned from the log when the respective transaction completes.

Let's look at what happens at the participant in terms of durability, when it's driven through the two-phase commit protocol, shown in Figure 1-7. We also use the term *original state* to mean the state the participant controls prior to the transaction starting, and *new state* to mean the state that exists when the transaction is about to commit.

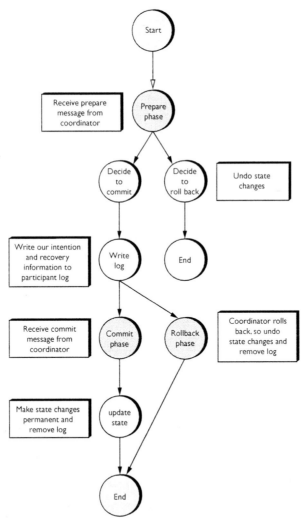

Figure 1-7 Participant log interactions.

As you can see, when the participant receives a prepare message from the coordinator it must decide whether it can commit or roll back. If it decides to roll back then it must undo any state changes that it may control (e.g., make sure that Mr. Smith's accounts are returned to their original state) and inform the coordinator; there is no requirement for durable access at this point. If the participant can commit, it must write its intentions to a durable store (*participant log*) along with sufficient information to either commit or roll back the state changes it controls. The format of this information is typically dependent on the type of participant, but may include the entire original and new states.

Once successfully recorded, the participant informs the coordinator that it can commit and awaits the coordinator's decision. When this second phase message arrives, the participant will either cancel all state changes (the coordinator wants to roll back), or if the coordinator wants to commit, make those state changes the current state (e.g., overwrite the original state with the new state). It can then delete the participant log and inform the coordinator.

Failure Recovery

Failures occur in all computing systems, both centralized and distributed. The more components that are involved with an application, the greater the chance of a failure occurring. As we mentioned earlier, in a distributed system failures are often independent—the failure of one component (process, machine, and so on.) does not necessarily cause the (immediate) failure of another.

Not only are transactions a good tool to use to ensure consistency in the presence of concurrent users or to obtain consensus between multiple participants/services, but they also offer an excellent fault-tolerance mechanism. Scoping work within a transaction, you immediately get the benefits of atomicity (all or nothing) despite failures: the transaction system must ensure that the work you do within the transaction either happens or appears to have never happened. All you will typically have to do is start and end the transaction.

However, failures can affect the transaction system itself. Although you may host your transaction system on more expensive (and hopefully more reliable) machines than your typical application, there can be no guarantees that those machines or the network connecting them to the rest of your environment won't fail. Enterprise-level transaction systems have usually had many man-years of effort put into their failure recovery and fault-tolerance capabilities. Without such capabilities, the benefits a transaction system offers are seriously downgraded. You will usually find that failure recovery is something that most open source or freeware transaction systems neglect entirely or simply don't consider to be important. Unfortunately, for a user it can often be the most important piece of the puzzle (Mr. Smith would be more than a little annoyed if the bank's transaction system lost his $400 due to a failure). It's something you don't want to discover that has been omitted until it is too late.

In order to cope with failures, transaction service implementations must possess some form of failure recovery subsystem. This subsystem ensures that results of a transaction are applied consistently to all resources affected by the transaction, even if any of the application processes or the machine hosting them crash or lose network connectivity. In the case of a machine (system) crash or network failure, the recovery will obviously not take place until the system or network is restored.

Importantly, the original application does not need to be restarted in order to perform recovery: the responsibility for recovery is typically delegated to a separate recovery process, although this will depend strongly on the transaction service implementation being used.

Recovery after failure requires that information about the transaction and the resources involved survives the failure and is accessible afterward: this information (the transaction log mentioned previously) is held in some durable state-store and therefore available upon machine recovery. Typically the transaction log (or logs, depending upon the implementation) is scanned to determine whether there are transactions mentioned in it that require recovery to be performed. If there are, then the information within the log is used to recreate the transaction and the recovery subsystem will then continue to complete the transaction. What action the recovery subsystem performs will depend upon which flavor of two-phase commit the transaction system uses; for example, in a presumed abort protocol, the fact that a log entry exists implicitly means that the transaction was in the process of committing.

We have already described the ACID properties that using transactions provide. One obvious consequence of ACID is that until the recovery procedures are complete, resources affected by a transaction that was in progress at the time of the failure may be inaccessible. For database resources, this may be reported as tables or rows held by "in-doubt transactions." To do otherwise could result in inconsistencies in the application or data.

N O T E What has been described so far assumes that recovery occurs from the transaction coordinator to the participant (top-down recovery). However, this is not necessarily always the case and in fact recovery may have to be driven from the participant to the transaction coordinator (bottom-up recovery).

So, for example, if a machine on which a participant resides fails and then recovers, the participant may need to enquire as to the status of the transaction. If participants waited for recovery to be driven from the coordinator then there are a number of issues that could cause problems. (This is not meant to be a complete list and is only presented to illustrate what a complex issue failure recovery can be and why many non-commercial implementations tend to undervalue it and underestimate how much effort is really required to do it justice.)

- If the coordinator has also failed and recovered, it may take some time before the recovery subsystem gets around recovering the specific transaction and hence resources may be inaccessible for longer than necessary.
- If a presumed abort protocol is used and the participant fails after having said it could prepare and the coordinator fails before it writes its log to say that it wants to commit, there will be no recovery on behalf of that transaction—no log entry for the transaction

means the transaction has rolled back as far as the recovery system is concerned. Hence, the participant will never get a termination message from the recovery subsystem.

Thus, most transaction systems require a failure recovery component to exist on both the coordinator and participant machines so that recovery can be driven in a bi-directional manner.

Implementing recovery is extremely complex and most public domain transaction service implementations (and some commercial products) don't provide it. So beware—find out about this feature before you invest time and money in using transactions. You don't want to discover that recovery is not supported after a critical failure has occurred. Without recovery mechanisms, atomic transactions may not be possible.

Let's consider our bank example and how a failure would affect it, as illustrated in Figure 1-8. When Mr. Smith begins to transfer his money he will (indirectly) start a transaction that will be used to manage the debit from the CurrentAccount and the credit to the SavingsAccount. Now let's assume that the debit/credit happens as per Mr. Smith's instructions. To do this, each

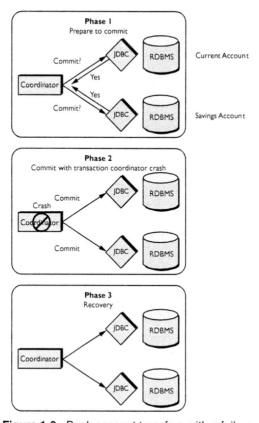

Figure 1-8 Bank account transfers with a failure.

of the bank account transactional services will have enlisted a participant with the transaction. When Mr. Smith informs the bank to perform the transaction, the bank will inform the transaction manager to commit. The transaction coordinator will execute the two-phase commit protocol among the registered participants. When it decides that it can commit, the transaction will write the log with information on the CurrentAccount and SavingsAccount participants; likewise, each of the two participants will previously have written enough information during the prepare phase to ensure that they can either commit or rollback the transfer should the coordinator inform them.

If a failure of the transaction coordinator occurs at this point (as shown in Figure 1-8) then the money (and the two bank accounts) will remain in a state of limbo. The money has not been transferred to the SavingsAccount but it also no longer resides in the CurrentAccount. Typically Mr. Smith won't be able to look at his accounts, because to do otherwise would break transaction semantics. However, because his bank uses an industrial strength transaction system, he can rest assured that his money hasn't been lost. Unfortunately, he'll just have to wait until the transaction coordinator machine recovers. When this eventually happens, the recovery subsystem will locate the transfer transaction in the log and essentially recreate the transaction. Once recreated, the transaction coordinator once again has the ability to complete the second phase of the two-phase commit protocol with the two account participants. At last Mr. Smith's money is transferred and he can check his accounts again.

Now let's consider a slightly more complex scenario, shown in Figure 1-9. During the post-prepare phase of Mr. Smith's transfer of money, a failure of the network stops the transaction coordinator from sending the commit message to the second database (the SavingsAccount); the CurrentAccount commits as instructed and Mr. Smith's $400 is removed. As we've already mentioned, the second database will have to wait for the second phase message before making a decision and the enlisted resources remain unavailable to other transactions. However, in this case the second phase message doesn't come quickly because of the network failure. So, after a period of time set by the administrator, the database makes a unilateral decision without waiting for the transaction coordinator; it decides to roll back the transaction updates (not accept to transfer of funds into the SavingsAccount) in order to free up the bank account (resources). This is obviously a heuristic decision, as the transaction has been committed and the $400 removed from the CurrentAccount.

Once the network connection is re-established, the crash recovery component will reconnect to the second database and will detect a heuristic exception, which will be transmitted to the administrator so that he/she can take the necessary compensatory action to bring the system back into a consistent state.

At this point we've covered many of the fundamentals of transaction processing, including optimizations and recovery from various failure scenarios. We've seen that transactions are an important tool that can be used to obtain fault-tolerance and ensure consistency in the presence of concurrent access to data. If you use transactions then you'll be placing your trust in these concepts as well as the specific service implementation. So, let's take a quick look at some trust implications that may not be immediately apparent, but which are important to understand.

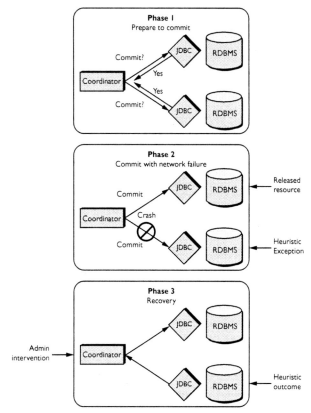

Figure 1-9 Recovery and heuristics.

Trust Implications

Something often overlooked by transaction implementers and users is that the two-phase commit protocol assumes a level of trust between the parties involved in the transaction. As we've seen, in any transaction there are essentially three actors:

- The participant that is driven through the two-phase commit protocol.
- The coordinator, with which participants register and that drives them through the commit protocol.
- The application logic that tells the coordinator whether it wants to commit or rollback the transaction.

Whatever the application logic might want (e.g., to commit) is never guaranteed by the coordinator, simply because failures can occur that force the transaction to roll back. In the earlier bank account example, if a transaction were used to control the transfer of money then the work only actually happens when the transaction is committed (after step 4); if a failure occurs during the transfer then the transaction system will rollback, putting the money back into the CurrentAccount.

Assuming that the coordinator and participants behave correctly and no failures occur, then whatever the application logic tells the coordinator to do, the participants will follow. If Mr. Smith informs his bank to commit the transfer, then it will happen.

However, what happens if someone else manages to get control of the transaction? Suppose for example that someone else (Mr. Jones) is capable of intercepting Mr. Smith's directions to the bank and replaces them with his own. If this is the case, then they can obviously tell the bank to roll back even if Mr. Smith is happy with the transfer. This is an unlikely scenario, but it illustrates that the coordinator can only do what it is told to by its users. By itself a transaction coordinator does not possess semantic information about the environment in which it runs or its users; it can't tell the difference between Mr. Smith and Mr. Jones.

Now consider the case where one of the participants decides to act maliciously. By being involved in a transaction the participant has knowledge of the outcome of that transaction: knowing that a specific transaction has committed or rolled back could be important to some people (e.g., insider share trading, where knowing that a specific deal has just occurred could gain you an advantage on buying shares). Furthermore, the participant can affect that outcome through the two-phase commit protocol, e.g., always forcing it to roll back. In effect, a suitably implemented participant could cause a denial of service attack by always refusing to allow a transaction to commit.

In addition, the two-phase commit methods a participant must implement (prepare, commit and rollback) require a certain level of trust in order to work. For example, when told to prepare and then to roll back it is assumed by the coordinator (and ultimately by the user of the transaction) that a participant will undo the work it was told to. There is no guarantee though—it could lie. Suppose that during prepare an application sends to a participant a decryption key for a document and then calls rollback assuming that the participant will destroy the key. The participant may say it has but could in fact lie and keep the key for later.

What if the coordinator is illegal? Being the coordinator allows you to have final say on the actual outcome of the transaction (assuming all other entities involved in the transaction are not being malicious). Just because the application logic says to roll back does not mean that the coordinator actually has to roll back the participants—it could lie. Likewise, if the application logic says to commit and all participants say they can commit, the coordinator could still roll them back. Even more threatening (especially to application consistency) is the fact that the coordinator could tell some participants to commit and others to roll back.

We're not mentioning these "holes" in the protocol to worry you. Most industrial strength transaction systems have been around for years and often incorporate audit trail mechanisms to keep track of which entity did what and when. However, we feel that it is important for you to realize that just because you're using a "transaction system" does not mean that all of your troubles have been solved. As we shall see in later chapters, there is much more to an enterprise transaction system than "just" the two-phase commit protocol and we want you to be forewarned about the possible risks you might take by making that assumption.

So far we've only considered one type of transaction: the so-called ACID transaction. It may surprise you to know that there are quite a few different types of transaction models, each with its own advantages and disadvantages that may make it better suited to certain use cases. In the following section we look at some of the better-known transaction models.

Types of Transactions

The most common form of transaction that people will use is typically called a *top-level transaction*. It exhibits all of the ACID properties mentioned previously. However, traditional transaction processing systems are sufficient if an application function can be represented as a single top-level transaction. Frequently this is not the case. Top-level transactions are most suitably viewed as "short-lived" entities, performing stable state changes to the system; they are less well suited for structuring "long-lived" application functions (e.g., running for minutes, hours or days). Long-lived top-level transactions may reduce the concurrency in the system to an unacceptable level by holding on to resources (e.g., locks) for a long time; further, if such a transaction aborts, much valuable work already performed could be undone. Several enhancements to the traditional flat-transaction model have been proposed and we shall briefly consider some of them in the following sections.

Nested Transactions

Given a system that provides transactions for certain operations, it is sometimes necessary to combine them to form another operation, which is also required to be a transaction. The resulting transaction's effects are a combination of the effects of the transactions from which it is composed. The transactions that are contained within the resulting transaction are *nested* (or *subtransactions*), and the resulting transaction is referred to as the *enclosing* transaction. The enclosing transaction is sometimes referred to as the *parent* of a nested (or *child*) transaction. A hierarchical transaction structure can thus result, with the root of the hierarchy being referred to as the *top-level transaction*, as shown in Figure 1-10, where each transaction is represented as an ellipse.

An important difference exists between nested and top-level transactions: the effect of a nested transaction is provisional upon the commit/roll back of its enclosing transaction(s), i.e., the effects will be recovered if the enclosing transaction aborts, even if the nested transaction has committed.

Subtransactions are a useful mechanism for two reasons:

1. *Fault-isolation*: If subtransaction rolls back (e.g., because an object it was using fails) then this does not require the enclosing transaction to roll back, thus undoing all of the work performed so far.
2. *Modularity*: If there is already a transaction associated with a call when a new transaction is begun, then the transaction will be nested within it. Therefore, a programmer who knows that an object requires transactions can use them within the object: if the

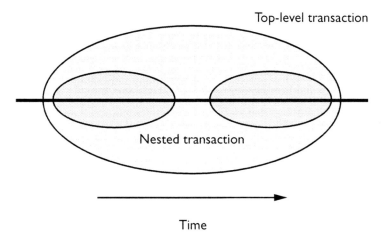

Figure 1-10 Nested transactions.

object's methods are invoked without a client transaction, then the object's transactions will simply be top-level; otherwise, they will be nested within the scope of the client's transactions. Likewise, a client need not know that the object is transactional, and can begin its own transaction.

NOTE   Because nested transactions do not make any state changes durable until the enclosing top-level transaction commits, there is no requirement for failure recovery mechanisms for them.

As far as isolation rules are concerned, locks that are acquired by a child transaction are inherited by the enclosing transaction when it commits. Typically those locks are then available for us in that transaction and any subsequently created children. However, there are other nesting models that restrict the availability of locks to only the parent, so that any newly created child transactions do not automatically have the same access rights on shared resources. This could mean that sibling transactions could conflict with one another.

Although nested transactions have been around in the literature for many years, they have not made much of an appearance in commercial transaction systems. There are a number of reasons for this and not least among them is that no commercial database supports subtransaction-aware participants. Since the majority of services use databases for persistence, this has always been a problem for the proponents of nested transactions. However, this is not to say that they aren't useful or that you can't find commercial transaction systems that support them. For example, the Arjuna Technologies Transaction Service supports nested transactions and provides nested transaction aware resources. The Encina transaction service available from IBM and IONA Technologies supports a limited form of nesting with X/Open XA transactions, by attempting to map them to top-level transactions.

One compromise that used to be common in some transaction systems was to allow a form of optimistic nesting when true nested transaction semantics were not available. Nested transactions could be started, but were grouped into the same top-level transaction such that nested commits would work fine, but a rollback in any nested transaction would require that the parent transaction would eventually be forced to roll back as well. This would allow things like workflow systems to start and end transactions, even if an underlying data store did not support nesting. As we see later in Chapter 3, the Object Transaction Service supports a similar model for its nested transactions.

Independent Top-Level Transactions

In addition to normal top-level and nested transactions, there are also such things as *independent top-level transactions* (also known as *nested top-level transactions*), which can be used to relax strict serializability in a controlled manner. With this mechanism it is possible to invoke a top-level transaction from within another transaction. An independent top-level transaction can be executed from anywhere within another transaction and behaves *exactly* like a normal top-level transaction, that is, its results are made permanent when it commits and will not be undone if any of the transactions within which it was originally nested roll back.

If the invoking transaction rolls back, this does not lead to the automatic rollback of the invoked transaction, which can commit or rollback independently of its invoker, and hence release resources it acquires. Such transactions could be invoked either synchronously or asynchronously. In the event that the invoking transaction rolls back compensation may be required.

Figure 1-11 shows a typical nesting of transactions, where transaction B is nested within transaction A. Although transaction C is logically nested within B (it had its Begin operation invoked while B was active), because it is an independent top-level transaction it will commit or rollback independently of the other transactions within the structure. Because of the nature of

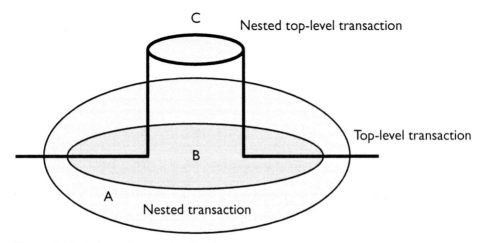

Figure 1-11   Independent top-level action.

independent top-level transactions they should be used with caution and only in situations where their use has been carefully examined.

Unlike nested transactions, nested top-level transactions can be found in the majority of commercial transaction systems. This is because you don't need any special support from your services or participants, i.e., there's no requirement for subtransaction-aware participants: ultimately a nested top-level transaction is a top-level transaction after all. And you might be surprised how useful they are and how relatively widely deployed nested top-level transactions are used.

Concurrent Transactions

Just as application programs can execute concurrently, so too can transactions (top-level or nested), i.e., they need not execute sequentially. So, a given application may be running many different transactions concurrently, some of which may be related by parent transactions, as shown in Figure 1-12.

We've already discussed the isolation rules for top-level and nested transactions. Whether those transactions are executed concurrently or serially does not affect the isolation rules: the overall affect of executing concurrent transactions must be the same as executing them in some serial order.

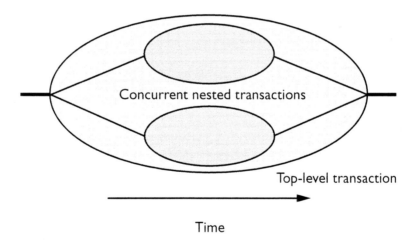

Figure 1-12   Concurrent transactions.

Glued Transactions

Top-level transactions can be structured as many independent, short-duration top-level transactions, to form a "logical" long-running transaction; the duration between the end of one transaction and the beginning of another is not perceivable and selective resources (e.g., locks on database tables) can be atomically passed from one transaction to the next, as shown in Figure 1-13. This structuring allows an activity to acquire and use resources for only the required duration of this long-running transactional activity. In the event of failures, to obtain transactional semantics for the entire long-running transaction may require compensation transactions that can perform forward or backward recovery.

As you might imagine, implementing and supporting glued transactions is not straightforward. Therefore, many (though not all) commercial transaction systems do not support them. However, as we shall see in Chapter 8, the advent of extended transaction mechanisms in general and specifically into J2EE may see that change.

So far we have assumed that transactions run in a local (non-distributed) environment. Although it is true to say that local transactions have their uses (e.g., updating a personal calendar), they really come into their own when used in a distributed manner. In the following section we'll describe those aspects of transactionality that are unique to distribution.

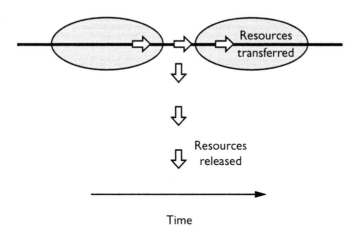

Figure 1-13   Glued transactions.

Distributed Transactions

In this section we look at what makes a transaction distributed. As you may imagine, as soon as you start to distribute transactions across a number of disparate machines (especially as the number of machines grows), many of the issues we've looked at (e.g., failure recovery) become much more complex. We're not going to be able to go into all of these details, but we touch on some of the more relevant aspects of distributed transactions.

The Transaction Context

In order for a transaction to span a distributed number of services/tasks, certain information has to flow between the sites or domains involved in the application. This is commonly referred to as the *context*. It is propagated in a distributed environment to provide a flow of information between remote execution environments, for example using the CORBA IIOP Service Context information. Typically this occurs transparently to the client and application services although in some cases the application programmer is able to explicitly propagate the context (e.g., as an extra parameter in a method call).

The context typically includes the following information:

- A transaction identifier that guarantees global uniqueness for an individual transaction.
- A coordinator location or endpoint address so participants can be registered by services.
- Implementation specific information, e.g., if the transaction system supports nesting of transactions, then this information may contain the transaction hierarchy that existed at the sending side in order that the importing domain may duplicate this hierarchy.

As shown in Figure 1-14, the context is propagated using whatever distribution mechanism is appropriate to the environment in which it is used (e.g., CORBA IIOP or SOAP). Many distribution infrastructures such as CORBA have a notion of message interceptors; as their name suggests, they intercept both incoming and outgoing messages and can add or remove information to/from the message. For example, at the application (client) an interceptor may be invoked prior to the remote service invocation going on to the network; when the message is taken from the network at the service-side, the corresponding interceptor is immediately invoked.

Transaction processing systems typically utilize interceptors to add the transaction context associated with the invoking thread to the outgoing application message. As shown in Figure 1-14, when the interceptor is called it asks the transaction service for the necessary information on the transaction (if any) associated with the application thread that is performing the remote service invocation. At the service side the transaction context is stripped off the message and associated with the thread that is about to do the work requested. As we see later, this may be an association with the original transaction resident at the client or may entail the domain importing the transaction context to create a local transaction proxy for the remote transaction. In either event, it appears as though the transaction seamlessly crossed process/machine boundaries.

The result of this is to produce what is typically called a transactional remote procedure call (TxRPC). A TxRPC has what is known as *exactly-once semantics*: if the remote call returns successfully it is guaranteed that it was executed once and only once. A basic, non-transactional RPC does not have this guarantee—such an RPC that fails may have been partially executed.

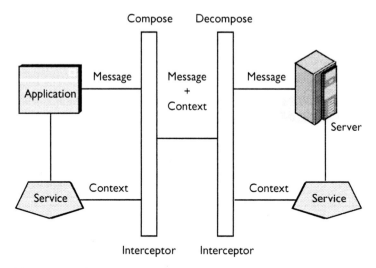

Figure 1-14 Services and context flow.

Interposition

Consider the situation depicted in Figure 1-15, where there is a transaction coordinator and three participants. For the sake of this example, let us assume that each of these participants is on a different machine to the transaction coordinator and each other. Therefore, each of the lines not only represents participation within the transaction, but also remote invocations from the transaction coordinator to the participants and vice versa:

- Enroll a participant in the transaction.
- Execute the two-phase commit protocol.

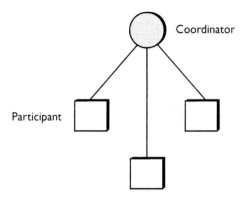

Figure 1-15 A distributed transaction.

In a distributed system there's always an overhead incurred when making remote invocations compared to making a purely local (within the same VM) invocation. Now the overhead involved in making these distributed invocations will depend upon a number of factors, including how congested the network is, the load on the respective machines, the number of transactions being executed, and so on. Some applications may be able to tolerate this overhead, whereas others may not. As the number of participants increase, so does the overhead for fairly obvious reasons.

A common approach to reduce this overhead is to realize that as far as a coordinator is concerned, it does not matter what the participant implementation does. For example, although one participant may interact with a database to commit the transaction, another may just as readily be responsible for interacting with a number of databases: essentially acting as a coordinator itself, as shown in Figure 1-16.

In this case, the participant is acting like a proxy for the transaction coordinator (the root coordinator): it is responsible for interacting with the two participants when it receives an invocation from the coordinator and collating their responses (and its own) for the coordinator. As far as the participants are concerned, a coordinator is invoking them, whereas as far as the root coordinator is concerned it only sees participants.

This technique of using proxy coordinators (or subordinate coordinators) is known as *interposition*. Each domain (machine) that imports a transaction context may create a subordinate coordinator that enrolls with the imported coordinator as though it were a participant. Any participants that are required to enroll in the transaction within this domain actually enroll with the subordinate coordinator. In a large distributed application, a tree of coordinators and participants may be created.

A subordinate coordinator must obviously execute the two-phase commit protocol on its enlisted participants. Thus, it must have its own transaction log and corresponding failure recov-

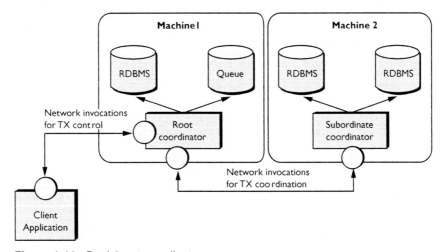

Figure 1-16 Participant coordinator.

ery subsystem. It must record sufficient recovery information for any work it may do as a participant *and* additional recovery information for its role as a coordinator. Therefore, it is impossible
for a normal participant to simply be a subcoordinator because the roles are distinctly different;
subcoordinators are tightly coupled with the transaction system.

> **N O T E** Not all transaction systems support interposition as
> many non-enterprise products see it as only being required for
> performance reasons. However, using interposed coordinators
> also allows an application to be broken down into administrative
> domains, where internal implementation details about partici-
> pants are not exposed to other parts of the distributed system.

So the question then becomes when and why does interposition occur?

1. *Performance*: If a number of participants reside on the same node, or are located phys-
   ically close to one another (e.g., reside in the same LAN domain) then it can improve
   performance for a remote coordinator to send a single message to a subcoordinator
   that is co-located with those participants and for that subcoordinator to disseminate the
   message locally, rather than for it to send each participant the same message.
2. *Security and trust*: A coordinator may not trust indirect participants and neither may
   indirect participants trust a remote coordinator. This makes direct registration impossible. Concentrating security and trust at coordinators can make it easier to reason about
   such issues in a large scale, loosely coupled environment.
3. *Connectivity*: Some participants may not have direct connectivity with a specific coordinator, requiring a level of indirection.
4. *Separation of concerns*: Many domains and services may simply not want to export
   (possibly sensitive) information about their implementations to the outside world.

So far we have talked about what transactions do and how they can benefit an application.
So what exactly happens when your application starts a new transaction? In the next section we
attempt to answer that question.

Controlling a Transaction

In order to talk about what happens when an application starts a transaction, we really need to
talk in general terms since there are many different implementation choices that could affect
what a specific transaction system does. Therefore, with this in mind, let's make a few initial
assumptions:

- All transactions will be managed by a separate process (let's call it a Transaction Factory);
  most modern implementations—and most J2EE servers—provide optimizations that

allow the factory to be co-located with users, but for the sake of our example it is easier to consider it as a separate entity. In J2EE terms this may be provided by the Java Transaction Service (JTS), which we describe in Chapter 3, but can be a proprietary implementation. So, although we might talk about JTS in the rest of this section, you shouldn't assume that it is a requirement; all transaction service implementations will have roughly equivalent terms and components.

- There is a transaction API that allows programmers to demarcate (start and terminate) transactions. This API will interface with the Transaction Factory. In J2EE terms this is the Java Transaction API (JTA), which we describe in Chapter 2.
- For each thread (unit of activity) in a process, the system maintains a mapping to the current transaction associated with that thread. When a thread creates a new transaction or terminates an existing transaction (e.g., via the API), this mapping is automatically updated. Luckily, if you use the JTA you won't need to worry about keeping track of which transaction is associated with which thread.
- All distributed invocations which occur within the scope of a transaction have the transaction context implicitly flowed between clients and servers so that remote invocations occur within the scope of the transaction that is active at the client. This is the domain of the underlying transaction service implementation; so, for example, a JTS implementation will use CORBA Portable Interceptors to augment the Service Context.

> **W A R N I N G** We'd better stress that the above assumption is purely for the purposes of our example. Some systems don't necessarily propagate transaction information (context) on remove invocations even if there is a transaction associated with the client thread performing the invocation. You'd better check what your implementation does if this is a requirement or you could find that service requests don't happen transactionally.

Given these assumptions, the general architecture of the transaction system we use in this description is shown in Figure 1-17.

The commands offered by the API that allow an application to control a transaction are typically:

- *Begin*: start a new transaction.
- *Commit*: commit the transaction and make permanent any work performed within its scope. Obviously even though an application may wish for a transaction to commit, the coordinator and its participants will determine the final outcome.
- *Rollback*: roll the transaction back and undo any work performed within its scope. Sometimes this is also called *aborting the transaction*.

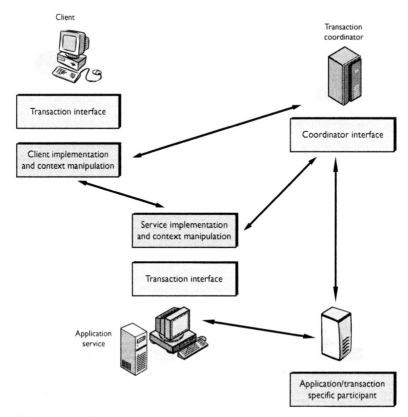

Figure 1-17   General transaction architecture.

As we've already mentioned, this control is typically provided to users through a suitable high-level API, such as the JTA or even the JTS (although as we see later, we would recommend against using the JTS raw as it offers a fairly low-level set of interfaces). However, there are some systems where no direct API exists and messages must be batched up by applications and sent to a transaction manager through a low-level API.

Using UML, Figure 1-18 illustrates what happens when the client issues *begin* on the transactional API (Tx API) to start a new top-level transaction. The Tx API first locates the Transaction Factory and issues a *create* request on it, which causes the factory to start a new transaction. Assuming the transaction is successfully started, the factory returns a reference to the client such that the client can use it for future requests and embed it within the transaction context.

When the transaction reference is returned to the client, the Tx API changes the invoking client thread's notion of what the current transaction is to this new transaction. If the system supported nested transactions, then the thread-to-transaction association would typically occur through a stack, where the new transaction was pushed onto the stack of transactions currently associated with the thread.

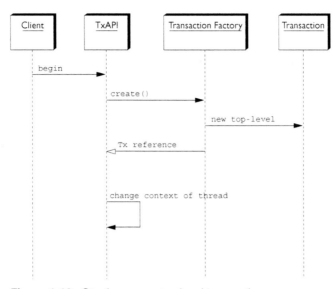

Figure 1-18   Starting a new top-level transaction.

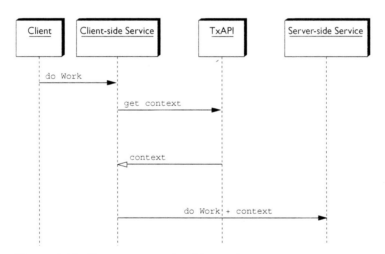

Figure 1-19   Remote transactional invocation.

Figure 1-19 illustrates the work involved when a remote invocation occurs within the scope of the transaction we have just created. Most distributed object models use client-side (local) proxies for remote services to make the fact of distribution transparent: both local and remote objects share the same interfaces and the client application interacts with the proxy which is then responsible for making the remote call. In this example, the client invokes the *doWork* method on the local proxy and its implementation is then required to determine if this invocation is occurring within the scope of an active transaction. Since it is, the reference to the transaction is obtained and the context is then sent to the remote (server) object. Not shown is that at the server, the context is stripped from the invocation and associated with the server-side thread that does the real work, i.e., the inverse occurs.

> **N O T E**   How this actually occurs will depend upon the system used for distributed objects. For example, in CORBA, the IIOP Service Context can be enhanced using Portable Interceptor technology.

When transaction processing systems first began there was no such thing as a multi-threaded application as you may know them today. Having multiple "threads of control" execute within a single operating-system process was often difficult to obtain. In the following section we'll examine what it means to mix transactions and threads.

Transactions and Threads

In this section we consider some of the issues involved when using transactions in a multi-threaded environment. Although Java is inherently a multi-threaded language, it shouldn't come as a surprise to learn that transactions have been around for a lot longer than threads, so when the two came together there were some subtle interactions.

Checked Transactions

When transaction systems were first developed they were *single-threaded* (where a *thread* is defined to be an entity which performs work, e.g., a lightweight process, or an execution context.) Executing multiple threads within a single process was a novelty. In such an environment the thread terminating the transaction is, by definition, the thread that performed the work. Therefore, the termination of a transaction is implicitly synchronized with the completion of the transactional work: there can be no outstanding work still going on when the transaction starts to finish.

With the increased availability of both software and hardware multi-threading, transaction services are now being required to allow multiple threads to be active within a transaction (although it's still not mandated anywhere, so if this is something you want then you may still have to look around the various implementations). In such systems it is important to guarantee that all of these threads have completed when a transaction is terminated, otherwise some work may not be performed transactionally.

> **W A R N I N G**   We can't ignore the fact that the transaction implementation must obviously be multi-thread safe!

Although protocols exist for enforcing thread and transaction synchronization in local and distributed environments (commonly referred to as *checked transactions*), they assume that communication between threads is synchronous (e.g., via remote procedure call). A thread making a synchronous call will block until the call returns, signifying that any threads created have terminated.

However, a range of distributed applications exists (and yours may be one of them) which require extensive use of concurrency in order to meet real-time performance requirements and utilize asynchronous message passing for communication. In such environments it is difficult to guarantee synchronization between threads, since the application may not communicate the completion of work to a sender, as is done implicitly with synchronous invocations.

As we've just seen, applications that do not create new threads and only use synchronous invocations within transactions implicitly exhibit checked behavior. That is, it is guaranteed that whenever the transaction ends there can be no thread active within the transaction which has not completed its processing. This is illustrated in Figure 1-20, in which vertical lines indicate the execution of object methods, horizontal lines message exchange, and the boxes represent objects. Figure 1-20 illustrates a client who starts a transaction by invoking a synchronous "begin" upon a transaction manager. The client later performs a synchronous invocation upon object *a* that in turn invokes object *b*. Each of these objects is registered as being involved in the transaction with the manager. Whenever the client invokes the transaction "end" upon the manager, the manager is then able to enter into the commit protocol (of which only the final phase is shown here) with the registered objects before returning control to the client.

However, when asynchronous invocation is allowed, explicit synchronization is required between threads and transactions in order to guarantee checked (safe) behavior. Figure 1-21 illustrates the possible consequences of using asynchronous invocation without such synchronization. In this example a client starts a transaction and then invokes an asynchronous operation upon object *a* that registers itself within the transaction as before. *a* then invokes an asynchronous operation upon object *b*. Now, depending upon the order in which the threads are sched-

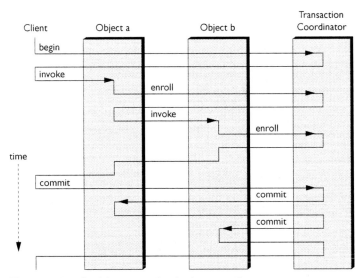

Figure 1-20 Synchronous checked transactions.

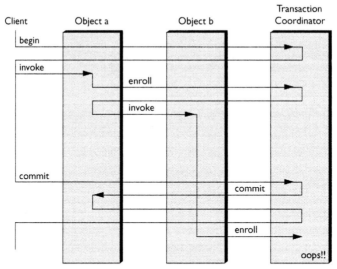

Figure 1-21   Asynchronous invocations.

uled, it's possible that the client might call for the transaction to terminate. At this point the transaction coordinator knows only of a's involvement within the transaction so it enters into the commit protocol, with a committing as a consequence. Then b attempts to register itself within the transaction, and is unable to do so. If the application intended the work performed by the invocations upon a and b to be performed within the same transaction, this may result in application-level inconsistencies. This is what checked transactions are supposed to prevent.

Some transaction service implementations will enforce checked behavior for the transactions they support, to provide an extra level of transaction integrity. The purpose of the checks is to ensure that all transactional requests made by the application have completed their processing before the transaction is committed. A checked transaction service guarantees that commit will not succeed unless all transactional objects involved in the transaction have completed the processing of their transactional requests. If the transaction is rolled back then a check is not required, since all outstanding transactional activities will eventually rollback if they are not told to commit.

As a result, most (though not all) modern transaction systems provide automatic mechanisms for imposing checked transactions on both synchronous and asynchronous invocations. In essence, transactions must keep track of the threads and invocations (both synchronous and asynchronous) that are executing within them and whenever a transaction is terminated, the system must ensure that all active invocations return before the termination can occur and that all active threads are informed of the termination. This may sound simple, but believe us when we say that it isn't.

Unfortunately, this is another aspect of transaction processing that many implementations ignore. As with things like interposition (for performance) and failure recovery, it can be an essential aspect that you really cannot do without in your application. Fortunately, J2EE places sever limitations on transactions and concurrency that result in checked transaction semantics on many of the typical ways in which transactions are used.

Not providing checked transactions is different from allowing checking to be disabled, which most commercial implementations support. In this case you typically have the ability to turn checked transactions off when you know it is safe (e.g., in a read-only application), to help improve performance. If you think there is the slightest possibility you'll be using multiple threads within the scope of a single transaction or may make asynchronous transactional requests, then you'd better find out whether your transaction implementation it up to the job.

Suspending and Resuming Transactionality

As we have seen, when a thread creates a transaction, typically that thread will then become associated with the transaction, i.e., if the thread subsequently asks, "what is my current transaction?" it will be returned as a reference to the one it has just created. As mentioned earlier, this is a bi-directional relationship, since the transaction needs to know which threads are running in it in order to ensure checked behavior.

In some applications, however, there may be a requirement for the thread to be disassociated from the transaction. For example, an application may require periods of non-transactional work for its threads, e.g., an update of a database that is not required to be undone should the enclosing transaction roll back. For that reason, most transaction systems provide a means whereby a thread can *suspend* its transaction association and later (or perhaps never) *resume* the association. This ability to modify a thread's transaction association can also be used to enable multiple threads to execute within the context of the same transaction and not just the creator.

Some distributed applications are what are often termed *loosely coupled*: their constituent components are often independent and execute over arbitrary lengths of time, with invocations often being made asynchronously. A client making an invocation on a service in such an application may not expect to get a response back for minutes, hours or days. Traditional top-level transaction semantics don't work efficiently in these applications. In the next section we examine how the introduction of queues (such as those found in JMS implementations) can solve this problem.

Transactions and Queues

So far we have discussed what can be considered *direct transaction management*: the application synchronously starts the transaction, does work within its scope and then terminates it. This is very much in line with the RPC model that most distributed object systems support. However, there are some applications where this mode of operation is not suitable. For example:

- Transactional activities that may take a (subjectively) long time to complete and would block the client until finished.
- If the server fails or communication problems prevent the client from interacting with the server, the client may have to block waiting for the server to become available, or the application must be written to resubmit the request later.

- What if the client fails after having successfully submitted the request for work to be performed to the server? After executing the request, the server will be unable to deliver the response and the transaction will fail. A recovering client will not know whether the server failed before executing the request, or whether the response was simply lost.
- What if there is a pool of servers all offering the same (popular) service? If all clients use the same server, then it will quickly become overloaded and response times may drop. However, what is the best load-balancing strategy to use? If the application randomly distributes requests across these servers, there is no guarantee that the load will be evenly shared. What if a particular request is high priority and should be executed above all others?

Using an indirect transaction management facility based on queues or buffers of requests and responses can solve these problems. Instead of a client sending requests directly to services, they are sent to a *transactional queue*, as shown in Figure 1-22, which may order them based on priorities set by the queue, the application, the client, and so on. Adding (inserting) a request on a queue is performed within the scope of a transaction and the insertion only actually happens if the transaction commits. Therefore, if the client fails before the transaction commits, it knows that the request has not been performed.

Because the queue is transactional, it maintains persistent state so that it too can tolerate failures. How this state is maintained and what the configuration of the queue is will depend upon the queue implementation. For example, some implementations may store individual requests as separate persistent state entries, whereas others may store all request entries within a single persistent state. There are trade-offs to be made in terms of performance and concurrency control.

Depending upon the system configuration, an arbitrary number of clients may be able to insert an entry within the queue (essentially connected to the *request-insertion end*). Likewise, an arbitrary number of services may be able to remove requests from the queue (essentially connected to the *request-removal end*). It's important to realize that the clients and services connected to a queue need not be identical

As with the client and shown in Figure 1-23, requests are removed from the queue within the scope of a transaction that may span the execution of the work by the service. Thus, only if the request successfully executes the request will it be permanently removed from the queue: the failure of a server either as it removes the request or as it executes it will cause the dequeue transaction to roll back and (appear to) re-insert the request, making it available for another service to dequeue.

But what happens when the service has successfully completed (and removed) the request, i.e., what happens to the response? In just the same way as with requests may be inserted to a transactional queue, so can responses. It will typically be implementation or deployment specific as to whether a different queue is used for the responses than for the requests. Most implementations will also by default tie the enqueue of the response with dequeuing of the request. Other-

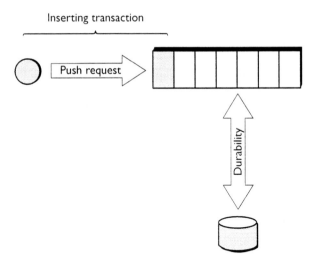

Figure 1-22 Transactional request enqueue.

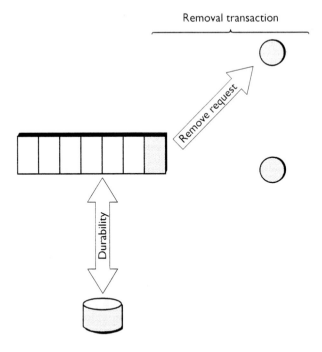

Figure 1-23 Transactional request dequeue.

wise, if two separate transactions are used a failure of the service could happen just after the request has been removed from the queue and before the response has been enqueued. This is illustrated in Figure 1-24.

Transactions ensure that only consistent state changes take place despite concurrent access and failures. However, they may be insufficient to ensure that an application makes forward progress, e.g., a transaction that rolls back because of a machine failure and then restarts may find that the machine has not yet recovered or fails again. It is possible to improve the probability that forward progress can be made by increasing the availability of an application's objects (resources) by replicating them on several machines and managing them through an appropriate replica-consistency protocol. The failure of a subset of these replicas may then be masked, allowing the application to continue. In the following section we give an overview of how replication and transaction techniques can combine to provide data consistency and forward progress in the presence of a finite number of failures.

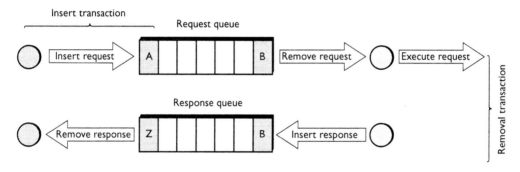

Figure 1-24 Request and response queues.

Transactions and Replication

What we're about to describe in this section is essentially concerned with replication of application-level objects and very few transaction systems (even commercial products) provide this kind of facility. However, as distributed systems grow in scale and complexity it is becoming more of an issue to improve availability for transactional applications and we believe that this sort of functionality will eventually become a critical requirement: you may already have the need today.

It is possible to construct fault-tolerant services (i.e., services capable of tolerating component failures) by replicating vital system components (both in software as well as hardware) and providing the notion of an *abstract component/service* to the users (one which exhibits the properties of a single component but is actually made up of many components). For simplicity we'll assume that replicated resources will reside on distinct nodes (workstations, or processors) in a distributed system (replicating on the same node has limited value, especially in terms of improving *availability* in the presence of node failures). Replication can be used for two main reasons in a distributed system: increased availability, and increased performance. It's also possible that replication can also be used to provide a means of tolerating software design failures.

The management of replicated objects is a complex operation. The main difficulty arises from the fact that an object is not just data, but data (*instance variables*) plus code (*methods* or *operations* which operate on the instance variables); furthermore, method executions can result in calls on other objects. Thus the problem of managing replicated objects really amounts to that of managing *replicated computations*.

This problem can be best formulated in terms of the management of object groups (where each group will represent a replicated object), which are interacting via messages. To avoid any consistency problems it is necessary to ensure that a group appears to behave like a single entity in the presence of concurrent invocations and failures. If not managed properly, concurrent invocations could be serviced in different order by the members of a group, with the consequence that the states of replicas could diverge from each other. Group membership changes (caused by events such as replica failures and insertion of new replicas) can also cause problems if these events are observed in differing order by the users of the group.

Maintaining Information on Persistent Objects

To be able to use an object in a distributed environment, an application must obviously have a reference to it. If that object is replicated, then the information must be managed to maintain consistency. In this section we look at a *typical* way in which a system may identify and access persistent objects in a distributed system. It's important to realize that different implementations of the architecture we describe are possible, although the essential functionality will be the same.

As shown in Figure 1-25, clients typically request this information from a naming service by presenting it the name of the object (message 1). The service maps this name to a previously registered reference to the object and the application then directs its invocations to the object (message 2). In order for a client to make use of a persistent object it is necessary for there to be at least one machine (say α) which is capable of running a server for that object (i.e., it has access to code for the object's methods).

The server for a persistent object and its state need not reside on the same machine. Therefore, there must be at least one machine (say β) whose datastore contains the persistent state of the object. In order to load/store its state (message 4), α may have to contact the naming service to obtain a reference to that node (message 3).

Given the above description, we can see that in a replicated environment a naming service must maintain two sets of data:

1. Sv_A: for an object A, this set contains the names of nodes each capable of running a server for A.
2. St_A: this set contains the names of nodes whose object stores contain states of A.

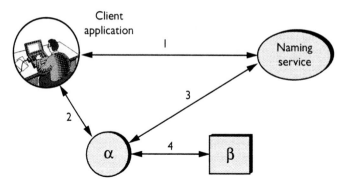

Figure 1-25 Object binding.

An object can become unavailable if all the nodes $\in Sv_A$ are down and/or all the nodes $\in$ St_A are down. In a non-replicated system, a common activation scheme for persistent objects activates an object at a fixed application server that also maintains the state. Therefore, a name server that maps an object name to the server location is all that is required. Exploitation of redundancy in the form of multiple application servers capable of hosting an object and multiple datastores capable of storing the state of an object is possible only after careful enhancements to the system.

Replication Protocols

We will consider the case of *strong consistency* which requires that the states of all replicas that are regarded as *available* be mutually consistent (so the persistent states of all available replicas are required to be identical). Object replicas must therefore be managed through appropriate replica-consistency protocols to ensure strong consistency. To tolerate K replica failures, in a non-partitionable network, it is necessary to maintain at least K+1 replicas of an object, whereas in a partitionable network, a minimum of 2K+1 replicas are necessary to maintain availability in the partition with access to the *majority* of the replicas (the object becomes unavailable in all of the other partitions). There are basically two classes of replication protocols:

- *Active replication*: more than one copy of an object is activated on distinct nodes and all copies perform processing, as shown in Figure 1-26. Active replication is often the preferred choice for supporting high availability of services where masking of replica failures with minimum time penalty is considered highly desirable. Since every functioning replica performs processing, active replication requires that they receive identical invocations in an identical order, and that the computation performed by each replica is deterministic.
- *Passive replication*: only a single copy (the primary) is activated, as shown in Figure 1-27; the primary regularly checkpoints its state to the object stores where states are

stored. One of the advantages of this form of replication is that it can be implemented without recourse to any multicast communication and does not require deterministic replicas; however, its performance in the presence of primary failures can be poorer than under no failures, because the time taken to switch over to a secondary is non-negligible.

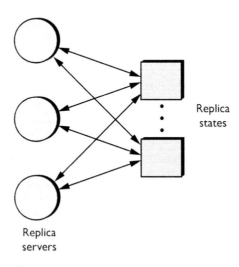

Figure 1-26   Active replication.

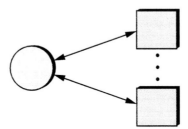

Figure 1-27   Passive replication.

Most replication protocols use replica group technology: A *group* is defined as a collection of distributed entities (objects, processes) in which a member can communicate with other members by multicasting to the full membership of the group. A desirable property is that a given multicast be *atomic*: a message is delivered to either all or none of the functioning members. An additional useful property is guaranteeing *total order*: messages are delivered in the same order to all the functioning members. These properties are ideal for replicated data management: each member manages a copy of data, and given atomic delivery and total order, it can be ensured that copies of data do not diverge.

There are three aspects of managing the replication of persistent objects that are common to both types of replication protocol:

1. *Object binding*: It is necessary to ensure that when an application activates a currently passive replicated object, it only uses those replicas that are (a) mutually consistent, and (b) contain the latest state of the object. If the object has been activated already, clients must be bound to the same replicas.

2. *Object activation and access*: A passive object must be activated according to a given replication policy. Part of object activation means locating the object state(s) and loading it/them into the correct object instance(s). Activated copies of replicas must be treated as a single group by the application in a manner that preserves mutual consistency. Communication between groups requires reliable distribution and ordering guarantees not associated with non-replicated systems: reliability ensures that all correctly functioning members of a group receive messages intended for that group and ordering ensures that these messages are received in an identical order at each member.

3. *Object passivation*: Once an application has finished using a replicated object, it is necessary to ensure that (a) new states of mutually consistent replicas get recorded to their object stores, and (b) information maintained by the system about which replicas are up-to-date remains accurate.

Integrating Replication and Transactions

The functionality provided by transactions and replication protocols overlap, requiring careful design of systems that wish to employ both techniques to avoid incurring unnecessary overheads. For example, many replication implementations rely upon reliable multicast communication to deliver invocations to each replica in the same order. However, the isolation property of transactions also imposes ordering guarantees (e.g., when concurrent clients attempt to perform conflicting invocations), and allows arbitrary interleaving of non-conflicting operations (e.g., concurrent read requests, or operations on different objects). Transactions impose ordering at the application level only when required. Multicast communication protocols typically enforce ordering at a lower level, where application specific knowledge is unavailable, and hence may consume system resources unnecessarily, e.g., ordering non-conflicting messages.

If you consider the three aspects of managing replicated objects mentioned above, then the typical way in which transactions and replication are integrated can best be illustrated with Figure 1-28. The shaded ellipses represent transactions that perform the binding or passivation phases and hence operate on the naming service information St_A and Sv_A mentioned previously. In the binding transaction, the naming service is contacted to either obtain a reference to the currently active object instances to use or, if the replicated object is not being used, those passive instances that can be used. Once the desired number of replicas has been activated, the transaction updates the naming service to inform subsequent clients.

The unshaded ellipse represents the application transaction that performs the real work on the replicated object, using whatever replica consistency protocol is deemed appropriate. As we mentioned earlier, this will typically involve multicast communication to ensure that all replicas get the same set of messages. Depending upon the replication protocol in use, the transaction may be able to commit in the presence of replica failures. If this is so, then when the transaction commits any replica failures must be recorded in order to prevent future users from using potentially out-of-date copies of the object. This is the job of the passivation transaction: it updates the St_A and Sv_A information.

So, we've seen how transactions and replication can be integrated together to provide consistency and forward progress. Although systems that conform to this style do exist, they are typically in the minority. In the next section we look at what you tend to find in terms of transactional high-availability offerings and also give an illustration of one system that does provide the kind of integration we've described.

Availability Measures in Current Application Servers

Commercial application servers tend to make use of multiple applications servers deployed over a cluster of machines in order to distribute load and improve availability in the presence of failures. In the case where specialist router hardware is used to mask server failures, all application servers are typically deployed over a cluster of machines. For example, a locally

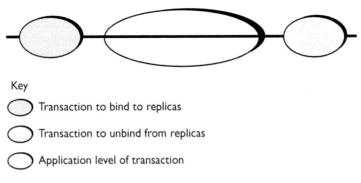

Key

Transaction to bind to replicas

Transaction to unbind from replicas

Application level of transaction

Figure 1-28 Transactions and replication scenario.

distributed cluster of machines with the illusion of a single IP address and capable of working together to host a Web site provides a practical way of scaling up processing power and sharing load at a given site.

Some commercially available application server clusters rely on specially designed gateway routers to distribute the load using a mechanism known as network address translation (NAT). The mechanism operates by editing the IP headers of packets so as to change the destination address before the IP to host address translation is performed. Similarly, return packets are edited to change their source IP address. Such translations can be performed on a per session basis so that all IP packets corresponding to a particular session are consistently redirected.

Alternately, load distribution and high availability can also be performed using a process group communication system as first supported by the ISIS system from Cornell University; for example, the JBoss open source application server has such a mechanism, called JGroups. There is a range of such group communication protocols (often termed *virtually synchronous*), each with its own guarantees on message delivery. For example, causal ordering, where only messages that are related to each other will be delivered in an order that preserves this relationship, and atomic ordering, where messages will always be delivered in the same order to all recipients, but this order may not preserve causality.

The market leaders in the commercial application server space, WebSphere from IBM, WebLogic from BEA and Oracle Application Server, have very similar approaches to clustering. They typically characterize clustering for:

- *Scalability*: The proposed configuration should allow the overall system to service a higher client load than that provided by the simple basic single machine configuration. Ideally, it should be possible to service any given load, simply by adding the appropriate number of machines.
- *Load balancing*: The proposed configurations should ensure that each machine or server in the configuration processes a fair share of the overall client load that is being processed by the system as a whole. Furthermore, if the total load changes over time, the system should adapt itself to maintain this load-balancing property.
- *Failover*: If any one machine or server in the system were to fail for any reason, the system should continue to operate with the remaining servers. The load-balancing property should ensure that the client load gets redistributed to the remaining servers, each of which will henceforth process a proportionately slightly higher percentage of the total load. Transparent failover (failures are masked from a client, who minimally might need to retransmit the current request) is an ideal, but rarely achievable with the current technology, for the reasons to be outlined below. However, the important thing in current systems is that forward progress is possible eventually and in less time than would be the case if only a single machine were used.

Transparent failover is easy to achieve for stateless sessions: any server in the cluster can service any request and if a client makes multiple requests in succession each may well be serviced by a different server. Failover support in this case is trivial: if a failure of the server occurs while it is doing work for the client then the client will get an exceptional response and will have to retransmit the request.

The situation is more complicated for a stateful session. If the same server instance is used for all requests from the client, the server failure will lead to loss of state. The approach adopted in commercial systems to avoid loss of state is to use the stateless session approach with a twist: the session is required to serialize its state to a datastore or one or more application servers within the cluster at the end of each client request and for the subsequent bean instance in the other application server to deserialize the state before servicing the new request. In some cases, the replication of the data is assumed to be the domain of the datastore or cluster itself. In this way, some of the functionality available for stateless sessions can be regained. However, even in this case, a failure during serialization of the session state (which could result in the state being corrupted) is typically not addressed. There is a more serious limitation: transactions cannot be supported: if transactional access to a stateful EJB is used, then the same server instance must be used for every invocation on that bean; in this case, failures may not be recoverable at all.

It's important to realize that there's a difference between replication of the application server and replication of the datastore. The former doesn't require persistence, whereas the latter does. Replicating only the in-memory application server can improve performance over replicating at the level of the datastore, but there's a tradeoff to be made: the ability to tolerate only a subset of types of failure, e.g., power failures and so on.

One system that provided transactional replication capabilities is the Arjuna transaction system that was developed at the University of Newcastle upon Tyne in the mid 1980s. This system was designed to provide a reliable infrastructure for the development of distributed applications and integrated transactions and replication in the manner we described earlier. The Arjuna system has been used for years to run the registration process for the University, tolerating machine failures, network outages and overloads.

So far we've talked mainly about *transaction systems*, or *transaction processing systems*. These enforce ACID properties for transactional resources by using a two-phase commit protocol in conjunction with two-phase locking. But most transaction products are sold as *transaction processing monitors* (TPM). So, just what is a transaction-processing monitor and how does it relate to a transaction system? In the next section we examine the traditional definition of a TPM.

Transaction Processing Monitors

A product that supports the development of transactional applications/systems is often identified as a *Transaction Processing Monitor* (TPM). It typically provides:

- Toolkits and APIs to allow transactions to be demarcated (created and terminated) and controlled in a distributed environment. Given our definition of a transaction system, we can say that it is at the heart of this part of the TPM.

- Integration of security requirements.
- An execution environment to manage transaction load to maintain high throughput as the number of transactions to be executed increases—transactions may be automatically distributed across a number of different execution environments.
- Ensure high-availability for transactions—if a transaction fails it may be automatically restarted on another machine or multiple copies (replicas) may be executed to mask failures.
- Administration services for configuring, monitoring and managing transactions and transactional applications.

In the world of J2EE, many of these services may seem familiar—they form the heart of application servers. A TPM is essentially a transaction-aware application server and in fact many of the features found in J2EE application servers have their basis in transaction processing monitors. Likewise, many modern day TPMs are Java application servers with transaction service cores.

Transactions as we have presented them are sufficient if an application function can be represented as a single top-level transaction. Frequently this is not the case, with application requests requiring more than one transaction. These multi-transactions are typically referred to as *workflows* and are coordinated and controlled by a *workflow system*. Let's now look at workflow systems.

Transactions and Workflow

There are a number of reasons why an application's activities may be structured as multiple independent transactions. Top-level transactions are most suitably viewed as "short-lived" entities, performing stable state changes to the system; they are less well suited for structuring "long-lived" application functions (e.g., running for hours, days or longer). Long-lived top-level transactions may reduce the concurrency in the system to an unacceptable level by holding on to resources for a long time; further, if such a transaction aborts, much valuable work already performed could be undone.

Workflows are rule-based management software that direct, coordinate and monitor execution of tasks arranged to form *workflow applications* representing business processes. *Tasks (activities)* are application specific units of work. A *workflow schema (workflow script)* is used to explicitly represent the dependency between the tasks.

The structure of many workflow management facilities is based on the Workflow Reference Model developed by the Workflow Management Coalition (WfMC). Figure 1-29 depicts the Reference Model.

This facility provides for the manipulation and execution of workflow instances (interfaces 2, 3 and 5) as well as for the definition and management of workflow schemas (interfaces 1 and 5).

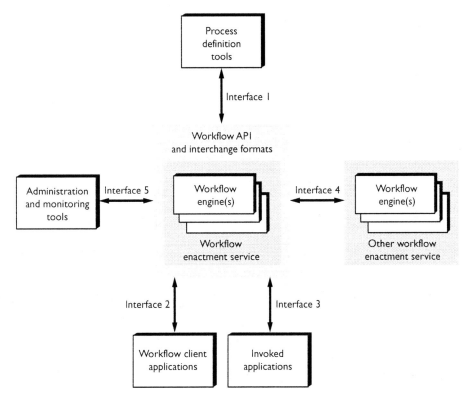

Figure 1-29 WfMC workflow reference model.

According to the base workflow model, a workflow application is modeled as a collection of tasks. A task is the unit of activity within a workflow application; typically you can equate a task with an independent, top-level transaction. The structure of the workflow application is expressed by the interdependencies between its constituent tasks. A dependency could be just a *notification (temporal)* dependency (shown by a dotted line in Figure 1-30, indicating that t2 can start only after t1 has terminated) or a *dataflow* dependency (shown by a solid line, indicating that, say t3, needs to be notified of the availability of input data from t1).

A task is typically modeled as a having a set of *input sets* and a set of *output sets*. The execution of a task is triggered by the availability of an input set. Only the first available input set will trigger the task; the subsequent availability of other input sets will not trigger the task (if multiple input sets became available simultaneously, then the input set with the highest priority may be chosen for processing). For an input set to be available it must have satisfied all of its constituent inputs and notifications.

A task can terminate producing one of a set of output sets, each output set producing a distinct set of outputs. The outputs of the produced output set and the inputs of the first available

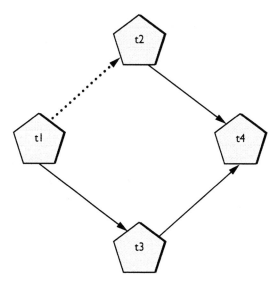

Figure 1-30 Inter-dependency tasks.

input will, if required, be propagated to other tasks as sources of input. In addition, a task can be composed from other tasks to form a compound task.

A workflow system allows the specification of task dependencies and their inter-relationships and then controls the execution of that workflow specification. Typically this specification will be maintained in a persistent manner such that failures of the workflow system or individual tasks will be recoverable to ensure that the required specification is executed to completion.

For example, let's consider a workflow application that involves processing a customer's order for a book from an online shop. It may be modeled as a compound task *processOrderApplication*, which contains four constituent simple task instances: *paymentAuthorisation*, *checkStock*, *dispatch* and *paymentCapture*. The relationship between the tasks is shown in Figure 1-31.

To process an order, *paymentAuthorisation* and *checkStock* tasks (top-level transactions) are executed concurrently. If both complete successfully then *dispatch* task is started and if that task is successful then the *paymentCapture* task is started.

Some workflow implementations allow the internal structure of a compound task to be modified without affecting the tasks that supply it with inputs or use it for inputs. In this case it would be possible to change the payment and stock management policies, for example, causing payment capture even if the item is not presently in stock, or the addition of a task that could check the stock levels of the suppliers of the company and arrange direct dispatch from them.

By now you should have a good grasp of the fundamentals behind transaction processing and many of the subtle (and often not so subtle) issues that arise when distribution, replication, threads and time are added into the equation. As we've seen, something that may initially seem relatively straightforward can quickly become extremely complex to understand, let alone

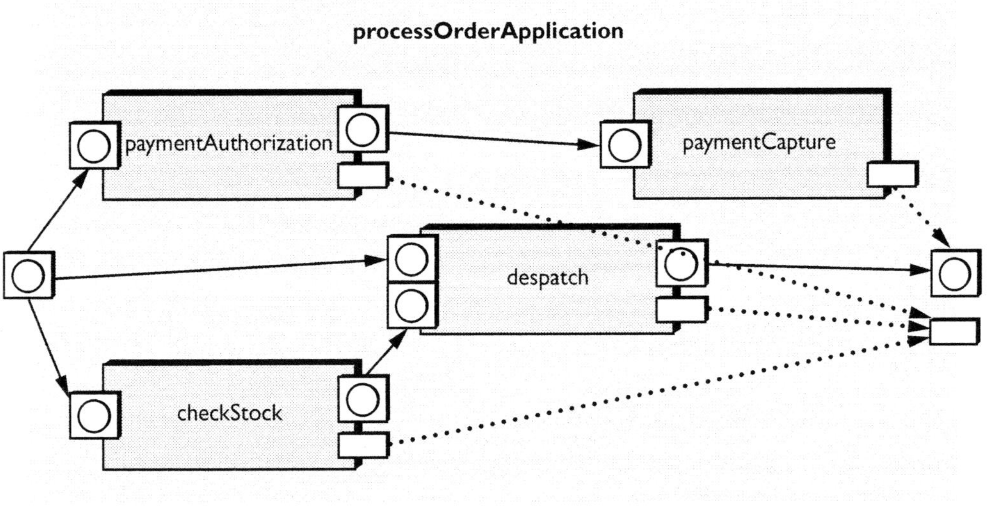

Figure 1-31 Process order application example.

implement. However, transactions have been around for many decades and there have been many commercial implementations and standards. In the following section we briefly look some of the more important events in the transaction timeline.

Summary

In this chapter we examined the main principles behind transactions and saw why they are typically needed. We looked at what ACID properties are and how they may be implemented, including some fairly subtle issues that can affect performance adversely. In order to ensure that all participants see the same outcome, the two-phase commit protocol is necessarily blocking; unfortunately blocking applications and holding on to resources is not practical in many cases so most transaction systems use heuristics to loosen the transaction's hold on resources. Obviously this can have dire consequences on consistency if the heuristic outcome is different than that ultimately taken by the transaction, but heuristics are usually only taken as a last resort.

Failures happen in distributed systems and these failures will often affect transactions. As a result, failure recovery mechanisms are necessary to ensure that transactional semantics occur. However, implementing recovery is extremely complex and most public domain transaction service implementations (and some commercial products) don't provide it.

We also looked at the different types of transactions, including nested and concurrent. Distributed transactions are extremely important and they present some challenging problems for failure recovery and performance. As with failure recovery, interposition is often overlooked by implementations and yet it is a critical component in improving performance.

Today's applications are inherently multi-threaded and it's inevitable that these threads will share transactions at some point. Therefore, we looked at how transactions and threads interact and the issues involved, especially in a distributed environment. Finally, we looked at some advanced transaction issues such as replication to improve availability and workflow systems that allow the gluing together of transactions to form long-running transactional applications.

CHAPTER 2

Foundation of Transactions in J2EE: The Java Transaction API

The transaction concept is powerful because it helps us to guarantee correct outcomes without imposing undo complexity on applications. Historically, different transaction monitors implemented their own variations of transaction processing messages, APIs, and completion routines. And as we've seen, the two-phase commit protocol itself can be implemented with different messages, semantics, and assumptions. Global transactions themselves are useless unless all participants can share the same framework for reaching a consensus. Proprietary implementations often allow unique optimizations for completely homogenous environments, but do not always work well for the complex, heterogeneous and distributed systems that are the hallmark of IT systems in large enterprises today. In order to make the transaction concept useful in the real world, applications, infrastructure and resource managers must share a common basis for coordinating transactional work.

The Java platform provides transactional capabilities by building on the widely adopted Distributed Transaction Processing (DTP) model defined by the Open Group. The leading relational databases, message queues, and even proprietary systems support the specifications based on DTP. Of special interest to Java programmers is the fact that all global transaction processing in the Java 2 Enterprise Edition is defined in terms of this model. In the world of enterprise Java applications, DTP is the cornerstone of transaction processing. So we're going to take a close look at the Open Group transaction model, the specifications that support it, and how they are applied in Java. Most of the technologies that we describe in the rest of the book build on these standards, including the crucial technologies to support relational database access and container managed transaction demarcations. In this chapter we also examine some of the important issues you should be aware of when using a DTP-based transaction manager in the Java environment.

What Is the DTP?

The Open Group defines standards for an integrated, high-value system software environment called the Common Application Environment (CAE). The goal of the CAE is to provide open systems that allow for portable, interoperable, and transactional applications. The primary products of the Open Group's work are specifications; these specifications rely on guides that define architectural models, terminology and common frameworks on which the specifications are based. DTP itself is a guide that provides a reference model for distributed transaction processing. The goal of the DTP guide is to provide an architecture that allows applications to work with shared and managed resources in the context of global transactions.

If you feel like you need to refresh your understanding of transaction processing basics, now is a good time to revisit Chapter 1. The concepts that we present there are realized in the DTP model in specific ways and it's important to understand how the model is defined to get a good grasp on the practical aspects of transaction processing in Java.

Before we get into details on the DTP, let's take a moment to consider some of the basics. The DTP reference model defines the participants in a transaction as an *Application Program, a Transaction Manager and a Resource Manager, as shown in Figure 2-1:*

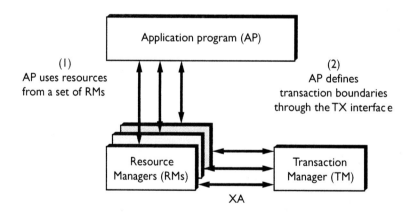

Figure 2-1　Distributed transaction participants.

- *An application program* manages the demarcation of transactions. This means that begin and commit operations are made available for use by an application through a specific API; the one defined in the original DTP specifications, TX, was C-based and we look at that briefly later. In Java, the model is modified slightly because there is an implicit assumption that a J2EE application server provides the infrastructure required to host transactionally aware components. The application server, in most application scenarios, performs the bulk of the transaction demarcation operations while the components focus on the business logic. So, together the application server and its hosted components comprise the *application program* role in a transaction. The component architecture most often deployed to an application server to support container-managed transactions is Enterprise JavaBeans (EJBs). The EJB model allows programmers to specify their transactional requirements both programmatically and declaratively using deployment descriptors. In most cases, the EJB server delineates the boundaries of the distributed transaction on behalf of the application and always manages the enlistment of resources with the transaction. We look at EJBs in considerably more depth later in the book. For now, it's important to understand that the combination of the container and the application business logic fulfill the role of the application program in DTP.

- A *transaction manger* provides the services and management functions required to identify, monitor, and either complete or recover global, top-level transactions. A *transaction manger* is not concerned with the actual implementation of the underlying transaction services of the resource manager. Rather, the transaction manager requires access to the interfaces that allow transaction demarcation, resource enlistment, synchronization, and recovery processes to occur. This is a critical piece of the J2EE infrastructure and we will explain these processes in detail. The transaction manager may be used directly by an application, or it may be used by a container hosting managed business components. As we shall see, the system-level interactions with resource managers are handled by the *transaction manager.* Crucially, the *transaction manager* assigns an identifier to transaction branches (essentially units of recoverable work within the transaction) and passes that identifier to the resource managers involved in the transaction, which is how resource managers associate their work with the given transaction.

  The *transaction manager* itself may run as a separate process that is remotely contacted by the other participants or it may, in a J2EE scenario, be co-located with application server instances. Although the standalone architectural choice is an option in most deployment scenarios, it can yield a significant performance bottleneck under the typical loads encountered by an Internet-based application. The distribution of the *transaction manager* functionality across multiple instances is a better choice for most applications that expect moderate to significant user loads. On the other hand, a standalone server may offer better management capabilities if it's shared across a large number of deployments.

- A *resource manager* provides the application with access to shared resources. Common examples of *resource managers* include relational database management systems like the Oracle 10g RDBMS, messaging systems such as Oracle Advanced Queues and IBM's WebSphere MQ (formerly MQSeries), and legacy transactional applications based on transaction monitors like BEA's Tuxedo. The *resource manager* also must interact with the transaction manager to manage the boundaries of work and to participate in the termination protocol. It is expected that numerous applications simultaneously request access to the resource manager and the services that it affords. A major advantage of transactions is the simplification of concurrency management.

In a typical application there may be multiple independent resource managers accessed within the scope of a single transaction. In this case, it is the responsibility of the transaction manager to work in concert with other resource managers to ensure the ACID properties of the transaction. The commitment of a resource manager's work not only depends on whether operations performed internally succeed but also whether the operations at other resource managers succeed as well. Moreover, a resource manager is typically unaware of the work performed at other resource managers. Transaction managers achieve this coordination for a common outcome by informing the resource managers of the existence of a global transaction. From that point on, the resource managers are subsequently responsible for mapping their work to the governing transaction. This is done so that, as we saw in Chapter 1, when the transaction terminates the resource manager can ensure that only the work performed within the scope of that specific transaction is affected.

Before we explain how the J2EE platform supports the DTP transaction model, we talk a bit about some of the specifications from the Open Group that are based on that model. It's important to have a basic understanding of these specifications because, as we've mentioned, they have influenced transaction development in Java and you may well come across them elsewhere if you are using J2EE to integrate with legacy systems. These specifications aim at providing the basis of the model we outlined previously by defining mechanisms for:

- Portable application code
- Interchangeable transaction managers and resource managers
- Interoperable transaction managers and resource managers.

You can think of the CAE as the basis for "Write Once, Run Anywhere" transactional applications. Java makes this even easier with its virtual machine and fully specified component models in J2EE. The DTP is the basis for several specifications that define the interfaces between applications, transaction managers, and resource managers. The two critical specifications based on the DTP model are the TX specification and the XA specification.

- The TX Specification defines the interfaces between a transaction manager and an application. The TX specification allows applications to begin, commit and rollback transactions.
- The XA Specification defines the interfaces between the transaction manager and resource managers. The XA specification allows the transaction manager to associate the work done on a resource manager by the application with a global transaction. It is also the basis for allowing the transaction manager to drive the two-phase commit protocol.

The interface between applications and resource managers is specific to the resource manager. An example of an open interface is the Call Level Interfaces (CLI) provided by Open Group for executing SQL commands on relational database management systems. Using libraries that conform to the XA specification requirements and a DTP compliant transaction manager, an application can create and use global distributed transactions in a heterogeneous environment. The DTP model defines both synchronous and asynchronous communication protocols for transaction processing, though Java only supports the synchronous processing model.

DTP's definition of a transaction is based on an earlier transaction model, the OSI DTP reference model. In the OSI model, a transaction is defined as a complete unit of work that modifies shared resources, which is a very generalized view of the problem domain. Put another way, a global transaction is used to describe all of the work across the system done in the context of a single unit. That transaction may have one or more branches, where a branch is defined as the recoverable work done by a resource manager on behalf of an application in the scope of a global transaction. And, in DTP, branches may not have additional work done on them once the completion protocol is initiated. You can think of branches as a way for an application to perform different (possibly concurrent) units of work within a single transaction and then have them all join in the final completion of that transaction.

In DTP, the commit protocol is described as two-phase commit with presumed rollback, though some distributed systems will in fact treat it as a "presumed nothing" variant of the protocol. The presumed rollback log optimization is typically implemented when participants can query the coordinator about a transaction. If a participant is in doubt and the coordinator doesn't know about the transaction, the participant will assume the transaction has been rolled back and resolve the branch; this allows the coordinator to skip a forced write to the transaction log at the start of the termination protocol. In practice, no provision is made in DTP or the XA specification for resource managers to query the coordinator for the status of a transaction; in fact a resource manager doesn't typically have a reference to the coordinator. As a consequence, some transaction managers in a pure XA environment cannot make the log optimizations associated with presumed abort that we discussed in Chapter 1.

Some application servers may implement an optimization where the coordinator identity is encoded in the data structure representing the transaction branch. Following a crash, the coordinator queries the participants for a list of branches that are in doubt and examines the branch identifiers for the specially encoded transaction branches to determine if the coordinator is responsible for the branches. If these branches are not present in a commit record in the transaction log, the coordinator will issue an abort message to the participant. This allows the coordinator to implement the presumed abort log optimization in an XA environment despite the fact that participants cannot query the coordinator. Transactions themselves are described by a unique global identifier, which is often referred to in shorthand as a TID. The XA specification also defines a transaction identifier called an XID that is assigned by the transaction manager and used by resource managers to map to the recoverable work done by them on behalf of a global transaction. The XID is composed of three elements: the global identifier or TID, a format identifier that describes how the TID is encoded, and a branch qualifier that uniquely distinguishes the transaction branch.

> **N O T E**   The format identifier can be any positive integer value, with 0 being reserved for the encoding scheme defined for OSI TP. Different implementations should use unique values and obviously these values need to be agreed upon (and understood) by the sender of such a transaction and its recipients. There is, however, no convention for guaranteeing uniqueness of format IDs for vendors. When you are building a system, it's worth verifying that each transaction manager uses a unique format ID.

The DTP model specifically restricts the initiation and termination of transactions to applications; in fact, the application that initiated a transaction is the only participant that may terminate the transaction. This restriction is related to the checked transaction semantics we discussed in Chapter 1. This differs from some protocols like IBM's LU6.2 where any participant may terminate a transaction. Also, nested transactions are not supported by the DTP model. As you may recall from Chapter 1, nested transactions are scoped by a top-level transaction. Though nested transactions support and solve many useful problems, they are not widely supported by established resource managers. Consequently, the DTP model supports top-level transactions only.

The other important point to be aware of is the importance of the thread of control in the DTP model. Once a thread is mapped to a global transaction, all work done on transactional resource managers will be scoped by the transaction. The XA routines we discuss that manage the association between a thread of control and the transaction must also be called on the same thread. This allows the application to interact with the native interfaces to the resource manager without explicitly passing transaction information; more complicated, multi-threaded transaction models often require explicit transaction parameters to be passed to participants in the transaction.

Java Transaction API

In 1999, Sun Microsystems defined the Java Transaction API (JTA) as a mapping of the Open Group specifications to Java. With the introduction of JTA, the Java platform gained standards-based closed, top-level, and concurrent transaction support. The mapping is object oriented, which departs from the firmly procedural TX and XA specifications. Additionally, the JTA provides support for only synchronous interactions between transaction participants.

JTA was originally conceived as an API that would be layered on top of existing transaction processing systems such as IBM's CICS product or those based on the CORBA Object Transaction Service; most application servers have native transaction managers, though many are also able to bridge into legacy Transaction Processing systems. In any case, most of the hard part of transaction processing is hidden from application developers, and JTA presumes that the majority of users will only interact with a small set of methods mapped from the TX specification. This is becoming less and less likely to be true.

As J2EE application servers mature and become used in more and more mission critical, high volume applications, solution architects and administrators have to understand the details of how they work and the assumptions on which they are built. New standards like the Java Connector Architecture require implementers to provide XA interface implementations for their resource adapters. We believe more and more programmers need to be able to program against these APIs directly. Developers also need to understand how their implementation choices may effect the transaction processing logic of different application servers. Unfortunately, the JTA specification is far from perfect. As a result, there are many issues that arise for infrastructure vendors and also for advanced users.

The JTA has three primary elements: an application transaction demarcation interface, a transaction manager interface intended for application servers, and a more direct mapping of the Open Group XA interface for implementation by transactional resource managers. In the following sections we look at these different elements in detail, show how they related to the original DTP specifications and give you some indications of issues that may arise when using JTA implementations.

Application Level Transaction Management in Java

The functionality of the Open Group TX specification is mapped to JTA through the `UserTransaction`, `TransactionManager`, and `Transaction` interfaces.

UserTransaction Interface

The `javax.transaction.UserTransaction` interface represents a limited portion of the Open Group TX specification and provides applications and application components with the capability to control transaction boundaries programmatically. This interface has methods for beginning, committing, and rolling back top-level transactions. The easiest way to think about `UserTransaction` is to consider it a simplified and user-friendly view of the transaction manager. It is up to a particular vendor's implementation as to whether a single instance of `UserTransaction` is available to all users (threads), or each thread has its own instance. In practice, it should not make a difference to an end user: each thread sees and controls its own transactions through the implementation of this interface and has no direct access to the other threads equivalents. The signature of the interface follows; we have omitted the exception declarations for clarity.

```
public interface UserTransaction
{
    void begin();
    void commit();
    void rollback();
```

```
void setRollbackOnly();
int getStatus();
void setTransactionTimeout(int);
}
```

The J2EE 1.3 specification indicates that components that may use the `UserTransaction` interface (e.g. EJB, Servlet, JSP) access the provided reference by performing a naming service lookup—in J2EE, the Java Naming and Directory Interface (JNDI) API is used—for `java:comp/UserTransaction`:

```
// create a JNDI Initial context
Context ctx = new InitialContext();
// obtain the UserTransaction
UserTransaction utx = (UserTransaction) ctx.lookup
("java:comp/UserTransaction");
// begin the transaction
utx.begin();
//  . . . do work
utx.commit();
```

N O T E This code sample is illustrative and does not include some of the exception handling that would be required for performing the steps indicated.

An EJB may also access the `UserTransaction` implementation via the `EJBContext.getUserTransaction()` method. Any such reference is only valid within the component instance that performed the lookup; the `UserTransaction` interface is only used in beans that are declared to use bean managed transactions.

This means that `UserTransaction` is leveraged by EJBs that demarcate transaction boundaries directly. Other J2EE components may perform transaction demarcation actions as well. For example, a servlet may actually initiate a transaction from the Web tier. Subsequent interactions with transactional resources in the course of servicing the Web request (e.g., calls to EJBs interacting with databases that have the appropriate declarative transactional attributes—we cover this in more detail in Chapter 6) can occur within the context of the transaction initiated by the calling servlet.

It is important to note that, unlike an EJB container, the J2EE web container has no facilities for handling the termination of a transaction should an exception be raised by the application code. If an exception is raised the application code must manage the transactional state appropriately:

```
try
{
  // begin the transaction
  utx.begin();
```

```
    //  . . . do work
    utx.commit();
}
catch ( Exception e )
{
    utx.rollback ();
}
finally
{
    if ( utx.getStatus() == Status.STATUS_ACTIVE )
    {
        utx.rollback ();
    }
}
```

It's also reasonable to ensure that error-handling servlets check for and if necessary roll back transactions active on the current thread. Some J2EE vendor tag libraries may allow transaction management to be used in Java Server Pages (JSPs). Many of the same considerations that apply to servlets apply to JSPs, though the vendor tag libraries may have some error handling built in. In general, it's a bad design decision to try to combine transaction management with a scripting technology and we advise against it.

J2EE also defines an application client container. This is a managed environment that provides system-level services related to transactions, JDBC DataSources, and other facilities that may be of interest to a standalone client application. The application client does not host EJBs or servlets, though it may leverage them as remote resources.

One of the things an application client may have access to is a UserTransaction instance, which may be used to scope work done on any transactional resource. The application client threads are controlled by the application, so the same care must be taken to disassociate the transaction and thread of control that are required for a servlet, though generally application client threads are managed by the application and not pooled. The application client container is not required to provide applications access to a UserTransaction handle.

There is another issue that may impact the behavior of an application: if remote EJB references are used, the semantics of the method invocation may not be invariant, depending on whether transaction context propagation across address space and machine boundaries is supported and configured. This means that some client applications may be able to include the resources of applications accessed by EJBs in a transaction initiated and terminated by the client while others may not. In general, we prefer to allow the container to manage the transaction and recommend that transactions be initiated on the server by an EJB container. This provides better error handling, guarantees of portable behavior and removes the burden of transaction management from the application developer.

However, as we see in Chapter 8, the thin-client approach to transactions is not always appropriate and end-to-end transactions incorporating client updates can be necessary. There is nothing in the JTA specification that prevents clients from starting and managing transactions:

this is purely an implementation restriction in some vendor platforms. If you think you may need this facility, you should understand whether or not the transaction service you are using can support it.

The UserTransaction interface is similar to the TransactionManager interface. Therefore, rather than detail these methods twice, we'll describe them in the following section.

TransactionManager Interface

An application server utilizes the javax.transaction.TransactionManager interface to demarcate transaction boundaries on behalf of an application and its associated components. This interface is the JTA representation of the Open Group TX specification. The TransactionManager, much like the UserTransaction interface, is responsible for maintaining the transaction context association with the thread of execution. At any given time a thread's transaction context may either be *null* or refer to a global transaction.

> **N O T E** As you see in the next section, the JTA specification allows a thread to suspend and later resume a transaction via the TransactionManager interface. A thread that suspends a transaction may then do work that isn't controlled by the transaction. Another side effect is that a thread is allowed to resume a transaction it did not suspend. Therefore, multiple threads may be associated with the same global transaction, although that is an implementation choice. In many implementations, concurrent transactions are also supported.

Each transaction is represented by a different javax.transaction.Transaction object, which is used to perform operations specific to the transaction. It's important to recognize this important difference between Transaction and UserTransaction or TransactionManager: as we've already mentioned these object references can be used to control different transactions. As we see later, Transaction references may be obtained in several ways.

The begin() method of TransactionManager starts a new top-level transaction and associates a transaction context with the calling thread. If the calling thread is already associated with a transaction, it throws the NotSupportedException exception because nested transactions are never allowed.

The getTransaction() method returns the Transaction object associated with the calling thread. This object, which is similar to the CORBA Object Transaction Service (OTS) Coordinator object, can be used to perform operations on the target transaction described later; we describe the OTS in detail in Chapter 3.

The commit() method is used to complete the transaction currently associated with the calling thread. After it returns, the calling thread is no longer associated with a transaction. If commit() is called when the thread has no associated transaction context, the transaction manager throws an `IllegalStateException`. In addition, some implementations restrict the commit operation to the originator of the transaction (checked transactions again). If the calling thread is not allowed to commit the transaction, the transaction manager may throw a `Securi-tyException`; this is a potential portability issue to be aware of. Although we said earlier that DTP imposes this limit, it wasn't carried across into JTA proper. It's possible for a Java-compliant implementation to relax these restrictions or to generate a different error.

The `rollback()` method is used to roll back the transaction associated with the current thread. After the `rollback` method returns, the thread is no longer associated with a transaction. As with `commit()`, if the thread is not associated with a transaction then an `Illegal-StateException` is thrown, and if the thread is not allowed to terminate the transaction, the implementation may throw a `SecurityException`, with the same portability proviso applying here as well.

An application server is generally the only user of the `TransactionManager` interface. Most notably, the application server uses this interface to interact with a transaction manager to support the transactional demarcation implied by the transactional attributes specified in an EJB's deployment descriptor. The application server, before invoking an EJB method, will determine the transactional requirements specified for the method and subsequently use the interface to obtain the current transactional state or perform the requisite operation on the transaction (e.g. commit, rollback, suspend, or resume). Some application servers may make the `TransactionManager` implementation available for use in JNDI; this is generally aimed at sophisticated ISVs that are integrating their products with the application server, e.g., Object Relational Mapping and caching product vendors.

Although client applications in a non-managed, non-J2EE environment may choose to manage transactions via the `TransactionManager` interface, it is much more common for clients to utilize the `UserTransaction` interface for transaction management; in implementations that support standalone access to the TransactionManager outside of J2EE, applications can be written against JTA directly. In general, this is a risky implementation strategy primarily because integrated transaction manager implementations may assume specific behavior on the part of the application server. We believe it is far better to allow the container to help deal with transactions when using an integrated J2EE platform. The only JTA transaction manager that we know of designed to be used as a standalone project is the Arjuna transaction service.

Suspending and Resuming a Transaction

The JTA supports the concept of a thread temporarily suspending and resuming transactions to enable applications to perform non-transactional work. The `suspend()` method is called to temporarily suspend the transaction that is associated with the calling thread. This method returns a `null` object reference if no transaction is associated with the thread; otherwise, it returns a valid `Transaction` object. The `Transaction` object can be leveraged as an argument to the `TransactionManager.resume()` method to restore the associated transaction context. This operation does not actually affect the transaction, but *only* the thread-to-transaction association; the transaction is *not* suspended, only the association with the thread. If the user (or typically application server) wishes to communicate this suspension to any enlisted participants, it must do so itself. This is a portability issue to be aware of, since some implementations may assume that branches should be automatically managed as well.

N O T E It is important to understand that `suspend` and `resume` don't affect the transaction at all. Unfortunately, we've come across several JTA implementations from groups that did not fully understand this, with the result that these implementations affect the transaction and its resources during `suspend` and `resume`. This isn't a portability issue as such, but it's worth being warned about. In a pure J2EE environment, this shouldn't be an issue as the application server will manage enlistment and delistment of resource managers in coordination with `suspend` and `resume` events transparently in order to maximize the availability of pooled resource adapters.

The `resume()` method re-establishes the suspended transaction context with the calling thread. If the transaction passed to this method is valid, it is associated with the calling thread. If the specified transaction is null then the thread is associated with no transaction; if it's an invalid transaction then an `InvalidTransactionException` is thrown:

```
Transaction tx = TransactionManager.suspend ();
 . . .
TransactionManager.resume (tx);
```

Additionally, the transaction manager throws an `IllegalStateException` if the thread is already associated with the transaction.

Additionally, the JTA (and most transaction manager implementations) allows a suspended transaction to be resumed by a different thread. This is required by an application server to support EJB declarative transactions and is the most common use case for `suspend` and `resume` in a multithreaded environment. This is a simple way to allow context switching between clients. As EJB methods are invoked the EJB container determines the current transactional state by querying the transaction manager. The container will subsequently decide whether the transaction needs to be suspended for the duration of the invocation based on the transactional attribute specified for the method. For example, if the method is designated as requiring a new transaction, the current transaction will be suspended, a new transaction will be initiated, and the method will be executed. After the method completes, the new transaction will be terminated and the previous transaction will be resumed. For a more detailed discussion of EJB transactional attributes, please see Chapter 6.

When a transaction is suspended, an application server must ensure that the resources in use by the application are no longer registered with the suspended transaction; it does this through the `delistResource` operation on the transaction. When a resource is delisted the transaction manager informs the resource manager to dissociate the transaction from work done on the thread of control. When the application's transaction context is resumed, the application server must ensure that the resources used by the application are re-enlisted with the transaction. When a resource is enlisted as a result of resuming a transaction, the transaction manager notifies the resource manager that it should re-associate the work done on the resource with the given transaction. These interactions are explained in our discussion of the `XAResource` interface.

Transaction Interface

The `javax.transaction.Transaction` interface allows applications to invoke operations on the transaction associated with the target object. The transaction manager associates every top-level transaction with a `Transaction` object. The `Transaction` object can subsequently be used to enlist transactional resources, register synchronization callbacks, commit or rollback the transaction, and obtain the transaction's status.

The `commit()` and `rollback()` methods allow the transaction to be committed or rolled back, respectively. The calling thread may have a different transaction context than the one associated with the object on which the methods are invoked. This API is used extensively by application servers to manage the transaction state for hosted components. As we see in the next chapter, using `Transaction` to manage transactions is similar to the *direct management* technique used within the OTS: no thread-to-transaction associations will be changed. As with the equivalent method of the `TransactionManager` interface, if the calling thread is not allowed to commit the transaction, the transaction manager may throw the `SecurityException` or `IllegalStateException` if it is enforcing checked transactions. This is an area where you may be concerned about portability.

In addition to the `TransactionManager` interface, the methods of the `Transaction` interface are used extensively by an application server to help manage the transactions for enterprise components. For example, an application server makes use of the `getStatus()` or `getTransaction()` methods to make decisions about whether a transaction should be initiated, suspended, resumed, committed, or rolled back based on the current status and the transactional attribute assigned to an EJB method. The processing an application server may undertake if an EJB method has the `Required` transactional attribute should include the following logic for a business method that has been declared to require a transaction:

```
Transaction tx = null;
TransactionManager tm = getTransactionManager ();
// see if a transaction is initiated and is
// associated with the invoking thread
    try
    {
        tx = tm.getTransaction();
    }
```

```
catch(SystemException e)
{
    // log exception
}

if(tx == null)
{
    // initiate a transaction since it is required
    try
    {
        tm.begin();
    }
    catch(NotSupportedException e)
    {
        // log exception
    }
    catch(SystemException e)
    {
        // log exception
    }
}
```

Transaction Status

Transactions are assumed to be state machines with the possible states defined in the `javax.transaction.Status` interface. The transaction may be described with the following states:

```
javax.transaction.Status.STATUS_ACTIVE
```

An active transaction is scoping work done on the thread of control to shared resources

```
javax.transaction.Status.STATUS_MARKED_ROLLBACK
```

Indicates that an active transaction has been marked for rollback; the transaction manager will not commit this transaction. In some sense, this is not an independent state.

```
javax.transaction.Status.STATUS_PREPARED
```

The transaction itself is in doubt. This typically occurs when the transaction is subordinate to an external coordinator. You may also see this value if you make an enquiry on the status as a transaction after it has completed the first phase of the commit protocol.

```
javax.transaction.Status.STATUS_COMMITTED
```

Indicates the transaction has been successfully committed.

```
javax.transaction.Status.STATUS_ROLLED BACK
```

Indicates the transaction has been rolled back.

```
javax.transaction.Status.STATUS_UNKNOWN;
```

The state of the transaction is unknown. This is a transient state and retrying to eventually result in one of the other values.

```
javax.transaction.Status.STATUS_NO_TRANSACTION
```

There is no transaction associated with the current thread.

```
javax.transaction.Status.STATUS_PREPARING
```

The transaction is in the prepare phase; this means either that not all branches have been prepared or that the commit decision has not been logged.

```
javax.transaction.Status.STATUS_COMMITTING;
```

The transaction is in the committing phase, but all branches have not been committed.

```
javax.transaction.Status.STATUS_ROLLING_BACK;
```

The transaction is in the rolling back phase, but all branches have not been rolled back. Depending on the transition path to this state, some branches (and potentially the transaction itself) may have been prepared.

Unfortunately, the transaction `Status` interface mixes thread of control semantics into its set of transaction states. In addition, the list of states is incomplete. It is entirely possible, for example, for a transaction that was prepared to enter a heuristic transition. None of the heuristic states are accounted for in the model, nor are inconsistent outcomes. Application servers may be forced to respond with misleading semantics to status requests if the `Status` interface is used; for this reason, it's best to regard the `Status` as a generalized reporting mechanism. In general, this means that distinctions between the outcome of a transaction due to normal processing and heuristic decisions cannot be determined. In most cases, this won't be of concern to an application.

Resource Enlistment

The application server typically manages transactional resources such as database connections by utilizing a resource adapter (e.g., database JDBC driver) in conjunction with a connection pool. For a transaction manager to coordinate the transactional work performed by the target resource managers, the application server must manage the association and dissociation of resources with the transaction as it progresses. This is important because connections may not be pooled while they are actively associated with a transaction. This means that the transaction manager is required to inform the resource that enlistment or delistment has occurred as we've already mentioned.

Each connection is tied to a specific resource manager and when association or disassociation occurs, the resource manager must be informed so it can ensure that work done using the resource manager is either associated or disassociated with the transaction at the appropriate boundaries. An application server registers each resource utilized by the application by invoking the enlistResource() method with an javax.transaction.XAResource object which identifies the resource. An enlistment request informs the resource manager to start associating the transaction with the work performed through the resource on the current thread of control. The transaction manager is responsible for passing a parameter representing the transaction state in its XAResource.start() method call to the resource manager.

The delistResource() method dissociates the specified resource from the transaction context and informs the resource manager that transactional use is ended (or suspended, meaning that the resource may later find itself active within that transaction again). The application server invokes the method with two parameters: the XAResource object that represents the resource, and a flag to indicate whether the operation is due to the transaction being suspended (TMSUSPEND), a portion of the work has failed (TMFAIL), or a normal resource release by the application (TMSUCCESS). A suspended transaction may later be resumed on the same resource manager. There is an important distinction between ending and suspending a transaction because once ended, the resource manager will not allow itself to be associated with that transaction again.

The delist request triggers the transaction manager to inform the resource manager to dissociate the transaction from the XAResource. A flag is passed as part of the invocation that indicates whether the transaction manager intends to come back to the same resource, thus requiring the resource states to be kept intact. The transaction manager passes the appropriate flag value in its XAResource.end() method call to the underlying resource manager.

Transaction Synchronization

In Chapter 1 we discussed the requirement for transaction synchronizations which are outside of the normal two-phase commit protocol; the transaction synchronization capability offered as part of the JTA API is not a part of the DTP transaction model. It is a protocol in and of itself, and as we see in Chapter 3, it first appeared in a standard form in the OTS specification. An application server utilizes transaction synchronization to be notified before and after a transaction completes, for example, to flush a cached copy of data used by the application back to the persistent database prior to commitment. For each transaction started, the application server may (and usually does) register a javax.transaction.Synchronization callback object. The Synchronization interface methods are invoked by the transaction manager as follows:

- The `beforeCompletion()` method is called prior to the start of the two-phase transaction completion protocol. This call is executed in the same transaction context of the caller who initiates the `TransactionManager.commit()/rollback()` or the call is executed with no transaction context if `Transaction.commit()` is used instead. If any `beforeCompletion` operation fails, then the transaction will be forced to roll back. This provides the application or application server a last opportunity to do work before the transaction is terminated. This is a standard signal to flush caches that have buffered data for the duration of a transaction.

- The `afterCompletion()` method is called after the transaction has completed. The status of the completed transaction is related by the method parameter. This method is executed without a transaction context. Any failures that occur during `afterCompletion` processing can be safely ignored by the transaction system, since the transaction has completed. This can be useful, for example, to determine whether updates were successful and optimistic caches may be maintained.

In some cases, application servers utilize the synchronization facility to manage the pooling of transactional resources that do not support the two-phase commit protocol, but have been enlisted in a transaction anyway; we explain why this might happen in Chapter 4 on JDBC. EJB containers also use synchronization callbacks to provide notification of transaction events to stateful session beans that implement the `javax.ejb.SessionSynchronization` interface and to manage data caches associated with entity beans. This is particularly important for container-managed persistence as it is the basis on which cache flushes to back-end storage are usually managed.

JTA-DTP Discrepancies

It is important to realize that there are a number of discrepancies between the model specified by the Open Group TX specification and the model supported by the JTA interfaces.

The `UserTransaction` interface uses heuristic exceptions that are not specified by the TX specification (recall that heuristics refer to resolution of "in doubt" transaction branches by some agent other than the coordinator), though it omits others. The heuristics that are included would only be received from a prepared resource manager that an application component does not interact with directly. Vendors interpret these discrepancies in varying ways so the exception handling of an application may vary on different platforms. Furthermore, the `SystemException` specified as part of the "throws" clauses for methods of the interface is semantically under-specified by the JTA specification. From the specification, it is not clear what a calling client is supposed to make of a `SystemException` nor what the responsibilities of the application server are. Whether different vendors return the exception to the application, mimic thread cancellation, return the transaction outcome as if it had been successfully completed or select some other solution is difficult to predict; for the most part it depends on the strategy preferred by the service implementer since the specification leaves it up in the air.

The TX specification defines a return code that indicates mixed outcome; JTA incorrectly maps this to a heuristic mixed code that is actually a part of the XA specification. On top of that, the transaction manager may elect not to report mixed outcomes at all; in general, there's nothing that the application itself can do about the mixed outcome and it is the responsibility of the administrator of a resource manager with an outcome inconsistent with the coordinator to rectify the problem. This may be important for the administration of an application, so it's important to determine how the transaction manager you are using behaves. Most of the implementations that we tested return mixed outcomes.

Note that the JTA says nothing about fully checked transaction semantics, except that an implementation may restrict the termination of a transaction to the creator. However, as we have seen in Chapter 1, in a multi-threaded environment the requirement on checked transactions goes beyond this, including the capability for ensuring all threads associated with a terminating transaction have previously completed their work. How, and if, this is dealt with will typically be in an implementation specific manner, e.g., some may deal with this transparently, by blocking the terminating thread until all other threads have completed, whereas others may throw a `SystemException` from `commit()` or `rollback()` and require the invoking thread to determine when it is appropriate to try again.

Transaction Manager to Resource Manager Interfaces

The functionality of the DTP XA specification is mapped to JTA through the `XID` and `XAResource` interfaces.

XID Interface

The `javax.transaction.xa.XID` interface provides a Java mapping of the XA specification's XID structure. Transaction managers and resource managers use the XID to identify a particular transaction branch. The `XID` interface provides methods that provide the transaction's format ID, a global transaction ID, and a branch qualifier. The `XID` is rarely if ever accessed by an application server in the context of transactional processing.

However, understanding the components of an XID is critical for architecting systems that include more than one system capable of initiating a distributed transaction. The XID format ID is an indicator of the encoding scheme used for the given XID. This format ID must be unique across the different transaction systems in order to provide guarantees that the transaction is uniquely identified; while it's highly unlikely to occur, a non-unique ID would lead to substantial problems for transactional scenarios and could lead to unrecoverable or inconsistent outcomes. Therefore, as a system architect or developer, it is imperative that you verify that the format IDs are in fact unique for architectures where multiple transactional coordination systems are interacting with the same resource manager.

XAResource Interface

Whereas the basic two-phase commit protocol does not impose any restrictions on the types of participants, `javax.transaction.xa.XAResource` interface is a Java mapping of the XA specification defined by the Open Group. The `XAResource` interface defines the relationship and interactions between a Resource Manager and a Transaction Manager as detailed by the XA Specification. The interface contains the following methods, all of which may throw an `XAException`:

```
public void commit(Xid, boolean);
public void end(Xid, int);
public void forget(Xid);
public int getTransactionTimeout();
public boolean isSameRM(XAResource);
public int prepare(Xid);
public Xid recover(int);
public void rollback(Xid);
public boolean setTransactionTimeout(int);
public void start(Xid, int);
```

A resource adapter that supports global transactions implements the `XAResource` interface. For example, each database connection utilized by an application or its components has an `XAResource` associated with it to allow the transaction manager to communicate with the underlying resource manager instance. As J2EE continues to grow and the standards become more complex, more developers are being required to both evaluate the capabilities of resource adapters and even to implement their own adapters. We try to give an appropriate level of detail to make this chapter of real use in those cases.

The transaction manager obtains and uses an `XAResource` for every resource manager participating in a global transaction. It uses the `start()` and `end()` methods to associate and dissociate the transaction, respectively, from the work performed on the resource. The resource manager is responsible for associating the transaction with all the work performed on its internal data between the `start()` and `end()` invocations. A transaction manager informs the resource managers at transaction termination time to prepare, commit, or roll back the transaction according to the two-phase commit protocol as we discussed several times.

All the methods of `XAResource` convey anomalies in processing via an `XAException`. Each `XAException` has an error code attribute that provides the specific semantics of the failure. It is crucial that the `XAException` include a correct error code. Unfortunately, the class has a constructor without an error code. If you are implementing an `XAResource` for a resource adapter, you must supply the appropriate error code with each failure case. If you do not, it may cause the coordinator to be unable to complete the transaction or to complete the transaction incorrectly: the two-phase commit and transaction processing in general are based on the assumption that each participant is accurate and honest. If a coordinator is confused by messages, it may stop processing rather than risk compounding a problem. This is the best case scenario. If the coordinator can't detect a problem, it can lead to compromised ACID properties or, worse, Byzantine outcomes. Unfortunately, even some widely deployed resource managers mis-report XA return codes, which is a major headache for transaction management.

> **N O T E**   Byzantine outcomes are the result of misleading or erroneous messages sent between transactional agents.

The error codes that should be returned for failure cases for each XAResource method are carefully delineated in the XA specification. If you are writing an XAResource, you must have the XA specification on hand. You cannot get by with the JTA specification as it is incomplete and sometimes inaccurate. We won't repeat the XA specification here—but we do urge you to rely on it as a single source of truth for accurately reporting return codes from XA methods.

With that in mind, in the following sections we examine the functions of the XARe-source interface from a practical perspective to help you understand how an implementation should work. We also indicate where appropriate the most notable differences between the JTA specification and the XA specification. If you're coming at JTA from an XA perspective then you'll find these differences important, and likewise if you need to approach an XA environment (perhaps for legacy reasons) from having known only JTA you will definitely need to appreciate these deviations from the original.

Thread of Control

The XA specification requires that XA calls responsible for transaction association are executed from the same thread of control in which work is being performed. This concept is central to the transaction manager's coordination of resource managers; a resource manager understands that a given work request pertains to a particular transaction branch because both the application and the transaction manager call it from the same thread.

Clearly, most distributed object environments (and specifically J2EE) involve multiple threads, since threads are generally dispatched dynamically during method calls, e.g., invocations on an EJB. In an application server, different threads may share the same connection; since each connection involved with a transaction will require an XAResource, these threads are also associated with the same XAResource object. Therefore, it is very possible that different threads invoke the start() and end() methods on an XAResource, which is different from the original XA specification where the *same* thread must invoke the start() and end() methods (on the xa_switch_t structure).

> **N O T E**   When the original XA specifications were written, multi-threaded environments were extremely rare. It was more common for applications to use multiple processes to dispatch concurrent units of work, a much heavier weight approach. However, as a result of this it was more natural to require the same entity do start() and end().

Because of the significant difference that an inherently multi-threaded environment such as J2EE provides, it is impractical and often impossible to require such a strict thread-to-XA mapping. However, it's also a fact that underlying legacy resource managers are XA-compliant and will continue to make this assumption about the same thread using start() and end(). It is the responsibility of the XAResource implementer to understand that multiple threads may be using any of the methods it provides and to ensure that they work.

It is the responsibility of the application server to ensure that although multiple threads may access a transactional resource, the thread of control association established for a transaction *branch* maps to only one *active* thread.

Transaction Association

At any given time, a connection to a resource manager is associated with a single transaction or no transaction at all. The association between a transaction and a transactional resource is established by a transaction manager by invoking the XAResource.start() method as we've already discussed; transactions are dissociated by invoking the XAResource.end() method. It is these methods that the Transaction.delistResource() and Transaction.enlistResource() methods mentioned earlier will use, with appropriate parameters to indicate to the underlying resource manager whether work is being started, resumed, suspended or ended.

It is possible to use the same XAResource to manage the work on behalf of multiple transactions; this dates back to the original XA specifications where an instance of a single C data structure was used to manage these interactions. Methods for preparing, rolling back or committing the transactions take XID instances, for example, to explicitly identify the transaction being prepared, rolled back or committed, respectively. One XAResource instance does not have to be tied to a single transaction. However, it is possible that a resource manager will include this restriction in a particular implementation.

In general it is possible to interleave multiple transactions using the same XAResource as long as each start() invocation is paired with an end() method call. In other words, each time a resource is used with a different transaction the end() method must be invoked for the previous transaction (either suspending or ending the transaction association) followed by the start() invocation for the current transaction. In all cases, the application server is responsible for managing the association of transactional resources to global transactions for the transactional applications it hosts via the enlistResource() and delistResource() methods.

If a global transaction is initiated by an application, any work it performs while utilizing a connection to a resource manager must be associated with that transaction; it is an error for an application server to allow such work to be performed outside the scope of the transaction. The application server, therefore, enlists all resources using the Transaction.enlistResource() method before making them available to application components.

Opening a Resource Manager

The XA specification requires a transaction manager to invoke the `xa_open()` function (on the aforementioned xa_switch_t C structure) to initialize a resource manager and prepare it for use in a distributed transaction environment. This method *must* be called before the transaction manager makes any other XA method calls.

However, this requirement has been removed from the JTA specification, which takes a more object-oriented approach than that available in the original procedural XA. The JTA assumes that a resource adapter (e.g., a JDBC driver) is a more appropriate place for performing the initialization of the associated resource manager. Therefore, the resource adapter is required to perform the required initialization when a connection with the resource manager is established: users don't have to do anything specific to accomplish this and can assume that it has happened by the time they can use the resource. Once the connection is established, the transaction manager is only required to indicate to the resource manager when to start, end, prepare, and so on, work associated with a global transaction.

Closing a Resource Manager

We've already discussed the fact that at the resource adapter level, a transactional resource involved in a global transaction is represented by an `XAResource` object and an associated connection object that allows an application to perform work on the target resource manager. The connection to the resource manager is kept open until invoking a connection's `close()` method explicitly closes it. This is equivalent to the original XA specification's requirement on users to perform the `xa_close()` operation. Once closed, the resource adapter invalidates the connection handle so it can no longer be used and informs any connection listeners (most notably, the application server) that the connection has been closed. It is this notification that allows an application server to realize that a connection is no longer in use and return it to its connection pool. In turn, the transaction manager invokes the `end()` method on the `XAResource` to dissociate the transaction from the connection.

Putting the JTA APIs Together

To summarize what we've learned so far about the JTA, let's take a look at the general procedure an application server follows in a transaction management scenario (Figure 2-2):

1. If the application request requires a transactional context (e.g. an EJB method invocation with the Required transactional attribute), the application server invokes the `TransactionManager.begin()` method.
2. The application requests a transactional resource (e.g. a JDBC connection) from a configured resource adapter (e.g. JDBC data source).
3. The application server intercedes in the resource request and requests the `XAResource` from the resource adapter being utilized.

4. The application server enlists the XAResource with the global transaction (`Trans-action.enlistResource()`).

5. The transaction manager invokes the `XAResource.start()` method to associate the resource manager's work with the transaction.

6. The application server requests the associated connection object from the resource adapter (e.g. `XAConnection.getConnection()`) and returns it to the application.

7. The application performs some work using the connection.

8. The application closes the connection.

9. The application server delists the resource when it receives the close notification from the resource adapter using Transaction.delistResource().

10. The transaction manager dissociates the transaction from the resource manager by invoking the `XAResource.end()` method.

11. The application servers request that the transaction manager commit the transaction.

12. The transaction manager invokes `XAResource.prepare()` to inform the resource manager that is should prepare the work it performed for committal.

13. The transaction manager invokes `XAResource.commit()` to commit the work associated with the transaction.

The final method with which you may need to be familiar is the `recover()` method. This method is used for transaction managers to resolve the state branches that are used to scope work within a resource manager in the event of failure and subsequent recovery. A call to `recover()` returns an array of XIDs, that represent branches that have either been prepared or heuristically completed. Combined with the state of the transaction itself, whether a particular XID is returned on a recovery scan is sufficient to model the state of the branch so that the transaction may be fully resolved.

There are two things to be aware of with respect to the `recover()` method. First, the `recover()` method API suggests paging semantics. A recover scan can be performed with a begin flag, a "no flag" flag, and an end flag. However, paging does not appear to be supported by all resource managers. It's best to assume that the list of XIDs returned from a recover call will be global to the resource manager or to some logical partition that is specific to the system. Secondly, the `recover()` method may require special security credentials to execute. This varies by resource manager and we examine the specific mechanisms for handling this issue in the chapters on JDBC and the Java Connector Architecture.

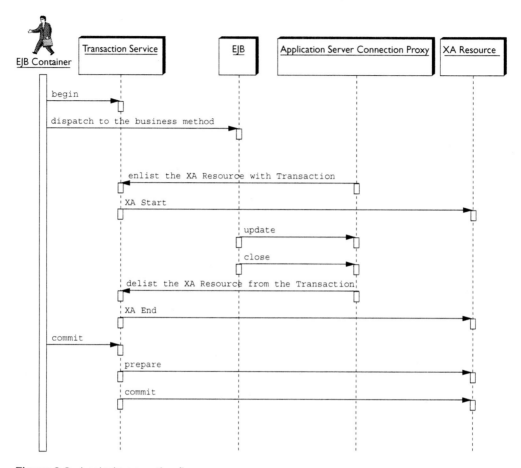

Figure 2-2   Logical transaction flow.

Architectural Considerations

Selecting an application server for an enterprise application requires careful analysis of the transaction support it affords. Some critical facets to consider are the level of support for failure recovery and distributed, heterogeneous component architectures, which we discuss in this section. We also explain some of the issues you should consider before employing the *last resource commit* optimization.

Failure Recovery

Consensus between participants is relatively simple to achieve and while the voting process is a key element of two-phase commit protocol, it does not in itself guarantee ACID properties, as we saw in Chapter 1. The crucial and more difficult component of the two-phase commit protocol revolves around recovery in the event of failure of either the coordinator or a participant. A viable transaction processing system must be able to cope with a variety of failures. In a distributed environment there are many nodes and paths that could possibly fail during the execution of a request. The transaction manager must be able to handle recovery for all these cases.

Failures that do not disrupt a transaction manager's commitment protocol generally do not adversely affect transaction processing. For example, a resource manager that is recovering from a failure will respond negatively to a prepare request on a branch that was active at the time of failure since the given XID is unrecognizable. The transaction manager handles this situation by rolling back the transaction.

However, more significant failures can disrupt the commitment of a transaction. In Chapter 1 we saw that the coordinator must log enough information at critical points in the protocol interactions to be able to reconstruct and complete the transaction. The resource managers have responsibility for creating a checkpoint of work and indefinitely holding open appropriate resources after they have voted during the prepare phase.

N O T E   As we saw in Chapter 1, the definition of "indefinitely" is implementation-specific and many implementations will use heuristics to break this blocking nature if the hold occurs for a long time.

In all cases, the transaction should be resolved consistently. It is therefore critical that the application server support recovery for multiple resources. Some application servers (today this applies mostly to experimental or open source projects rather than enterprise-quality servers) do not provide recovery capabilities and should not be used for applications that interact with multiple recoverable resources that require transactions. We cover this in more detail in Chapter 8.

Since the XA specification defines a "presumed nothing" protocol driven from the coordinator toward the participant, recovery is always the responsibility of the coordinator. For the case of XA transactions, if a participant fails, the coordinator is responsible for re-contacting the participant when it becomes available and communicating the appropriate message to the branch, depending on the state of the global transaction and the branch. If no failure or restart has occurred in the coordinator, it should be able to complete the branch using internal data structures in place when the transaction was created. If the coordinator has experienced a failure or a restart, it must reconstruct its view of the transaction. Although the coordinator maintains a transaction log, it can only do so with the help of the participant; the XAResource interface provides a recover() method that the transaction manager invokes to request from a resource manager all prepared or heuristic completed branches. The coordinator will treat all these branches as though they were prepared and issue either a rollback or a commit for those involved in unresolved transactions it owns. Heuristic decisions will be reported at this time, but as we saw in Chapter 1, how this happens will be implementation-dependent.

When a coordinator fails, the participants in XA may complete their branches in one of two ways:

1. They may wait for a recovery agent or a restarted coordinator to communicate how to resolve the transaction, which will ultimately result in a completed, consistent global transaction.

2. An administrator may intervene and instruct the participant on how to resolve the transaction. This option requires a heuristic decision to be made, either through an automated mechanism like a timeout in the participant or the more likely case of intervention by a system administrator. Since the decision may be made with imperfect (or no) knowledge, it may result in an inconsistent outcome for the transaction (a heuristic outcome). This is highly undesirable, and it is the responsibility of the owner of the heuristically completed resource manager to correct this situation.

As noted, ultimately the heuristic information is communicated back to the coordinator. This may be useful since it may raise alarms that help to rapidly rectify inconsistencies. However, it does not change the outcome of the decision that was made by the coordinator. Therefore, it's possible that the transaction manager will never allow an application to see a mixed result.

It may make sense to code defensively in the event of a mixed result, but counting on the code to be executed is probably a poor choice. Handling mixed results is difficult: since you don't necessarily know what resources were used within the transaction, where the participants were, a clean "reboot" may be impossible to obtain automatically and you may well have to resort to offline mechanisms. Most transaction service implementations provide a suite of administration tools to help in this situation. It may be appropriate to raise administrative alarms within your application in this scenario.

Another critical element of recovery revolves around security. Recall that the transaction manager must be able to resolve the transaction based on information acquired from the resource manager and the coordinator log. The JDBC and JTA literature both indicate that the transaction recovery agent may use any `XAResource` that points to the resource manager managing the branch to resolve a transaction.

However, assuming this is the case in practice is both dangerous and wrong. During recovery the resource adapter utilized to communicate with the resource manager may not necessarily be the one that initiated the transaction. The associated resource manager may require that a resource adapter utilized for recovery be configured with a special set of security credentials in order to terminate transactions that it did not initiate. Therefore, it is important that the application server provide the ability to logically map from a resource identified in the recovery log to a resource adapter configured with the appropriate security credentials. If an application server does not provide this capability it may be deficient in its support for failure recovery in some resource managers.

Tree of Process Model

DTP supports the notion of a "tree of process" model to define a transaction that migrates from node to node in a distributed architecture. In this case, the transaction itself is defined by an a-cyclic, directed graph (a tree) where the root node acts as a coordinator, but all of the transaction managers in subordinate nodes are participants just like any other resource manager. Inner nodes are viewed as coordinators with respect to the participant transaction managers that they enlist as resources. This is essentially what was discussed in Chapter 1 when we talked about distributed transactions and interposition.

Great care should be taken when deploying this application architecture. Because of all the distributed communication, the tree of process will take longer to complete than in a centralized system. In XA, the recovery process in this tree is driven from the root node. This means that there is opportunity for latency during recovery if a node in the middle of the tree is unavailable. While it's possible for a system of homogeneous transaction managers to optimize this, in a heterogeneous environment a failure within the tree of process may wind up blocking the completion of a transaction. In addition, because there are many coordinators participating in the two-phase commit protocol, the probability of experiencing a problem is increased.

Transaction Interoperability

If a heterogeneous architecture is used, you will need to decide on a remote communication protocol between servers. The original X/Open DTP model provided a *Communications Resource Manager* (CRM) to infect different address spaces with a transaction started on a remote server, with three separate implementations based on popular transaction systems at that time. However, each of these implementations was only interoperable with itself.

In Chapter 1 we discussed how in order to achieve distributed transaction semantics, the application server must serialize the transaction context associated with the thread of control and include it in some kind of wire-level message. This is what the CRM was intended to do. Unfortunately the DTP does not define a protocol for interactions across heterogeneous implementations.

As we see in Chapter 3, OTS provides this support, and in fact, J2EE servers are supposed to achieve transaction interoperability by using OTS service contexts in RMI-IIOP calls. It is entirely possible to marry OTS and JTA in more complicated ways to provide a general programming model in terms of JTA but support more complete transaction context propagation and recovery based on OTS; this was how we built the HP Application Server. Nevertheless, you should be very careful to thoroughly test transaction interoperability between heterogeneous application servers; this is an optional part of J2EE and not well supported. We recommend that you do not rely on this feature unless you have the support of all vendors.

The interoperability scenarios supported by J2EE are defined in the EJB 2.0 specification. We discuss these in more detail in Chapter 6. In addition, many vendors support a proprietary mechanism for context propagation. This is a reasonable approach, but it reaches its limit when more than one vendor's application server is deployed in a solution that requires distributed transactions.

You should also be aware that OTS support is not in and of itself a guarantee of interoperability; early testing of EJB interoperability using just the GIOP messages from CORBA had quite a few hiccups when EJB 2.0 was in the works. Although OTS provides the basis of J2EE interoperability, this doesn't mean that J2EE servers can do transaction interoperability seamlessly in the real world. In particular, the semantic mismatches of synchronization events may cause serious problems, including memory leaks, or even potential problems with two-phase locking. Let's look at both of these cases.

First of all, both the OTS and JTA specifications state that beforeCompletion() will occur prior to the prepare phase of the transaction. This means that a beforeCompletion() notification doesn't occur for transactions marked for rollback or that are rolled back explicitly when termination is requested.

This makes sense. For example, caches that manage their state via synchronization events don't need to flush the cache to persistent store if the transaction is to be aborted. Cache cleanup is presumed to occur in the afterCompletion() call. However, it's important to understand that in both JTA and OTS, the afterCompletion() synchronization event is a courtesy call that may never occur. Why is this?

In the event of a failure a transaction service may be required to complete a transaction using a recovery mechanism. Synchronizations are not defined to be recoverable objects. Since none of the recovery infrastructure supports persistence of registered synchronization objects, there is no way to complete the last synchronization event. This means that caches in the application server may have a condition that can allow a resource (usually a memory) leak.

Some application servers will handle this by calling beforeCompletion() regardless of whether the transaction is being rolled back and the cache will cleanup at this stage; while this works it is not a portable solution if you are implementing synchronization objects (a rather rare occurrence in J2EE). Others may have their cache try to query the transaction manager on behalf of synchronization objects that have been around for a while. Yet others allow synchronizations to be recoverable objects and participate in failure recovery, but this is even less portable. Since this is a gray area, it can be a problem for system interoperability since each application server may try to address this problem differently.

Secondly, as seen in Figure 2-3, the combination of synchronization and the two-phase commit protocol results in four phases of communication during the termination of a transaction

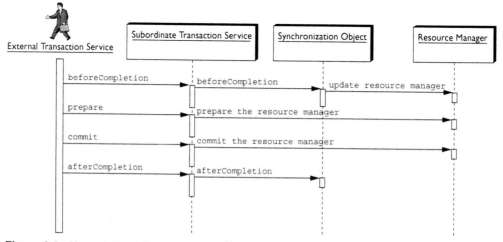

Figure 2-3 Normal distributed termination sequence.

(beforeCompletion, prepare, commit, afterCompletion). However, some JTA implementations may be built on legacy transaction systems that don't support synchronization events. In distributed scenarios, this means that the `beforeCompletion()` call may have to be introduced locally by the application server since it won't be generated by the legacy transaction service driving the transaction (Figure 2-4). In general, this means that work may have to be done locally after the remote legacy transaction service has initiated the prepare phase of the global transaction. If multiple nodes in the transaction are acting upon the same resource manager, this additional work may generate an error (or in the worst case, a reactivation of the prepared branch). It also means that transaction interoperability may be a problem if the parent coordinator never sends a `beforeCompletion()` message as expected. In this case, data management is likely to be corrupted.

It's our recommendation that you use a single transaction service for distributed transactions over IIOP at the present time as a rule. If for some reason you find that you must bridge transaction services when connecting two different vendors' EJB containers, you will in all likelihood need cooperation and help from at least one vendor to ensure that all aspects of the implementations are compatible.

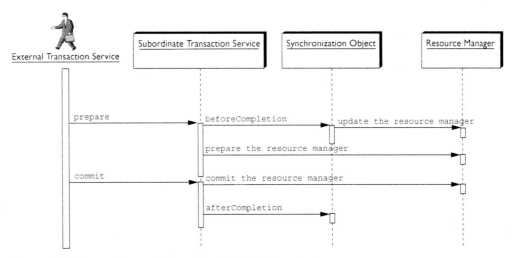

Figure 2-4   Legacy transaction service distributed termination sequence

Protocol Bridges

Resource managers that support two-phase commit do not need to understand XA or its particular recovery semantics to participate in global transactions coordinated by a J2EE application server. It's possible to provide a bridge between the two protocols using adapter classes, if need be. This can be accomplished by with custom `XAResource` implementations using the Java Connector Architecture. If you're using an OTS then you get this bridging natively because the OTS was not designed to be XA specific, but was designed to interoperate with XA, LU 6.2 and other transaction service implementations/standards.

External EIS systems that start distributed transactions but don't natively use XA can call into an application server and enlist the resources accessed by EJBs in a transaction. This is now possible with the Java Connector Architecture 1.5 and its transaction inflow mechanism that can be used to infect the application server with the remote systems transaction context; the resource adapter is responsible for mediating into the XA semantics. We discuss this in Chapter 7 when we talk about transactional resource adapters. To accomplish this properly, you need to understand the concepts discussed in this chapter.

Transaction interoperability may be important for systems that aren't entirely composed of J2EE servers. EJBs may be invoked with transaction contexts from heterogeneous systems that use the CORBA Object Transaction Service. We look closely at OTS in Chapter 3 and discuss its role in EJB interoperability in Chapter 6.

Last Resource Commit

You may have read about the last resource commit optimization in the J2EE literature; some of the specifications, for example, the Java Connector Architecture, make reference to it repeatedly. We discussed this optimization in general terms in Chapter 1. Many application servers support last resource commit as a mechanism to allow transactional resources that do not support two-phase commit to participate in a global transaction. How this is achieved is a proprietary implementation detail of the transaction manager and is generally not exposed as anything more than a configuration option.

In the vast majority of cases, this will work without a problem. Normal processing will occur where the coordinator prepares all the resources that support two-phase commit and then transfer the coordination decision to the last resource. If that resource commits, the coordinator will log a successful commit record and issue a commit to all of the prepared resources. However, if a failure occurs (whether it be a failure of the coordinator, a failure of the resource, a disk failure on the commit write, or a network communication failure) during the transfer of control to the last resource, the coordinator will not know how to consistently resolve the transaction on recovery. Although the transaction manager will in all likelihood roll back the prepared branches, it is usually impossible to determine how to resolve the transaction consistently since there is no mechanism to determine the state of a local transaction. This is a serious liability: we have lost the ACID guarantees that transactions help to provide and risk data inconsistency (heuristic outcomes again).

In some cases, you may be able to use this feature as an optimization for resource managers that do support the full two-phase commit protocol. You should beware that XA does not support the required semantics of this optimization to recover consistently; the one-phase commit option in XA doesn't prepare and then perform the equivalent of a heuristic commit on the work done within the transaction branch. In this case, the work is simply committed and the branch is promptly forgotten by the resource manager. This means that application server transaction managers that support it for XAResources cannot guarantee ACID properties. As we pointed out above, if a failure occurs during transfer of control to the last resource, there is no way to determine if or what decision was made by that resource on recovery.

Last resource commit has another wrinkle for distributed transactions that involve multiple coordinators. If the optimization is used at all, it can only be used once in the tree of transaction managers. For this reason, we strongly advise caution when using this optimization in distributed transactions: make sure that the transaction manager you are using restricts the optimization to the root coordinator.

One of our colleagues jokes that "last resource commit exists only because IMS couldn't support transactions." You may be wondering at this point why anyone would ever use this optimization. There are advantages that last resource commit provides and they are often pragmatic considerations that may lead you to use this feature. For one thing, last resource commit will allow much better reliability when committing work done on multiple resource managers, one of which does not support two-phase commit. In the vast majority of failure cases, the optimization will not present a problem. Even when all resources support XA, last resource commit can be used as a means to achieve quality of service enhancements for critical systems. For large, critical databases, it is highly undesirable for the resource manager to remain in doubt and to ever lock access to resources for an extended period of time. This is precisely why administrators are often forced to make heuristic decisions. Last resource commit can be used to ensure that your critical resource manager is never in doubt, and this may well be worth the compromise on recovery.

> **N O T E**   There are no hard and fast rules here, but you need to be aware that the use of last resource commit has serious consequences for your IT solutions.

On a somewhat related note, you should be aware that certain J2EE application server and enterprise information system vendors may not truly support the two-phase protocol due to technical limitations or the fact that a particular legacy resource may not support distributed transactions. Since transactional behavior in J2EE is tied to the DTP model, some vendors have resource adapters that attempt to mimic XA semantics through local transactions. In these instances the XAResource interface implementation supplied may simply return the XA_OK response when the prepare() method is invoked by the transaction coordinator. This lightweight emulation of the role played by a resource manager participating in a distributed transaction can lead to the loss of the ACID properties when multiple resource managers are involved.

But don't write them off either: they also provide very real performance gains in systems where two-phase commit is not needed.

In Chapter 1, Transaction Fundamentals we saw that the two-phase protocol consists of more than just a series of messages exchanged between a coordinator and participating resource managers. Rather, the protocol requires logging by the transaction manager and check pointing by the recoverable resource managers (participants). These fake XA resources simply do not fulfill the latter requirement because they do not get driven through the prepare phase, the time when participants should save recoverability information. It is therefore imperative that a software architect validates the completeness of the `XAResource` implementations and ensures that the server does complete real two-phase commit where required.

Conclusion

Transaction management is at the heart of J2EE; it is, today, based almost entirely on the DTP model and the mapping of the TX and XA specifications provided by the Java Transaction API. In the early days of J2EE, transaction support was haphazard, often incorrect, and generally hidden behind the machinery of the EJB container. This has all changed. The market-leading J2EE application servers support global transaction management, the transaction managers are reasonably sophisticated, and J2EE developers require more detailed knowledge of the how JTA works. This latter point is becoming even more important as new specifications that are now being finalized for J2EE 1.4 provide hooks for resource adapter authors to write their own `XAResource` implementations; XA-aware resource managers are ubiquitous and mature. At the same time, understanding how an application server can be used reliably and the consequences of different options like last resource commit is mandatory for solutions architects.

CHAPTER 3

The Java Transaction Service

In this chapter we look at one of the transaction specifications we briefly mentioned in Chapter 1, "Transaction Fundamentals," and see how many of those issues have been addressed by a real-world specification; this should help to make concrete some of the things we discussed earlier and give you an indication of just how much effort is involved in turning principles into practice. However, we're not looking at just any specification; we examine the one that is of most importance to J2EE: the Object Transaction Service from the Object Management Group. We look at the transaction service component of CORBA because that first became the standard for transactions in distributed object systems. It later became the standard for distributed transactions in J2EE when the Java Transaction API (JTA) recommended it for its underlying transaction system implementation (subtly renaming it the Java Transaction Service, or JTS). In this book we use the terms OTS and JTS interchangeably.

Although you are extremely unlikely to encounter OTS directly when writing your J2EE applications, you may be using it indirectly. The JTA that your beans or container actually uses may be layered on OTS for the purposes of interoperability with other transaction services or simply because of the legacy of the underlying transaction system; the JTA specification does not mandate the JTS but recommends it. Knowing whether or not there is a JTS operating in your favorite application server can be important, especially if you want to talk to foreign application servers/transactional applications.

> **NOTE** We shall only be able to give an overview of OTS, since the actual specification is over 100 pages. Although we concentrate on the recent 1.4 version of the specification, we endeavor to indicate differences between it and the 1.1 version, which forms the basis of many existing implementations used in application servers.

The Common Object Request Broker Architecture (CORBA), as defined by the Object Management Group (OMG), is a standard derived by an industrial consortium including IBM, BEA and Hewlett-Packard, which promotes the construction of interoperable applications that are based upon the concepts of distributed objects. The architecture principally contains the following components:

- Object Request Broker (ORB), which enables objects to transparently make and receive requests in a distributed, heterogeneous environment. This component is the core of the OMG reference model.
- Object Services, a collection of services that support functions for using and implementing objects. Such services are considered to be necessary for the construction of any distributed application. Of particular relevance to this chapter is the Object Transaction Service (OTS).
- Common Facilities are other useful services that applications may need, but which are not considered to be fundamental such as desktop management and help facilities.

Now you may think that this sounds similar to J2EE and in many respects it is. You'll also find that much of the work the OMG did on various services such as transactions or messaging has found its way into J2EE: why reinvent the wheel when what exists works well?

N O T E   Although we assume a basic level of CORBA under-standing (particularly about IDL) you should be able to under-stand most of the concepts and interfaces described in this chapter without any prior knowledge.

CORBA predates J2EE by a decade and is not restricted to a single implementation language. Importantly for us, CORBA was the standard development platform for enterprise applications before Java and J2EE came along. Despite what you might have been lead to believe, there are a lot of legacy components and applications out there written in languages other than Java. In an enterprise application, you typically have to interact with these components sooner rather than later. As a result, interoperability between J2EE and CORBA quickly became important in J2EE.

The J2EE specification addressed this by requiring Java Remote Method Invocation (RMI) to utilize the CORBA message format IIOP (Internet Inter-ORB Protocol). This allows Java applications to invoke methods on CORBA objects written in any language. Transaction interoperability was obtained by recommending that JTA implementations use transaction services written using the JTS.

The OTS in a Nutshell

The OTS provides interfaces that allow multiple, distributed objects to cooperate in a transaction such that all objects commit or abort their changes together. However, the transaction service does not require all objects to have transactional behavior. Instead objects can choose not to support transactional operations at all, or to support it for some requests but not others. Transaction information may be propagated between client and server explicitly, or implicitly, giving the programmer finer-grained control over an object's transactionality. Objects supporting (partial) transactional behavior must reside within domains (Portable Object Adapters in CORBA parlance) that have appropriate transaction *policies* defined on them. The OTS specification allows transactions to be nested. However, an implementation need not provide this functionality. Appropriate exceptions are raised if an attempt is made to use nested transactions in this case.

> **N O T E**   In the 1.1 version of OTS specification objects had to have interfaces derived from the `TransactionalObject` interface. This was deprecated in 1.2.

The transaction service also distinguishes between *recoverable objects* and *transactional objects*:

- Recoverable objects are those that contain the actual state that may be changed by a transaction and must therefore be informed when the transaction commits or rolls back (aborts) to ensure the consistency of the state changes. This is achieved be registering appropriate objects that support the `Resource` CORBA interface (or the derived `SubtransactionAwareResource` interface) with the current transaction. Recoverable objects are also by definition transactional objects.
- In contrast, a simple transactional object need not necessarily be a recoverable object if its state is actually implemented using other recoverable objects. A simple transactional object need not take part in the commit protocol used to determine the outcome of the transaction since it does not maintain any state itself, having delegated that responsibility to other recoverable objects that will take part in the commit process.

The OTS is simply a *protocol engine* that guarantees that transactional behavior is obeyed but does not directly support all of the transaction properties given above. As such it requires other co-operating services that implement the required functionality, including:

1. *Persistence/Recovery Service*. Required to support the atomicity and durability properties.
2. *Concurrency Control Service*. Required to support the isolation properties.

The application programmer is responsible for using these services to ensure that transactional objects have the necessary ACID properties.

N O T E   It is important to understand that OTS does not define how to implement a transaction service, only what is expected of an implementation at the interface level and (roughly) behavior that is visible through these interfaces.

What this means is that many of the issues we discussed in Chapter 1, "Transaction Fundamentals," such as transaction logs, two-phase concurrency control and so on are assumed by OTS: you won't find anywhere in its 120+ pages a description of how to write a transaction log that performs well under load, for instance. So, although just taking the OTS specification and trying to write a conformant implementation is possible, it is unlikely to result in an implementation that performs or even works under all failure scenarios. Unfortunately, many new entrants to the field of transaction processing have failed to understand this, so you should beware: just because something is OTS compliant doesn't mean it is resilient, performs well, scales or can tolerate failures.

The Java Transaction Service

As with all OMG specifications, the Object Transaction Service is not language specific, i.e., it can be implemented just as easily in C++ as COBOL. Therefore, the Java Transaction Service specification is a Java language mapping of OTS. The advantage of using a JTS-compliant implementation is that, in theory at least, it allows interoperation with other JTS implementations.

Unfortunately, OTS interoperability has never been high on the agenda of transaction service vendors and hence the definers of the specification: it's not in their interests to allow you to buy implementations from different vendors. Problems with interoperability began to be addressed with truly interoperable versions of CORBA and then with OTS 1.2. So look out for implementations based on this version of the specification as you're much more likely to not suffer from vendor lock-in in the future.

N O T E   Although the CORBA specification is now at version 1.4, the JTS specification only references OTS 1.1. Although transaction service implementations compliant with 1.2 and above provide the potential for better interoperability, unfortunately there is no requirement for JTS compliant implementations to support these versions.

Relationship to Other Transaction Standards

The OTS specification was developed by some of the main players in the transaction processing arena. Although it was meant as the model for next generation transaction processing systems, it was impractical to believe that existing systems (e.g., IBM's CICS) would be replaced by new implementations based on OTS. Much trust in the reliability, performance and functionality of these systems has been built up over many years and for many critical applications it is this trust that is more important than the underlying model on which they are based.

Therefore, one of the important aspects of OTS was that it should be able to interoperate with the main legacy transaction processing implementations and their associated models. OTS implementations can therefore interact with many of the transaction systems we presented in Chapter 1, "Transaction Fundamentals." It is slightly ironic that interoperability with legacy systems was supported from the beginning whereas interoperability with other OTS implementations was not.

The OTS Architecture

The architecture of OTS is captured in Figure 3-1. The OTS defines interfaces to a transaction service implementation. That implementation may be a pre-existing system, based on another standard or vendor-specific protocol, or it may be written from scratch based on the requirements dictated by OTS. However, the OTS interfaces can essentially be grouped into those available to a client (shown in the box beneath the transaction originator in the figure) and those available to the server (shown in the box below the recoverable server). You'll notice that there is some overlap between these interfaces; as we see later this is because there are situations where these interfaces need to be available to both the client and the server.

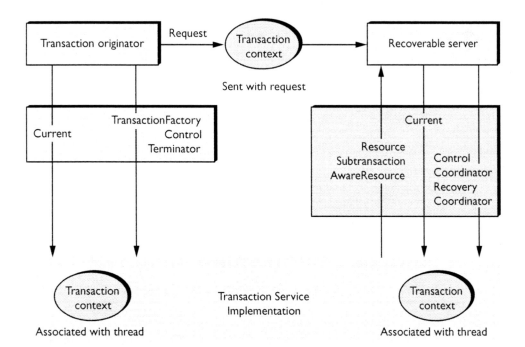

Figure 3-1 The OTS architecture.

We now briefly describe the roles that these various interfaces play in the OTS specification:

- `Current` is the application programmers' typical way to interact with the transaction implementation and allows transactions to be started and ended. Transactions created using `Current` are automatically associated with the invoking thread. It is a per-thread object, so that it must remember the transaction associated with each thread that has used it. The underlying implementation will typically use the `TransactionFactory` for creating top-level transactions. Nested transactions are an optional extra.
- The `Control` interface provides access to a specific transaction and actually wraps the transaction `Coordinator` and `Terminator` interfaces which are used to enlisting participants and ending the transaction respectively. One of the reasons for splitting this functionality into two interfaces was to allow a transaction implementation to have finer control over the entities that could terminate the transaction.
- The `Resource/SubtransactionAwareResource` interfaces represent the transaction participants and have a deliberately generic interface to allow any (two-phase) compliant implementation to be registered with the transaction rather than just an XA compliant implementation.
- Each top-level transaction has an associated `RecoveryCoordinator` that is available to participants in order for them to drive failure recovery. As we mentioned earlier, recovery after a crash will almost certainly be driven from the transaction coordinators' end but allowing participants to drive it as well can improve recovery time.
- The transaction context is fundamental to any distributed transaction system and OTS is no different in this respect.

In the following sections we look at these different interfaces and how they are used within OTS.

Application Programming Models

A client application program may use *direct* or *indirect* context management to manage a transaction. With indirect context management, an application uses `Current` to associate the transaction context with the application thread of control. In direct context management, an application manipulates the `Control` object and the other objects associated with the transaction: the application threads are not automatically associated with transactions through this mechanism, which gives the application more control over thread-to-transaction association.

Furthermore, OTS allows an object to specify whether transactions should be explicitly or implicitly propagated to its operations:

- *Explicit propagation* means that an application propagates a transaction context (defined by what OTS calls a `PropagationContext`) by passing objects defined by the transaction service as explicit parameters. How the context is explicitly propagated is not mandated by OTS: for example, a `PropagationContext` or `Control` object may be used.
- *Implicit propagation* means that requests are implicitly associated with (share) the client's transaction. The context is transmitted implicitly to the objects, without direct client intervention. Implicit propagation depends on indirect context management, since it propagates the transaction context associated with `Current`. An object that supports implicit propagation would not typically expect to receive a `PropagationContext` (for example) object as an explicit parameter.

A client may use one or both forms of context management, and may communicate with objects that use either method of context propagation. This results in four ways in which client applications may communicate with transactional objects:

1. *Direct Context Management/Explicit Propagation*: The client application directly accesses the `Control` object, and the other objects that describe the state of the transaction. To propagate the transaction to an object, the client must include the context as an explicit parameter of an operation.

2. *Indirect Context Management/Implicit Propagation*: The client application uses operations on `Current` to create and control its transactions. When it issues requests on transactional objects, the transaction context associated with the current thread is implicitly propagated to the object.

3. *Indirect Context Management/Explicit Propagation*: For an implicit model application to use explicit propagation, it can get access to the `Control` using the `get_control` operation provided by `Current`. It can then use an instance of `PropagationContext` as an explicit parameter to a transactional object. This is explicit propagation.

4. *Direct Context Management/Implicit Propagation*: A client that accesses the transaction service objects directly can use the `resume` operation provided by `Current` to set the implicit transaction context associated with its thread (set up the thread-to-transaction association). This allows the client to invoke operations of an object that requires implicit propagation of the transaction context.

The main difference between direct and indirect context management is the effect on the invoking thread's transaction context. If using indirect, the thread's transaction context *will* be modified automatically by OTS, e.g., if `begin` is called then the thread's notion of the current transaction will be modified to the newly created transaction; when that is terminated, the transaction previously associated with the thread (if any) will be restored as the thread's context (assuming nested transactions are supported by the OTS implementation). However, if using direct management, no changes to the thread's transaction context are performed by OTS: the application programmer assumes responsibility for this.

Let's now look at the various components of OTS in more detail. We start at the top, with the entity that is responsible for creating transactions: the transaction factory.

The Transaction Factory

The `TransactionFactory` interface is provided to allow the transaction originator to begin a top-level transaction. Nested transactions must be created using the `begin` method of `Current`, or the `create_subtransaction` method of the parent's `Coordinator`. Operations on the factory and `Coordinator` to create new transactions are direct context management, and as such will not modify the calling thread's transaction context.

The `create` operation creates a new top-level transaction and returns its `Control` object, which can be used to manage or control participation in the new transaction. When an application invokes `create` it can also provide an application specific timeout value, in seconds: if the transaction has not completed before this timeout has elapsed then the transaction service will roll it back. If the parameter is zero, then no application specified timeout is established.

> **N O T E**   Nested transactions do not have a timeout associated with them and so will only be automatically rolled back if their enclosing top-level transaction is rolled back.

This sequence of operations can be represented in UML as shown in Figure 3-2:

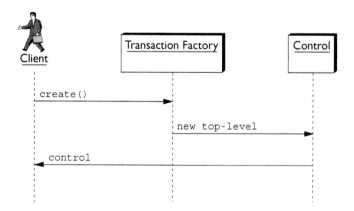

Figure 3-2   Top-level transaction creation (direct mode).

The client contacts the `TransactionFactory` and invokes the `create` method. This causes the factory to create and start a new top-level transaction and eventually return a `Control` reference to the client for the transaction. As we see, the client can then use this reference later to manipulate the transaction.

The specification allows the `TransactionFactory` to be a separate server from the application (e.g., a typical Transaction Monitor), which transaction clients and services share and which manages transactions on their behalf. However, the specification also enables the `TransactionFactory` to be implemented by an object within the same process (JVM) as the clients/services that use it. This has obvious performance and fault-tolerance benefits but can be a management nightmare. Nearly all OTS implementations support the Transaction Monitor approach, with several also offering the co-located option. In our experience, a well-designed transaction service that offers both styles is the best of both worlds, allowing you to choose the location of the transaction factory to best suit your applications. Remember that the choice may well vary from application to application, so only being given one option may severely limit your scope for future transactional developments.

Managing Transaction Contexts

As we saw in Chapter 1, "Transaction Fundamentals," the *transaction context* is fundamental to any distributed transaction architecture and OTS is no different. Each thread is potentially associated with a context and this association may be null, indicating that the thread has no associated transaction, or it refers to a specific transaction. The OTS explicitly allows contexts to be shared across multiple threads. In the presence of nested transactions a context remembers the stack of transactions started within the environment such that when the nested transaction ends the context of the thread can be restored to that in effect before the nested transaction was started.

This relationship is shown in Figure 3-3 in UML where, as we've already seen, `Current` is the object used by a thread for manipulating its transaction context information (represented by `Control` objects) and performing the thread-to-transaction association:

What this diagram shows is that `Current` maintains a hierarchy of transactions (zero-to-many transactions) for every thread in the application. These transactions are represented by `Control` objects.

As we mentioned earlier, management of transaction contexts may be undertaken by an application in either a direct or an indirect manner. In the direct approach the transaction originator issues a request to a `TransactionFactory` to begin a new top-level transaction. The factory returns a `Control` object that enables two further interfaces to be obtained. These latter interfaces allow an application to end the transaction (via a `Terminator`), to become a participant in the transaction, or to start a nested transaction (both via a `Coordinator`). These interfaces (shown in Code Listing 3-1) may be passed as explicit parameters in operation invocations since transaction creation using these interfaces does not change a thread's current context.

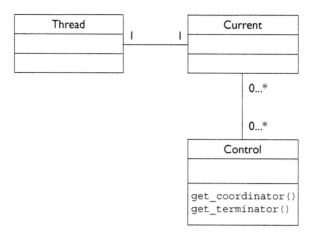

Figure 3-3 Thread and context relationship.

Code Listing 3-1 Direct context management interface.

```
interface Terminator
{
    void commit (in boolean report_heuristics) raises (HeuristicMixed,
HeuristicHazard);
    void rollback ();
};

interface Coordinator
{
    Status get_status ();
    Status get_parent_status ();
    Status get_top_level_status ();

    RecoveryCoordinator register_resource (in Resource r) raises
(Inactive);
    Control create_subtransaction () raises
(SubtransactionsUnavailable, Inactive);
    void rollback_only () raises (Inactive);
    . . .
};

interface Control
{
    Terminator get_terminator () raises (Unavailable);
    Coordinator get_coordinator () raises (Unavailable);
};
```

```
interface TransactionFactory
{
        Control create (in unsigned long time_out);
};
```

The relationship between a `Control` and its `Coordinator` and `Terminator` interfaces is shown in Figure 3-4. For every `Control` there is exactly one `Coordinator`, and every `Coordinator` is associated with exactly one `Control`. However, the same cannot be said for the `Terminator`. The OTS allows a `Control` to have no `Terminator` (the implementation may wish to restrict who can end a transaction, for example, and so could ensure that the `Control` has a null `Terminator`).

As mentioned earlier, when a transaction is created by the factory it is possible to specify a timeout value in seconds; if the transaction has not completed within this timeout then it is subject to possible rollback. If the timeout value is zero then no application specific timeout will be set.

In contrast to explicit context management, implicit context management is handled by the `Current` interface (shown in Code Listing 3-2), which provides simplified transaction management functionality and automatically creates nested transactions as required. Transactions created using this interface do alter a thread's current transaction context, i.e., the thread's notion of the current transaction changes appropriately.

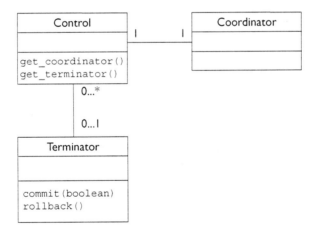

Figure 3-4 Control relationship.

Code Listing 3-2 Indirect Context Management Interface

```
interface Current : CORBA::Current
{
    void begin () raises (SubtransactionsUnavailable);
    void commit (in boolean report_heuristics) raises
(NoTransaction, HeuristicMixed, HeuristicHazard);
    void rollback () raises (NoTransaction);
    void rollback_only () raises (NoTransaction);
    . . .
    Control get_control ();
    Control suspend ();
    void resume (in Control which) raises (InvalidControl);
};
```

Nested Transactions

We saw in Chapter 1, "Transaction Fundamentals," how nested transactions can be a useful structuring tool for modularity and fault-tolerance. The OTS was the first industrial transaction specification to include support for nested transactions. Unfortunately, the provision of nested transaction by an OTS implementation is optional, so just because you find an implementation of OTS doesn't necessarily mean you've found something that supports nested transactions. Remember also that you'll need to have subtransaction-aware resources in order to actually be able to do anything useful with your newly found nested transactions.

When nested transactions (subtransactions) are provided, the transaction context forms a hierarchy. Resources acquired within a subtransaction should be inherited (retained) by parent transactions upon the commit of the subtransaction, and (assuming no failures) only released when the top-level transaction completes, i.e., they should be retained for the duration of the top-level transaction. If a subtransaction rolls back, it can release any resources it acquired, and undo any changes to resources it inherited.

Unlike top-level transactions, in OTS subtransactions behave differently at commit time. Whereas top-level transactions undergo a two-phase commit protocol, nested transactions in OTS do not perform any commit protocol: when a program commits a nested transaction, the transaction is considered committed and it simply informs any registered resources of its outcome. If a resource cannot commit then it raises an exception, and the OTS implementation is free to ignore this or attempt to roll back the subtransaction. Obviously rolling back a subtransaction may not be possible if some resources have already been told that the transaction has committed.

Because a two-phase commit protocol is not used by OTS, this can lead to non-atomic behavior. Therefore, most sensible implementations will either cause the enclosing transaction (which may or may not be a subtransaction) to rollback, thus guaranteeing that all work will be undone, or will extend the protocol and (in an implementation-specific manner) actually run a two-phase commit protocol on all subtransaction-aware resources. (Several systems that do support nested transactions use a two-phase commit protocol to terminate them.)

If you use an OTS with subtransactions, you should certainly attempt to verify which, if any, mechanism the implementation uses to ensure the integrity of your application and its data. If there is no such mechanism is in place, then nested transactions should be used with extreme care.

Transaction Propagation

So you've written your transactional object/service and you now want to make sure that remote transactional clients can use it within the scope of their transactions, i.e., you need to ensure that transaction contexts are propagated between clients and services. How do you accomplish this? In this section we look at how things used to work in older versions of the OTS specification and how they're now supposed to work. The reason for comparing and contrasting is that at the time of writing most existing implementations of OTS still use the original, older form of context propagation.

The OTS supports both implicit (system driven) propagation and explicit (application driven) propagation of transactional behavior. In the implicit case transactional behavior is specified in an operation signature or Portable Object Adapter (POA) policy and any transaction context associated with the calling thread is automatically sent with each operation invocation.

With explicit propagation, applications must define their own mechanism for propagating transactions. This allows two options:

- A client can control whether its transaction is propagated with any operation invocation. When using POA policies, it is assumed that all methods of the invoked object are transactional, which may not actually be the case. If there are some non-transactional methods, propagating the context will be an unnecessary overhead.
- A client can invoke operations on both transactional and non-transactional objects within a transaction.

Note that transaction context management and transaction propagation are different things that may be controlled independently of each other. Furthermore, mixing of direct and indirect context management with implicit and explicit transaction propagation is allowed. Use of implicit propagation requires co-operation from the ORB, in that the current context associated with the thread must be sent with any operation invocations by a client and extracted by the server prior to actually calling the target operation.

In the following sections we look at how implicit context propagation occurs. This uses the `PropagationContext` structure defined by OTS. As you might be able to guess from what we saw in Chapter 1, "Transaction Fundamentals," this structure contains a reference to the transaction coordinator and the timeout value associated with the transaction; if the transaction is nested, then the entire hierarchy is also defined.

TransactionalObject Interface

In the 1.1 version of the OTS specification, the empty `TransactionalObject` inter-face is used by an object to indicate that it is transactional. By supporting this interface, an object indicates that it wants the transaction context associated with the client thread to be associated with all of its operations.

An OTS implementation is not required to initialize the transaction context of every request handler. It is required to do so only if the interface supported by the target object is derived from `TransactionalObject`. Otherwise, the initial transaction context of the thread is undefined. A transaction service implementation can raise the `TRANSACTION_REQUIRED` exception if a `TransactionalObject` is invoked outside the scope of a transaction, i.e., the transaction context is null.

In a single-address space application (i.e., all objects reside within the same process), transaction contexts are implicitly shared between "clients" and objects, regardless of whether or not the objects support the `TransactionalObject` interface.

OTSPolicy

Although the use of `TransactionalObject` is maintained for backward compatibil-ity, explicit transactional behaviors are now encoded using `OTSPolicy` values, which are inde-pendent of the transaction propagation rules used by the infrastructure. These policies are similar in many respects to those possessed by J2EE containers.

The main problem with `TransactionalObject` was that it was an attribute of the type of object and not of its deployment. What this meant was that if you wanted a transactional and non-transactional instance of the object you'd be required to have two different types. With the advent of the CORBA POA, it was possible to remove this restriction and make transaction-ality a property of the way in which the object is deployed.

The POA policies and their OTS 1.1 equivalents are defined as shown in Table 3-1.

Table 3-1 OTS 1.2 transaction behaviors

OTSPolicy	Policy Value	OTS 1.1 equivalent
Reserved	0	Inheritance from `TransactionalObject`
REQUIRES	1	No equivalent
FORBIDS	2	No inheritance from `TransactionalObject`
ADAPTS	3	No equivalent

- REQUIRES—The behavior of the target object depends on the existence of a current transaction. If the invocation does not have a current transaction, a TRANSACTION_REQUIRED exception will be raised.
- FORBIDS—The behavior of the target object depends on the absence of a current transaction. If the invocation does have a current transaction, an INVALID_TRANSACTION exception will be raised.
- ADAPTS—The behavior of the target object will be adjusted to take advantage of a current transaction, if one exists. If not, it will exhibit a different behavior (i.e., the target object is sensitive to the presence or absence of a current transaction).

Examples

To aid in comprehension of the above discussions, Code Listing 3-3 illustrates a simple transactional client using both direct context management and explicit transaction propagation.

Code Listing 3-3 Simple transactional client using direct and explicit

```
{
    . . .
    org.omg.CosTransactions.Control c;
  org.omg.CosTransactions.Terminator t;
    org.omg.CosTransactions.PropagationContext pgtx;

  c = transFact.create(0);          // create top-level transaction

    pgtx = c.get_coordinator().get_txcontext();
  ...
    trans_object.operation(arg, pgtx);              // explicit
propagation
    ...
    t = c.get_terminator();          // get terminator
    t.commit(false);              // so it can be used to commit
    ...
}
```

> **N O T E** Many of the examples we use in this chapter are only partial code fragments, illustrating the pertinent aspects. If you want to see working examples and the later demonstration code, then take a look at the Arjuna reference from **websiteURL**#Need URL

In contrast, Code Listing 3-4 shows the same program using indirect context management and implicit propagation. This example is considerably simpler since the application only has to be concerned with starting and then committing or aborting actions.

Code Listing 3-4 Simple transactional client using indirect and implicit

```
{
    .  .  .
    ...
    current.begin();              // create new transaction
    ...
    trans_object2.operation(arg);             // implicit propagation
    ...
    current.commit(false);           // simple commit
    ...
}
```

Finally, Code Listing 3-5 illustrates the potential flexibility of OTS by using both direct and indirect context management in conjunction with explicit and implicit transaction propagation.

Code Listing 3-5 Mixed transactional client

```
{
    .  .  .
    org.omg.CosTransactions.Control c;
    org.omg.CosTransactions.Terminator t;
      org.omg.CosTransactions.PropagationContext pgtx;

    c = transFact.create(0);            // create top-level transaction
      pgtx = c.get_coordinator().get_txcontext();

    current.resume(c);              // set implicit context
    ...
    trans_object.operation(arg, pgtx);             // explicit
propagation
    trans_object2.operation(arg);             // implicit propagation
    ...
    current.rollback();            // oops! rollback
    ...
}
```

Handling Heuristics

In Chapter 1, "Transaction Fundamentals," we saw how transaction heuristics are an inevitable component of transaction systems and the OTS specification is no different. To recap, heuristics are the means whereby the traditional blocking nature of a transaction two-phase commit protocol can be unblocked: prepared participants can take autonomous decisions about whether to ultimately commit or rollback if they do not get the coordinator's final decision or it is not received in a timely manner. However, it's important to remember that heuristics should be used with care and only in exceptional circumstances since there is the possibility that the decision will differ from that determined by the transaction service and will thus lead to a loss of integrity in the system.

In terms of OTS, if a heuristic decision is made by a participant then an appropriate exception is raised during commit/rollback processing. The OTS supports an exception for each type of heuristic, i.e., `HeuristicRollback`, `HeuristicCommit`, `HeuristicMixed` and `HeuristixHazard`. Heuristics are ordered such that `HeuristicMixed` takes priority over `HeuristicHazard`.

Rather than always being told about heuristics, a client can choose to ignore them; we'd obviously not recommending this approach unless you are sure about the resources that will participate within your transactions and how they will behave in the event a heuristic occurs. The commit operation of `Current` or the `Terminator` takes a Boolean parameter that allows the caller to specify whether or not heuristic reporting is required.

> **N O T E**   As we saw in Chapter 2, the JTA took the approach of not allowing applications to ignore heuristics. If a heuristic occurs, you're application will be informed.

However, heuristics could occur after the transaction has officially terminated: for example, if not all participants can be contacted during the second phase of the commit protocol, the failure recovery system may be responsible for completing the transaction later. If that happens, any heuristic outcomes cannot be reported directly to the application, which may have long since terminated. Early versions of the OTS specification allowed heuristic outcomes to be reported via the CORBA Event service. However, this was removed in more recent versions. As such, heuristic notification can be something that is overlooked or provided in an implementation-specific manner. We recommend that you do a little investigation in this area to determine exactly what your favorite implementation does, especially in the event of heuristics occurring during failure recovery: if they aren't reported, we suggest going elsewhere.

Transaction Controls

The `Control` interface allows a program to explicitly manage or propagate a transaction context. An object supporting the `Control` interface is associated with one specific transaction. The `Control` interface supports two operations, `get_terminator` and `get_coordinator`, which return instances of the `Terminator` and `Coordinator` interfaces respectively. Both of these methods throw the `Unavailable` exception if the `Control` cannot provide the requested object, e.g., the transaction has terminated. An OTS implementation can restrict the ability for the `Terminator` and `Coordinator` to be used in other execution environments or threads; at a minimum the creator must be able to use them.

The `Control` object for a transaction can be obtained when the transaction is created either using the `TransactionFactory` or the `create_subtransaction` method defined by the `Coordinator` interface. In addition, it is possible to obtain a `Control` for the current transaction using the `get_control` or `suspend` methods provided by `Current`.

The Terminator

Each transaction has an individual `Terminator` and applications can use the `Terminator` to commit or rollback the transaction. Typically these operations are used by the same thread that started the transaction. As we mentioned earlier, you can use the `Terminator` to manage your transactions (direct context management) but if you do it will mean that the invoking thread's notion of the current transaction will not be changed.

It is possible for a transaction to be terminated directly (i.e., through the `Terminator`) and then an attempt to terminate the transaction again through `Current` can be made (or vice versa). In this situation, an exception will be thrown for the subsequent termination attempt.

The `commit` operation attempts to commit the transaction: as we saw in Chapter 1, "Transaction Fundamentals," to successfully commit, the transaction must not have been marked as rollback only (e.g., the `rollback_only` method provided by `Current`) and all of its participants must agree to commit. Otherwise, the transaction will be forced to rollback and the `TRANSACTION_ROLLEDBACK` exception will be thrown by `commit` to indicate this fact to the application.

If the `report_heuristics` argument is `false`, the `commit` operation can complete as soon as the `Coordinator` has made its decision to commit or rollback the transaction, i.e., as soon as the prepare phase has completed. The application is not required to wait for the transaction coordinator to complete the second phase of the protocol. This can significantly reduce the elapsed time for the `commit` operation, especially where participant `Resource` objects are located on remote network nodes. However, no heuristic conditions can be reported to the application in this case. So, as we said before, you'd better be confident that ignoring heuristics, as this does, will not adversely affect your application. You should weigh the possible performance gains against the fact that you may not know about loss of application consistency until much later (if at all).

The `report_heuristics` option set to `true` guarantees that the `commit` operation will not complete until the coordinator has completed the `commit` protocol with all `Resource` objects involved in the transaction. This guarantees that the application will be informed of any non-atomic outcomes of the transaction via the `HeuristicMixed` or `HeuristicHazard` exceptions, but increases the application-perceived elapsed time for the `commit` operation. You might wonder why `HeuristicRollback` isn't one of the possible exceptions that can be thrown by `commit`: if a participant heuristically rolls back, the coordinator will either be able to roll back all other participants (if the heuristic participant was the first one encountered during the second phase of the commit protocol, for instance), or it will have told the other participants to commit. In the former case, the `TRANSACTION_ROLLEDBACK` exception is thrown, whereas in the latter it will be `HeuristicMixed` or `HeuristicHazard`.

When a transaction is committed, the coordinator will drive any registered `Resources` using their `prepare/commit` methods. It is the responsibility of these `Resources` to ensure that any state changes to recoverable objects are made permanent to guarantee the ACID properties, as described in Chapter 1, "Transaction Fundamentals."

When `rollback` is called, the registered `Resources` are responsible for guaranteeing that all changes to recoverable objects made within the scope of the transaction (and its descendants) is undone. All resources locked by the transaction are made available to other transactions as appropriate to the degree of isolation enforced by the resources. Remember that no heuristics can occur here because there is no prepare phase.

The Coordinator

As you might guess from the name, the `Coordinator` is the main interface to the transaction coordinator. Each `Coordinator` represents a specific transaction and is obtained by the `get_coordinator` method of `Control`. For a number of reasons, including architecture and compatibility with existing transaction service implementations, the `Coordinator` does not actually contain operations for starting or ending the transaction. What it does contain, however, are operations needed by servers to enable them to enlist participants (resources) in the transaction represented by the `Coordinator`. These participants are typically either recoverable objects or agents of recoverable objects, for example a resource controlling updates on a database. In addition, as we saw in Chapter 1, "Transaction Fundamentals," these participants could be subordinate coordinators for interposition.

The operations supported by the `Coordinator` interface of interest to application programmers are:

- `get_status`, `get_parent_status`, `get_top_level_status`: these operations return the status of the associated transaction. At any given time a transaction can have one of the following status values representing its progress:
  - `StatusActive`: The transaction is currently running and has not been asked to prepare or been marked for rollback.
  - `StatusMarkedRollback`: The transaction has been marked for rollback. This is the only possible outcome for the transaction.
  - `StatusPrepared`: The transaction has been prepared, i.e., all subordinates have responded `VoteCommit`.
  - `StatusCommitted`: The transaction has completed commitment. It is likely that heuristics exist, otherwise the transaction would have been destroyed and `StatusNoTransaction` returned.
  - `StatusRolledBack`: The transaction has rolled back. It is likely that heuristics exist, otherwise the transaction would have been destroyed and `StatusNoTransaction` returned.
  - `StatusUnknown`: The transaction service cannot determine the current status of the transaction. This is a transient condition, and a subsequent invocation will ultimately return a different status.
  - `StatusNoTransaction`: No transaction is currently associated with the target object. This will occur after a transaction has completed successfully (either commit or rollback).

- StatusPreparing: The transaction is in the process of preparing and has not yet determined the final outcome.
- StatusCommitting: The transaction is in the process of committing.
- StatusRollingBack: The transaction is in the process of rolling back.

- is_same_transaction: This operation and a number of similar operations can be used for transaction comparison. Resources may use these various operations to guarantee that they are registered only once with a specific transaction.

- hash_transaction, hash_top_level_tran: This operation returns a hash code for the specified transaction.

- register_resource: This operation registers the specified Resource as a participant in the transaction. The Inactive exception is raised if the transaction has already been prepared: it makes no sense to enlist a participant with a transaction that has already completed the first phase of the commit protocol, since the new participant wouldn't be able to take part in the termination protocol. The TRANSACTION_ROLLEDBACK exception is raised if the transaction has been marked rollback only; the OTS designers decided that there was little point in being able to enlist a participant with a transaction when the transaction was guaranteed to rollback. If the Resource is a SubtransactionAwareResource *and* the transaction is a subtransaction, then this operation registers the Resource with this transaction and indirectly with the top-level transaction when the subtransaction's ancestors have committed. Otherwise, the Resource will only be registered with the *current* transaction. This operation returns a RecoveryCoordinator that can be used by this Resource during recovery, as we see later. Note that there is no ordering of registered Resources implied by this operation, i.e., if Resource A is registered after Resource B, OTS is free to operate on them in any order when the transaction terminates. Therefore, Resources should not be implemented that assume (or require) such an ordering to exist.

> **N O T E**   Some implementations of OTS do allow users to specify orderings of resources (the Hewlett-Packard/Arjuna Technologies Transaction Service, for example) where this is required, but obviously this is not a feature of the standard and may not exist if you are migrating code between implementations.

- register_subtran_aware: This operation registers the specified subtransaction-aware resource with the current transaction such that it will be informed when the subtransaction commits or rolls back. This method does not register the resource as a participant in the top-level transaction, however. The NotSubtransaction exception is raised if the current transaction is not a subtransaction. As with register_resource, no ordering is implied by this operation.

- `register_synchronization`: This operation registers the `Synchronization` object with the transaction such that it will be invoked prior to prepare and after the transaction has completed. `Synchronizations` can only be associated with top-level transactions and an exception (`SynchronizationsUnavailable`) will be raised if an attempt is made to register a `Synchronization` with a subtransaction. As with `register_resource`, no ordering is implied by this operation.
- `rollback_only`: This operation marks the transaction so that the only possible outcome is for it to roll back. The `Inactive` exception is raised if the transaction has already been prepared or completed. This could happen if one thread terminates the transaction while another one (possibly in another process) tries to mark it or roll back only.
- `create_subtransaction`: A new subtransaction is created whose parent is the current transaction. The `Inactive` exception is raised if the current transaction has already been prepared or completed. As we mentioned earlier, an implementation of the transaction service need not support nested transactions, in which case the `SubtransactionsUnavailable` exception is raised. It's unlikely you're going to write subtransaction-aware applications without first determining that the transaction service you are using supports subtransactions, so you may never see this exception.

Current

We've seen the interfaces that define the transaction coordinator and control the interactions with it, but how do application programs actually start or end transactions, and in a multithreaded environment, how are transactions associated with specific threads? The answer to this question is simple: the `Current` interface. We've seen that applications (clients or servers) could create transactions through the `TransactionFactory` and terminate them via the associated `Terminator`: direct context management as OTS calls it. However, as we mentioned earlier, transactions manipulated in this way don't affect the thread. Also, having to go through all of these various interfaces to start or end a transaction, especially if you want to create nested transactions, can be cumbersome.

`Current` defines operations that allow a client to explicitly manage the association between threads and transactions, i.e., indirect context management. Importantly, it also defines operations that simplify the use of the transaction service. For example, starting a transaction is extremely simple via `Current`, regardless of whether or not that transaction is nested.

As you might imagine, `Current` supports many of the same operations of the `Terminator` and `Coordinator`. However, there are several important differences and omissions: `Current` was designed with clients in mind, so there is no direct way to register resources – you can register them, but you'll first have to get the `Control` and then the `Coordinator` from it. Transaction comparison isn't possible directly—again, you'll need to get the `Coordinator` if you want to do this.

With this in mind, we now examine the operations:

- `begin`: A new transaction is created and associated with the current thread. If the client thread is currently associated with a transaction and the OTS implementation supports nested transactions, the new transaction is a subtransaction of that transaction. Otherwise, the new transaction is a top-level transaction. If the OTS implementation does not support nested transactions, the `SubtransactionsUnavailable` exception may be thrown. The thread's notion of the current context will be modified to this transaction.

- `commit`: The transaction commits; if the client thread does not have permission to commit the transaction, the `NO_PERMISSION` exception is raised. The effect is the same as performing the `commit` operation on the corresponding `Terminator`. The thread's transaction context is returned to the state prior to the `begin` request. As with the `Terminator`, heuristic reporting can be turned on or off depending upon the Boolean parameter to `commit`.

- `rollback`: The transaction rolls back; if the client thread does not have permission to terminate the transaction, the standard exception `NO_PERMISSION` is raised. The effect is the same as performing the rollback operation on the corresponding Terminator object. The client thread transaction context is returned to the state prior to the `begin` request.

- `rollback_only`: The transaction is modified so the only possible outcome is for it to rollback. If the transaction has already been terminated (or is in the process of terminating) an appropriate exception will be thrown.

- `get_status`: This operation returns the status of the current transaction, or `StatusNoTransaction` if there is no transaction associated with the thread.

- `set_timeout`: This operation modifies the timeout associated with *top-level transactions* for subsequent begin requests *for this thread only*. Subsequent transactions will be subject to being rolled back if they have not completed after the specified number of seconds. It is implementation dependant as to what timeout value will be used for a transaction if one is not explicitly specified prior to begin. Most implementations impose a default value of tens of seconds, although some may not impose a timeout value at all. You should obviously find out what the implementation you are using does.

- `get_timeout`: This operation is used for obtaining the current timeout associated with a thread. Because timeouts may be changed at any time, this value isn't necessarily the value associated with a transaction created by the same thread. Unfortunately the specification doesn't define an easy way in which to get the timeout value of a transaction. You can, however, get hold of the `PropagationContext` for the current transaction and read the timeout from there.

- `get_control`: If the client thread is not associated with a transaction, a null object reference is returned. Otherwise, a `Control` object is returned that represents the current transaction. The operation is not dependent on the state of the transaction, so you can get hold of the transaction `Control` no matter its state; of course, what you can do with it afterward will depend upon the state.

- `suspend`: If the client thread is not associated with a transaction, a null object reference is returned. Otherwise, the `Control` that represents the transaction context is returned. This object can be given to the `resume` operation to re-establish this context in a thread. The operation is not dependent on the state of the transaction. When this call returns, the current thread has no transaction context associated with it.
- `resume`: If the parameter is a null `Control`, the client thread becomes associated with no transaction. Otherwise, if the parameter is valid in the current execution environment, the client thread becomes associated with that transaction. Any previous transaction will be forgotten by the thread.

If we consider the creation of a top-level transaction using `Current`, the course of events within OTS can be represented as shown in Figure 3-5.

The client starts the transaction via `Current`, which will invoke the `create` method on a `TransactionFactory`. How the reference to the factory is obtained will depend on the OTS implementation. For example, it might be co-located with the client or it might be published in some naming service. The factory creates and starts a new top-level transaction and returns the reference to that transaction (the `Control`) to `Current`, which associates it with the client's thread.

Likewise, creation of a subtransaction through `Current` can be represented as shown in Figure 3-6. As you can see, this is different to the first case because the creation of a subtransac-

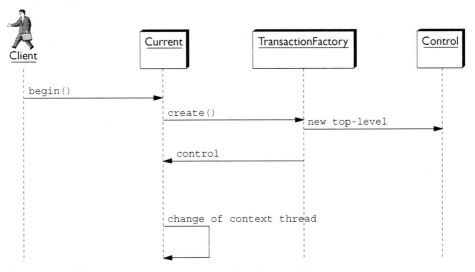

Figure 3-5 Using `Current` to create a top-level transaction

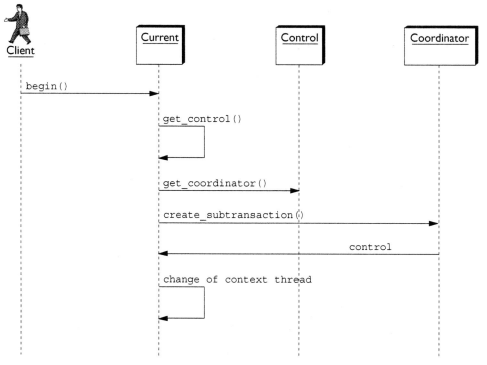

Figure 3-6   Using `Current` to create a nested transaction (subtransaction).

tion does not involve the `TransactionFactory`—the parent transaction (whether it's a top-level transaction or another subtransaction) is responsible for creating and starting the new sub-transaction. That's why `Current` gets the `Coordinator` from the current transaction `Control` and then invokes the `create_subtransaction` operation on that.

Participating in an OTS Transaction

We've looked at how transactions can be created, terminated and propagated, but what kind of participants can you register with them? In the following sections we look at the three different types of participants that OTS allows.

Resource

To take part in the two-phase commit protocol, a participant must support the `Resource` interface. Remember, nested transactions in OTS don't use two-phase commit, so any `Resource` will only be driven by the completion of the top-level transaction. As you can see from Code Listing 3-6, the `Resource` supports all of the operations you'd expect. When a `Resource` is registered with a transaction a `RecoveryCoordinator` is returned by the transaction system; as we'll see later, this object can be used to drive failure recovery.

Code Listing 3-6 The `Resource` Interface

```
interface Resource
{
    Vote prepare ();
    void rollback () raises (HeuristicCommit, HeuristicMixed,
                             HeuristicHazard);
    void commit () raises (NotPrepared, HeuristicRollback,
                           HeuristicMixed, HeuristicHazard);
    void commit_one_phase () raises (HeuristicRollback,
HeuristicMixed,
                                     HeuristicHazard);
    void forget ();
}
```

Each `Resource` object is implicitly associated with a single top-level transaction. A given `Resource` should not be registered with the same transaction more than once. This is because when a `Resource` is told to prepare, commit or roll back it must do so on behalf of a specific transaction; however, the `Resource` methods do not specify the transaction identity and neither is the transaction context propagated to the `Resource`. So, the only way a Resource can know which transaction is it being driven by is because it can only be associated with a single transaction.

Transactional objects must register objects that support the `Resource` interface with the current transaction using the `register_resource` method of the transaction's `Coordina-tor`. An object supporting the `Coordinator` interface will either be passed as a parameter (if explicit propagation is being used) or may be retrieved using operations on `Current` (if implicit propagation is used). If the transaction is a subtransaction, then the `Resource` will not be informed of the subtransaction's completion, and will be registered with its parent upon commit.

This is illustrated in Figure 3-7 where, for simplicity, we assume the hierarchy is only two deep.

As shown in the activity diagram, the client (or server) gets the `Coordinator` for the current transaction and then invokes its `register_resource` operation, passing it the `Resource`. As part of this enlistment process, the transaction will return a reference to a `RecoveryCoordinator` object. We describe what this is for later, but for now all you need to know is that this is a critical component in the way OTS defines failure recovery. The client, or whoever registered the `Resource`, is responsible for ensuring this reference is stored in a durable manner, so that it can be used in the event of a failure. When the client commits the transaction, the coordinator for the nested transaction will propagate participants (`Resources`) to its parent.

A single `Resource` or group of `Resources` is responsible for guaranteeing the ACID properties for the recoverable object they represent. The work `Resources` should perform can be summarized for each phase of the commit protocol:

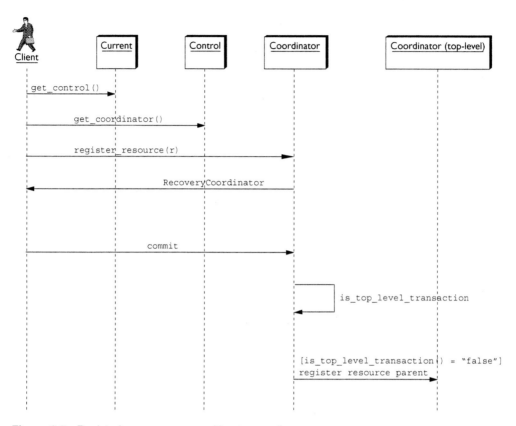

Figure 3-7 Registering a `Resource` with a transaction.

- `prepare`: If no persistent data associated with the resource has been modified within
  the transaction, then the `Resource` can return `VoteReadOnly` and forget about the
  transaction; it need not be contacted during the second phase of the commit protocol
  since it has made no state changes to either commit or roll back. If the resource is able
  to write (or has already written) all the data needed to commit the transaction to stable
  storage, as well as an indication that it has prepared the transaction, it can return
  `VoteCommit`. After receiving this response, the transaction service will eventually
  either commit or roll back. To support recovery, the `Resource` should store the
  `RecoveryCoordinator` reference in stable storage. The resource can return
  `VoteRollback` under any circumstances; after returning this response the
  `Resource` can forget the transaction. Inconsistent outcomes are reported using the
  `HeuristicMixed` and `HeuristicHazard` exceptions. Heuristic decisions must
  be made persistent and remembered by the `Resource` until the transaction

coordinator issues the `forget` method; this essentially tells the `Resource` that the heuristic decision has been noted (and possibly resolved).

- `rollback`: This operation can either be invoked after `prepare` (the first phase of the `commit` protocol has failed for some reason and the coordinator is now rolling back), or if the client explicitly rolls back the transaction. If necessary, the resource should undo any changes made as part of the transaction. Heuristic exceptions can be used to report heuristic decisions; but as we've already mentioned, this can only occur if `prepare` had already been received. If a heuristic exception is raised, the resource must remember this outcome until the `forget` operation is performed so that it can return the same outcome in case `rollback` is performed again. Otherwise, the resource can forget the transaction.

- `commit`: If necessary, the resource should commit all changes made as part of this transaction. As with `rollback`, heuristic exceptions can be raised. The `NotPrepared` exception is raised if the `Resource` has not been prepared.

- `commit_one_phase`: This is used when only a single resource is registered with the transaction; the one-phase optimization we discussed in Chapter 1, "Transaction Fundamentals." Since there is only a single participant, the `HeuristicHazard` exception is used to report heuristic decisions related to that resource. This may be important if, for example, the participant is masking multiple subresources from the coordinator (e.g., if interposition is being used).

- `forget`: This operation is performed if the `Resource` raised a heuristic exception. Once the coordinator has determined that the heuristic situation has been addressed, it will issue `forget` on the resource. The resource can then forget all knowledge of the transaction.

What work a participant in the two-phase protocol does when instructed by the coordinator is typically not of interest to the coordinator. It may update a database, modify a file on disk, etc; it depends upon the type of transactional resource it is responsible for manipulating. Some older transaction implementations place restrictions on the types of participants that can be used within the two-phase protocol; for example, as we saw in Chapter 1, "Transaction Fundamentals," in the X/Open DTP standard participants must support the XA protocol, which imposes restrictions on the underlying participant implementations, typically resulting in only databases being used. From the outset, OTS was designed to allow arbitrary participant implementations to be enrolled with transactions. Therefore, the `Resource` interface does not imply or mandate a specific implementation. It is possible to drive XA compliant database if necessary, but it is certainly not a requirement.

SubtransactionAwareResource

Recoverable objects that wish to participate within a nested transaction may support the `SubtransactionAwareResource` interface, which is a specialization of the `Resource` interface.

```
interface SubtransactionAwareResource : Resource
{
    void commit_subtransaction (in Coordinator parent);
    void rollback_subtransaction ();
}
```

Only by registering a `SubtransactionAwareResource` will a recoverable object be informed of the completion of a nested transaction. Generally, a recoverable object will register `Resources` to participate within the completion of top-level transactions and `SubtransactionAwareResources` to be notified of the completion of subtransactions. The `commit_subtransaction` method is passed a reference to the parent transaction in order to allow subtransaction resources to register with these transactions, e.g., to perform propagation of locks.

It is important to remember that `SubtransactionAwareResources` are informed of the completion of a transaction *after* it has terminated, i.e., they cannot affect the outcome of the transaction. It is implementation-specific as to how the OTS implementation will deal with any exceptions raised by `SubtransactionAwareResources`. As we discussed earlier, this can lead to non-atomic outcomes and sensible implementations will always err on the safe side and ensure data and application integrity by forcing the enclosing transaction to roll back.

As we've already mentioned, traditionally nested transactions are terminated using the same two-phase protocol that top-level transaction termination uses. The reason for the difference in OTS is a combination of performance (running a two-phase protocol imposes an overhead) and adoption (most of the companies involved in defining OTS could not support nested transactions, did not intent to support them and so were not concerned with the reliability aspects). As such, the nested transaction support in OTS is unfortunately less than perfect.

A `SubtransactionAwareResource` is registered with a transaction using either the `register_resource` method, or the `register_subtran_aware` method. Both methods have subtly different requirements and effects:

- `register_resource`: If the transaction is a subtransaction then the `Resource` will be informed of its completion and automatically registered with the subtransaction's parent if it commits.
- `register_subtran_aware`: If the transaction is not a subtransaction, then an exception will be thrown. Otherwise, the participant will be informed of the completion of the subtransaction. However, unlike `register_resource`, it will *not* be propagated to the subtransaction's parent if the transaction commits. If the participant requires this it must re-register using the supplied parent parameter.

Both of these registration techniques are illustrated in the following diagrams.

N O T E   It's important to understand the differences between these enlistment mechanisms—you might be surprised at the number of OTS implementations (commercial and open source) that get this wrong.

Figure 3-8 shows how a `SubtransactionAwareResource` is registered with a subtransaction using the `register_subtran_aware` method. As you can see in the activity diagram, this is different from the act of registering a `Resource` that we saw earlier: obviously the `register_subtran_aware` operation is invoked on the corresponding `Coordinator`, but when the transaction is committed, its `Terminator` invokes the `commit_subtransaction` operation on all `SubtransactionAwareResources`. A reference to the parent is passed to each such participant in case they wish to register another participant with the parent.

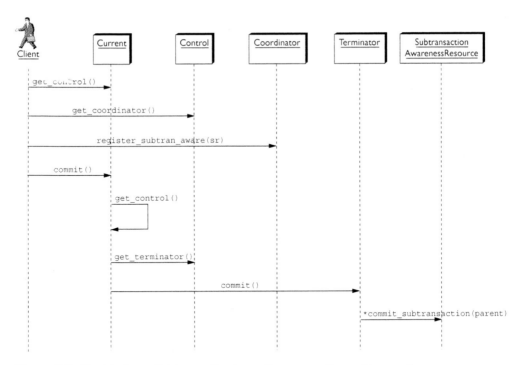

Figure 3-8   Registering a SubtransactionAwareResource with a subtransaction.

Figure 3-9 illustrates the mechanisms involved when a `SubtransactionAwareRe-`
`source` is registered using the `register_resource` operation. In this case, when the
transaction commits, the `Terminator` invokes `commit_subtransaction` on each `Sub-`
`transactionAwareResource` and then automatically registers that participant with the
parent transaction.

In either case, the participant cannot affect the outcome of the transaction completion. It is
only informed of the transaction decision, and should attempt to act accordingly.

Synchronization

In Chapter 1, "Transaction Fundamentals," we saw how many enterprise transaction systems
introduced the notion of participants that take part in the transaction protocol before and after the

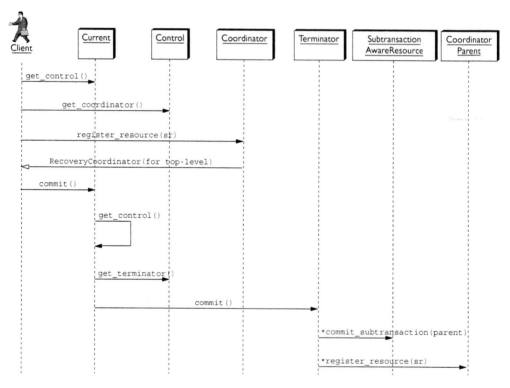

Figure 3-9 Registering a `SubtransactionAwareResource` with a subtransaction as a
`Resource`.

two-phase commit protocol: *synchronizations*. The OTS incorporates this notion in the Synchronizations, which are enlisted with the transaction using the register_synchronization operation of the Coordinator. Synchronizations are typically employed to flush volatile (cached) state, which may be being used to improve performance of an application, to a recoverable object or database prior to the transaction committing.

N O T E Synchronizations can only be associated with top-level transactions and an exception will be raised if an attempt is made to register a Synchronization with a subtransaction. Each object supporting the Synchronization interface is associated with a single top-level transaction.

```
interface Synchronization : TransactionalObject
{
    void before_completion ();
    void after_completion (in Status s);
}
```

The method before_completion is called prior to the start of the two-phase commit protocol, and after_completion is called after the protocol has completed (the final status of the transaction is given as a parameter). If before_completion raises an exception, the transaction will be forced to roll back. Any exceptions thrown by after_completion will have no effect on the outcome of the transaction.

Participant Relationships

Given the previous description of Control, Resource, SubtransactionAwareResource, and Synchronization, the UML relationship diagram shown in Figure 3-10 can be drawn:

What this shows is that each transaction Control can have any number of Synchronizations, Resources or SubtransactionAwareResources registered with it. However, each of those resources can only be associated with a single transaction.

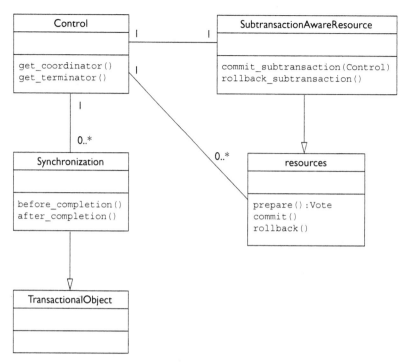

Figure 3-10   The relationships among the various OTS interfaces.

Transactions and Registered Resources

In this section we look at some example interactions between transactions and various types of participants. We also use UML activity diagrams to try to better illustrate exactly what is going on and what we've just described.

Figure 3-11 shows the course of events when committing a subtransaction that has both `Resource` and `SubtransactionAwareResource` objects registered with it; we assume that the `SubtransactionAwareResources` were registered using `register_subtran_aware` so they won't be automatically registered with the parent transaction when it commits. Remember that the `Resources` are not informed of the termination of the subtransaction, whereas the `SubtransactionAwareResources` are. However, only the `Resources` are automatically propagated to the parent transaction.

It should be relatively easy to see what happens when the subtransaction rolls back. Any registered `Resources` are discarded and `SubtransactionAwareResources` are informed of the transaction outcome.

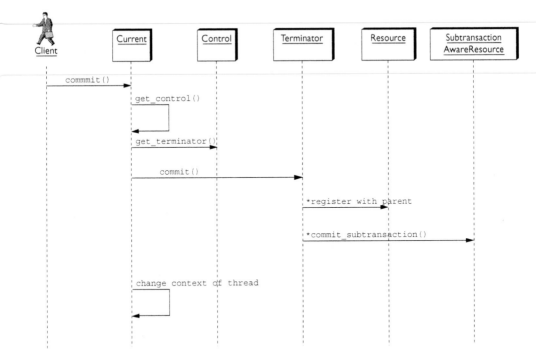

Figure 3-11 Committing a subtransaction.

Figure 3-12 shows the activity diagram for committing a top-level transaction; those sub-transactions within the top-level transaction that have also successfully committed will have propagated `SubtransactionAwareResources` to the top-level transaction, and these will then participate within the two-phase commit protocol. As can be seen, however, prior to `prepare` being called, any registered `Synchronizations` are first contacted. Because we are using indirect context management, when the transaction commits, the transaction service changes the invoking thread's transaction context.

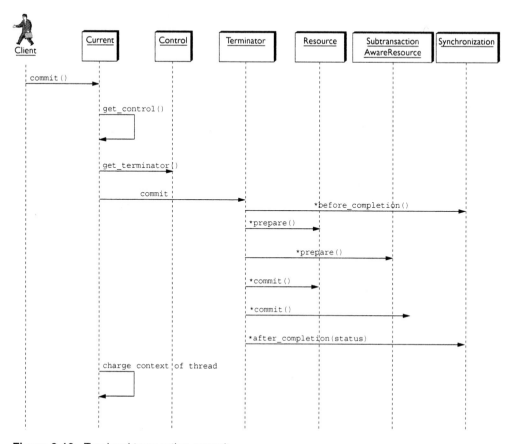

Figure 3-12 Top-level transaction commit.

The RecoveryCoordinator

We saw in Chapter 1, "Transaction Fundamentals" how failure recovery is extremely important to transaction systems (and distributed systems in general) and also how it is typically overlooked or neglected by most public domain and some commercial implementations. In the OTS specification recovery is described in some detail and although not optional in the way nested transactions are, you'll still find supposedly "OTS compliant" implementations that don't implement it. Beware!

In order to drive recovery, a participant needs a reference to the transaction (or transaction system) it is registered with. You might think that the `Coordinator` would play that role but it can't for a number of reasons including:

- The CORBA object that supports the `Coordinator` interface doesn't need to be durable; the entity that the `Coordinator` represents may well be durable, however. So, a reference to the `Coordinator` doesn't have to remain valid after recovery has occurred and in most cases it won't be valid.

- We saw in Chapter 1, "Transaction Fundamentals," how a transaction coordinator maintains an intentions list of participants that is made durable after the `prepare` phase succeeds so that failure recovery at the coordinator can be driven if necessary. If a participant fails and recovers and then enquires about the transaction status, the transaction coordinator should be able to tie up the enquiry with the specific participant so that it can begin to prune the intentions list. You might think that the `Resource` could be passed as a parameter (e.g., to `get_status`). Unfortunately, due to the CORBA architecture the same object may be represented by multiple interfaces and there is no guaranteed equality operator in CORBA. The only sure way to do this when OTS was originally defined is to tie a specific participant to a specific coordinator interface: then the coordinator knows implicitly which participant is enquiring about the status since only one participant can use that interface. Unfortunately, the general `Coordinator` interface does not have this property, since the same interface can be propagated to any number of participants.

As a result, the OTS specification introduced a very special interface on the transaction coordinator: the `RecoveryCoordinator`. A reference to a `RecoveryCoordinator` is returned as a result of successfully calling `register_resource` on the transaction `Coordinator`. This object is recoverable so that it remains valid after the transaction it represents fails and recovers and is implicitly associated with a single `Resource`. It is intended to be used to drive the `Resource` through recovery procedures in the event of a failure occurring during the transaction.

As you can see from Figure 3-13, the `RecoveryCoordinator` has a single method `replay_completion` that takes a reference to a `Resource` and returns the current transaction status. The operation is supposed to be non-blocking, which means that although the reception of `replay_completion` may cause the transaction coordinator to start recovery procedures, it must return the status immediately and do any other work afterwards. Each `Resource` is tied to a specific `RecoveryCoordinator`.

Given that each `RecoveryCoordinator` is tied to a specific `Resource`, you may be wondering why `replay_completion` takes a `Resource` parameter. The reason is that participants need not recover at the same location making the original corresponding `Resource` invalid; the coordinator can thus use the parameter provided to redirect invocations meant for the old `Resource`.

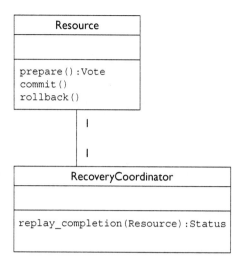

Figure 3-13   Resource and RecoveryCoordinator relationship.

Interposition

In Chapter 1, "Transaction Fundamentals," we saw how interposition of subordinate coordinators can be used in distributed transaction systems to improve performance. OTS objects supporting the interfaces such as the `Control` interface are simply standard CORBA objects. This implies that when an interface is passed as a parameter in some operation call to a remote server only an object reference is passed. This ensures that any operations that the remote server performs on the interface are correctly performed on the real object. However, this can have substantial penalties for the application due to the overheads of remote invocation.

To avoid this overhead, an implementation of OTS *may* support interposition. This permits a server to create a local control object, which acts as a local coordinator fielding registration requests that would normally have been passed back to the originator. This surrogate must register itself with the original coordinator to enable it to correctly participate in the commit protocol.

Unfortunately as with nested transactions, interposition isn't mandated by the specification. You may need to check with your friendly OTS vendor to determine whether or not performance optimizations are possible when using distributed transactions.

As we mentioned earlier, the `PropagationContext` contains the timeout for the transaction. An interposed coordinator can use this value to optimize the termination protocol and (essentially) start a local timer so that if it goes off, the interposed coordinator can roll back its portion of the transaction hierarchy. Some transaction service implementations use this fact to optimize the entire transaction termination protocol: the root coordinator may not even send a roll back message since it knows that subordinates have already rolled back (e.g., the Hewlett-Packard Transaction Service (now marketed by Arjuna Technologies).

Shared and Unshared Transactions

The introduction of asynchronous messaging into CORBA was a relatively late develop-ment and required a new form of transaction model similar to that we considered in Chapter 1, "Transaction Fundamentals," in the section on Transactions and Queues. The model supported by OTS specification 1.0, the *shared transaction model*, provides an end-to-end transaction shared by the client and the server. This model cannot be supported by asynchronous messaging. Instead, a new model was introduced (the *unshared transaction model*) in version 1.2, which uses a store and forward transport between the client and server. In this new model, the commu-nication between client and server is broken into separate requests, separated by a reliable trans-mission between routers (queues). When transactions are used, this model uses multiple shared transactions, each executed to completion before the next one begins.

Checked Transaction Behavior

In Chapter 1, "Transaction Fundamentals," we saw how in a distributed, multi-threaded environ-ment checked transactions are essential to ensure integrity of your applications. So it shouldn't come as a surprise to learn that OTS supports both checked and unchecked transaction behavior. If you remember, checked transactions have a number of integrity constraints including:

- Ensuring that a transaction will not commit until all transactional objects involved in the transaction have completed their transactional requests.
- Ensuring that only the transaction originator can commit the transaction.

Checked behavior is only possible if implicit propagation is used since the use of explicit propagation prevents OTS from tracking which objects are involved in the transaction with any certainty: the propagation of the transaction context happens at the application level out of the control of the transaction service to monitor.

In contrast, unchecked behavior allows relaxed models of atomicity to be implemented. Any use of explicit propagation implies the possibility of unchecked behavior since it is the application programmer's responsibility to ensure the correct behavior.

There are many possible implementations of checking in a transaction service. One pro-vides equivalent function to that provided by the request/response inter-process communication models defined by X/Open. The X/Open transaction service model of checking is particularly important because it is widely implemented and this is the one favored by OTS. In X/Open, completion of the processing of a request means that the object has completed execution of its method and replied to the request. X/Open DTP Transaction Managers are examples of transac-tion management functions that implement checked transaction behavior.

When implicit propagation is used, the objects involved in a transaction at any given time may be represented as a tree: the request tree for the transaction. The beginner of the transaction is the root of the tree. Requests add nodes to the tree; replies remove the replying node from the tree. Synchronous requests, or the checks described below for deferred synchronous requests, ensure that the tree collapses to a single node before commit is issued.

Applications that use synchronous requests implicitly exhibit checked behavior. For applications that use deferred synchronous requests, in a transaction where all clients and objects are in the domain of a checking transaction service, the transaction service can enforce this property by applying a *reply check* and a *commit check*. The transaction service must also apply a *resume check* to ensure that the transaction is only resumed by application programs in the correct part of the request tree.

1. *Reply check*: Before allowing an object to reply to a transactional request, a check is made to ensure that the object has received replies to all its deferred synchronous requests that propagated the transaction in the original request. If this condition is not met, an exception is raised and the transaction is marked as rollback only, that is, it cannot be successfully committed. A transaction service may check that a reply is issued within the context of the transaction associated with the request.

2. *Commit check*: Before allowing commit to proceed, a check is made to ensure that (1) the commit request for the transaction is being issued from the same execution environment that created the transaction, and (2) the client issuing commit has received replies to all the deferred synchronous requests it made that caused the propagation of the transaction.

3. *Resume check*: Before allowing a client or object to associate a transaction context with its thread of control, a check is made to ensure that this transaction context was previously associated with the execution environment of the thread. This would be true if the thread either created the transaction or received it in a transactional operation.

Transaction Interoperability

We mentioned at the start of this chapter that the original intention of the OTS specification was that it would be the next generation of transaction service standard. However, interoperability with existing implementations and standards was a major requirement. As such, OTS defines possible interactions with the following:

- X/Open TX interface for transaction demarcation. There is a lot of overlap between these interfaces and the OTS `Current` interface.
- X/Open XA interface for resource manager interactions. Given the discussions in this chapter and Chapter 2, you might be able to see the possible mappings between the XA resource manager and the OTS `Resource` interface. However, full XA interoperability for OTS goes beyond this mapping.
- OSI TP protocol is the transaction protocol defined by ISO and selected by X/Open to allow the distribution of transactions by one of the communication interfaces (remote procedure call, client-server, or peer-to-peer).

- SNA LU 6.2 protocol is a transactional protocol defined by IBM and widely used for transaction distribution.
- ODMG standard is defined by the Object Database Management Group and described a portable interface to access Object Database Management Systems.

It's outside the scope of this book to describe how interoperability between these various protocols and OTS is achieved, but it is important that you realize it is possible. Although interoperability between OTS implementations may still be less than ideal, interoperability with protocols such as those mentioned above has always had a higher priority. The sheer number of transaction systems and applications that use one or more of these protocols made this an obvious necessity.

However, although interoperability with these protocols is possible, it is not a mandated part of the OTS specification. Therefore, a compliant OTS implementation need not provide interoperability at all, or may only be interoperable with a subset of the protocols. It is worth noting that all of the commercial implementations of OTS that we know about support interoperability with some of these protocols (usually at least X/Open).

Writing Applications Using OTS Interfaces

So far we've looked at how the OTS specification supports the transaction fundamentals we discussed earlier in this book. However, we haven't seen how you could actually use the specification to implement a transactional application. In the following sections we look at this aspect.

The first things to note are that to develop a transactional application that has transactional clients and objects, a programmer must be concerned with:

- Creating `Resource` and `SubtransactionAwareResource` objects for each object that will participate within the transaction/subtransaction. These resources are responsible for the persistence, concurrency control and recovery for the object. The OTS will invoke these objects during the prepare/commit/rollback phase of the (sub)transaction, and the `Resources` must then perform all appropriate work.
- Registering `Resource` and `SubtransactionAwareResource` objects at the correct time within the transaction, and ensuring that the object is only registered once within a given transaction. As part of registration a `Resource` will receive a reference to a `RecoveryCoordinator` which must be made persistent so that recovery can occur in the event of a failure.
- Ensuring that, in the case of nested transactions, any propagation of resources such as locks to parent transactions is correctly performed. Propagation of `SubtransactionAwareResource` objects to parents must also be managed.
- In the event of failures, the programmer or system administrator is responsible for driving the crash recovery for each `Resource` which was participating within the transaction using the `RecoveryCoordinator`.

- The OTS does not provide any `Resource` implementations. These must be provided by the application programmer or the OTS implementer. The interfaces defined within the OTS specification are too low-level for most application programmers.

As you can see, there's quite a lot that involved and most of it is error-prone, which is one reason why most implementations provide high-level interfaces to abstract away the complexity. The most common high-level API is the Java Transaction API that we saw in Chapter 2. However, this can have its disadvantages, such as the fact that your participants are limited to being XA-aware. So, just in case you do want to program at the level of OTS, we look at the issues involved in more detail in the following sections.

Transaction Context Management

If implicit transaction propagation is being used, the programmer should ensure that appropriate objects are located within a POA with the correct transaction policies specified; otherwise, the transaction contexts must be explicitly passed as parameters to the relevant operations.

A Transaction Originator: Indirect Context Management and Implicit Propagation

In the code fragments below, a transaction originator uses indirect context management and implicit transaction propagation; `txn_crt` is the `Current` interface; the client uses the `begin` operation to start the transaction which becomes implicitly associated with the originator's thread:

```
. . .
txn_crt.begin();
// should test the exceptions that might be raised
...
// the client issues requests, some of which involve
// transactional objects;
BankAccount1.makeDeposit(deposit);
. . .
```

The program commits the transaction associated with the client thread. The `report_heuristics` argument is set to `false` so no report will be made by the transaction service about possible heuristic decisions; not necessarily a great idea, but all right for the purposes of our example.

```
. . .
txn_crt.commit(false);
. . .
```

Transaction Originator: Direct Context Management and Explicit Propagation

In the following example, a transaction originator uses direct context management and explicit transaction propagation. The client uses a transaction factory to create a new transaction and uses the returned `Control` object to retrieve the `Terminator` and `Coordinator` objects.

```
   . . .
org.omg.CosTransactions.Control c;
org.omg.CosTransactions.Terminator t;
org.omg.CosTransactions.Coordinator co;
org.omg.CosTransactions.PropagationContext pgtx;

c = TFactory.create(0);
t = c.get_terminator();
pgtx = c.get_coordinator().get_txcontext();
   . . .
```

The client then issues requests, some of which involve transactional objects. When invoking transactional objects the client explicitly propagates the context as an extra parameter in each operation. The `Control` object reference is passed as an explicit parameter of the request:

```
transactional_object.do_operation(arg, pgtx);
```

The transaction originator uses the `Terminator` object to commit the transaction; the `report_heuristics` argument is again set to `false`:

```
t.commit(false);
```

Implementing a Recoverable Server

Hopefully by now you have some idea of what a recoverable server is, but let's spend a bit of time just going over what we mean by this term. In OTS a recoverable server is essentially a deployment environment for at least one transactional object and one `Resource` (participant). For example, if you remember the bank account example we first examined back in Chapter 1, "Transaction Fundamentals," we might imagine a recoverable server for each bank account, as shown in Figure 3-14.

In that recoverable server we assume that there is a transactional object representing the actual account and containing operations to add, remove and inspect operations (there could well be others, but those will be sufficient for this example). Whenever an operation is performed on the account object within the scope of a transaction (e.g., removing money), the transactional object will be responsible for registering a participant with the transaction so that it can ultimately control the outcome of the work. In OTS terms, this participant is a `Resource`.

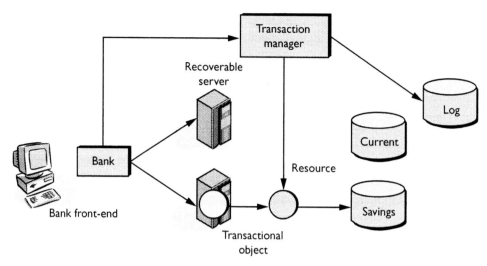

Figure 3-14 Recoverable servers and the bank account.

Hopefully, you can now see that the concept of a recoverable server is fundamental to transactional applications. Whether you know it or not, if you've written server-side objects that use transactions, such as EJBs residing in an application server, this combination (of application server and EJB) is the equivalent of the OTS recoverable server. As we've seen in earlier chapters, if that EJB uses a JDBC driver, the application server will be getting XAResources and registering them with the transaction at appropriate times: the equivalent of the OTS Resource. So, with that in mind, let's look at the responsibilities of each of these objects in more detail in the following sections.

Transactional Object

The responsibilities of the transactional object are to implement the object's operations and to register a Resource object with the Coordinator so commitment of the resources, including any necessary recovery, can be completed.

Remember that the Resource object identifies the involvement of the recoverable server in a particular transaction so it can only be registered in one transaction at a time. A different resource object *must* be registered for each transaction in which the server is involved. Because a transactional object may receive multiple requests within the scope of a single transaction it should only register its involvement once per transaction. In order to ensure that this is the case, you can use the is_same_transaction operation of the Coordinator to do transaction comparison. The hash_transaction operation allows you to reduce the number of transaction comparisons it has to make: the is_same_transaction operation need only be done on Coordinators which have the same hash code as the Coordinator of the current request.

Resource Object

We saw earlier that the responsibilities of a `Resource` object are to participate in the completion of the transaction, to update the recoverable server's resources in accordance with the transaction outcome, and ensure termination of the transaction, including across failures.

N O T E In the following examples of transactional objects some form of concurrency control implementation will be required to ensure isolation. Typically this will depend upon the deployment environment and is beyond the scope of OTS to mandate. As such, we simply assume concurrency control is available.

An Example of a Recoverable Server

In this example, `BankAccount1` is an object that is directly responsible for its own state, so it is a transactional object and explicitly uses a `Resource`. It inherits from both the `TransactionalObject` and the `Resource` interfaces (for the purposes of this example it is easier to revert to the 1.1 way of doing things rather than show you how to initialize a POA):

```
interface BankAccount1 : CosTransactions::TransactionalObject,
CosTransactions::Resource
{
    ...
    void makeDeposit (in float amt);
    ...
};
```

The corresponding Java class is:

```
public class BankAccount1 extends
org.omg.CosTransactions.TransactionalObjectImplBase, extends
org.omg.CosTransactions.ResourceImplBase
{
public void makeDeposit(float amt);
public float get_balance ();
public void set_balance (float amt);
    ...
};
```

When an invocation on `makeDeposit` is made, the context of the transaction is implicitly associated with the thread doing the work by virtue of the fact that the `BankAccount1` interface is derived from the `CosTransactions::TransactionalObject` interface. From the previous discussion of `TransactionalObject`, you'll remember that this is works as a flag to the transaction service and ORB to ensure that any transaction context present at the client is implicitly propagated to the server and made available to the object doing the work (via `Current`). You don't have to worry about how this happens—that's the responsibility of the

OTS implementation you're using to figure out. All you have to know is that it will happen and you can program accordingly.

For those readers who are interested in how this context propagation and thread association occurs, we give a brief overview. Anyone who's not interested can skip the next paragraph.

When a thread with a transaction associated with it makes a call on a remote object, the transaction service and ORB cooperate to ensure that the transaction context is propagated with the invocation. At the receiver, this additional context information is plucked off the incoming invocation and associated with the thread that will do the work—which, just to add more complexity, may not actually be the thread that received the invocation! This transaction association occurs in collaboration with Current such that if that thread were then to use Current to get the transaction, Current would return a reference to the imported transaction (or to a local subordinate coordinator if interposition is being used).

Current is used to retrieve the Coordinator object associated with the transaction. In this example, the variable txn_crt is assumed to point to an instance of Current – we won't show how this variable is set up simply because that can depend upon the implementation of the transaction service and the version of the OTS specification you're using.

```
void makeDeposit (float amt)
{
    org.omg.CosTransactions.Control c;
    org.omg.CosTransactions.Coordinator co;
    c = txn_crt.get_control();
    co = c.get_coordinator();
    . . .
```

As we saw earlier, because Current was developed with client interactions in mind, it is not suitable for all server-side requirements. That's the reason that the above code fragment has to use Current to get the Coordinator via the Control so that it can then register the Resource.

> **N O T E** In this example the object registers itself as a Resource. This imposes the restriction that the object may only be involved in one transaction at a time. For obvious reasons this is not the recommended way for recoverable objects to participate within transactions and is only used as an example. If more parallelism is required, separate resource objects should be registered for involvement in the same transaction.

```
RecoveryCoordinator r;
r = co.register_resource(this);

// get a WRITE lock on the object state; only proceed if
```

```
        // that lock is granted.

        balance = balance + f;
        num_transactions++;
        ...
        // end of transactional operation
    };
```

It's typical to register the Resource before any work is performed by the transactional object. The reason for this is that the resource may need to perform some initialization on the state that the transactional object is about to manipulate. For example, if the state is obtained from a database, then the Resource implementation may need to associate the transaction with the database connection prior to it being used.

What we haven't shown in the above fragment is what happens with the RecoveryCo-ordinator returned by the Coordinator when the object registers the Resource. As has been mentioned previously, the RecoveryCoordinator is the hook into the transaction recovery subsystem that the recovering object has (recovering BankAccount1 object in our case). So, making sure this hook (reference) is saved away successfully is very important, because without it, recovery may take a long time to complete or in some circumstances may never be able to happen.

We now show the other two important operations on the bank account. They are surprisingly similar to makeDeposit.

```
        float get_balance ()
        {
            org.omg.CosTransactions.Control c;
            org.omg.CosTransactions.Coordinator co;
            c = txn_crt.get_control();
            co = c.get_coordinator();

            RecoveryCoordinator r = co.register_resource(this);

            // get a READ lock on the object state; only proceed if
        // that lock is granted.

            num_transactions++;

        return balance;     // end of transactional operation
        };

        void set_balance (float amt)
        {
            org.omg.CosTransactions.Control c;
            org.omg.CosTransactions.Coordinator co;
            c = txn_crt.get_control();
            co = c.get_coordinator();
```

```
RecoveryCoordinator r = co.register_resource(this);

// get a WRITE lock on the object state; only proceed if
// that lock is granted.

num_transactions++;

balance = amt;     // end of transactional operation
};
```

Example of a Transactional Object

In this example, BankAccount2 is an object that delegates all state manipulation and control to other objects (perhaps implementations of BankAccount1). Therefore, it's not a recoverable server, but simply a "pure" transactional object (it does not use Resources). However, in order to ensure that any transaction context present on client invocations is implicitly propagated, the BankAccount2 interface derives from TransactionalObject interface:

```
interface BankAccount2 : CosTransactions::TransactionalObject
{
    ...
    void makeDeposit(in float amt);
    ...
};

public class BankAccount2 extends
org.omg.CosTransactions.TransactionalObjectImplBase
{
public void makeDeposit(float amt);
    ...

private BankAccount1 res1;
private BankAccount1 res2;
};
```

The makeDeposit operation performs some transactional requests on external, recoverable servers which, as you can see above, we assume are implementations of BankAccount1. The objects res1 and res2 are recoverable objects, but the BankAccount2 object isn't—it does not maintain any state that is affected by the transaction, so it doesn't need to save or restore anything in the event of a failure (or recovery). The current transaction context is implicitly propagated to these other recoverable objects because we remembered to make sure that BankAccount1 derives from TransactionalObject.

```
void makeDeposit (float amt)
{
    balance = res1.get_balance(amt);
    balance = balance + amt;
    res1.set_balance(balance);
    res2.increment_num_transactions();
} // end of transactional operation
```

So the `makeDeposit` implementation looks a lot simpler in this case than previously. However, if you think about it, all we've done is passed the responsibility of recoverability to something else (in our case `BankAccount1`). Someone must be responsible for ensuring `Resources` are enlisted with transactions at the appropriate time, `RecoveryCoordinators` are saved away and that recovery procedures are instigated when required. There is no such thing as a free lunch. However, what this example does show is that it is entirely possible to construct one transactional application using objects from another.

Worked Example

The following example illustrates the concepts and the implementation details for a simple client/server example that uses implicit context propagation and indirect context management. It is relatively simplistic in that only a single unit of work is included within the scope of the transaction; consequently, a two phase commit is not required, but rather a one phase commit.

The IDL interface for this example is as follows. For the purposes of this worked example, we have defined a single method (see line 9 in Code Listing 3-7) for the `DemoInterface` interface. We use this method in the `DemoClient` program.

Code Listing 3-7   The Demo IDL

```
1    #include <idl/CosTransactions.idl>
2    #pragma javaPackage ""
3
4
5    module Demo
6    {
7        exception DemoException {};
8
9        interface DemoInterface :
CosTransactions::TransactionalObject
10       {
11           void work() raises (DemoException);
12       };
13   };
```

Resource

Here, we have overridden the methods of the Resource implementation class; the DemoResource implementation includes the placement of System.out.println statements at judicious points, to highlight when a particular method has been invoked.

As mentioned previously, only a single unit of work is included within the scope of the transaction; consequently, we should not expect the prepare() at line 6 in Code Listing 3-8, or the commit() at line 20 to be invoked. However, we should expect the commit_one_phase() method at line 26 to be called.

Code Listing 3-8 Example OTS Resource implementation

```
1     import org.omg.CosTransactions.*;
2     import org.omg.CORBA.SystemException;
3
4     public class DemoResource extends  org.omg.CosTransactions
._ResourceImplBase
5     {
6         public Vote prepare() throws HeuristicMixed, HeuristicHazard,
7         SystemException
8         {
9             System.out.println("prepare called");
10
11            return Vote.VoteCommit;
12        }
13
14        public void rollback() throws HeuristicCommit, HeuristicMixed,
15        HeuristicHazard, SystemException
16        {
17            System.out.println("rollback called");
18        }
19
20        public void commit() throws NotPrepared, HeuristicRollback,
21        HeuristicMixed, HeuristicHazard, SystemException
22        {
23            System.out.println("commit called");
24        }
25
26        public void commit_one_phase() throws HeuristicHazard,
SystemException
27        {
28            System.out.println("commit_one_phase called");
29        }
30
31        public void forget() throws SystemException
32        {
33            System.out.println("forget called");
34        }
35    }
```

Transactional Implementation

At this stage, let's assume that the Demo.idl has been processed by the ORB's idl compiler to generate the necessary client/server package.

Line 13 in Code Listing 3-9 returns the transactional context for the Current object. Once we have a Control object, we can derive the Coordinator object (line 15).

Line 16 creates a resource for the transaction.

Line 18 uses the Coordinator to register a DemoResource object as a participant in the transaction. When the transaction is terminated, the resource will receive requests to commit or rollback the updates performed as part of the transaction.

Code Listing 3-9 Example transactional object implementation

```
1     import Demo.*;
2     import org.omg.CosTransactions.*;
3     import org.omg.*;
4
5
6     public class DemoImplementation extends
Demo._DemoInterfaceImplBase
7     {
8         public void work() throws DemoException
9         {
10            try
11            {
12
13                Control control = get_current().get_control();
14
15                Coordinator  coordinator = control.get_coordinator();
16                DemoResource resource    = new DemoResource();
17
18                coordinator.register_resource(resource);
19
20            }
21            catch (Exception e)
22            {
23                throw new DemoException();
24            }
25        }
26
27    }
```

Server Implementation

It is the servant class DemoImplementation that contains the implementation code for the DemoInterface interface. Furthermore, it is ultimately the responsibility of the servant to service a particular client request. Line 13 in Code Listing 3-10 instantiates a transactional object (servant) for the subsequent servicing of client requests.

Lines 15 through to 19 take the servant and obtain a CORBA reference (IOR) for it. This is a string representation of the reference that can be passed between users via a file or name service, for example, and allow multiple users to share the same object implementation. In our example, this IOR is written to a temporary file. This IOR will be subsequently used to construct the object in the `DemoClient` program.

Finally, line 23 places the server process into a state where it can begin to accept requests from client processes.

Code Listing 3-10   Example server implementation

```
1       import java.io.*;
2       import com.arjuna.OrbCommon.*;
3
4       public class DemoServer
5       {
6           public static void main (String[] args)
7           {
8               try
9               {
10                  // initialise the ORB using args from command line
11                  // initialise the POA
12
13                  DemoImplementation obj = new DemoImplementation();
14
15                  String ref  = orb.object_to_string(obj);
16                  BufferedWriter file =
17                  new BufferedWriter(new
FileWriter("DemoObjReference.tmp"));
18                  file.write(ref);
19                  file.close();
20
21                  System.out.println("Object reference written to
file");
22
23                  for (;;);
24              }
25              catch (Exception e)
26              {
27                  System.err.println(e);
28              }
29          }
30  }
```

Client Implementation

Once a server process has been started and it has written the IOR of the servant to a temporary (and shareable) file, our client can read that IOR (lines 17 to 22 in Code Listing 3-11).

Once we have the IOR, we can reconstruct the servant object. Initially, this string to object conversion returns an instance of `org.omg.CORBA.Object` (see line 24). However, if we want to invoke a method on the servant object, it is necessary for us to narrow this instance to an instance of the `DemoInterface` interface (line 26).

Once we have a reference to this servant object, we can start a transaction (line 28), perform a unit of work (line 30) and commit the transaction (line 32).

Code Listing 3-11 Example client implementation

```
1       import Demo.*;
2       import java.io.*;
3       import org.omg.*;
4       import org.omg.CosTransactions.*;
5
6
7
8       public class DemoClient
9       {
10          public static void main(String[] args)
11          {
12              try
13              {
14                  // initialise the ORB using args
15                  // initialise the root POA
16
17                  String ref = new String();
18                  BufferedReader File =
19                  new BufferedReader(new
FileReader("DemoObjReference.tmp"));
20
21                  ref = file.readLine();
22                  File.close();
23
24                  org.omg.CORBA.Object obj =
25                  orb.string_to_object(ref);
26                  DemoInterface d = (DemoInterface)
DemoInterfaceHelper.narrow(obj);
27
28                  get_current().begin();
29
30                  d.work();
31
32                  get_current().commit(true);
33              }
34          catch (Exception e)
```

```
35              {
36                  System.err.println(e);
37              }
38          }
39      }
```

Sequence Diagram

The activity diagram in Figure 3-15 illustrates the method invocations that occur between the client and server.

The following aspects are worthy of further discussion:

1. The transactional context does not need to be explicitly passed as a parameter (as we are using implicit context propagation since `DemoInterface` is a `Transaction-alObject`) in the `work()` method.

2. We assume the use of interposition when the client and server processes are started. The interposed coordinator is automatically registered with the root coordinator at the client (indicated by the `Control` object at the client).

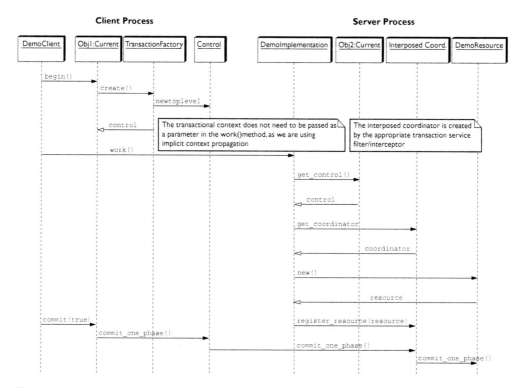

Figure 3-15 Example activity diagram.

3. The resource that is responsible for committing or rolling back modifications made to the transactional object is associated ("registered") with the interposed coordinator.

The `commit()` invocation in the client process calls the root coordinator. The root coordinator calls the interposed coordinator, which in turn calls the `commit_one_phase()` method for the resource.

Choosing an OTS Implementation

We've looked at what's involved in providing an implementation of the OMG's OTS specification. In this section, we try to distill this information and our own experiences into some important questions to consider and ask if you are looking at an OTS implementation. This list is by no means exhaustive and you may come up with your own questions after re-reading this chapter.

- Has the implementation been written from scratch, and if so, what are the credentials of the implementers? This may seem like a strange question, but let's look at an analogy. If you were going to buy a car would you get one from a reputable dealer or from someone who's only just started in the business? Now the answer is not straightforward, as it will depend upon a number of factors. But, if you do go to the newbie car manufacturer, you'd be sensible to determine before hand what their track record is in the area of building cars. Unfortunately, this analogy doesn't quite hold up because there are laws governing who can build and market cars and all cars have to go through stringent safety tests. The same cannot be said of OTS implementations. So, doing your homework beforehand is your first and best line of defense against shoddy implementations.
- Has the implementation been deployed elsewhere? Although there has always got to be a first customer for an OTS, it's worth asking whether or not the implementation has been used before and if this was successful. Systems that have been used before and have survived are often more reliable than those that have only been tested by the developers.
- Which version of the specification does it support? As we said at the start of this chapter, most implementations are OTS 1.1 compliant, but the current version of the specification is 1.4. Backward support for interoperability between 1.4 and 1.1 is available, but upward interoperability is not possible.
- How compliant is it with the specification? It may be surprising to learn that there are implementations of OTS that do not support failure recovery, or only support it in very limited situations.
- Does it support the optional parts of the specification, such as nested transactions and interposition? Although you may never need nested transactions, interposition can be extremely important in any large-scale deployment in improving the performance of your applications. If the implementation does not support interposition then it may be

an indication that performance considerations haven't been high on the developer's agendas.

• The OTS specification is written in such a way as to provide flexibility in implementations. This is primarily so that it can be layered on existing transaction processing systems that may have taken slightly different implementation choices. For example, OTS allows an implementation to always have a separate transaction factory process/server, or the factory can be co-located within the process of the transaction creator. The former implementation choice can affect performance adversely, but may allow for better management. It is worthwhile considering what design-time choices the OTS implementers have taken in these, and other areas. At the moment we know of only one implementation that supports *all* of the flexible choices at runtime, the Hewlett-Packard/Arjuna Technologies Transaction Service.

• The OTS isn't perfect and there are a number of places where there are obvious errors, as we've already seen (remember the issue of subtransactions and heuristics?). However, workarounds and non-standard solutions are possible. You should check to see if the developers have considered these issues and what solutions they have proposed for the implementation. If they do not know about any problems with OTS then we would recommend that you look elsewhere.

• As we saw at the start of this chapter, OTS simply defines the raw two-phase protocol engine. It doesn't specify how to implement or use concurrency control or persistence, for example. So, if you have to implement transactional applications at the level of OTS you're going to need more than just an OTS: at the very least you'll need some kind of Resource implementation, and possibly a concurrency control service. Does the implementation you're considering provide any support in these areas? Most assume that you'll be using OTS to control transactions operating on a database and *may* therefore provide a Resource that can drive a specific type of database (though even that's not guaranteed); they assume that the concurrency control is then provided by that database. If you're not interested databases, then you may have to worry about implementing your own Resources. And if you want nested transactions, you'll have to look at implementing SubtransactionAwareResources. There are several commercial implementations that offer good support to developers working at the level of OTS, including IBM and Hewlett-Packard. However, we know of no open source implementations that compare favorably.

• Performance is always an issue with transaction systems, and particularly with OTS. This is because the CORBA specification has evolved over time to provide as much distribution transparency to applications as possible. In the early days of CORBA, it was possible to have different invocation behavior if the object you were calling resided in the same process as opposed to if it resided in a separate process. The latest versions of CORBA solve this issue, but it often results in purely local implementations performing as though all invocations (including those on local objects) are remote. There are ways around this that can be provided by the ORB or the application (in our case, OTS). So you would be wise to determine beforehand whether or not this issue has been solved by the implementation you are considering.

Summary

In this chapter we looked at probably the most important distributed transaction specification for J2EE: the Object Transaction Service. This is the specification that J2EE recommends for interoperability of its JTA implementations, so you may already by using an OTS implementation whether you know it or not. We looked at how the principles of transaction processing we discussed earlier in the book have been applied in a real-world specification, including failure recovery, heuristics and distribution. In Chapter 1, "Transaction Fundamentals," we discussed the nested transaction model and in this chapter we saw how OTS was the first industrial strength specification to support them, albeit optionally. The fact that nested transactions are supported at all means that you may well find implementations that provide them, which could be important for you.

Through many example scenarios and UML activity diagrams we've seen how much work is actually involved in turning theory into practice for an implementer of OTS, and why issues such as performance and failure resiliency are important. As we also saw, actually using an OTS to implement a transactional application is not trivial, as there is much work involved in writing clients and transactional services. This is perhaps the main reason why most commercial implementations provide higher-level APIs (such as the JTA) to isolate users from the programming intricacies.

Finally, we reiterate something that we said at the start of this chapter: OTS does not define how to *implement* a transaction service. It will not teach you the fundamental principles of transaction processing or how to create an implementation that scales, that performs or is fault tolerant. As someone looking to purchase or use an OTS you should be extremely cautious of implementations that have been written from scratch by people relatively new to the field of transaction processing; this is not to say that transaction processing is an elitist field and only those who have been involved in it for decades can ever be right, because that is obviously wrong as well: it is simply unlikely that an implementation based on the details given in the OTS specification will be best-of-breed. You should be able to use the contents of this book to determine the right questions to ask and what answers to expect.

Likewise, if you are thinking of implementing a transaction service you can do a lot worse than starting with OTS. It is a good specification to conform to, but it is not sufficient to help you through all of the many pitfalls that may occur. We would strongly recommend that you not only use the contents of this book but other texts such as *Transaction Processing: Concepts and Techniques* by Jim Gray and Andreas Reuter and *Principles of Transaction Processing* by Philip Bernstein and Eric Newcomer before implementing a single line of code: forewarned is forearmed.

PART 2

Transactions in J2EE

The next four chapters of the book deal with the tools you will use directly to build transactional applications in J2EE. This includes the Enterprise JavaBeans (EJB) component model and the APIs used to access resource managers that support transaction semantics. EJBs are used directly by application developers to write business logic that relies on transactions. In both cases, we pay special attention to how these tools can be used with transactions. We also look at how the J2EE infrastructure behaves under the covers and point out idiosyncrasies to watch out for in existing implementations.

JDBC is the API that is used for accessing relational databases, a requirement of virtually any serious business application. Chapter 4 focuses on JDBC, with a general overview of the programming model, how applications servers integrate JDBC to support a range of system services, and a special focus on transactional behavior. This material is critical to a majority of business applications. JDBC also provides a model for the management of physical connections to resource managers that is used throughout the J2EE platform.

Message-oriented middleware is another important kind of infrastructure software for developing responsive and highly available applications. In Chapter 5, we examine message services and the kinds of problems they can be used to solve. We then look at the Java Message Service specification, an API for accessing messaging services. The main thrust of the chapter revolves around how JMS can be used to send messages reliably in the face of possible failures. As you may expect, transactions play a key role in robust message-based solutions.

Both Chapters 4 and 5 include a demo application that you can execute locally. We explain how the application server will manage the connections, transactions, and resource manager enlistment.

Enterprise JavaBeans are the centerpiece for transactional applications written for the J2EE platform. The EJB model described in Chapter 6 allows developers to write business logic that relies on distributed transactions without having to manage transactions explicitly. A major strength of the EJB model is the aid it provides in maintaining correct semantics for applications, even in the face of failure. We provide the details of how the application server behaves and why this is important for applications.

Section Two closes with a look at the J2EE Connector Architecture, a generalized framework for building adapters to resource managers that cannot be accessed through one of the existing APIs defined for the J2EE platform. Connectors are the basis for talking with back-end systems using their native protocols. As the integration space and Web services heats up, The J2EE Connector Architecture continues to grow in importance. Chapter 7 focuses on details required to use and implement transaction support in resource adapters.

CHAPTER 4

JDBC and Transactions

The Java Database Connectivity (JDBC) API defines a set of interfaces and classes that together allow for vendor independent access to a wide range of relational database platforms. As such, JDBC serves to abstract the relational data access of an application through its call-level API for dynamic SQL. JDBC is loosely based on ODBC, though it is more object-oriented and intuitive. Like ODBC, it draws directly on the Open Group Call Level Interface to provide a normal mechanism for accessing relational database systems. Thus, developers can utilize JDBC to write enterprise applications that can potentially leverage different databases without modifying their code. By far, JDBC is the standard mechanism for interacting with database systems from the Java platform. Because it's flexible and easy to use, JDBC is in fact one of its most powerful features. Even Object Relational mapping runtime engines that are often used to provide transparent persistence typically use JDBC under the covers.

Accessing information in databases while maintaining data integrity is a fundamental requirement of virtually every enterprise application. Of course, transactional capabilities are a part of maintaining data integrity; the JDBC API provides both the ability to create local transactions to a single resource as well as the capacity to scope the work done on behalf of an application into distributed, global transactions. Most relational databases support the DTP model and the XA interfaces. JDBC provides a mapping to XA for application servers to use to implicitly manage enlistment and control of global transactions in J2EE applications.

This chapter examines the support in JDBC for both local and distributed transaction models. In addition, the way in which other J2EE components leverage JDBC and interact with its transactional capabilities is explored.

The Basic JDBC Model

Before we start to look at transaction facilities in JDBC, it's important that you have a basic understanding of the client APIs and programming model. For many Java programmers with enterprise programming experience, this will be review material and you may skip to the next section. However, if you are familiar with programmatic use of relational databases but new to the Java platform, this material will provide an overview of the fundamental ideas behind JDBC.

Since JDBC is a thin wrapper around standard SQL, it's relatively straightforward. The JDBC programming model is described in detail in the *JDBC API Tutorial and Reference, Second Edition.* We recommend this book, though there are several errors and omissions with respect to transaction processing. To date, it is the definitive guide to JDBC.

java.sql.Connection

All database access revolves around a Connection object that represents a physical connection to a database. The connection typically points to an external process, probably running on a different machine. The Connection is used to create Statement objects that are used to execute queries against the database. These queries return ResultSets that contain the results of the SQL execution; we'll look at these interfaces in more detail below. But first, let's look at some key methods of the Connection interface:

```
public interface java.sql.Connection {
    public static final int TRANSACTION_NONE;
    public static final int TRANSACTION_READ_UNCOMMITTED;
    public static final int TRANSACTION_READ_COMMITTED;
    public static final int TRANSACTION_REPEATABLE_READ;
    public static final int TRANSACTION_SERIALIZABLE;
    public Statement createStatement( );
    public PreparedStatement prepareStatement(String sql)
    public CallableStatement prepareCall(String sql)
    public String nativeSQL(String sql);
    public void setAutoCommit(boolean autoCommit);
    public boolean getAutoCommit();
    public void commit();
    public void rollback();
    public void close();
    public void setTransactionIsolation(int level);
    public int getTransactionIsolation();
    ....
```

The Connection implementation is the main handle the application has to a specific database. This implementation is a proxy to the actual physical connection and comes in one of two flavors: PooledConnection and XAConnection (more on these later). In J2EE scenarios, the Connection instance that an application holds is typically a wrapper provided by the application server to the logical connection from the database driver vendor. It is through this wrapper that the application server detects events triggered by the application that allow the application server to manage pooling of connections, sharing of physical connections across multiple `Connection` proxies in the same transaction, enlisting `Connections` transparently with transactions, and similar functions. The `XAResource` used to manage global transactions associated with a physical connection works in the same ways (see Figure 4-1).

If you have a need to work directly with the raw database `Connection` – sometimes necessary to access database platform proprietary features – the application server will typically provide a mechanism to allow you to acquire a `Connection` without a wrapper. This means the `Connection` cannot benefit from the services provided by the application server and should be used only when strictly required. Even in this case, you should still think of a `Connection` as a logical channel to a database.

The `Connection` is generally used to create `Statements`. A `java.sql.Statement` is an abstraction for a SQL query. Statements can be created and used to submit dynamic

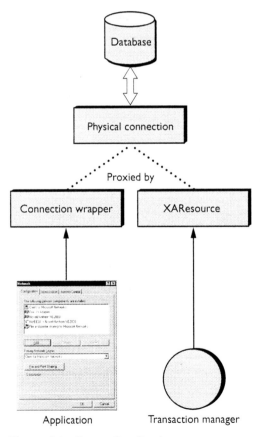

Figure 4-1 Connection Proxies.

SQL queries to the database. There are several kinds of Statement subclasses available in Java. For example, a PreparedStatement can be used to compile and cache statements that are used over and over frequently. Typically, the application server will handle the caching of prepared statements to optimize query execution.

If the query returns a result, the rows are encapsulated in ResultSets. The Result-Set represents an abstract database row and multiple rows may be referenced in sequence by calling the next( ) method. If you want to examine the data in a ResultSet, it's as simple as calling rs.getString(1) to reference the first column in the row. We look at some examples that use these features.

To start using JDBC, you have to first get a hold of a Connection. This can be accomplished in one of two ways, either via a java.sql.DriverManager object or via a javax.sql.DataSource object. Both are connection factories. The DriverManager is the original JDBC connection factory defined in the first release of Java 2. We discuss it first. Unlike some of the component models in J2EE that have been deprecated and abandoned, the DriverManager abstraction is still in use and still relevant for users today.

So what is a DriverManager? The class looks like this, with implementation details omitted:

```
public class DriverManager {
    static final SQLPermission SET_LOG_PERMISSION;
    public static PrintWriter getLogWriter();
    public static void setLogWriter(PrintWriter logWriter);
    public static synchronized Connection getConnection(String url,
Properties info);
    public static synchronized Connection getConnection(String url,
String user, String password);
    public static synchronized Connection getConnection(String url);
    public static synchronized Driver getDriver(String url);
    public static synchronized void registerDriver(Driver driver);
    public static synchronized void deregisterDriver(Driver driver);
    public static synchronized Enumeration getDrivers();
    public static void setLoginTimeout(int seconds);
    public static int getLoginTimeout();
    public static synchronized void setLogStream(PrintStream
logStream);
    public static PrintStream getLogStream();
    public static void println(String message);
    static void initialize();
```

DriverManagers provide a static mechanism to use Drivers. The Driver is the main abstraction provided by the database vendor for creating and using Connections. As long as the VM is configured properly, the DriverManager will transparently hide the interactions with the Driver from the programmer, who need only use a variant of the getConnection() method to obtain a handle to a physical connection to a database. Aside from some of the problems discussed above, the class isn't object oriented, which is something of an irritant.

DriverManagers can be configured via properties files that are used by the VM. This is an awkward bootstrap mechanism and not something we would recommend. As a matter of course properties files can be picked up anywhere and lead to problematic and confusing configuration of virtual machines.

The alternative is the slightly more reliable use of the Class.forName("my.driver.class") construct. This guarantees the expected driver in a reliable and controllable fashion. However, it also means that your application will either be hard-coded to a particular database or that it will require some custom configuration scheme.

In any case, the Driver needs to establish the physical connection to a database instance: this is virtually always done via a socket, regardless of the location of the database process. The Driver creates a Connection using a connection URL of the form:

```
jdbc:subprotocol:subname
```

An example connection URL for an Oracle database instance is:

```
jdbc:oracle:thin:@host:port:sid
```

Note that this URL indicates that the Oracle thin driver uses a proprietary protocol to connect to a database listener for the particular *sid* at the specified host and port. The *sid*, or *system identifier*, is an Oracle proprietary mechanism for encapsulating a workspace within the relational database. A Connection URL is similar for other vendors' database systems. For the DriverManager class, Connection URLs are hard-coded.

JDBC 2.0 introduced the javax.sql.DataSource interface as a replacement for the DriverManager. Because the JDBC specification is meant to be used both with and without application servers, the specification equivocates on the responsibility of implementing the DataSource. If you take only one thing away from this chapter, it should be this: for a J2EE application, the appropriate DataSource to use is the implementation provided by the application server infrastructure; this is also true for application clients that have access to the client libraries provided by JDBC vendors. We see why as we examine the benefits of using the DataSource implementation itself. The DataSource interface is defined as:

```
public interface DataSource
{
    public Connection getConnection();
    public Connection getConnection(String user, String password);
    public PrintWriter getLogWriter() throws SQLException;
    public void setLogWriter(PrintWriter logWriter) throws
SQLException;
    public void setLoginTimeout(int seconds);
    public int getLoginTimeout();
}
```

The `DataSource` abstraction was designed to be registered with a JNDI registry context. To do so, application server code (or in extreme cases, application bootstrap logic) is responsible for creating, configuring and registering the `DataSource` with a lookup name. In J2EE, this context is accessed via a URL string prefixed by "`java:comp/env`" followed by the logical name. The following is an example from the `data-sources.xml` file used to configure `DataSources` for the Oracle Application Server Containers for J2EE (OC4J) server. In this case the application server provides a `DataSource` implementation that utilizes the driver's `DriverManager` implementation; this `DataSource` will "emulate" XA semantics using local transactions:

```
<data-source
        class="com.evermind.sql.DriverManagerDataSource"
        name="OracleDS"
        location="jdbc/OracleCoreDS"
        xa-location="jdbc/xa/OracleXADS"
        ejb-location="jdbc/OracleDS"
        connection-driver="oracle.jdbc.driver.OracleDriver"
        username="scott"
        password="tiger"
        url="jdbc:oracle:thin:@localhost:5521:oracle"
        inactivity-timeout="30"
    />
```

We include this as a representative example based on the application server we are currently building. Other J2EE application servers have similar facilities and configuration, each adapted to the implementation details of the server. Of course, most application servers allow `DataSources` to be configured via a management tool.

The `DataSource` above is accessed as in the following example:

```
Context ctx = new InitialContext();
DataSource ds = ( DataSource )ctx.lookup( "java:comp/jdbc/OracleDS" );
Connection conn = ds.getConnection();
```

Exception handling is omitted. We assume that the infrastructure has registered and created the `DataSource` based on user configuration.

The second advantage of the `DataSource` abstraction is that, unlike the `DriverManager`, it does not necessarily return a direct link to a physical connection to a database. The `DataSource` may be configured to return `Connection` handles that support pooling (supported by virtually all commercial application servers) and enlistment in global transactions. These are intimately related—pooled connections cannot be shared between multiple active transactions—and `Connections` created by the `DataSource` are the main focus of this chapter.

Types of JDBC Drivers

When we showed the example connection URL to an Oracle database instance, we mentioned that this was a "thin" driver. You're probably wondering what that means. JDBC defines four classifications of drivers:

Type 1 drivers are JDBC-ODBC bridges. These drivers are essentially a legacy approach to rapidly supporting database access in the Java platform. When the APIs were introduced around 1998, most databases supported ODBC. An ODBC bridge is not the most efficient driver and should probably be avoided.

Type 2 drivers, on the other hand, leverage existing C libraries via the Java Native Interface (JNI), which allows the JVM to link platform native code into the virtual machine to be accessed by Java classes. These drivers require libraries compiled to a particular hardware platform. As such, they often have some portability constraints, but the native libraries are often highly optimized and very fast. The well-known Oracle OCI drivers are type 2 drivers.

Type 3 drivers use a common middleware component to normalize the protocol that drivers use. The special middleware acts as a bridge and translates the JDBC requests from the normal protocol to a protocol used natively by the database.

That leaves us with the last, category of drivers, the so-called "thin" drivers. Type Four drivers are written entirely in Java, are platform portable, and require no special native libraries. The type 4 driver is reliable and surprisingly performant: as the Java virtual machine has been made increasingly efficient and vendors gain more experience writing efficient Java code these drivers have become popular.

While a resource manager may have the capability of acting as a participant in a global transaction, this functional capability must be exposed through the driver you have available. Not too many years ago this was a problem. However, in general it is not a problem today.

Support for transactions is independent of the driver type. As a practical matter, almost all relational databases support XA, though specifics of the behavior may vary. Some databases will not support tight coupling of branches; others will automatically detect relationships between branches and introduce optimizations. For example, Oracle's database will return a read-only return code to the coordinator on subsequent branches enlisted in a global transaction during the prepare phase. This allows the coordinator to use a single commit for multiple branches.

Application servers are often used to support database access across multiple databases, sometimes from different vendors. At the same time, the J2EE platform is expected to work with any database, not just one supplied by the application server vendor. For this reason, many application servers bundle the DataDirect JDBC drivers, which were recently acquired by Progress Software, to connect out of the box to most enterprise-quality databases. The DataDirect product line provides JDBC 2.0 compliant drivers that support XA for most relational databases.

Before we talk about detailed transaction characteristics of JDBC `Connections`, let's expand on our early discussion of isolation concepts and see how they apply to SQL databases.

Transaction Isolation Levels

In general, database support for transactions is not limited to the ability to group application updates. It also covers the management of potential conflicts that may arise when a database handles simultaneous transactions from multiple clients. How the database manages transaction isolation can be changed by developers by setting the transaction isolation level for the `Connection`.

Java defines transaction isolation levels ranging in severity from no transactional support to strict serialized access. As the transaction level gets stricter there is greater isolation of data in a transaction. As you may expect, stricter isolation levels can yield slower execution times because of increased database locking and decreased concurrency between clients. Thus, careful consideration is required when selecting the isolation level for a given application because of the inherent performance implications.

There is actually no default isolation level defined for a JDBC connection. Rather, the default level will depend on the default for the target database. You can determine the default isolation level with the following code (where `con` represents an object that implements the `java.sql.Connection` interface):

```
con.getMetaData().getDefaultTransactionIsolation ();
```

In addition, you can ascertain the transaction isolation level for the current connection with the following:

```
con.getTransactionIsolation ();
```

If the above methods indicate that the isolation level is inappropriate for the application it can be modified; be aware that isolation levels cannot be altered while the connection is involved in a transaction:

```
con.setTransactionIsolation (TRANSACTION_READ_COMMITTED);
```

The isolation levels defined for the JDBC `Connection` interface are:

- TRANSACTION_NONE
- TRANSACTION_READ_UNCOMMITTED
- TRANSACTION_READ_COMMITTED
- TRANSACTION_REPEATABLE_READ
- TRANSACTION_SERIALIZABLE

Not all databases support all of the defined isolation levels. Generally they support a core subset that is sufficient to support most client applications. Table 4-1 lists some of the major database vendors and the isolation levels they support.

Table 4-1 JDBC Supported Isolation Levels

Isolation Level	Supporting Databases
NONE	DB2
READ_UNCOMMITTED	Informix, SQL Server, Sybase
READ_COMMITTED	DB2, Informix, Oracle, SQL Server, Sybase
REPEATABLE_READ	Informix, SQL Server, Sybase
SERIALIZABLE	DB2, Oracle, Informix, SQL Server, Sybase

Implications of Relaxed Isolation

Before we examine isolation levels in detail it's important to understand the problems that emerge when isolation constraints are relaxed.

Dirty Reads

A dirty read occurs when changes made in the context of a transaction are visible to other transactions prior to the original transaction being committed. While this means that the underlying resource manager can minimize locking and maximize system throughput, dirty reads can easily compromise data integrity. If a transaction fails to complete and rolls back, concurrent transactions are able to act on invalid data.

As an example, consider a banking application that provides a transfer of funds function and allows dirty reads. If a person transfers funds from a savings account to an empty checking account the funds may appear in the checking account prior to a formal commit on the transaction. At this time, the funds appear as useable to a family member. If that family member makes a withdrawal and the original transfer subsequently fails, a withdrawal will have been made against an empty account.

For most systems, data integrity is critical. Generally speaking, dirty reads should not be allowed and some resource managers (Oracle RDBMS springs to mind) will not allow sufficiently loose isolation constraints to support dirty reads at all.

When should you allow dirty reads? If you know that concurrent access to data in the underlying resource managers is not going to occur. You may still be interested in coordinating multiple accesses with all-or-nothing semantics, possibly to multiple resource managers. In that case, transactions are still appropriate. Allowing dirty reads can trim the cost of access considerably. Dirty reads are also typically used by apps to increase performance—to avoid the cost of locking—in read-only or very infrequent write systems when the data is not expected to change or when the client can permit occasional data irregularities.

Non-repeatable Reads

This condition occurs when an application in the context of a transaction reads data from a resource manager, does some work, rereads the data and the data has changed due to another transaction which has committed. This is different from the dirty read problem in that the data change made in the context of the second transaction is not visible until the transaction itself has committed. Again, this can lead to subtle data integrity problems.

Once again consider a banking application, this time assuming that the application allows for non-repeatable reads. A bank employee queries for the account balance of a customer just prior to a deposit to the account. If the bank employee now queries for the balance again (within the same transaction) he will see the new account balance. The read performed by the bank employee is therefore a non-repeatable read.

Non-repeatable reads can be acceptable if the application logic is not rereading data repeatedly. However, if you are using O/R mapping tools or CMP implementations, it can be more difficult to determine whether repeat reads are performed in transactions.

Phantom Reads

Phantom reads occur when new data suddenly appears within the context of a unit of work. With relational databases, this is likely to occur if an application reads a set of rows from a database, another transaction adds a new row to the database and commits, and the original transaction rereads the set of rows using the same condition. When a phantom read occurs, there will be a new row of data that was not available in the original result set. This is different from a repeatable read where data has changed; phantom reads occur when new data is added to the system.

Let's, once again, consider the banking example, this time assuming that phantom reads are not precluded by the application. A bank employee performs a query for a list of customers at a branch location. Subsequently, a new customer is added to the database. If the employee performs his query again he will suddenly see a new customer—a "phantom" customer, if you will.

Now that we understand the various problems that can occur as a consequence of relaxing isolation constraints let's take a close look at each of the isolation constraints available.

Isolation Constraints

Since correctly configuring the database driver isolation levels is fundamental to ensuring data integrity, we explain what the four isolation levels are and their implications for transactional database access.

While isolation is a key part of the ACID properties we described while discussing transaction fundamentals, enforcing isolation can be expensive. Allowing variation in isolation levels provides a mechanism to "relax" the isolation requirements associated with data within a transaction, which can often provide significant improvements in system throughput and help to eliminate potential deadlocks in the system. The relaxation of isolation levels must be carefully coordinated with application logic so that data corruption does not result.

TRANSACTION_NONE

This is the most relaxed isolation level and effectively indicates that transactions are not supported.

Strictly speaking this level is not valid since transactional support is expected from a compliant JDBC driver. However, in certain cases is still appears that vendors have utilized this level for specific database scenarios. For example, when accessing an IBM DB2 database via the AS/400 interface for native JDBC, this isolation level, in conjunction with an auto-commit setting of "true," provides access to triggers, stored procedures and large object columns.

TRANSACTION_READ_UNCOMMITTED

This isolation level allows all three problems we discussed. If you don't have concurrent changes to data, this may be acceptable and will almost certainly boost performance. Use this isolation level with great care, however; it is rarely a safe choice.

TRANSACTION_READ_COMMITED

This isolation level is supported by most databases and is generally the default level for a database session (e.g., it is one of only two isolation levels supported by Oracle's RDBMS). The isolation provided by this level is adequate for many applications. However, for applications that require complex database interaction, you may require a more rigorously isolated view of the database than this level provides.

This setting allows non-repeatable and phantom reads while precluding "dirty" reads. In other words, this isolation level ensures that an executing query sees only data that has been entered or changed in the system by another completed transaction (it will obviously see the effects of previous updates done within the same transaction). The possibility does exist that two successive queries in the same transaction could see different results if other queries committed data between the execution of the two queries. Applications that take snapshots of data for processing that don't care about concurrent changes can use `TRANSACTION_READ_COMMITTED` with satisfactory results.

Different database platforms provide different levels of transaction set consistency for an isolation level. A query is transaction set consistent if all read operations return data written by the same set of committed transactions. If an operation is not transaction set consistent, different reads return inconsistent results from varying sets of transactions.

For example, Oracle transactions executing in `READ_COMMITTED` mode are transaction set consistent on a per-statement basis; the rows read by a query must be committed before the query begins. However, other databases are known to return results that are not transaction set consistent for this isolation level. In this case it is possible, for example, that a join of a master table with a detail table will see a master record without the corresponding detail records.

TRANSACTION_REPEATABLE_READ

Beyond the isolation provided with `TRANSACTION_READ_COMMITTED` isolation, this level ensures that executing the same query multiple times will result in the same data set even if another transaction modifies the data. In other words, it eliminates the non-repeatable read problem. However, it does not eliminate the possibility of phantom reads, but for many applications, that is acceptable.

TRANSACTION_SERIALIZABLE

The serializable isolation level promises that the effect of a transaction will be the same as if concurrent users had exclusive access to the data being acted on. At first glance, it may appear that other concurrent transactions can neither write nor read the same data. Be aware that it is an oversimplification to assume that this isolation level is supported in databases by literally serializing data access. Rather, the goal of the serializable isolation level is to emulate serial processing of database transactions, as we saw in Chapter 1. It is very possible that a particular database will support concurrent modifications to the underlying data. For example, Oracle uses an optimistic concurrency strategy in supporting this isolation level. Therefore the database does not report serialization problems until a transaction commit is attempted. The message returned is:

```
java.sql.SQLException: ORA-08177: can't serialize access for
this transaction
```

Clients may receive exceptions at commit time if contention occurs between them for the same rows; the second committed transaction will receive the exception above. To handle these problems an application should catch and examine the generated exceptions (the messages will be platform-specific). If a serialization problem is detected the application can take an appropriate action such as restarting the transaction. Note that transactions executing in this mode are transaction set consistent on a per-transaction basis since the statements execute on an image of the database as of the beginning of the transaction.

Bear in mind that when using the serializable isolation level, the transaction has no view into data modifications performed by other concurrent transactions; the data view of the transaction does not change from when the data was first modified in the transaction. While often overly restrictive for many applications, this isolation level in essence eliminates all the problems we discussed.

Local Transactions

For our discussion of transactional capabilities, we start with the simplest case. The term "local transaction" refers to a transaction that is created and committed against a single resource manager. Local transactions can be used for a large number of applications. As long as a unit of work does not need to scope multiple resource managers, local transactions are an appropriate and fast solution.

You can expect the ability to create and manage local transactions against all enterprise database vendors. Note that it is possible to use global transactions to organize a single unit of work, since the overhead is greatly diminished by the one-phase commit optimization discussed in Chapter 1. However, it does add complexity to the solution.

When a JDBC `Connection` object is created it is, by default, in autocommit mode. This means that each SQL statement executed through the connection is treated as an autonomous transaction and will be committed automatically. In order to associate more than one statement with a transaction this mode must be disabled. The following code, where `con` represents an object that implements the `java.sql.Connection` interface, shows how the auto-commit mode is disabled:

```
con.setAutoCommit (false);
```

This operation cannot be used when the connection is already involved in a transaction. Once autocommit is set to false no updates will be committed until the code calls the connection's `commit()` method explicitly. All of the updates that were executed after the last invocation of the `commit()` method on the connection will be committed as a single unit of work. The following code illustrates the general sequence for committing multiple statements simultaneously:

```
// turn off auto-commit mode
con.setAutoCommit (false);
// create a statement
Statement update1 = con.createStatement ();
// execute an update
update1.executeUpdate (. . .);
// create a second statement
Statement update2 = con.createStatement ();
// execute a second update
update2.executeUpdate (. . .);
// commit the transaction
con.commit ();
```

In this example the autocommit mode is disabled for the connection. Subsequently, two different updates are executed within the context of the same transaction since both statements are associated with the transactional connection. When the `commit()` method is invoked both of the updates will be made permanent in the target database.

Aside from atomic updates, there are important performance advantages to using local transactions to scope multiple interactions with databases. If autocommit is enabled for a connection and multiple updates are executed during application processing, a lot of disk updates have to occur. There is an inherent input/output overhead associated with database commits that may degrade the performance of an application. In this situation a developer may choose to set the autocommit mode to "false" in order to attain performance gains.

However, the database locks associated with transactional processing may cause performance degradation in a situation where multiple users are accessing a database simultaneously. In this context it may be necessary to enable autocommit so that the database locks are not held for long durations. In general, a developer needs to consider carefully where to place the transactional boundaries for statement execution in order to optimize the application's throughput.

JDBC 2.0 Advanced Features

The JDBC 2.0 release introduced some new advanced features for manipulating relational data. These capabilities include the ability to perform a batch update in which multiple queries are performed as a single group or modify a row set returned by a query. While we don't want provide a tutorial on JDBC APIs, there are some subtle implications to performing these operations in the scope of a transaction that require some consideration during your application design and development that you're unlikely to learn about in other books.

Batch Updates

With the JDBC 2.0 API, `Statement`, `PreparedStatement`, and `CallableStatement` objects have been enhanced to allow for the grouping of SQL commands that can be executed as a single operation. SQL commands are added to the list with the method `addBatch()` or are removed from the list with the method `clearBatch()`. Once a list of operations is assembled it is sent to the database by invoking the method `executeBatch()`:

```
// turn off autocommit
con.setAutoCommit(false);
Statement stmt = con.createStatement();
stmt.addBatch("INSERT INTO roles VALUES (1000, 'Administrator')");
stmt.addBatch("INSERT INTO groups VALUES (260, 'Employees')");
stmt.addBatch("INSERT INTO users VALUES (100, 'John', 'Smith' )");
// submit a batch of update commands for execution
int[] updateCounts = stmt.executeBatch();
```

In the example, the connection's autocommit mode is disabled to prevent the driver from committing the transaction upon the invocation of `executeBatch()`. Disabling autocommit allows the application to manage the associated transaction and dictate how to handle errors in the event that some of the commands in a batch cannot be processed successfully. It is therefore extremely important for application developers to ensure that batch updates are not executed with autocommit enabled. Moreover, the commit behavior of `executeBatch()` with autocommit enabled is implementation dependent and, therefore, could result in disparate behavior across vendor drivers.

Updateable Result Sets

The ResultSet object was enhanced with the release of JDBC 2.0 and now provides the ability to update the underlying data set. Rows in an updateable result set may be updated, inserted, and deleted. The ResultSet.updateXXX() methods are used to modify the value of an individual column in the current row, but do not update the underlying database until the updateRow() method is called:

```
rs.first();
rs.updateString(1, "Joe");
rs.updateFloat("balance", 10000.0f);
rs.updateRow();
```

The key to utilizing this new feature appropriately lies in understanding the visibility of changes made by others afforded to a ResultSet. This visibility is primarily based on the isolation level of the encompassing transaction and the type of the result set.

A scroll-insensitive result set does not make any changes made by others visible once the result set is opened; there is no modification to the ordering, membership, or row values of the result set. However, a scroll-sensitive result set will make all updates that are visible to its enclosing transaction visible (the level of visibility is dictated by the isolation level that is set for the given JDBC connection). It is possible that inserts and deletes will not be visible based on a particular vendor's driver implementation. Once again, it pays to be familiar with the platform you are using.

Distributed Transactions

By now, you should be familiar with the concept of global transactions and how they are used to scope work across multiple resource managers. The remainder of the chapter is focused on two goals: providing a basic understanding of the XA components of JDBC and explaining how they are used in the application server to provide transparent enlistment and coordination in transactions.

Unlike the local transaction scenario, the boundaries of a global transaction must be controlled by a separate transaction manager that coordinates the work across multiple connections. The transaction management in the JDBC API is designed to work in concert with the Java Transaction API (JTA), and we'll take a look at how they work together in J2EE.

The JDBC support for distributed transactions actually requires an infrastructure composed of these elements:

1. A JTA compliant transaction manager is required in order to control the transactional boundaries and guide the transactions through the two-phase protocol.
2. A JDBC driver that implements the XAResource, XAConnection, and XADataSource interfaces is required in order to interact with the JTA transaction manager.

3. The application server provides a `DataSource` implementation that is accessible to the client tier. It decorates the underlying driver's implementation of the `XAData-Source` interface and provides the application access to transaction-capable connections. At the same time, it encapsulates the plumbing that manages the complexities of interacting with the transaction manager.

4.   A relational database that supports the distributed transaction semantics is required in order to participate in a global transaction.

Before we drill into more detail, there are some restrictions on the application's use of `Connections` that must be observed when using global transactions. It is an error for a client application to invoke the `setAutoCommit(true)`, `commit()`, and `rollback()` methods of the JDBC connection while in the scope of a transaction; executing these methods will result in `SQLExceptions`. In addition, applications should refrain from invoking the

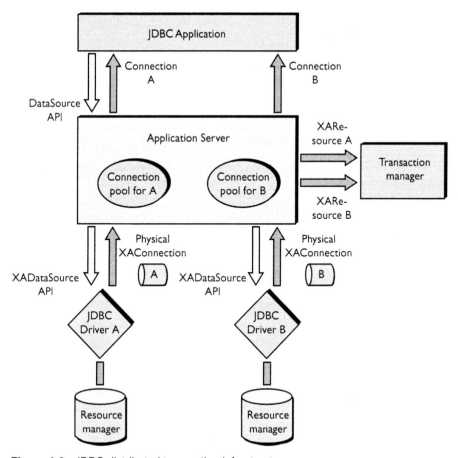

Figure 4-2   JDBC distributed transaction infrastructure.

setTransactionIsolation() method while in a transaction—the behavior may vary from vendor to vendor and result in potentially non-portable code. Finally, if autocommit mode is enabled when a global transaction is initiated it will be ignored. The autocommit behavior should resume when the connection is returned to local transaction mode.

XADataSource and XAConnection Interfaces

JDBC drivers that support distributed transactions are required to provide implementations of the javax.sql.XADataSource and javax.sql.XAConnection interfaces. These are the major components provided by the driver to expose the XA capabilities of the database. The XAConnection represents a physical connection to the database—it is an extension of the javax.sql.PooledConnection interface that provides the additional method getX-AResource(). This method provides the caller with an XAResource that is utilized by the transaction manager to demarcate the beginning and end of work done on the resource and to include the connection in the termination protocol.

Since the XAConnection interface extends the PooledConnection interface, the driver implementations of these interfaces are required to support all of the inherited behaviors. PooledConnections represent reusable physical connections to an underlying database platform. A PooledConnection is used to provide a logical Connection handle. However, this logical handle is wrapped by the application server: the application itself will not use a connection from the driver. The application server is responsible for providing access to these logical connections via its DataSource implementation, which typically uses the XAData-Source under the covers to create and pool physical connections. An application developer will almost never have cause to work directly with an XAConnection or PooledConnection object.

In almost all cases, connection pooling is intimately connected to XA support in the application server. This allows the server to provide physical connections on an as-needed basis. When a physical connection is not required by the Connection handle used by the application, the Connection is typically returned to a pool. However, if the application or application server is managing a transaction—either global or local—the physical Connection is maintained in a cache associated with the transaction. In this case, the Connection handle keeps the physical Connection out of the pool for the duration of the transaction. We don't want to re-pool the Connection when it's enlisted in the transaction. If this were allowed, another application thread could use the Connection and the work would be scoped by the original user's transaction!

One related point about pooled connections: while it is the responsibility of the application server to manage the details of pooling and the isolation from other clients, it is crucial that the application code close the Connection—it's a fundamental signal to release resources in the Connection handle. In some implementations, failure to close a Connection will result in a Connection leak. It's often a good idea to close the Connection in a final block.

```
Connection conn = null;
try {
      conn = ds.getConnection( );
      //do work...
} finally {
      if (conn != null ) conn.close( );
}
```

Deployment of XADataSources within an application server varies for each platform. Each vendor will have some unique configuration files that indicate the information the server requires to bootstrap the driver's DataSource. Typically, these files will include information on the XADataSource implementation class, a user name, a password, and a database connection URL. The servers will generally instantiate the XADataSource, set some vendor dependent attributes, and then make the XADataSource available to the server's client-facing DataSource implementation. After deployment, the DataSource will obtain a Connection and wrap it for the application's use. If a pooled connection is not available, the code in an application server might look like this:

```
// Obtain the XADataSource.
XADataSource xads = getXADataSource ();
// obtain the XAConnection implementation
XAConnection xacon = xads.getXAConnection("user",
"password");
// Get a logical connection to wrap for the client.
Connection con = xacon.getConnection();
```

Of course, the client's view of things is very different. To get a connection, the client simply does a JNDI lookup for the DataSource and requests a Connection, as illustrated in Figure 4-3:

```
Context ctx = new InitialContext();
DataSource ds = (DataSource)ctx.lookup("jdbc/ds");
Connection con = ds.getConnection("user","password");
```

The application code gives no indication that a XADataSource or an XAConnection was used. In fact, the application doesn't see any of the details of transaction management as it relates to the Connection. All the application has to do is make sure to begin and commit the global transaction at the appropriate points. If EJBs are used, the container will even take care of that.

XAResource Interface

So far, we've indicated that physical connections are maintained in a pool. We've seen how they are used to service applications, but how are they enlisted in transaction? The application server uses the XAResource available from the XAConnection. As we indicated, the

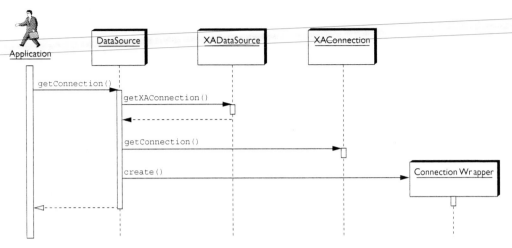

Figure 4-3 Connection Retrieval Sequence Diagram.

XAResource is nothing but another view into the actual connection. It provides the functionality that is required to demarcate work in a transaction and to perform the two-phase commit protocol. When an application accesses a Connection wrapper in the scope of a transaction, the application server code will enlist the XAResource with the transaction. The code to perform this work looks like this:

```
// XAResource obtained from XAConnection object retrieved
javax.transaction.xa.XAResource xares = xacon.getXAResource();
. . .
// current transaction is retrieved from
// javax.transaction.TransactionManager implementation
javax.transaction.Transaction tx = tm.getTransaction ();
// XAResource is enblisted with transaction
boolean success = tx.enlistResource ( xares );
```

The transaction manager will subsequently use the XAResource object to guide the related resource manager through the transaction, as shown in Figure 4-4:

```
// Begin working with the resource manager.  The second
// argument generally indicates whether the transaction
// is being initiated, joined in progress, or resumed. In
// this example, it is being initiated.
xares.start(xid, javax.transaction.xa.TMNOFLAGS);
// do work with resource manager A
...
// tell resource manager that it's portion of the
// transactional work is done, and no errors
```

```
// have occurred
xares.end(xid, javax.transaction.xa.TMSUCCESS);
. . .
// the transaction manager initiated the two phase
// protocol by asking the resource manager to vote
// for confirming the transaction.  A resource manager
// votes to rollback by throwing an XAException.
xares.prepare (xid);
. . .
// if all enlisted resources have voted to commit
// the transaction manager indicates to all enlisted
// resources to go ahead and commit the transaction.
// If any resource had voted to rollback this invocation
// would be replaced with xares.rollback (xid).
xares.commit (xid);
```

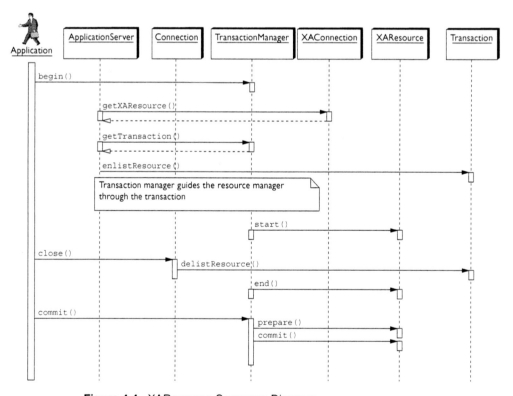

Figure 4-4 XAResource Sequence Diagram.

The transaction manager uses the XAResource exclusively; it never calls directly on the associated XAConnection. Moreover, as illustrated by the code above, a transaction manager may coordinate the work of multiple XAResource objects, each of which represents a participant in a distributed transaction.

An XAResource may be associated with at most one transaction at a time because it is providing the association between the transaction and the physical connection. Remember: the JDBC driver maintains a one-to-one correspondence between an XAResource and an associated XAConnection.

Connection Management

We've frequently mentioned that the Connection reference that the application uses is a proxy provided by the application server. The application itself never deals directly with a physical connection and normally never deals with the Connection provided by the driver. This allows the application server to introduce a number of optimizations transparently. Some of those optimizations include lazy binding of a physical connection to the logical handle, usage timeouts forcing bound connections back into the pool, and "connection sharing."

Connection sharing occurs when multiple Connection handles attained from the same DataSource are used in a transaction. This can occur, for example, if the application logic calls getConnection() to retrieve two Connection objects, or if separate collocated EJBs access the same database through different Connection handles. In these cases, the application server detects that a single physical connection may service both Connection handles since they are acting in the same unit of work. This optimization allows both the application server and the database to do less work because only one transaction branch has to be created. It also optimizes the commit protocol. You will find that connection sharing can provide measurable performance gains.

As a general rule, if you are using a Connection provided by the application server, do not assume that each interaction occurs over the same physical link to the database. In many cases, this is unlikely to be true, particularly across transaction boundaries. For example, when a transaction ends, the underlying connection that the application server uses may be returned to a pool. If connection sharing was used, it's likely that all binding to the physical connection used will be undone.

In order for the application server to coordinate the resources involved with a distributed transaction, it must be notified when a connection is closed by a client application. Therefore, the application server will generally register as a ConnectionEventListener and get notified when the application invokes the Connection.close() method. The application server may use any number of mechanisms to intercept the connection close event; for example, it's likely to wrap the connection objects it returns to the client to intercept the close of a connection. Once the close of a connection is detected, the application server may notify the transaction manager that the transactional branch associated with the given XAResource may be ended. In addition, the connection pool module will generally receive a notification so that the connection may be made available to other clients.

Theoretically, this is correct behavior. However, in many cases, application servers support the use of non-XA aware `DataSources` for historical reasons as we discussed in Chapter 2. In this case, two-phase commit is "faked" and local transactions are being used by the coordinator in lieu of global transaction branches. In this case, there is no way to designate the end of a unit of work short of a commit. If the application server were to re-pool the connections in this scenario, other threads could acquire the `Connection` and perform work within the unterminated local transaction. To accommodate this, most application servers will not, in practice, re-pool connections until the transaction is terminated. In this case, the commit or rollback operation may result in the re-pooling of the connection. Many application servers will include an option to allow you to force this behavior for all `Connections` derived from a particular `Data-Source`.

We've given an overview of how things work in an application server. To make this discussion more concrete, we've provided a simple `Servlet` application that can be deployed in any application server. The code, deployment instructions and an application server download instructions can be found on the Web site for this book. The application allows an HR administrator to transfer an employee record from one database to another. The code for the transfer looks like this:

```
1   package book.ch4.sample.xa;
2   import javax.servlet.http.HttpServlet;
3   import javax.servlet.http.HttpServletRequest;
4   import javax.servlet.http.HttpServletResponse;
5   import javax.servlet.ServletException;
6   import javax.servlet.ServletConfig;
7   import javax.servlet.ServletContext;
8   import javax.sql.DataSource;
9   import javax.naming.Context;
10  import javax.naming.InitialContext;
11  import javax.naming.NamingException;
12  import javax.transaction.*;
13  import java.io.IOException;
14  import java.io.PrintWriter;
15  import java.sql.*;
16  import java.text.SimpleDateFormat;
17
18  /**
19   * This servlet demonstrates the creation of a
20   * distributed transaction that scopes work performed
21   * against two different databases.
22   */
23  public class SampleJDBCServlet extends HttpServlet {
24
25    private Context m_ctx;
26    private ServletConfig m_cfg;
27    private DataSource m_division1DS;
```

```
28    private DataSource m_division2DS;
29    private static final String DIVISION1_DS_LOOKUP_STR =
30    "java:comp/env/jdbc/hr1";
31    private static final String DIVISION2_DS_LOOKUP_STR =
32    "java:comp/env/jdbc/hr2";
33    private static final String USER_TX_LOOKUP_STR =
34    "java:comp/UserTransaction";
35
36    /**
37     * Initializes the JNDI context and JDBC datasources.
38     */
39    public void init ( ServletConfig servletConfig )
40    throws ServletException
41    {
42        m_cfg = servletConfig;
43        try
44        {
45            m_ctx = new InitialContext ();
46            initDataSources ();
47        }
48        catch ( Exception e )
49        {
50            throw new ServletException( e );
51        }
52    }
53
54    /**
55     * Looks up and stores the datasources.
56     */
57    private void initDataSources () throws NamingException
58    {
59        m_division1DS = (DataSource) m_ctx.lookup (
60            DIVISION1_DS_LOOKUP_STR );
61        m_division2DS = (DataSource) m_ctx.lookup (
62            DIVISION2_DS_LOOKUP_STR );
63    }
64
65    /**
66     * Returns the component JNDI context.
67     */
68    protected Context getJNDIContext ()
69    {
70        return m_ctx;
71    }
72
73    /**
74     * Responds to the HTTP POST request.
75     */
```

```
76  public void doPost (
77     HttpServletRequest httpServletRequest,
78     HttpServletResponse httpServletResponse )
79     throws ServletException, IOException
80  {
81        doTransfer ( httpServletRequest,
82            httpServletResponse);
83  }
84
85  /**
86   * Executes the employee transfer.
87   */
88  private void doTransfer ( HttpServletRequest request,
89     HttpServletResponse response )
90     throws ServletException
91  {
92        // get empNo to transfer
93        boolean success = false;
94        UserTransaction tx = null;
95        int empNo = 0;
96
97        try
98        {
99           empNo = Integer.parseInt
100              ( request.getParameter( "empNo" ) );
101
102           // lookup the user transaction reference
103           tx = (UserTransaction) m_ctx.lookup
104              ( USER_TX_LOOKUP_STR );
105
106           // begin the transaction
107           tx.begin ();
108
109           EmployeeBean employee = removeEmployee
110              ( empNo );
111           addEmployee ( employee );
112           success = true;
113        }
114        catch ( NumberFormatException e )
115        {
116           throw new ServletException ( e );
117        }
118        catch ( NamingException e )
119        {
120           throw new ServletException ( e );
121        }
122        catch ( NotSupportedException e )
123        {
```

```
124              throw new ServletException ( e );
125          }
126      catch ( SystemException e )
127      {
128          throw new ServletException ( e );
129      }
130      finally
131      {
132          // if the two database interactions were
133          // successful, commit the transaction.
134          // Otherwise, roll it back.
135          if (!success)
136          {
137              rollback ( tx );
138          }
139          else
140          {
141              commit ( tx );
142          }
143          printOutput ( success, response, empNo );
144      }
145  }
146
147  /**
148   * Prints the results of the transfer.
149   */
150  private void printOutput ( boolean success,
151      HttpServletResponse response, int empNo )
152      throws ServletException
153  {
154      response.setContentType ( "text/html" );
155      try
156      {
157          PrintWriter out = response.getWriter();
158          out.println ( "<HTML><HEAD><TITLE>Funds " +
159              "Transfer</TITLE></HEAD>" );
160          out.println ( "<BODY>" );
161          out.println ( "<H3>Your transfer of " + empNo +
162              " was " + ( success ? "" : "not " ) +
163              "successful.</H3>" );
164          out.println ( "</BODY>" );
165          out.println ( "</HTML>" );
166          out.close ();
167      }
168      catch ( IOException e )
169      {
170          throw new ServletException ( e );
171      }
```

```
172  }
173
174  /**
175   * Adds the employee record to the target database.
176   */
177  protected void addEmployee ( EmployeeBean employee )
178      throws ServletException
179  {
180      Connection conn = null;
181      Statement stmt = null;
182
183      try
184      {
185          conn = m_division2DS.getConnection ();
186          stmt = conn.createStatement ();
187          String insertStmt =
188              "INSERT INTO EMP (EMPNO, ENAME,"+
189              "JOB, MGR, HIREDATE, SAL, COMM, DEPTNO) " +
190              "VALUES ("+( employee.getEmpNo() + 1000 ) +
191              ", '" + employee.getEname() +
192              "', '" + employee.getJob()  +
193              "', " + employee.getMgr() +
194              ", TO_DATE('" +
195              formatDate ( employee.getHireDate () ) +
196              "', 'DD-MON-YYYY'), " +
197              employee.getSal() +
198              ", " + employee.getComm() +
199              ", " + employee.getDeptNo() + ")";
200          m_cfg.getServletContext().log
201            ( "Insert statement:" +
202            insertStmt );
203          int affectedRows = stmt.executeUpdate
204            ( insertStmt );
205          if ( affectedRows == 0 )
206          {
207              throw new SQLException ( "Insert of employee "
208                  + employee.getEmpNo() + " failed" );
209          }
210
211      }
212      catch ( SQLException e )
213      {
214          throw new ServletException ( e );
215      }
216      finally
217      {
218          closeResources ( conn, stmt );
219      }
```

```
220  }
221
222  /**
223   * Formats the date into a database usable string.
224   */
225  protected String formatDate ( Date hireDate )
226  {
227     SimpleDateFormat format = new SimpleDateFormat
228        ( "dd-MMM-yyyy" );
229     return format.format ( hireDate );
230  }
231
232  /**
233   * Removes the employee record from the original
234   * database.
235   */
236  private EmployeeBean removeEmployee ( int empNo )
237     throws ServletException
238  {
239     // get a connection
240     EmployeeBean employee = null;
241     Connection conn = null;
242     Statement stmt = null;
243     try
244     {
245        conn = m_division1DS.getConnection ();
246        employee = getEmployee ( conn, empNo );
247        stmt = conn.createStatement ();
248        int affectedRows = stmt.executeUpdate (
249           "DELETE from EMP where EMPNO = " + empNo );
250        if ( affectedRows == 0 )
251        {
252           throw new SQLException ( "Delete of employee "
253              + empNo + " failed" );
254        }
255
256     }
257     catch ( SQLException e )
258     {
259        throw new ServletException ( e );
260     }
261     finally
262     {
263        closeResources ( conn, stmt );
264     }
265     return employee;
266  }
267
```

```
268  /**
269   * Returns the employee record.
270   */
271  private EmployeeBean getEmployee ( Connection conn,
272     int empNo ) throws SQLException
273  {
274     Statement stmt = conn.createStatement ();
275     ResultSet rs = stmt.executeQuery (
276        "select * from emp where empNo = " + empNo );
277     EmployeeBean employee = new EmployeeBean ( rs );
278     return employee;
279  }
280
281  /**
282   * Closes the JDBC resources.
283   */
284  private void closeResources ( Connection conn,
285     Statement stmt ) throws ServletException
286  {
287     ServletContext servletCtx =
288        m_cfg.getServletContext ();
289     try
290     {
291        if ( stmt != null )
292        {
293           servletCtx.log ( "Closing stmt" );
294           stmt.close ();
295        }
296        if ( conn != null )
297        {
298           servletCtx.log ( "Closing conn" );
299           conn.close ();
300        }
301     }
302     catch ( SQLException e )
303     {
304        throw new ServletException ( e );
305     }
306  }
307
308  /**
309   * Commits the transaction.
310   */
311  private void commit ( UserTransaction tx )
312     throws ServletException
313  {
314     try
315     {
```

```
316        tx.commit ();
317     }
318     catch ( RollbackException e )
319     {
320        throw new ServletException ( e );
321     }
322     catch ( HeuristicMixedException e )
323     {
324        throw new ServletException ( e );
325     }
326     catch ( HeuristicRollbackException e )
327     {
328        throw new ServletException ( e );
329     }
330     catch ( SecurityException e )
331     {
332        throw new ServletException ( e );
333     }
334     catch ( IllegalStateException e )
335     {
336        throw new ServletException ( e );
337     }
338     catch ( SystemException e )
339     {
340        throw new ServletException ( e );
341     }
342  }
343
344  /**
345   * Rolls back the transaction.
346   */
347  private void rollback ( UserTransaction tx )
348     throws ServletException
349  {
350     try
351     {
352        tx.rollback ();
353     }
354     catch ( IllegalStateException e )
355     {
356        throw new ServletException ( e );
357     }
358     catch ( SecurityException e )
359     {
360        throw new ServletException ( e );
361     }
362     catch ( SystemException e )
363     {
```

```
364              throw new ServletException ( e );
365      }
366   }
367   }
```

We're going to walk through what happens in the application server when the Servlet executes. Let's first assume that both DataSources are configured to provide Connections to two different databases; further, let's assume that the application server isn't pooling physical Connections for simplicity's sake.

When the getConnection() method is executed in the removeEmployee() method (line 244), the application server will create a connection wrapper to return the servlet. The data source implementation may, however, choose not to bind the wrapper immediately to a physical Connection—it may defer this binding until work is performed. When the binding is performed, the application server will use the XADataSource to create an XAConnection. From that XAConnection, it will retrieve a Connection to associate with the Connection wrapper. Since the Connection is being used in the scope of a global transaction, the application server will also retrieve an XAResource from the XAConnection.

Before control is returned to the application, the application server will enlist the XARe-source with the transaction. The transaction manager will in turn call start() on the XARe-source, assigning the branch an XID. At this point, the physical connection is associated with the transaction branch. Any work performed through the Connection that is now bound to the Connection wrapper will be scoped by the transaction. This physical channel will remain transacted until the transaction manager uses the XAResource to invoke the end() method to demarcate the end of work. In most implementations, this allows the XAConnection to be released for use by other transactions. In our example, the end method is called as a by-product of the close() method being called on the connection wrapper (line 298). This notifies the application server that there will be no more work performed through the Connection wrapper. In most cases, this will invalidate the wrapper altogether.

The exact same process will in turn occur when the addEmployee() method is executed. This means two Connections will be used in the same transaction. When the commit method is called, the transaction manager will see that multiple XAResources have been registered with the transaction and it will run through the two-phase commit protocol. Both branches will be asked to prepare. If the branches are prepared successfully, they will be committed.

Now what happens if the two employee tables are in the same database? Many application servers will detect that the Connections are in the same transaction and share the same underlying physical Connection. This means in practice that a second XAResource would not be enlisted in the transaction. Moreover, the two-phase commit process won't occur. Instead, the transaction manager will be able to use the XAResource to call commit with the "one-phase" flag set. As you can see, this can save quite a number of round trips to the database, and avoids having to write a transaction log altogether.

Summary

Transactions in JDBC are one of the most important and useful features of the J2EE platform. Simply having the ability to scope multiple updates within a local transaction is incredibly powerful in and of itself. Fortunately, JDBC provides robust support for global transactions, extending the applicability of the transaction concept to units of work that involve more than just a single database. As you can see, the application server does a lot of work to support transaction enlistment, scoping of global transactions as units of work, pooling, and other system services. Most of this is accomplished by unpublished internals of the application server—it helps to be as familiar as possible with how application servers manage `Connections`. In some cases, JDBC drivers may provide some of these capabilities as well (e.g., connection pooling). Because of the interdependencies between pooled `Connections` and transactional `Connections`, we recommend that the application server facilities be relied on exclusively for J2EE applications.

CHAPTER 5

JMS and Transactions

The Java Message Service (JMS) specification defines an API that is used to access message-oriented middleware, or MOM, systems. This chapter begins with a discussion of some key concepts of messaging technologies: what kinds of capabilities they provide, why they are so important, and why transactional capabilities fit so well with message bus and queue architectures. We then provide an overview of the interfaces and messaging semantics provided by JMS. The chapter then explores the facilities this specification provides for achieving reliable communications: message acknowledgement modes, local transactions, and distributed transactions, including a working example of transacted interaction with message queues. We explore the ramifications of the under-specified transactional contract defined in the JMS specification between J2EE containers and JMS providers and the means for addressing this limitation provided by the upcoming Java Connector Architecture release. Finally, we look at some ways to use message queues and relational databases reliably without the overhead and pitfalls involved with the two-phase commit protocol.

What Is Message-Oriented Middleware?

Most software developers' first experiences with distributed systems revolve around synchronous interactions between separate processes using some kind of inter-process communication facilities. If the application is distributed and meant to interoperate across different operating systems, the most familiar programming construct is the stream-based TCP/IP socket abstraction.

Socket-level programming can often be replaced with higher-level middleware like Remote Procedure Calls (RPC), CORBA, or the Simple Object Access Protocol (SOAP) RPC facility. Middleware is generally less error-prone and not so tedious to use, especially when using a native system programming language like C. RPC-based middleware technologies are for the most part used to create tightly coupled systems with synchronous interactions.

However, RPC-style middleware has some fairly significant limitations. Because systems are tightly coupled, they are not resilient to change. If a method on a remote interface needs to change, all clients have to be updated; until each client is updated, it will not be able to interact with the system.

Another significant problem is lack of scalability. To interact with an RPC service each of the clients usually maintains an open connection to the system for the duration of the request-response process; moreover, requests have to be handled as they arrive. This tends to scale poorly; it is even less appropriate for extremely high-volume event-driven applications. Scalability problems also occur for RPC systems that have to deal with sending information to many clients of a service, since synchronous interactions with hundreds, thousands or even millions of clients are profoundly inefficient.

Finally, RPC-style interactions are just not practical for long-running operations as clients are forced to block for the duration of the request. Locking up the service for prolonged periods will further degrade the performance and functionality of the application and may potentially yield deadlocks in critical back-office resources.

It should be clear that these limitations are not only significant; they arise in virtually every distributed application of even moderate complexity. Messaging systems provide an alternative interaction pattern that doesn't suffer from these drawbacks.

The difference between message and RPC systems isn't based on a choice of communication protocols or implementation strategies, which vary between products. Rather, it's based on the fundamental unit of exchange between applications and services within the system: the message itself.

A message is composed of data of interest to applications and a set of message headers. Some of the headers may provide network-level information that may or may not be visible to applications and may be used for routing within the MOM infrastructure. A message represents an event or occurrence that merits attention, for example, a message might be a purchase order that needs to be processed. The message system is equivalent to the queuing systems we discussed in Chapter 1, "Transaction Fundamentals."

This approach solves several problems that occur with RPC interactions. For one thing, the client and server are not coupled. Instead, a client is sending a message to a stateless channel (or "destination"). The client doesn't need to have any knowledge about the service that will handle the purchase order. The only thing the client needs to know is the structure of the purchase order message.

Secondly, the client doesn't need to block while the purchase order is handled by the purchase order processing system. Once the client application has submitted the purchase order, it may continue processing immediately. A message service can be the basis for a scalable and highly available system; in fact, as long as there is a guarantee of delivery, the client may continue to submit purchase orders even if the purchase order processing service is down for a time.

This is not a contrived scenario: consider the last time you placed an order with Amazon.com. When you submit a purchase order, it is placed on a queue and processed asynchronously. The system tells you the order has been placed. Some time later you receive an e-mail that your purchase order has been processed.

The scenario above illustrates the flexibility of point-to-point messaging, which is typically implemented with message queues. With this kind of MOM service, applications can perform reliable one-way messaging and asynchronous communication.

Broadcast messaging is another paradigm supported by many MOM products. This is also referred to as a publish-and-subscribe ("pub-sub") model. With broadcast models, the message is written to a channel on which there may be an arbitrary number of listeners. This messaging scheme allows for very scalable delivery and consumption models: consumers may tune in and out of a channel to detect messages when required. Similarly, publishers may push out messages with great frequency independent of the number of consumers. A common example for a publish-and-subscribe use case is a stock exchange that needs to push out near-real time data to large numbers of clients.

In both models, there are quality-of-service guarantees that can be used to ensure that messages are delivered. Reliable messaging is important for business applications that use messages for critical functions like billing and purchase orders. Most message brokers support reliable message delivery for both point-to-point and broadcast models.

It should come as no surprise that many MOM implementations support both local and global transactions. For message systems, local transactions are incredibly powerful. Like the ability to scope multiple SQL statements in a single unit of work, message server transactions allow publication of groups of messages as a single unit of work. Some systems allow the receipt of a message to be "undone" if a transaction rolls back. Support for global transactions adds even more flexibility. For example, messages delivered to heterogeneous or distributed queues, relational database table inserts, and other modifications to resource managers can be scoped within the same distributed unit of work.

Messaging products are not new and in fact have been used for a long time in many large enterprises. Well-known and widely used products include IBM Websphere MQ (formerly MQSeries), Tibco Rendezvous, and Oracle Advanced Queuing. Since the release of the JMS specification lighter-weight MOM implementations have become available from companies like Sonic Software, Fiorano Software and Arjuna Technologies. In addition, J2EE application servers are required to include their own JMS implementation as a native message broker integrated into the product. The level of transaction support may vary, so it's important to determine exactly what features are implemented in the MOM product you intend to use. For JMS, support for global transactions is optional.

Even though messaging products provide significant advantages, we don't want to leave you with the impression that they are the key to all architecture problems. Message-based solutions are not always appropriate, especially for highly interactive systems where progress is dependent on the synchronous completion of distributed services.

In addition, MOM products have serious limitations of their own. One is interoperability: each message system has its own protocol and unique implementation, and will not interoperate with other systems. This is why EAI projects based on a messaging architecture require significant investments in a message broker.

Finally, it's important to note that asynchronous programming is hard, especially when message correlation is required. A vastly more complicated programming model may not be a reasonable tradeoff for some of the advantages gained from message systems. In practice, many solutions will involve a combination of asynchronous and synchronous interactions.

Now that we have a better understanding of MOM systems, let's examine JMS in a little more detail.

Java Message Service

The Java Message Service defines a set of interfaces and the associated semantics that facilitate communication between Java applications and message service implementations. By leveraging the JMS API, applications can create, send, receive and read messages in both the point-to-point and broadcast paradigms. For J2EE applications, JMS enables communication that is loosely coupled, asynchronous, and reliable.

The main focus of this chapter is on using transactions with JMS. First, let's take a look at the basic concepts in the JMS specification for some necessary background.

The broadcast model that we discussed above is captured in JMS as a topic abstraction. A topic is a virtual channel that allows a message producer to send messages to any number of message consumers.

Point-to-point interaction is modeled by the Queue abstraction. The queue is a reliable virtual channel that allows both message producers and consumers to write and read from it, respectively. While there may be many message consumers reading from queue, a single message can be read by only one consumer. Queues are generally used for reliable messaging between applications. However, topics may also have reliable delivery semantics since they can be made durable.

JMS provides a fairly straightforward programming model for accessing topics and queues. For illustrative purposes we discuss how to connect to a queue as a message producer and as a consumer. Later we look at some examples using transactions that you may download and execute.

In J2EE, the standard mechanism for looking up a JMS administered object (an administered object is a pre-configured JMS object created by an administrator for use by clients) is via JNDI. To support this, application servers will allow you to map the client view of JMS into their managed naming environment. To communicate with a `Queue` or `Topic` requires that two objects be looked up: the `QueueConnectionFactory` and the `Queue` itself. The `Queue-ConnectionFactory` interface contains the following methods:

```
public QueueConnection createQueueConnection() throws JMSException;
public QueueConnection createQueueConnection (String userName, String
password);
```

Here's what the code looks like to acquire a `QueueConnectionFactory` instance:

```
InitialContext ctx = new InitialContext( );
QueueConnectionFactory qcf =
(QueueConnectionFactory)ctx.lookup("java:comp/env/jms/
OracleQueueConnectionFactory" );
```

Note that the code examples above omit exception handling.

Once you have a reference to the `QueueConnectionFactory`, it can be used to create a `QueueConnection`. The `QueueConnection` is a logical connection to the JMS provider environment—remember, nothing mandates a connection-oriented protocol be used to implement JMS. Notice that the factory methods for creating connections to a given server allow security credential management to be applied on a per-connection basis. The `QueueConnection` provides the ability to start the delivery of messages to registered consumers, but it is not used directly to create, send or receive messages. This is accomplished with the `QueueSession`, which is created via the connection:

```
public QueueSession createQueueSession(boolean transacted,
int acknowledgeMode) throws JMSException;
```

The `transacted` flag indicates that the session will be used to deliver messages within the context of a local transaction; the `acknowledgeMode` is used to control the reliability semantics of message delivery or receipt. Note that many sessions, each with its own transaction and acknowledgement semantics, can be created from a single connection. We talk more about these aspects later. For now, bear in mind that it is possible to have multiple sessions to provide finer grained control of the behavior of senders and receivers associated with a connection. The `createQueueSession()` method allows automatic local transaction initiation by the JMS client code. We deal with transactions in much greater depth below.

You will notice that neither the `QueueConnection` itself nor the `QueueSession` is associated with any particular queue. The session is used to publish or consume messages from a particular queue in a two-step process. A reference to the queue itself is generally registered in a JNDI context by an administrator and acquired as follows:

```
InitialContext ctx = new InitialContext( );
Queue poQueue = ( Queue )ctx.lookup( "java:comp/env/jms/
PurchaseOrderQueue" );
```

Once the `Queue` is acquired, a `QueueSender` can be created from the `QueueSession`:

```
QueueSender sender = queueSession.createSender( myQueue );
```

The `QueueSender` can then be used to write messages to the virtual channel represented by the `Queue` object. At this point, message delivery is quite simple:

```
sender.send( message );
```

Message receipt is somewhat more complicated. A message receiver may block synchronously waiting to dequeue a message, a relatively uncommon scenario for most enterprise applications. More often a receiver will register a `MessageListener` for asynchronous receipt of messages. The `MessageListener` contains business logic that is used to process the message on receipt.

> **N O T E** As a general rule, we recommend that you use Message-Driven Beans as a mechanism for receiving JMS messages. We discuss this alternative programming model in quite a bit of detail in Chapter 6. For now, we want to point out that the Message-Driven Bean is actually much simpler to write than a custom implementation of a `MessageListener`. When you use Message-Driven Beans, the application server takes care of thread management, object pooling, and transaction management automatically.

The full capabilities of JMS and the entire API set are beyond the scope of this chapter. We recommend the useful book *Java Message Service* by Richard Monson-Haefel and David Chappell as a good overview of JMS. But even without a deep familiarity with JMS, you should be able to follow our discussion with the background we've provided. The remainder of the chapter is primarily focused on the reliability and transaction facilities that are provided by JMS and what they mean for applications.

Message Acknowledgement

JMS supports several alternatives for message delivery and receipt semantics based on acknowledgement modes. The acknowledgement modes determine the degree to which the client and server interact to guarantee delivery and receipt of a message and are set during the creation of a JMS session. For example, a queue session leveraging the auto acknowledgment mode can be created with the following code:

```
Session queueSession = queueConnection.createQueueSession (
false, Session.AUTO_ACKNOWLEDGE );
```

It's that simple. Let's look at the possible message acknowledgement modes and what they mean.

AUTO_ACKNOWLEDGE Mode

In this mode, the JMS provider is explicitly made responsible for guaranteeing delivery; the client is not in direct control of message acknowledgement. Message delivery is implemented as a synchronous, blocking interaction under the covers. In general, AUTO_ACKNOWLEDGE will have "once and only once" delivery semantics. However, some failure conditions will allow duplicate messages to move through the system, so it's important to have integrity checks for replicated messages in your application logic when relying on negotiated guarantees of delivery.

DUPS_OK_ACKNOWLEDGE Mode

This is a more relaxed mode that allows the server to improve performance by reducing the extent to which it attempts to negotiate with clients to both guarantee delivery and prevent redelivery of messages. The extent to which performance gains may be realized is heavily implementation specific. Coupled with the fact that most applications that want reliable delivery are better off without multiple copies of the same message flowing through the system, DUPS_OK_ACKNOWLEDGE may be of limited use.

CLIENT_ACKNOWLEDGE Mode

As the name suggest, CLIENT_ACKNOWLEDGE allows message recipients to indicate explicitly when the message acknowledgement is sent to the JMS server. Message consumers can leverage this mode to insure reliable processing of messages.

An important capability of reliable messaging is the ability to acknowledge the receipt of groups of messages. This differs subtly from the normal transacted delivery of messages that we examine below since a transaction typically revolves around the receipt and processing of a single incoming message.

JMS message recipients accomplish reliable receipt of a group of messages using the CLIENT_ACKNOWLEDGE mode and an explicit call on the Message object:

```
message.acknowledge();
```

The acknowledge() call applies to all messages received in this session. Many people trip over the fact that the Session holds channel-specific state. If you have many consumers in a session, acknowledge() applies to all messages consumed by all consumers.

As with AUTO_ACKNOWLEDGE, it remains possible for messages to be sent multiple times following certain kinds of failures. It's important that recipient applications are prepared to deal with duplicate messages. Specifically, an application can query the Message for an indication of whether the given message is being redelivered:

```
boolean redelivery = message.getJMSRedelivered();
```

Reliable messaging achieved via the acknowledgment modes can be very important, but it is semantically distinct from transacted message server interactions. With transactions, you are able to associate multiple actions within the same unit of work. In the context of a transaction, JMS message delivery or receipt has implicit reliability guarantees. Moreover, message acknowledgement is handled automatically when a transaction is committed. Let's explore transacted sessions in greater detail.

JMS Local Transactions

A JMS client can use local transactions (as with JDBC, we use the term local transactions to refer to transactions that are local to the JMS provider) to group message sends and receives. The client interaction with the transaction is facilitated via the `Session` interface.

A messaging provider maintains the messages sent and consumed within the session until the transaction is committed or rolled back. By invoking the `commit()` method the client indicates that all produced messages are to be sent and all consumed messages are to be acknowledged and removed from the messaging server (The message may not be removed from the server if it was sent to a durable topic and all subscribers have not received the message). Similarly, an invocation of the `rollback()` method indicates that all produced messages are to be destroyed and all consumed messages are to be recovered and redelivered by the JMS provider.

A JMS transacted session is always associated with a local transaction. The JMS provider creates an initial transaction when the session is created. Subsequent commits or rollbacks trigger the creation of a new local transaction. In addition, closing a transacted session before committing or rolling back the given transaction forces the rollback of the transaction.

Using the local transaction facilities of the JMS API is prohibited in the context of a distributed transaction. If you are using EJBs with container-managed transactions, you need to be careful not to attempt to use local transaction demarcation calls when a global transaction is associated with the current thread of control. Invoking the session `commit()` or `rollback()` methods from within an JTA transaction will likely result in a JMS `TransactionIn-Progress` exception.

You can combine multiple message sends and receives in a single JMS API local transaction. However, there are a few issues you should consider if you plan to combine these functions in the scope of one transaction. There are no inherent problems if the client application only performs message sends or receives during a transaction, or if the message receives occur before the sends. However, the program will hang if the application implements a request-reply scenario where a message is sent and then an attempt is made to receive a reply to the sent message in the same transaction. A message send cannot take place until the associated transaction is committed because a message produced during a transaction is not actually sent until the transaction is committed; the transaction cannot contain any receives that depend upon a message sent during the same transaction.

As with much else in J2EE, there are exceptions to this guideline. The scenario above is not true for all JMS providers. Message visibility—which indicates if messages produced inside a session are visible to consumers before a commit—is highly provider specific. For instance, for Oracle's Advanced Queuing provider, messages sent in a transacted session are visible to consumers. In addition, the JMS provider bundled with the Oracle Application Server by default has the same behavior (though here the message visibility can be changed to "not visible"). So it is a good idea that you check with the documentation of your JMS provider before attempting message delivery and receipt within the scope of a local transaction.

Another critical point: JMS local transactions do not cross session boundaries. The reason for this is that the JMS provider intervenes between the production and consumption of messages; there is no direct communication or link between distributed JMS clients. This separation highlights a fundamental difference between synchronous invocations and messaging; applications communicate asynchronously by relying on the delivery guarantees afforded by the messaging provider.

As seen in Figure 5-1, the sending of messages from one client can occur in the scope of one transaction and similarly the receipt of multiple messages by another client can also fall under the scope of a single transaction. However, the two transactions are completely unrelated.

So how do you start a local, transacted session? A JMS session is designated as transacted during its creation. The first argument to the `TopicConnection.createTopicSession()` and `QueueConnection.createQueueSession()` methods is a boolean argument indicating whether the session is transacted:

```
QueueSession queueSession = queueConnection.createQueueSession
( true, Session.AUTO_ACKNOWLEDGE );
```

Note that since we are creating a transacted session, the second argument, indicating the message acknowledgment mode, is ignored (by convention the `AUTO_ACKNOWLEDGE` mode is utilized as the value for this argument). In JMS, you cannot control reliability semantics for sessions that are created to use a transaction. In a transacted session the message acknowledgment is handled automatically by the execution of `commit()`.

An example helps to illustrate the step required to create and utilize a transacted `QueueSession`. In this case we demonstrates how multiple messages are created and sent to a queue within the context of a local transaction. Note that there is no "begin" method used to start the local transaction. All work done on the queue through the session is transactional. This code can be used inside a J2EE application or within a standalone application:

```
// the required administered objects are
// retrieved from the component context:
Context ctx = new InitialContext ();

// lookup the queue
```

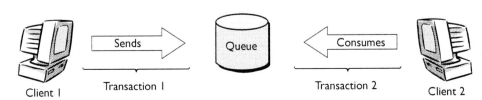

Figure 5-1 JMS API Local Transactions.

```
Queue queue = (Queue) ctx.lookup ( "myQueue" );

// lookup the queue connection factory
QueueConnectionFactory qcf = (QueueConnectionFactory) ctx.lookup
("myQueueConnectionFactory");

// create the queue connection
QueueConnection connection = qcf.createQueueConnection ();

// create a transacted queue session.  The second argument
// really isn't used by a transacted session since message
// acknowledgement is handled by the commit.
// by convention it is set to zero.
QueueSession session = connection.createQueueSession (true, 0 );

// create a queue sender
QueueSender sender = session.createSender (queue);

// create the messages to send as part of the transaction
TextMessage msg1 = session.createTextMessage ("message1");
TextMessage msg2 = session.createTextMessage ("message2");

// in the code below, the messages are sent and committed.
// If an unexpected error occurs the transaction will be
// rolled back
try
{
    sender.send (msg1);
    sender.send (msg2);

    // commit the send which actually makes the messages
// visible at the queue
    session.commit ();
}
catch ( Exception e)
{
    session.rollback ();
}

// close the connection
connection.close ();
```

A single JMS session is assumed by the specification to be acted on by a single thread. The only method on the Session interface that can be called from a different thread is `close()`. Some JMS providers do a better job at this and allow different threads to use the same Session and provide thread safe implementations, but you shouldn't count on the availability of this behavior.

JMS 1.1 Improvements

Prior to the release of the JMS 1.1 specification the association of a local transaction to the JMS Session implied that transactional boundaries could not be used to scope work on both queues and topics together. For example, you could not receive a message from a queue and publish to a topic within the scope of a single transaction since the associated queue receiver and topic publisher were accessed from separate sessions. However, if you created receivers and senders from the same transactional session you could potentially send and receive from one queue to another or from one topic to another within the scope of the same local transaction.

The latest JMS release addressed the unification of the programming interfaces for the topic and queue messaging domains by changing the APIs. Many of the `TopicSession` and `QueueSession` methods were moved up the class hierarchy to the `Session` interface to add the ability to create a session that could be used with both topics and queues.

These changes mean that you can use local transactions more flexibly. For example, an application can create a transacted `Session`, and then receive messages from a `Queue` and send messages to a `Topic` within the same transaction. Since the changes simply require promoting methods to a superclass there is no impact on existing applications.

Now that we've examined local transactions let's explore the distributed transaction facilities afforded by the JMS specification.

Global Transactions

Support for XA transactions is not required by the JMS specification—the specification defines a global transaction model, but states that support is optional. The good news is that the ability to participate in global transactions is supported by a growing number of JMS providers. We assume that most JMS vendors will continue to bolster their support for distributed transaction functionality in the near term given the growing popularity of Message-Driven Beans as an interface to message-oriented middleware—since MDBs are a kind of EJB, they are quite useful for managing global transactions.

> **N O T E** If you plan to use JMS with global transactions, the first thing you need to do is validate that the implementation you are using supports XA. We also recommend that you validate that the transaction capabilities have been proven in a production environment.

The JMS specification assumes that an application server, rather than a standalone application, will leverage the XA facilities of a JMS provider. An application will rarely be responsible for the acquisition of the XA-enabling JMS interfaces and the enlistment of the `XAResource` with a JTA-compliant transaction manager. As a general rule, client applications will be shielded entirely from the mechanics of transaction management.

However, we are going to review the interfaces that are defined to support XA in detail. We think they are important for several reasons:

Expert application developers are not precluded from emulating the steps undertaken by an application server to participate in a distributed transaction.

Receiving messages in a global transaction can be problematic due to flaws in the specification.

It's important to have insight into what's happening inside the application server in order to make good decisions in product selection and application design. These interfaces are the basis for how application servers and JMS providers work together to support transactions.

Parts of this discussion may seem fairly low-level. After we have gained an understanding of how JMS providers work together with applications servers to support transactions, we examine a real application scenario that uses JMS and JDBC together in a transaction.

In one sense, sessions enlisted in a global transaction provide functionality similar to the local-transacted sessions described previously. JMS operations performed in the scope of an XA transaction are conditional on the commit of the transaction. The main difference is the party acting as the transactional coordinator. In the case of local transactions the JMS provider itself manages the execution of the transaction. Using XA transactions, the outcome of the JMS transaction is dependent on the decision of the transaction manager into which the JMS `XAResource` is enlisted.

And, as with local transactions, since JMS 1.1 was released, a global transaction can be used to scope operations on queues and topics accessed through the same session. In addition, the two existing sets of parallel interfaces were maintained for interacting with queues or topics separately while in the scope on a distributed transaction, which maintains backward compatibility.

Let's examine the JMS APIs for participating in a global transaction. As we discuss the interfaces, bear in mind that the application server will usually wrap the session provided to the application in order to intervene and manage the enlistment of `XAResources` with a transaction. This is similar to how an application server manages JDBC connections, which we examined in Chapter 4.

XAConnectionFactory

A JMS provider will expose its support for XA in `XAConnections`, which are created via methods in the `XAConnectionFactory` interfaces for both the topics and queues. Much like the equivalent non-XA interfaces, the XA connection factories are administered objects that are generally retrieved using JNDI. An application server (or much less likely, a standalone application) will use the `XAConnectionFactory` to create `XAConnections`. For example, the process for creating XA queue connections in an application server might look be as follows:

```
// create the JNDI context
Context ctx = new InitialContextFactory ()

// lookup an XA queue connection factory
```

```
XAQueueConnectionFactory factory = (XAQueueConnectionFactory)
ctx.lookup ( "jms/xa/QueueConnectionFactory" );

// create an XA queue connection
XAQueueConnection xaConnection =
factory.createXAQueueConnection();
```

We cannot emphasize strongly enough that J2EE applications do not look up XAConnectionFactory implementations directly. As with JDBC, the application server will register its own ConnectionFactory implementation for applications to use. The application server's ConnectionFactory will in turn use the vendor's XAConnectionFactory under the covers when it is required. J2EE applications get these benefits for free, but it may be very important to configure your application server such that it knows how to find the XAConnectionFactory for the JMS provider when it needs to use it.

XAConnection

XA connection objects extend the functionality of non-XA connections by providing the facilities for creating XA sessions:

```
XAQueueSession session = xaConnection.createXAQueueSession ();
```

In surveying some existing JMS XA-compliant implementations it appears that the creation and utilization of an XA connection is one of the areas in which developers can expect to encounter some vendor dependencies. For example, although the XAQueueConection or XATopicConnection interfaces extend the standard Connection interface and would therefore appear to inherit the associated connection functionality, Sonic Software's SonicMQ JMS provider requires the creation of not only the XAConnection object but also a standard Connection object:

```
progress.message.jclient.xa.XAQueueConnectionFactory
xaQfac= new XAQueueConnectionFactory("aHost:2506");

XAQueueConnection xaQcon =
xaQfac.createXAQueueConnection("myname", "mypassword");

QueueConnection qConnect =
((progress.message.jclient.xa.XAQueueConnection)xaQcon).getQueueConnect
ion();
(Source: SonicMQ V5 Programming Guide, Chapter 13)
```

XASession

XASession objects extend the functionality of the standard session object to provide access to an XAResource that can be enlisted with a transaction manager.

When the application server determines that a session needs to be enlisted with a global transaction, it uses the getXAResource( ) method on the XASession. The XAResource is used enlist the session with the transaction manager. The transaction manager will in turn uses the XAResource to demarcate, commit, or rollback work the JMS provider performed within the scope of the transaction. An XAResource can be thought of as a handle to the XASession.

XASessions are not used directly. Rather, a Session interface is obtained from the XASession and used to perform the standard JMS operations involved in message receipt or sending (similar to the way JDBC Connection proxies obtained from XAConnections are utilized). For example, an application server integrated with a JMS provider will use the XASession object to create an XAResource and to create a Session that will be used by the application.

To summarize, the general sequence of events for enlisting a JMS session with a distributed transaction follows; these interactions occur "under the hood" of the application server:

```
/* initiate the transaction, let's assume the application server does
this using some internal reference to the Transaction Manager */
tm.begin();
Transaction txn = tm.getTransaction();
. . .
// create the XA connection
XATopicConnectionFactory xatcf = (XATopicConnectionFactory)
jndiCtx.lookup ("XATopicConnectionFactory");
XATopicConnection xatc =
xatcf.createXATopicConnection( user, password );
. . .
// create the XA session and obtain XAResource
XATopicSession xats = xatc.createXATopicSession();
XAResource xart = xats.getXAResource();
. . .
// enlist the resource
txn.enlistResource(xart);
. . .
// application performs JMS operations and closes session
. . .
// delist the resource
txn.delistResource ( xart, XAResource.TMSUCCESS );
. . .
// commit the transaction
tm.commit ();
```

Figure 5-2 illustrates the interactions that occur within an application that uses JMS sessions in a transaction.

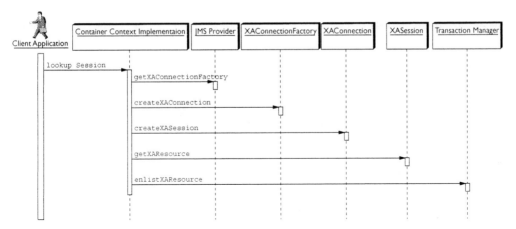

Figure 5-2   Transactional interaction diagram.

Remember: application servers provide integration facilities for JMS and a managed JMS session will hide the details of transaction enlistment and the JMS XA interfaces from end users. You'll note that our examples are really built around transacted message delivery. You really need to have an application server to support transacted message receipt, as we explain in the next section. Fortunately, Message-Driven Beans are a perfect, lightweight, and simple way to manage JMS message receipt—in fact, far simpler than dealing with JMS directly. We talk about MDBs at length in Chapter 6.

In order to support the interactions above, an application server vendor will generally incorporate a JMS provider into its offering. Let's examine the nature of this integration.

Application Server Integration

Since the release of the J2EE 1.3 specification, application servers are required to make available a JMS provider that supports both reliable point-to-point messaging as well as the publish-subscribe model. A J2EE-compatible platform is expected to integrate a JMS provider into the application server and make it available as a runtime service to deployed J2EE components. Unfortunately, integration between application servers and JMS is under-specified, so some JMS implementations may integrate with your application server better than others.

For one thing, while the application server is typically responsible for thread pool management, the JMS specification defines a message consumption model in which the application server's `ServerSessionPool` implementation winds up using threads that are managed within a special `ConnectionConsumer` class provided by the JMS provider.

Since much of the application server internals and all of the transaction processing are based on per-thread semantics, this is a poor design; normally the application server manages pooled threads and may decorate the threads as part of its implementation strategy. This is an area where application servers may require special integration code with JMS providers.

In addition, and of primary interest here, there's no standard way to associate a global transaction with the receipt of a message.

A common runtime scenario will help illustrate the difficulties vendors have encountered in implementing support for JMS and Message Driven Beans. Assume that a client wishes to consume a message using an MDB with Container-Managed Transactions (CMT) enabled. This means that the EJB container will need to start a transaction before it receives the message. This is a common scenario: within the `MessageListener`'s `onMessage()` method the application will often need to perform some entity bean updates or direct JDBC interaction and expect all of the operations to execute in the same global transaction. However, once the message has been delivered to the container it is too late to create the transaction and enlist the JMS provider as the message has already been received prior to the initiation of the transaction.

One of the major benefits of message driven beans is the ability to receive a message in the scope of a global transaction that subsequently may scope additional work on other resource managers. When vendors pointed out that the specification was lacking, Sun took the position that the specification deals strictly with the client view of JMS within the platform. Each application server vendor is therefore required to define an integration strategy that meets all of the transactional requirements in the specifications in an ad hoc manner.

Different vendors have addressed this problem in three different ways; let's look at examples of the three possible approaches:

- Oracle Application Server doesn't bother to use the `ConnectionConsumer` construct defined as part of the application server integration model presented by the JMS specification. Instead, it creates a global transaction and does a synchronous receipt with a timeout while waiting for a message to be delivered to a `Queue` or `Topic`. If the message is delivered before the timeout period expires, the application server will process the message. If the message receipt does time out, the transaction is completed and a new transaction is started before calling the blocking receive again. This guarantees that the message is delivered to the application server in a transacted context. This kind of integration relies on a client-based polling mechanism.
- Some other custom integrations are designed to force the JMS model to work. Consider one example that we worked on directly, HP Application Server 8.0. It integrated Sonic Software's SonicMQ version 4 JMS provider by leveraging the SonicMQ capability for promoting local transactions to global transactions. The HP Application Server container obtained locally transacted sessions from the SonicMQ XA connection. When the associated `XAResource` was registered with the HPAS JTA transaction manager, the local transaction managed by SonicMQ was transitioned to the application server's transaction manager.
- BEA WebLogic Server v 6.1 defined an interface that a JMS provider could implement to allow the EJB container to invoke a method that informs the provider that the original message was to be included in the global transaction. Although the interface was publicly available no vendors other than BEA provided an implementation.

The custom integrations are problematic because each JMS vendor and each application server must be integrated on a case-by-case basis to accommodate either's idiosyncrasies (e.g. the need to create two connections for SonicMQ as illustrated above). This is unlikely to be used widely in the industry moving forward, but you should be aware that it is present in versions of some servers that are widely in use, and may limit the extent to which they can work effectively with JMS providers for transacted delivery of messages.

A developer leveraging a J2EE environment unfortunately cannot rest assured that the receipt of a message within the MDB occurs within the scope of a global transaction irrespective of the integration details. In some cases, it may be that the behavior of the applications varies depending on the capabilities of the JMS provider and the application server. This is one of the areas where J2EE is less mature and the transactional integration capabilities of each paired JMS implementation and application server may vary. It's important to do your homework and make sure that the two implementations can be used together successfully.

The J2C expert group has made an attempt to alleviate these integration woes in the Java Connector Architecture 1.5 release. Generally, we have tried to avoid dwelling on future, unimplemented developments in the J2EE platform throughout the main body of this book. We believe it's far more useful to provide a realistic overview of what's currently available in the J2EE platform and also to point out potential pitfalls you may encounter.

However, one area of work that has been finalized in the specification process right now is support for adding integration capabilities to the Java Connector Architecture to support asynchronous resource managers. In practice, this means that a clearly defined path for integrating JMS providers with application servers in a standard way is under development. While we don't recommend you rely on this being available in the short term, it promises to be a potential solution to the mismatch between J2EE and JMS. This is something to watch for since it may broaden the scope and flexibility of JMS providers to application server integrations.

Another integration issue that you should be aware of relates to optimizations. As we've noted, it's quite common to require the ability to scope a database change along with a read or write of a message queue within the same transacted unit of work. This can occur in a case as simple as a database insert to create an audit trail for message delivery.

At first this requirement may appear to be the perfect use case for the two-phase commit protocol; in fact, many application architects assume they have no choice but to use two-phase commit, despite reservations about using a blocking completion protocol and the relative overhead involved. As it turns out, an alternative exists.

Some vendors provide a database resident message queue that can be accessed as a part of a local database transaction. This means that message delivery and database changes can be done together without the need for two-phase commit. How does this work?

In a nutshell, the message server is implemented as a database application. This means that from the resource manager's perspective, the message queue is just another set of relational database tables. To take advantage of this, the J2EE application server must provide a JMS client library that sits on top of a managed JDBC data source. Assuming the application server properly implements connection sharing for JDBC, it is possible to access the message queue and the database in the context of the same local transaction. The Oracle database, Oracle Advanced Queue technology, and the Oracle Application Server support this capability. The optimization is generally only available in an integrated product stack. For cases where different vendors' products are being used two-phase commit is necessary.

Example Application

Most of our survey of support for global transactions in JMS has dwelt on XA interfaces that are not used by applications directly. Let's look at how you use JMS sessions in a real application that sends messages and makes modifications to a relational database within a transaction. Our application implements an employee transfer and is similar to the one we examined in Chapter 4. In this case, however, the employee insert operation is implemented by sending a message to a Queue. As before, an employee may be deleted from a table maintained in a database. The use of transactions guarantees that the transfer as a whole respects the ACID properties. The source code can be downloaded directly from the book's Web site in a packaged form that is ready to execute.

```
1   package book.ch5.sample.xa;
2
3   import book.ch4.sample.xa.SampleJDBCServlet;
4   import book.ch4.sample.xa.EmployeeBean;
5
6   import javax.servlet.ServletException;
7   import javax.naming.Context;
8   import javax.naming.NamingException;
9   import javax.jms.*;
10
11  /**
12   * This servlet demonstrates the deletion of an
13   * employee and the sending of a message in a
14   * single, distributed transaction.
15   */
16  public class SampleJMSServlet
17      extends SampleJDBCServlet {
18
19    private static final String
20        QUEUE_CONNECTION_FACTORY_LOOKUP =
21        "java:comp/env/jms/XAQCF";
22    private static final String QUEUE_LOOKUP =
23        "java:comp/env/jms/QUEUE1";
24
25    /**
26     * Sends a message to add an employee. Recall
27     * that this method is invoked in the context of
28     * the transfer() method within the scope of a
```

```
29          * transaction.
30          */
31         protected void addEmployee
32            ( EmployeeBean employee )
33             throws ServletException
34         {
35           Context ctx = getJNDIContext ();
36           QueueSession session = null;
37           QueueConnection conn = null;
38           try
39           {
40             QueueConnectionFactory qcf =
41               (QueueConnectionFactory) ctx.lookup
42               ( QUEUE_CONNECTION_FACTORY_LOOKUP );
43             Queue queue =
44               (Queue) ctx.lookup ( QUEUE_LOOKUP );
45             conn = qcf.createQueueConnection();
46             session = conn.createQueueSession
47               ( false, Session.AUTO_ACKNOWLEDGE );
48             QueueSender sender = session.createSender
49               ( queue );
50             StreamMessage msg =
51               session.createStreamMessage ();
52             fillMessage ( msg, employee );
53             sender.send ( msg );
54           }
55           catch ( NamingException e )
56           {
57             throw new ServletException ( e );
58           }
59           catch ( JMSException e )
60           {
61             throw new ServletException ( e );
62           }
63           finally
64           {
65             try
66             {
67               session.close ();
68               conn.close ();
69             }
70             catch ( JMSException e )
71             {
72               throw new ServletException ( e );
73             }
74
75           }
76
```

```
77        }
78
79        /**
80         * Fills the employee information in the message.
81         */
82        private void fillMessage ( StreamMessage msg,
83           EmployeeBean employee ) throws JMSException
84        {
85           msg.setIntProperty ( "empNo",
86              employee.getEmpNo() );
87           msg.setStringProperty ( "ename",
88              employee.getEname () );
89           msg.setStringProperty ( "job",
90              employee.getJob () );
91           msg.setIntProperty ( "mgr",
92              employee.getMgr () );
93           msg.setStringProperty ( "hiredate",
94              formatDate ( employee.getHireDate () ) );
95           msg.setDoubleProperty ( "sal",
96              employee.getSal () );
97           msg.setDoubleProperty ( "comm",
98              employee.getComm () );
99           msg.setIntProperty ( "deptno",
100             employee.getDeptNo () );
101       }
102  }
```

We're going to walk through what happens in the application server when the servlet executes. Again, let's assume that the application server isn't pooling physical connections for simplicity's sake. When the deleteEmployee() method executes (this method is defined in the super class we introduced in Chapter 4), the application server will create a Connection. Before the Connection is returned to the client, the XAResource associated with the physical database Connection is returned and enlisted with the transaction. This in turn causes the transaction manager to generate an XID and assign it to the transaction branch in the resource manager. This behavior is exactly the same as we discussed our example in Chapter 4 for JDBC, where we provide even more detail about database connection management.

An analogous process will occur when the addEmployee() (line 31) method is executed, but in this case the JMS Session will be associated with the transaction. When the application requests a Session (line 46), the application server will detect that a transaction is associated with the current thread. The application server will acquire an XAConnectionFactory from which it will create an XAConnection. It will then use the XAConnection to create an XASession which represents the link to the message system. The application server will use the XASession to create both a Session and an XAResource. The XAResource will be enlisted with the transaction manager, which in turn will call the start() method with a new XID on the XAResource, instructing the XASession to treat subsequent interactions with the `Queue` as a part of the global transaction. Then the application server will wrap the `Session` and return it to the application. The JMS message will then be sent in the context of the global transaction. When the application calls `close()` on the `Session` (`line 67`), the application server will delist the `XAResource`. The transaction manager will invoke the `end()` method on the `XAResource`, signaling that the `Session` is no longer associated with transactional work.

When the application commits the transaction, the transaction manager will execute the two-phase commit protocol. The database and the JMS service will be asked to prepare their branches. If both resource managers are able to commit, they will in turn be instructed to do so.

For transacted receipt of messages, we strongly recommend you use Message-Driven Beans. We describe MDBs in greater detail in Chapter 6.

Summary

The Java Message Service provides a rich mapping of MOM capabilities into the Java environment, including the support of both local and global transactions. However, because of the early and independent development of JMS, the integration between application servers and JMS implementations is sometimes problematic, and must be evaluated on a case-by-case basis. The good news is that this situation is improving and there are important alternatives to global transactions that allow message queues and databases to be tied together.

Message-Oriented Middleware has been, and continues to be, a critical part of many enterprise solutions. Transactions are a key component of the value proposition offered by these messaging systems. The reliability and data integrity of message leveraging enterprise applications would not be possible if not for the evolving transactioning capabilities of these systems.

Enterprise JavaBeans and Transactions

The primary model for building business components that support transactions in the Java platform is provided by the Enterprise JavaBeans (EJB) specification. This chapter provides a basic summary of the EJB model, explains the support for transactions that is included with all of the different EJB component types, and takes a close look at how the containers help programmers to manage correct outcomes for applications.

N O T E In order to describe how transactions fit into the EJB model it's obviously important to have at least a basic understanding of what EJBs are—we've already covered the basics of transactions. If you already know about EJBs then you can skip this introductory section.

What Are EJBs?

The Enterprise JavaBeans specification defines a standard component model that reifies several important patterns in distributed enterprise software environments. These patterns are based largely on experience derived from building distributed object-based solutions and from years of experience with transaction monitor platform evolution. The separate EJB component types help to encapsulate the lifecycle events and system-level services that previously had to be coded by developers on a per-solution basis. This kind of ad hoc, low-level development is error prone and difficult, requiring an expertise not only in the business domain of the application, but also in distributed objects, transactional theory and security. While EJBs are a major innovation for the Java community, they represent a trend in software systems infrastructure that has been underway for some time.

In the mid-1990s, the enterprise software industry saw the development of a set of server technology offerings called Object Transaction Monitors (OTM). This infrastructure hosted distributed objects within "containers" that managed the object's lifecycle and provided intervention between client requests to inject system-level functions like transactions into the execution context for the business logic. The containers grew out of a convergence between transaction monitor technology based on procedural RPC or message queuing and distributed object paradigms like CORBA and Microsoft DCOM. In fact, Microsoft MTS and COM+, introduced in 1996, can be thought of as an early OTM offering. Similarly, BEA introduced an OTM called M3 based on CORBA and implemented in C++. Products like M3 were not commercially successful, but they heralded the development of a Java-centric container model for distributed, transactional components.

When the EJB model appeared, it was able to leverage the publicity torrent around Java and find adoption where other OTM application servers had failed. One reason for this success was that EJBs were based on a standard, whereas previous OTM offerings were proprietary and the components they hosted were not even close to being portable between different vendor offerings. In addition, EJBs benefited from aggressive marketing campaigns by Sun and other J2EE platform vendors during the height of technology investment in the late 1990s into 2000.

While the Object Management Group (OMG) was working on defining a CORBA standard for managed components, the Java Community Process (JCP) was working on the fourth major revision of the EJB specification. The adoption of a normal component model for encapsulating business logic and supporting system services is a major step forward in the industry.

The basic idea behind the component model for all EJBs is that the application server controls the actual bean instance that contains the business logic throughout its lifecycle. This also means that the application server will intervene in the calling client's method invocation (or message delivery). At this point, system services like transactions can be managed. The application server—or "container"—also takes care of error handling semantics. This may sound like the EJB model just provides an interception point to inject transactions. Not so: the container is responsible for creating, pooling, and destroying bean instances based on well-defined rules and lifecycle events; the EJB specification provides a contract for both containers and for bean implementers that helps to guarantee correct outcomes, especially in the face of failures or error—this is especially important when transactions are involved. It also provides an `EJBContext` that is accessible to the bean instance at runtime and allows the bean instance to be an active participant in the container-managed services.

There are three types of EJBs that can be accessed directly by method invocations: stateless session beans, stateful session beans, and entity beans. Stateless beans contain business logic that does not rely on per-client state; note, though, that a bean instance may contain state or hold on to resources like database connections across method invocations. Stateful session beans are defined for use by a single client and maintain conversational state. They may be thought of as analogous to Servlet sessions and have fixed lifespans controlled by timeout mechanisms and managed by the container. Entity beans are persistent objects that have the full declarative capabilities of EJBs. Developers leveraging entity beans may write their own persistence logic directly using the Bean-Managed Persistence (BMP) model or may rely on the persistence facilities provided by the application server using the Container-Managed Persistence (CMP) model.

The EJB CMP model was significantly refined in EJB 2.0. In that release as well, the specification introduced a new kind of bean, the message-driven bean, which was driven by the receipt of JMS messages. EJB 2.1 generalizes the model to accept messages from other kinds of EIS systems besides MOM implementations via new capabilities in the Java Connector Architecture, following an approach pioneered by Bluestone Software a number of years earlier.

It turns out that many applications use EJBs in combination with Servlets and other EJBs together in the same address space. Because EJBs were originally defined as remote objects with location transparency requirements, the EJB model required copy-by-value semantics for method parameters. However, in order to accommodate these co-location use cases and to make the new persistence model defined in EJB 2.0 useable, a local view of the EJB component was introduced. The local interface still involves indirect access to the bean via the container, but it provides a semantically valid way to relax the location transparency requirements.

If you need more in-depth coverage on the EJB model as an OTM solution, there are a number of books that cover the specification. We recommend either the EJB specification itself or the latest edition of the more comprehensible *Enterprise JavaBeans* by Richard Monson-Haefel; we have also provided links to an application server download with EJB tutorials and examples on the Web site for this book. As you read this chapter concerning the transactional aspects of the EJB component model, keep in mind that you should carefully consider the prudence of using EJBs in your applications. EJBs are an important tool to have at your disposal, but they are heavyweight components that have the potential to place significant latency and scalability constraints on your application if used improperly.

As a consequence, there is a recent movement afoot to introduce lightweight frameworks or even Aspect Oriented Programming (AOP) techniques as a replacement for EJBs in J2EE. While we believe some of these approaches may evolve in maturity to have their place in transactional applications, the lightweight frameworks we have seen so far overlook or fail to provide the kinds of semantic aid for transactional applications that is built into the EJB model. AOP, on the other hand, is based on the idea of applying functions to objects that are "oblivious" to the new behavior. We have serious reservations about this model for transactions; most of the early prototyping we've examined has shown a lack of grounding in the kinds of fundamentals this book focuses on. As a practical matter, you will probably want to take a wait-and-see attitude to these new techniques as they relate to transaction management.

Which brings us to a fundamental question about EJBs: when should you contemplate using them?

The general rule of thumb is to use EJBs when global transaction management is important for your application. In building three generations of EJB containers and using most major commercial and open source application servers we have concluded that you should predicate your use of EJBs on strong requirements for the system capabilities they provide. Don't avoid them when you need them and don't use them when they don't add value to your application. Trying to roll your own equivalent to EJB, on the other hand, is a mistake.

Since this book is about transactions, we spend a lot of space on EJBs. That doesn't mean they are the cure-all for every problem: one of our biggest complaints with J2EE is that the only object persistence mechanism on the platform is EJB entity beans with Container-Managed Persistence (CMP), leaving many architects looking at more mature and lightweight object-relational mapping tools like TopLink that can be used without entity beans.

Transaction Support

The current EJB transaction semantics were first introduced in the EJB 1.1 specification. This revision of the specification introduced a fairly substantial number of changes and improvements, swelling the specification to nearly triple the size of EJB 1.0. The deployment descriptor was recast from a Java class definition into an XML document that was both human-readable and writeable with standard XML tools or even text editors. This deployment descriptor supports the definition of two container types for session beans, stateful and stateless. In addition, the XML deployment descriptor allows session beans to be defined as having either bean or container-managed transactions. Bean-managed transactions are demarcated by the application logic in the bean instance itself. Container-managed transactions are started and ended by the container, though the bean instance can participate in the transaction management as well. The transaction management strategy is defined in the EJB XML DTDs as

```
<!ELEMENT transaction-type (#PCDATA)>
```

This element is a required child element for the session element. For example, a typical session bean may define its transaction type with the following descriptor segment:

```
<session>
    …
    <transaction-type>container</transaction-type>
    …
```

On the other hand, entity beans always have container-managed transactions.

If a bean is declared to have container-managed transactions, a separate container-transaction element should also be specified:

```
<!ELEMENT container-transaction (description?, method+, trans-
attribute)>
```

This indicates that the container transaction element may have an optional description, one or more methods specified, and a single transaction attribute. (For some reason, the EJB 1.1 Expert Group thought it was a good idea to truncate transaction to "trans;" we spell things out and avoid that confusing idiom).

Container-managed transactions are used in a majority of bean deployments. Let's explore them in greater detail.

Container-Managed Transactions

Container-managed transactions are at the heart of the EJB component model. Instead of writing difficult and error prone system code for controlling distributed transactions, the EJB model allows the container to handle the initiation of transactions, the termination of transactions, and the recovery from errors based on well-defined rules. In fact, the container even plays an important role with beans that are labeled as supporting bean-managed transactions, which is required in order to properly support error recovery and management of state-transaction association for stateful session beans. We discuss this behavior in detail below, as it is critical to successfully managing transactional behavior with EJBs.

There are a number of transaction attributes defined by the EJB specification that may be specified for a bean method declared as requiring container management of its transactions. They are `NotSupported`, `Supports`, `Required`, `RequiresNew`, `Mandatory`, and `Never`.

NotSupported

This attribute indicates that a business method should never be executed in the context of a transaction by the container. However, the caller is allowed to invoke the bean's remote (or local) interface with an active transaction context. In that case, the container will suspend the transaction for the duration of the method dispatch and resume the transaction when the method completes. Recall that suspended transactions are still active, but they are no longer associated with the current thread of control.

Technically, the method is executed in an unspecified transaction context, which provides the container several options for how to deal with access to underlying resource managers from a transactional standpoint. In practice, many containers will simply assume that no container intervention is required or desired. However, according to the EJB specification it is entirely permissible for the container to follow one or any combination of the following strategies:

- The container may invoke the method without any transaction context.
- The container may treat each call of an EJB instance to a resource manager as a single transaction. In the case of JDBC, this means that the container would set the auto-commit flag to "true" on the connection.
- The container may merge multiple calls of an EJB instance to a resource manager into a single transaction.
- The container may merge multiple calls of an EJB instance to multiple resource managers into a single transaction.
- If the bean instance invokes other EJBs that run in an unspecified transaction context, the container may merge the resource manager calls for all EJBs into a single transaction.

The EJB specification recommends that bean developers write beans "conservatively" so as not to rely on a particular container behavior. In the case of the `NotSupported` transactional attribute it is best to assume no container intervention. If you do deploy a bean to a container that implements one of the optional strategies above (and your logic depends on one of these strategies) you should be aware that problems may arise if you port your application to a different container. One serious anti-practice we have observed is for developers to write EJB applications on an open source or reference implementation EJB container and deploy to production-quality commercial application servers: get to know as much about your intended deployment platform as early as possible in the development process.

Generally speaking, we have not seen many use cases where `NotSupported` makes sense. You might use it when the bean is dependent on the use of a resource manager that lacks transactional capabilities or well-defined integrations with the application server product. In that case all methods on the bean most likely should use this attribute.

Supports

The `Supports` attribute indicates that the container should defer the creation of a transaction to the bean method caller. Thus, the container may allow the invocation of the business method within the transaction context of a caller. However, the method may also be called with no transaction context associated with the caller. In that case, the method will be invoked in an unspecified transaction context according to the semantics we explained for the `NotSupported` transaction attribute. `Supports` is best used for methods that do not require a transaction but can be used in conjunction with one. For example, a method that simply reads a database table doesn't need to be executed in a transaction if used by itself, but can be made dependent on a larger unit of work when appropriate.

The `Supports` attribute is commonly the default transaction attribute for enterprise beans in most vendor EJB container implementations.

Required

This attribute indicates that the business method must be invoked in the context of a transaction. If there is a transaction associated with the caller, that transaction is associated with the method invocation. If the caller does not have an associated transaction, the container starts a new transaction prior to invoking the business method on the bean instance, and subsequently terminates the transaction when the business method has returned.

The `Required` attribute assumes that the method will do non-atomic updates and that it is appropriate to include these updates in a unit of work initiated by another bean.

RequiresNew

`RequiresNew` indicates that the bean will always be invoked in the context of a new transaction. If the caller invokes the method within a transaction, the container will suspend that transaction and start a new transaction before calling the actual business method. When the business method completes, the container will terminate the existing transaction and resume the caller's transaction. This means that the outcome of the transaction associated with the business method has no effect on the transaction of the caller.

RequiresNew creates an independent transaction. Use this attribute if the method can result in non-atomic changes to shared resources but should not be dependent on an externally managed unit of work. You should have a very good reason for using RequiresNew; it is a poor choice for a default.

Mandatory

If this transaction attribute is specified for a bean method, callers without a transaction context will receive a subclass of java.rmi.RemoteException, the JTA exception javax.transaction.TransactionRequiredException (or, in the case of a local client invocation, the javax.ejb.TransactionRequiredLocalException). The container will not attempt to start a transaction on behalf of the caller.

This attribute should be used when a failure of the business method needs to be correlated closely with the transactional integrity of resources associated with the caller's transaction. In other words, this attribute should be used to guarantee that changes to shared resources are always changed in the context of a larger unit of work. A transaction attribute like Required cannot enforce this because it only provides a guarantee that a transaction will exist. It does not require that a client initiate the transaction.

Never

The Never attribute was added with the release of the EJB 1.1 specification. If a bean method assigned the Never attribute is invoked while the caller is part of a transaction, the container will throw a RemoteException to remote client or an EJBException to local clients and the method will never execute. However, if the caller is not associated with a transaction, the container will dispatch the method on the bean instance and the method will execute normally. The method will be invoked in an unspecified transaction context according to the semantics we described for the NotSupported transaction attributes. Never, however, has stronger semantics and may be used as a runtime check to ensure that the calling client does not misuse the bean method, assuming that a successful method invocation results in changes scoped within the clients transaction.

Table 6-1 summarizes the behavior associated with each of the EJB transaction attributes.

Table 6-1 Transaction Attribute Summary

Transaction Attribute	Client's Transaction	Transaction Associated with Business Method	Transaction Associated with Resource Manager
NotSupported	None	None	None
	T1	None	None
Required	None	T2	T2
	T1	T1	T1
Supports	None	None	None
	T1	T1	T1
RequiresNew	None	T2	T2
	T1	T2	T2
Mandatory	None	ERROR	N/A
	T1	T1	T1
Never	None	None	None
	T1	ERROR	N/A

Specifying Container-Managed Transactions

A typical container transaction element in an EJB deployment descriptor looks like the following:

```
<container-transaction>
    <method>
      <ejb-name>EmployeeBean</ejb-name>
      <method-name>provideRaise</method-name>
    </method>
    <trans-attribute>Required</trans-attribute>
<container-transaction/>
```

The EJB specification states that the assignment of transaction attributes is the job of the application assembler and goes to great length to define roles for each stage of the development lifecycle to attempt to provide flexibility and separation of concerns between bean developers and application "assemblers," or architects. This is also aimed at trying to ensure reusability of components, but often doesn't map to real-life use case scenarios. In practice, the transaction semantics of the bean will often need to be determined by the developer.

It is possible to omit the transaction attribute of a method, since the DTD does not enforce any rules that all methods must be mapped. The resulting behavior is container-dependent. Most containers will default to the Supports transaction attribute, but you should take care to avoid this ambiguity and ensure that beans developed for a specific project have completed deployment descriptors that explicitly specify the transaction attributes for all bean methods.

Authors of beans using container-managed transactions should not attempt to access the JTA `UserTransaction` object from either the `javax.ejb.EJBContext` instance corresponding to the EJB or the JNDI context that defines the bean's environment (i.e., from a JNDI lookup of the string "`java:comp/UserTransaction`"). This will result in the container throwing a `java.lang.IllegalStateException`.

Finally, when programming with container-managed transactions, there are several important rules to be aware of with respect to the invocation of the methods defined for the `javax.ejb.EJBContext` object. If the `EJBContext.setRollbackOnly()` method is called from a business method whose transaction attribute is either `Required`, `RequiresNew` or `Mandatory` then the container must make sure that the transaction will not commit. Most implementations will communicate directly with the transaction manager to mark the transaction for a rollback. If the container initiated the transaction, the container itself must roll back the transaction. While the transaction itself will be rolled back, the container will not affect the reply from the bean instance method to the calling client. If the method returns a value to the client, the container will allow the reply to proceed independent of whether the transaction was marked for rollback by the bean instance.

However, access to the `EJBContext.setRollbackOnly()` method from within a method with a transaction attribute of `Supports`, `NotSupported`, or `Never` will result in a `java.lang.IllegalStateException` since the container does not initiate a transaction when one of these is specified. The same rule applies to the `EJBContext.getRollbackOnly()` method: if the method transaction attribute is `Supports`, `NotSupported`, or `Never`, the container will generate a `java.lang.IllegalStateException`.

In addition to container-managed transactions, bean developers do have the option of managing their own transactions for certain bean types. This alternate scheme makes use of bean-managed transactions.

Bean-Managed Transactions

As the name implies, EJBs that use bean-managed transactions manage their own transaction initiation and termination. However, the container still has an important role to play since it enforces well-defined rules that limit how bean developers can use transactions, principally to ensure that transactions that are initiated by bean developers are terminated correctly. Most importantly, only session beans and message driven beans may use the bean-managed transaction demarcation.

For bean-managed transactions, bean instances establish and manage transactions via the JTA `javax.transaction.UserTransaction` interface, which can be acquired from either the `EJBContext` associated with the bean instance or from the environment via a JNDI lookup. The container is responsible for ensuring enlistment of resource manager drivers and for the coordination of the commit or rollback:

```
Context initCtx = new InitialContext();
UserTransaction utx = (UserTransaction)initCtx.lookup(
"java:comp/UserTransaction");
utx.begin();
...
utx.commit();
```

When a client invokes a business method on a bean with bean-managed transactions via the home, remote or local interface, the container will always suspend any transaction associated with the client's request. However, the container behaves differently when managing transactions for stateful vs. stateless session beans with bean-managed transactions.

If the bean instance for a stateful session bean had previously initiated a transaction, then the transaction is associated with the request after the caller's transaction has been suspended. This condition occurs when a business method completes without terminating the transaction it has initiated; because stateful session beans are associated with a single client and maintain conversational state, this is allowed. When the method returns, the container must suspend any transaction associated with the bean instance, and if a transaction was associated with the original client request, the container must resume the original transaction. The container is responsible for managing and maintaining the associations, illustrating that the container still has a lot of work to do for bean-managed transaction scenarios.

On the other hand, a stateless session bean must terminate any transactions it initiates within a business method prior to returning. Stateless session bean instances are interchangeable between business method invocations and may, for example, be pooled. Maintaining an association between the instance and a transaction across multiple requests would be a serious error that would likely affect data integrity since the same bean may be shared by many clients serially. For example, a pooled stateless session bean that maintained a transaction association across requests could modify data for two clients in the context of the same transaction. So if the container finds that a stateless session bean returns from a business method without committing or rolling back a transaction it has initiated, the container must do the following in order:

1. Log an application error to alert the system administrator.
2. Roll back the started transaction.
3. Discard the instance of the session bean because it is erroneously maintaining state associated with a client.
4. Throw a `java.rmi.RemoteException` if the client is remote or a `javax.ejb.EJBException` if the client is local.

For either stateful or stateless session beans, the container must allow the bean instance to start and terminate any number of transactions serially within the business method. If a bean instance attempts to start a transaction while already in a transaction by invoking `begin()` on the `UserTransaction` interface (or any other method, for that matter), the container will throw a `javax.transaction.NotSupportedException` from the `begin` method:

this would mean that the container supported nested transactions, which are disallowed in EJBs. If a bean attempts to use `setRollbackOnly()` or `getRollbackOnly()` methods on the `EJBContext` object, the container will generate a `java.lang.IllegalStateException` as these methods are reserved for beans with container-managed transaction demarcation.

Given the availability of both container-managed and bean-managed transactions, a developer should consider a number of factors in deciding which transactioning scheme is appropriate.

BMT vs. CMT

If you've worked with EJBs for some time, you may have heard complaints or discovered that early versions of Container-Managed Persistence (CMP) often provided less satisfactory results than alternative forms of object persistence in terms of scalability and performance. But when people were questioning the usefulness of early CMP implementations, we were often asked if developers should also be wary of container-managed transactions.

We'd have to say the answer to that is a resounding "no." It's unlikely that you will gain an appreciable increase in performance or scalability attempting to manage distributed transactions yourself, and in fact, the container still has to do a lot of work when processing an EJB with bean-managed transactions. Moreover, the container's support for declarative transactions encapsulates all of the use cases that you are likely to require for a managed component. Since a widely deployed container also is likely to be battle-hardened from vendor testing, J2EE compatibility testing, and customer use, you're also likely to have much less room for error if you choose to rely on the container to manage the transactional behavior of your application. Even simple transaction processing code can be error prone, and mistakes are likely to effect data integrity and application invariants that compromise correctness.

When you program with declarative transactions, you can largely omit any code from the system that deals with transactions. In fact, even the choice of whether to roll back or commit a transaction can be delegated to the container based on error handling characteristics of the EJB model. Our rule of thumb is that you should strongly prefer using container-managed transactions for EJBs unless you have a compelling reason not to.

Once the appropriate transaction behavior is chosen, it's important to have a solid understanding of the error handling behavior of the EJB container to properly design and implement your application's beans. We emphasize repeatedly that the automated assistance in error handling and recovery semantics the container provides is an important aid to achieving correct outcomes in your application. This is something you will be unlikely to benefit from in homegrown transaction management solutions.

Error Handling

The EJB container defines normal error handling models for transaction handling that varies by bean type, whether or not the container is managing transactions. This means that developers do not have to explicitly write the same error handling and recovery routines over and over, and ensures that the rules are sensible—a nontrivial task. On the other hand, both bean developers and EJB clients must understand these rules, as they will be enforced without exception in a standard conformant container. The rules for transaction handling are shown in Table 6-2 and Table 6-3:

Table 6-2 Handling of exceptions thrown by a business method of a bean with **container-managed** transaction demarcation (From EJB 2.1 Specification, Section 18.3.1, Table 15)

Method Condition	Method Exception	Container's Action	Client's View
Bean method runs in the context of the caller's transaction (`Required`, `Mandatory`, and `Supports` attributes)	`AppException`	Re-throw `AppException`	Receives `AppException` Can attempt to continue computation in the transaction, and eventually commit the transaction (the commit would fail if the instance called `setRollbackOnly()`)
	All other exceptions and errors	Log the exception or error Mark the transaction for roll back Discard instance Throw `TransactionRolledBackException` to remote client or `TransactionRolledbackLocalException` to local client.	Receives `TransactionRolledBackException` or `TransactionRolledbackLocalException` Continuing transaction is pointless.
Bean method runs in the context of a transaction the container started immediately before business method dispatch (`Required` and `RequiresNew`)	`AppException`	If the instance called `setRollbackOnly()` roll back transaction and re-throw `AppException`. Otherwise, attempt to commit the transaction and re-throw `AppException`.	Receives `AppException` Can attempt to continue computation in the transaction, and eventually commit the transaction (the commit would fail if the instance called `setRollbackOnly()`)
	All other exceptions and errors	Log the exception or error Mark the transaction for roll back Discard instance Throw `RemoteException` to remote client or `EJBException` to local client.	Receives `RemoteException` or `EJBException` If client executes in a transaction it is not marked for roll back and client can continue work.

Table 6-2 Handling of exceptions thrown by a business method of a bean with **container-managed** transaction demarcation (From EJB 2.1 Specification, Section 18.3.1, Table 15) (continued)

Method Condition	Method Exception	Container's Action	Client's View
Bean method runs with an unspecified transaction context (`NotSupported`, `Never`, and `Supports` attributes)	`AppException`	Re-throw `AppException`	Receives `AppException` If the client executes in a transaction, the client's transaction is not marked for roll back, and client can continue work.
	All other exceptions and errors	Log the exception or error Discard instance Throw `RemoteException` to remote client or EJBException to local client.	Receives `RemoteException or EJBException` If the client executes in a transaction, the client's transaction may or may not be marked for roll back

Table 6-3 Handling of exceptions thrown by a business method of a session with **bean-managed** transaction demarcation (From EJB 2.1 Specification, Section 18.3.1, Table 16)

Method Condition	Method Exception	Container's Action	Client's View
Bean is stateful or stateless.	`AppException`	Re-throw `AppException`	Receives `AppException`
	All other exceptions and errors	Log the exception or error Mark for rollback a transaction that has been started, but not yet completed, by the instance. Discard instance Throw `RemoteException` to remote client or `EJBException` to local client.	Receives `RemoteException or EJBException`

These rules have implications for bean developers and EJB clients. For application exceptions, the bean developer needs to ensure that the exception does not leave the bean in an unusable state. Application exceptions do not indicate that the bean is invalid; rather, they indicate that there is an exceptional condition or error anticipated by the developer—bear in mind that the container has no way to validate application semantics and will not enforce a transaction roll back. The bean developer might need to do additional work to clean up database changes or mark the current transaction for rollback; moreover, the bean developer should leverage the standard EJB application exceptions for recoverable problems during creates, finds or removes.

If the transaction is initiated by or propagated from the client and the business method throws an application exception, the client must make a decision as to whether the transaction should roll back or continue. If the client did not initiate the transaction, it may still mark the transaction for rollback if appropriate or ensure through some other means that the container will roll back the transaction:

```
try {
    // attempt a given business method
    bean.method1();
} catch ( AppException e ) {
    // mark the transaction for roll back due to receipt of
    // application exception
    bean.getEJBContext().setRollbackOnly ();
}
```

System exceptions are generally unexpected `RuntimeExceptions`, `java.rmi.RemoteExceptions`, JVM errors, and so on. System exceptions are interpreted differently by the container, which assumes that something fundamentally unanticipated has occurred in the system for which there may not have been a recovery mechanism. For this reason, bean instances are discarded and stateful session beans are completely invalidated. Since the container must assume that data inconsistency may result, it will always set a rollback on the current transaction. This is a subtle but important mechanism to help application developers maintain the consistency aspect of ACID properties.

If the client propagated the transaction into the container, then that transaction will be marked for rollback and the client will either receive a `javax.transaction.TransactionRolledBackException` (a subclass of `java.rmi.RemoteException`) or a `javax.ejb.TransactionRolledbackLocalTransaction` (a subclass of `javax.ejb.EJBException`) if it is local. This assures the client that the transaction was in fact rolled back. If a generic exception is returned to the client, it may have insufficient information about the transaction's status, as there is not a strict guarantee that the request failure occurred within the container. It may have failed, for example, in the transport layers. At this point, it's best to roll back the transaction explicitly or to mark the transaction for roll back if it was initiated by another caller.

Bean Types and Transactions

Each of the different EJB types that represent component patterns for request-response interactions (stateful, stateless, and entity beans) demonstrate similar behavioral characteristics in transactional scenarios.

For session beans with bean-managed transactions, transactional behavior varies based on the capacity of the type to participate in conversational state management. If a transaction is initiated within the component for a stateless session bean and that transaction is not committed before the business method returns, the container will intervene by rolling back the transaction and generating a `RemoteException or EJBException` that is propagated to a remote or local client, respectively; the bean instance is then disposed of by the container.

Recall that a stateless session bean is not permitted to maintain state related to a particular client. For this reason many containers manage a pool of stateless session beans so that beans may be efficiently recycled to service different client invocations. If a transaction remained associated with the bean instance when it was pooled, the bean would execute in the context of the transaction on behalf of another client, which would be a serious error.

On the other hand, since stateful session beans are explicitly associated with a single client and are designed to maintain conversational state, they are explicitly permitted to remain associated with a transaction between requests. This will occur when the bean instance initiates a transaction, but does not terminate the transaction before the method returns control to the container. In this case, the container will do nothing and the transaction will remain associated with the bean.

For example, the following stateful session bean code that retains a transaction across two methods (invoked in sequence by the client) is allowed (note that some of the exception handling is omitted to make the example clearer):

```
1    public class SampleSessionEJB implements SessionBean {
2        EJBContext ejbContext;
3        DataSource ds1, ds2;
4        Connection conn1, conn2;
5
6        Public void method1() {
7          Statement stmt;
8          // obtain the component JNDI context
9          Context ctx = new InitialContext();
10
11          // obtain the UserTransaction
12          UserTransaction ut =
13                  ejbContext.getUserTransaction ();
14          // start a transaction
15          ut.begin ();
16
17          // execute database updates
18          ds1 = (DataSource) ctx.lookup ( "jdbc/ds1" );
```

```
19          conn1 = ds1.getConnection();
20          stmt = ds1.createStatement ();
21          stmt.executeUpdate (. . .);
22
23          stmt.close();
24          conn1.close();
25
26          // note that the transaction has not been
27          // committed or rolledback.  Therefore, the
28          // container maintains the association
29              // between the bean and the transaction for
30              // subsequent method invocations.
31      }
32
33      public void method2() {
34          Statement stmt;
35          // obtain the component JNDI context
36          Context ctx = new InitialContext();
37
38          // obtain the UserTransaction
39          UserTransaction ut =
40                  ejbContext.getUserTransaction ();
41
42          // execute database updates against another
43          // database
44          ds2 = (DataSource) ctx.lookup
45                  ( "jdbc/ds2" );
46          conn2 = ds2.getConnection();
47          stmt = ds2.createStatement ();
48          stmt.executeUpdate (. . .);
49
50          // the transaction initiated is method1
51              // is now committed
52          ut.commit();
53
54          stmt.close();
55          conn2.close();
56      }
57  }
```

Note in the example that a client invoking method1() initiates a transaction (line 15) that does not terminate until the client invokes method2() (line 52).

A complete example of an application utilizing a BMT bean such as the one above is available for download from the Oracle Technology Network (http://otn.oracle.com/tech/java/oc4j/htdocs/how-to-ejb-tx-X-Calls.html).

While associated with a transaction, including while the bean is not servicing requests, the bean instance is ineligible for "passivation" by the container. Passivation is a mechanism the container can use to release resources held on behalf of an inactive client. Beans in transactions may not be passivated both because there is no mechanism for externalizing a reference to the transaction and because the state of the bean may be tied to the outcome of the transaction.

For these same reasons, the clustering of stateful session beans engaged in a transaction should also be avoided unless the cluster replication mechanism in the application server can behave as a transactional resource manager as well. So while maintaining a transactional association across multiple business methods is a valid usage scenario for stateful session beans, it is not something that we recommend employing as it actually compromises the application server's ability to manage the scalability, replication and lifecycle of the EJB without adding clear benefits.

Stateful session beans also may optionally implement the `SessionSynchronization` interface:

```
public interface javax.ejb.SessionSynchronization
{
    void afterBegin() throws javax.ejb.EJBException,
java.rmi.RemoteException;
    void beforeCompletion() throws javax.ejb.EJBException,
java.rmi.RemoteException;
    void afterCompletion(boolean committed) throws
javax.ejb.EJBException, java.rmi.RemoteException;
}
```

This interface provides beans with notification about the lifecycle of the transaction with which they are associated. This can be helpful if the transaction is coordinating database access and behavior, especially if it is delegating logic to other EJBs. We have seen this used most frequently as a mechanism for setting initial state in the data members of stateful session beans. The bean is said to be in the Transactional Method-Ready State when the container invokes the callback methods on the `SessionSynchronization` interface. If you are using the `SessionSynchronization` interface your bean methods should have transaction attributes `Required`, `RequiresNew` or `Mandatory` to ensure the execution of the synchronization logic since it is dependent on a transaction being in place during execution.

Entity beans have different transaction management requirements primarily because they are designed to provide object models on top of different kinds of data stores. Since they are inherently linked to data access, they are the component type that most often requires transactions, though in many applications, the transactions can be limited to one-phase commit. Beans that use Container-Managed Persistence should execute in a transaction. Since multiple entity beans may be chained together to form a persistent object model, the `Required` attribute is most commonly used for the methods of CMP entity beans.

Similarly, transactions may need to scope multiple method invocations on a single bean. The transaction needs to be present from initial interaction with the bean, as entity beans are often pooled, but the state within the bean in the pool is meaningless. Therefore, when the bean is retrieved from the pool, the container must invoke the `ejbLoad()` method to initialize the state for the request or transaction.

Entity beans are not allowed to have bean-managed transactions and the behavioral characteristics of entity beans with respect to lifecycle and transactions are the same for both entities with bean-managed persistence and container-managed persistence. The most interesting aspects of bean-managed transactions involve the data synchronization strategies associated with potentially shareable state. This is generally addressed by the container's locking strategy.

Optimistic Locking

Optimistic locking assumes that data collisions occur infrequently, i.e., rarely will two records in the database be accessed simultaneously. Given this assumption a system will not attempt to prevent these collisions but will simply choose to detect and resolve them in those rare instances when they occur.

Application servers may provide many implementation strategies for optimistic locking. As an example, we examine the straightforward case where the optimistic locking strategy is implemented by utilizing a "lock column" added to a database table. This column holds a value, such as an integer value or timestamp that is altered each time changes are committed to the given row in the database. This column is checked during an update to the record to see whether an optimistic transaction should succeed or fail.

For example, a database table representing customer orders may include a version column. When a given row is selected its version number is recorded. In order to modify the number of items in an order whose version number was 1 the container would generate the following update statement:

```
UPDATE ORDERS SET NUM_ITEMS=3, VERSION=2 WHERE ORDER_ID=1 AND VERSION=1
```

The container considers an affected row count of zero an optimistic lock failure (whether the failure is due to the lack of an existing record or a version mismatch is inconsequential – both are considered error conditions).

Regardless of the implementation strategy, when an optimistic lock implementation detects a contention issue for a dataset, the first update is successful but all subsequent update attempts scoped by contending transactions result in an exception.

Optimistic locking may be employed in conjunction with a distributed cache mechanism for clustered application servers—although it can be used with a single server quite effectively. In this scenario, the local cache can be used in lieu of database access in many cases. Optimistic locking is often more efficient in applications that are extremely read intensive and do not have much contention with respect to changes in the persistent state modeled by the entity beans.

At first this kind of aggressive caching seems very attractive. However, there are implications to this approach that need to be considered. If an application server employs this kind of optimistic locking and cache combination, it's important that the underlying data store not be changed by anything outside of the EJBs participating in the cache environment, unless a cache callback trigger can be used to alert the cache to the change. This is important because the application server is taking responsibility for the data and changes to the underlying data store will result in corruption of the data in the cache. Obviously, this can affect data consistency if the application is making changes based on a stale cache. It's not uncommon for data stores to be modified by batch jobs scheduled at odd hours: if this is the case, it could spell trouble for your application if you are relying on this kind of cache strategy.

Some application servers allow optimistic locking to be managed directly by a database. For example, Oracle Application Server supports delegating locking to the Oracle database and relies on a close integration with the database. It can be much more efficient than timestamp or versioned optimistic locking, since it occurs natively in the database. This option also relies on database specific behavior. As always, there's a tradeoff between performance and portability.

Pessimistic Locking

Pessimistic locking takes a different view of the underlying data store: it assumes that someone is going to mess with your data, and always engages the data store in a transaction for both data retrieval and updates. This doesn't necessarily mean that the data is retrieved from the store on every request and written to the store at the end of the business method, though this is often the case for pessimistic locking of entity beans when no global transaction is involved. Even this "tight loop" of data synchronization does not provide a guarantee against data corruption since the data store itself is not locking data against concurrent access and modification.

Most application servers provide a pessimistic locking scheme by deferring the locking to the underlying database. In some cases, this may be initiated on the first interaction with the database, even for "select" statements. With Oracle's database, for example, the container may force the database lock by utilizing the "select for update" SQL predicate in CMP beans. This query will lock the selected record until the transaction is committed; without these extra semantics, a lock will only be initiated by a database change or update.

It's important to understand that the container is likely to cache the state of the bean without updating the database for the duration of the transaction when one is in place. In other words, the EJB container typically reads from the database as beans are accessed throughout a transaction and writes the data back to the database when the transaction is committed. This guarantees that the business methods may operate on the data without manipulation of the data set in the underlying store. Applications that modify shared data frequently should consider using pessimistic locking.

A frequent point of confusion for many developers is the fact that many application servers allow multiple entity beans in memory or within a cluster for a single primary key concurrently. For most scenarios—the exceptional case is a fully transacted system with serializable isolation levels—this is an important implementation detail for ensuring adequate request throughput in the system. Because the data stores maintain isolation semantics, the container can rely on the underlying data store to manage the correctness of the data based on the isolation constraints that we discussed earlier, so independent, "competing" clients are actually dealing with different views of the data.

The selection of a locking strategy will be proprietary to each application server. In some cases, it may be dependent on the persistence engine if a third-party CMP implementation is used. The EJB specification itself has adopted a less than adequate terminology and categorization for transaction data management schemes: Commit Option A, Commit Option B, and Commit Option C. While we find these categorizations most unhelpful, we explain them so you will know what the terminology means if you see it used. We recommend you dig deeper into any vendor's product implementation to really understand what kind of data cache, locking and bean management is occurring in reality.

Commit Options

Commit Option A indicates that the container caches a "ready" bean instance between transactions. In addition, the container knows that the bean instances have exclusive access to the objects in the database. Therefore, the container does not have to synchronize the instances' state to or from persistent storage at the beginning of a transaction.

Commit Option B requires the container to cache "ready" bean instances between transactions as well. However, in this case, the container recognizes that it does not have exclusive access to the objects in the database. Therefore, the container must synchronize the state of the instance from the database at the beginning of a transaction if its state has changed in the database; a transaction, to be successfully committed, must only operate on data that is in sync with the database at the beginning of the transaction.

Commit Option C relies on entity pooling and data refreshes on transaction boundaries. This is in some sense the simplest, cluster-friendly implementation strategy (although somewhat costly in terms of performance).

As you might imagine, the richness of interactions between caches, data stores, and containers isn't quite captured in the specification. In addition to understanding and employing the correct locking scheme, a bean provider must ensure that the proper isolation levels are utilized to guarantee the application's data integrity.

Isolation Levels

While isolation is a key part of the ACID properties we described while discussing transaction fundamentals, enforcing isolation can be expensive in terms of application performance. Allowing variation in isolation levels provides a mechanism to "relax" the isolation requirements associated with data within a transaction, which can often provide significant improvements in system throughput performance and help to eliminate potential deadlocks in the system. The relaxation of isolation levels must be carefully coordinated with business logic so that data corruption does not result.

The EJB specification is a little disingenuous in this area. For example, the specification makes the claim that in general the API for managing isolation levels is specific to a given type of resource manager and therefore, the EJB specification itself does not define an isolation level management API. This could be normalized, of course, and is the least problematic part of controlling isolation levels within a container or application code. As we've noted, container management of isolation levels doesn't work.

In addition, the EJB specification does state that a bean developer may choose to set different isolation levels for the interactions with different resource managers in a transaction programmatically. However, great care should be taken when doing so; allowing a variation in isolation could potentially lead to unpredictable results particularly if another bean or method attempts to access the same resource manager. Changing isolation levels in the midst of a transaction will more than likely lead to undesirable results. In most cases, it is not allowed and in some extreme cases a sync point may be set by the resource manager, which is an implicit commit of work done to that point. While the specification states that the developer must ensure that the isolation level of a resource manager is not altered programmatically when multiple beans interact with the given resource manager in single transaction, this is error prone at best.

As we've noted previously, CMP classes may alter isolation levels to achieve locking strategies. Unfortunately, this can lead to a conflict generated by a calling transaction with enlisted resources. For this reason, it's best to isolate database accesses solely to CMP beans when using this strategy and to make sure all beans that may interact in a persistence relationship use the same locking strategy.

As a general strategy for controlling isolation levels, we recommend setting fixed isolation levels for resource adapters via configuration.

Message-Driven Beans

Message-Driven Beans (MDB) is a new component model introduced in EJB 2.0. We treat it separately from the other bean types because it is fundamentally different: it has no client-facing view. Message-Driven Beans reside in an application server's EJB container and act as asynchronous message listeners (see Figure 6-1). They can leverage all of the enterprise facilities afforded by the container, such as security, concurrency, and transactioning, while simultaneously supporting a simpler programming model for message consumers than is the one defined in the JMS specification directly.

The MDB model can also support concurrent processing of a stream of messages by leveraging application server thread pools and pools of bean instances. The MDB allows developers to leverage the robust infrastructure of an application server to create secure, fault-tolerant, and scalable JMS consumers. If you haven't read our discussion of JMS in Chapter 5, now is a good time to familiarize yourself with the JMS model and its transactional capabilities.

Message-Driven Beans are anonymous, stateless beans that have no client-visible identity of any sort. A client application has no direct knowledge of an MDB but rather sends messages to a given JMS destination for which the MDB acts as a message consumer. Since the bean has

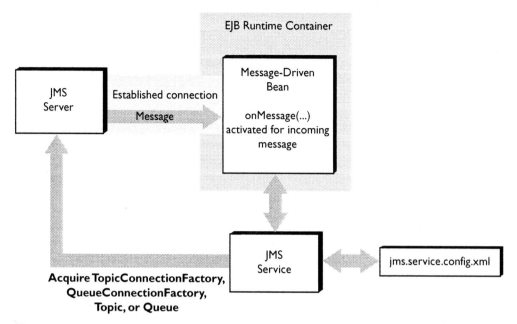

Figure 6-1   Message-Driven Bean in an EJB container.

no business methods that are invoked directly by EJB clients there is no need for the home and remote interfaces required of other enterprise bean types.

Creating a message receiving application using MDBs is simpler than a corresponding pure JMS application since the container performs a number of the required preliminary steps. While an MDB is instantiated and initialized the container creates a message consumer (`TopicSubscriber` or `QueueReceiver`) to receive the bean's messages based on the configured destination and connection factory. The bean is subsequently registered with the given message consumer. A developer may optionally also specify a durable subscription for topics or use a message selector during deployment. The message-driven bean itself only needs to implement the following methods:

```
public void ejbRemove();
public void setMessageDrivenContext(MessageDrivenContext
context);
```

In order to receive JMS messages, the bean must also implement the `javax.jms.MessageListener` interface, which defines the `onMessage( Message message )` method. We discuss JMS message listeners in more depth in Chapter 5.

The runtime management of messaging interactions is also simplified with message-driven beans. The container is responsible for handling message acknowledgement for the deployed bean. The form of message acknowledgement is dependent on the transaction mode utilized by the bean.

If the bean is using container-managed transactions the container will perform the message acknowledgement as part of the transaction commit. However, if bean-managed transactions are used the container will perform the acknowledgement as dictated by the acknowledgement mode specified in the deployment descriptor, which may be set to either `AUTO_ACKNOWLEDGE` or `DUPS_OK_ACKNOWLEDGE`; if nothing is specified, `AUTO_ACKNOWLEDGE` JMS semantics are assumed. One important difference is that a message-driven bean developer should not attempt to use the JMS API for message acknowledgement, which means that message grouping is not supported.

In order to properly code and deploy message-driven beans it is important to understand the means by which the EJB container manages the transaction context associated with a bean invocation.

Managing MDB Transactions

A message driven bean's deployment descriptor can specify that the container's invocation of the `onMessage()` method occur with no transactional context, with container-managed transaction demarcation, or bean-managed transaction demarcation. If the bean deployer chooses one of the two transactional modes the bean can participate in a distributed transaction.

Bean-Managed Transactions

An MDB with bean-managed transaction demarcation can initiate a transaction during the container's invocation of the `onMessage()` method. The bean developer can initiate, commit, or roll back a transaction via the `javax.transaction.UserTransaction` interface accessible via the bean's `javax.ejb.EJBContext` interface or by looking it up in the bean's JNDI context under the name `java:comp/UserTransaction`.

The `UserTransaction` interface provides methods for initiating (`begin()`), committing (`commit()`) or rolling back (`rollback()`) bean-managed transactions. The container is responsible for enlisting all resource managers accessed during the transaction with the JTA transaction manager. Once committed, the transaction manager will perform the two-phase commit across all enlisted resource managers. If only a single resource manager is employed and connection sharing is allowed by the bean descriptor the container may actually choose to use the one-phase commit optimization.

The general responsibilities of a bean with bean-managed transaction demarcation are illustrated in the following code snippet:

```
public void onMessage () {
    try {
      // obtain the user transaction
      UserTransaction ut = ejbCtx.getUserTransaction();
      // initiate the transaction
      ut.begin ();
      // perform some logic such as database access
```

```
        . . .
        // commit the transaction
        ut.commit ();
    } catch ( Exception e ) {
        ut.rollback ();
    }
  }
```

Note that it is the bean developer's responsibility to either commit or roll back the transaction initiated before the onMessage() method returns. If the bean does not complete the transaction the container is required to handle this as an error condition by logging the condition, rolling back the transaction, and discarding the given bean instance.

For a message-driven bean with bean-managed transaction demarcation, the message receipt that causes the bean to be invoked is not part of the transaction. The message is received and acknowledged by the container before it is passed to the bean instance; the transaction is initiated from within the bean's onMessage() method.

If the developer wishes to have the message receipt be part of the transaction then container managed demarcation must be used.

Container-Managed Transactions

A message-driven bean with container-managed transactions is only allowed to specify the NotSupported or Required transactional attributes. Utilizing other transactional attributes is not meaningful since there can be no pre-existing transactional context denoted by the RequiresNew and Supports attributes or a client that needs to observe transactional invariants implied by the Mandatory and Never attributes.

If the NotSupported transaction attribute is specified in a message-driven bean's deployment descriptor then the onMessage() method executes in what the specification terms an "unspecified transaction context." The semantics are identical for message-driven beans to the behavior defined for other EJBs that use the NotSupported attribute. It's important to bear in mind that other beans called by the message-driven bean will execute with no transactional context from the caller.

On the other hand, a bean with the Required transaction attribute specified is invoked with a valid transaction context. Since there is never a client transaction available for a message-driven bean the container will always initiate a new transaction before the message is delivered by the provider to the bean's onMessage() method. The container is also responsible for enlisting the resource manager associated with the incoming message with the transaction manager. If the onMessage() method calls other enterprise beans the container will propagate the transaction context with the invocations. When the onMessage() method returns the container is responsible for committing the associated transaction. If the method does not complete successfully or the container rolls the transaction back then JMS message redelivery semantics apply.

Remember from our discussion of JMS in Chapter 5, it is the enlistment of the message resource manager with a global transaction before message delivery that presents the greatest challenges for current J2EE implementations. Since the interface between the J2EE container and the JMS provider is underspecified with respect to transactions specific integrations may exist between the two elements to facilitate pre-delivery enlistment.

Beyond support for all defined bean types, infrastructure vendors have additional requirements for distributed transaction support. Foremost among these it the optional support for transaction context propagation.

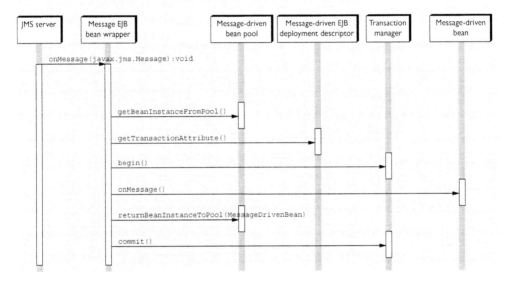

Figure 6-2 Object interactions for MDB with `Required` container-managed transaction demarcation.

Transaction Context Propagation

Support for transaction context propagation between distributed containers is specified, but not mandated, by the EJB 2.0 specification. By contrast, transaction context and distributed transaction support was not addressed at all in EJB 1.1. Within a single application server environment, that meant that vendors could choose to handle transaction context propagation in whatever manner they wished. In practice, this meant that most application servers didn't support context propagation at all.

EJB 2.0 has a relatively short chapter on interoperability and distribution. Despite its brevity, this section of the specification is both extremely important and filled with complicated requirements for infrastructure providers. The basis for interoperability, both at the wire protocol layer and at the system concept level, is CORBA. That means that all EJB containers have to make themselves available to RMI-IIOP clients; there is nothing to preclude C++ interoperability as well.

The server-side programming model is not similarly constrained, and most containers will be implemented by programming directly against the Portable Object Adapter (POA) model defined for CORBA servers. Aside from transaction context propagation, the specification requires support for Common Secure Interoperability, version 2 (CSIv2) conformance level 0 to address interoperable security identity assertions between clients and containers (it leaves unspecified the sticky problem of establishing and verifying trust relationships between servers). In fact, the EJB 2.0 specification incorporated CSIv2 support before the specification was complete in the OMG.

There's a similar story for transaction interoperability and distribution. The EJB 2.0 specification-based support for distributed transactions on OTS 1.2 before it was completed within the OMG, though the EJB specification was not completed until well after the OTS 1.2 work was released (there is a slight ambiguity in the J2EE world because the JTS specification still references OTS 1.1). EJB 2.0 requires that vendors follow certain rules depending on whether or not the container supports transaction interoperability. The rest of the material on transaction interoperability that we discuss in this chapter is heavily dependent on our presentation in Chapter 3.

Recall that the OTS transaction context is defined by the IDL for `CosTransactions::PropagationContext`. EJB containers supporting interoperability must be able to use, produce, and consume this context information according to well-defined rules; this requirement pertains to Web containers as well. The EJB specification itself shows in detail how the container can interact with the OTS transaction manager to support transaction context propagation as shown in Figure 6-3. To understand how distributed transactions work in a multi-application server environment, it's important to have a familiarity with the OTS specification.

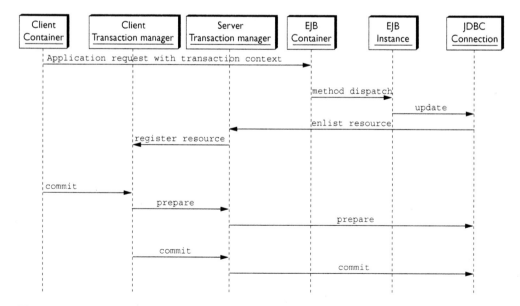

Figure 6-3   Sequence diagram showing EJB interoperability scenario based on OTS.

The key point to note is that containers performing work within an OTS transaction must register an OTS `Resource` object with the coordinator referenced in the propagated context.

In the simplest case, an application server vendor can opt not to support transactional interoperability. In this case, in order to protect the application's data integrity, the client transaction will be rolled back as a result of a `java.rmi.RemoteException` thrown by the server container upon receipt of the client's transactional request.

If a client container doesn't support OTS transaction interoperability, it may take one of two possible approaches.

The first approach requires the client to send a `CosTransactions::Propagation-Context` structure in the IIOP request with `CosTransactions::Coordinator` and `CosTransactions::Terminator` object references set to null. This informs the server that the client is incapable of propagating a context, which allows the container to determine how to handle the request. This is a generally valid approach for implementations that don't support context propagation.

Alternately, clients that support propagation but not interoperability may take another tack. In that case, if the client container recognizes that the EJB reference is from another vendor's container, it throws a CORBA system exception (not formally specified in the EJB 2.0 specification) when the client container attempts the `Coordinator::register_resource` call. It verifies this by checking the server's `Resource` object reference. The RMI-IIOP layers will wrap the CORBA system exception within a `java.rmi.RemoteException`. Since the containers cannot interoperate in a way that guarantees consistent and well-defined behavior, data integrity is maintained by blocking an RPC call that would jeopardize the ACID properties of the OTS transaction.

The server side container behavior is also clearly specified. In all cases, EJB containers must put special information into the IOR for the EJB references they create. The IOR must include the `CosTransactions::OTSPolicy` and optionally may include the `CosTransactions::InvocationPolicy` tagged components for both `javax.ejb.EJBHome` and `javax.ejb.EJBObject` references.

As we described, the OTS specification deals with transactions at the object level, while the EJB model specifies transactional attributes at the method level. The EJB 2.0 specification defines rules that result in the propagation of the OTS transaction context at least when it is required.

`EJBObject` and `EJBHome` references must have either `CosTransactions::SHARED` or `CosTransactions::EITHER` as the `InvocationPolicy`, though clients should interpret `CosTransactions::EITHER` as the default. In addition, all IORs should have the `OTSPolicy` value as `CosTransactions::ADAPTS` to support client invocations with or without transaction contexts as the EJB container enforces whether transactions are required or allowed by clients, not the ORB infrastructure or the transaction service.

These rules of course may result in context propagation when it is not needed. For example, a bean that has `RequiresNew` for every business method except one that is defined as

`Mandatory` will result in the context propagation occurring unnecessarily for the `RequiresNew` attribute.

Transaction interoperability is something that shouldn't be taken for granted, even if the EJB containers fulfill the requirements of the specification. We highly recommend that you gain a careful understanding of what both containers are supposed to do and verify that behavior. It's also a good idea to try to get a commitment from one or both vendors to analyze failure recovery scenarios to ensure that transactions will be resolved.

N O T E   We discussed J2EE interoperability issues in depth in Chapter 2.

Many containers will offer transaction context propagation without the promise of interoperability. In some cases, context propagation will be supported over protocols other than IIOP. If you do not require interoperability, this may provide a workable solution for scoping work on multiple application servers within a single transaction. Application servers may be able to provide optimizations in this environment.

Summary

The EJB specification provides the enterprise developer with a component framework for creating transactional enterprise applications in a relatively straightforward manner. At its core the specification aims to allow developers to focus on their business logic while relegating the details of system-level services, including transaction support, to the underlying EJB container; in this case, the required transaction semantics can simply be specified declaratively for the bean methods in XML based deployment descriptors.

The EJB model is rich, building on previous distributed object and TPM experiences, but refined by many years of EJB-specific experience. It has also been extended to provide transactional MOM integrations. We've covered in some detail the semantic model based on the transactional capabilities of application servers in the EJB component models.

Despite the simplicity of the transaction model in EJB, developers should be certain to give the transactional aspects of their applications careful attention. Although there is very little for a developer to do in terms of actual coding to use transactions, the assignment of transaction attributes to his bean does require care. Moreover, the behavior of the containers needs to be well understood. Does the JTA implementation really support two-phase commit and in what circumstances? Are distributed transactions supported? Are they required?

It has been our experience that OTS-based transaction managers can provide great flexibility, but that CORBA ORBs tend to be a major problem for system throughput. In addition, EJB containers support isolation strategies in conjunction with caches and resource managers in different ways that can have significant impact on the performance of a system. This is an area where you want to adopt a mature, hardened platform, since all these issues can have major implications for the successful operation of your application. The most widely deployed containers are marketed by BEA, IBM and Oracle. Because of the variations in implementations we strongly recommend you develop on the platform to which you intend to deploy, as this approach will support accurate, in-depth testing at an early stage of development. Currently, there are not really any free or open source alternatives that provide a mature platform for transactional applications, though Arjuna offers a commercial, reliable transaction service that may be integrated with the JBoss server in a product called Arjuna+JBoss.

Overall, we like the EJB model for transactional applications. It's imperfect and far from appropriate for all applications, but it has benefited from years of implementation experience on the part of vendors and end users. Because the component model defines a contract that must be observed for maintaining appropriate transaction semantics for both the bean and the container, it is a relatively safe technology to use. By this, we mean that EJB programming is much less error prone than many alternative approaches to programming transactions; the container contract helps to maintain application specific correctness. This is significant since transactions are about achieving correct outcomes. If you have transactional requirements for your business logic, EJB transaction management is most likely the way to go.

J2EE Connector Architecture and Transactions

Until recently, application servers provided proprietary interfaces to access and integrate legacy systems. One implementation we helped to develop was included in Bluestone Software's Sapphire/Web product, one of the first available Web application servers. Sapphire/Web provided Sapphire Integration Modules (SIMs) to enable connectivity to legacy Enterprise Integration Systems (EIS). The Integration Modules allowed developers to push EIS content to the Web by providing request-response instructions through a SIM to the EIS. This proved to be a popular and powerful mechanism for integrating legacy systems with the Internet.

The principal disadvantages of this approach were that it was proprietary and non-portable. Essentially, solutions like the SIM architecture were unique for every application server. This approach forced application server vendors to try to extend their expertise to every EIS system to which integration was desired and locked developers into a closed model for connecting to back-end systems in their enterprise.

In addition, these sorts of custom integration infrastructures generally did not support high-level quality of service capabilities such as the notion of global or distributed transactions or a normal security model. For some systems (e.g., SAP) that do not support the ability to act as participants within a global transaction this was not a significant drawback. However, this was a formidable drawback for systems that supported XA or other transaction models.

The J2EE Connector Architecture (which we refer to as J2C) was introduced to standardize access from Java application server environments to existing EIS applications via resource adapters. The importance of this functionality cannot be overstated when you consider what EIS systems represent.

Most business developers are familiar with legacy EIS applications like CICS, various Enterprise Resource Planning and Customer Relationship Management systems like those offered by Oracle, Seibel and SAP, or relational database management systems that are typically accessed today through JDBC. These kinds of systems are critical to any large enterprise; in many cases, they represent systems that have been installed and in use for decades and therefore embody processes and contain data that are at the core of the business. Much of the business productivity gains from Internet technologies in the 1990s were driven by Web-enabling EIS functions. In most cases replacing the existing systems is not a viable option: they embody hundreds or thousands of man-years of customization and adaptation to a particular enterprise environment.

Many EISs either provide J2C modules now or will certainly have resource adapters available in the near future. In many cases, there are multiple, competing vendor offerings for access to a single EIS system, with J2C vendors competing based on functionality, price, performance and reliability.

In this chapter we take a close look at the circumstances that led to the creation of J2C, explore the connector architecture, and detail the transactional capabilities that can be used with the Java Connector Architecture. We also provide a glimpse at some of the new functionality that is in the works for the next revision of the J2C specification as it relates to transactions.

To give you some more concrete background on J2C, let's look at some important use cases.

Enterprise Application Integration

Enterprise Application Integration (EAI) is a driving use case for the J2C standard. Most analysts agree that one of the largest problems in the modern enterprise is coping with the proliferation of legacy software systems in a coherent and reusable manner. EAI offerings were developed as an attempt to provide a systematic approach to integration. These applications abstract the interactions between systems and ensure that integrations are built using techniques that can be recycled to other integration efforts.

There are many approaches that are often used for EAI solutions. Some methods mandate a tight coupling of systems using EIS-specific APIs and shared databases; these solutions are typically hard to extend and maintain. Conversely, large-scale EAI solutions may rely on an asynchronous messaging backbone that provides extensive flexibility and peak performance.

In particular, messaging systems allow system boundaries to ignore variations and changes in the underlying infrastructure. However, the flexibility comes at a cost since distributed transactions and security context propagation are difficult to implement in messaging solutions.

Emerging Web Services standards, as well as J2C resource provider vendors, are currently attempting to address these problem areas in order to bolster the viability of these approaches. As integration and EAI continue to move to the top of IT priority lists, the "integration server" is emerging as a new and important application for J2C.

Integration Servers

Integration servers combine J2C resource adapter toolkits, workflow engines, metadata repositories, routing capabilities and message transformation capabilities. These servers combine core business processes with multiple applications running on different operating systems that may use disparate communication protocols. Using integration servers, organizations benefit from increased productivity and efficiency by more readily automating business processes across the enterprise's information systems. Most infrastructure vendors—including Oracle, BEA and IBM—are offering integration servers of various capabilities and maturity today. These servers sit on top of J2EE infrastructures and leverage J2C as an important mechanism for communicating with EIS systems. The vendors provide various value-adds beyond J2EE that are required to support real-life EAI deployments.

In conjunction with J2C, Web services are emerging as another solution to the problems posed by the integration of multiple, disparate systems.

Web Services

Web services provide an important component of the solution to today's integration issues since they, at their core, define interoperability protocols for exchanging data between different services. However, it is unrealistic to expect all EIS systems to expose themselves as Web services—it's much more likely that XML messaging will be translated to a J2C request on a back-end system that interfaces directly to an EIS. Rather than a replacement for traditional integration technologies, Web services are going to be a complement that enables interoperability between loosely coupled systems.

With J2C becoming an integral part of a large number of integration projects, and with the likelihood that it will continue to grow in importance, it is critical to understand how the J2C architecture is structured and what transactional aspects are available for building reliable, fault tolerant systems. Let's look at the architecture in more depth.

Inside J2C

The Connector Architecture is built around the concept of a resource adapter, which encompasses the classes and metadata that together provide the client's communication channel to an EIS system. A simple analogue for a J2C resource adapter is a JDBC driver implementation since the blend of connection, statement, and result set classes provides a client-facing API for interacting with databases. As a matter of fact, the J2EE Test Compatibility Kit (TCK) provides resource adapters that leverage JDBC as the basis for its J2C tests. In addition, a JDBC resource adapter is packaged with the J2EE Reference Implementation. At heart, J2C is simply a framework for resource adapters. WebSphere, for example, has rebuilt their JDBC support on top of J2C.

Resource adapters are either deployed within an Enterprise Archive (EAR) file (much like other J2EE components such as EJBs and servlets) or as a standalone module for use within a J2EE application. The deployment unit, or file, for a resource adapter is known as a Resource Adapter Archive (RAR) file, and typically has a .rar extension.

J2EE components interact with the resource adapter via contracts defined by the J2C specification. The specification also provides contracts detailing how an application server can manage connections to provide valuable system services like transaction enlistment, connection pooling and sharing, and security credential management.

Resource adapter vendors are required to supply client-facing interfaces for the EIS system with which the adapter is intended to communicate. These interfaces may leverage either the Common Client Interface (CCI), a generic interface that is independent of the EIS, or proprietary, vendor-specific interfaces. J2EE application components such as EJBs leverage these interfaces to interact with the EIS system. Our discussion focuses on the CCI since it is the preferred client mechanism for resource adapters and a universal model for programming with resource adapters based on J2C. The underlying mechanics of transaction support are the same in either case.

There are two fundamental components of the J2C that we'll discuss in some detail in order to establish a basis for a thorough examination of the support for transactions in the architecture. First, we look at the Common Client Interface visible to application programmers. Second, we explore the J2C Service Provider Interface (SPI) used by resource provider vendors to build implementation classes that manage the physical connections to a resource and fulfill the system contracts centered on connection management, transactions and security. Depending on the development project, you may be called upon to use resource adapters, to build them, or both. While vendors are providing adapters for commercial products, many enterprise applications are homegrown and require custom adapters.

CCI

The Common Client Interface (CCI) defines a set of interfaces that are implemented by the resource adapter provider. These interfaces are in turn utilized directly by the client application to programmatically access EIS systems. An exhaustive examination of all the CCI interfaces is beyond the scope of this book. We focus on the six interfaces that play an important role in accessing EIS systems and the management of transactions in those systems. After we introduce the interfaces, we give an example to better illustrate their use. You will find it much easier to understand the concepts in CCI if you are already familiar with JDBC.

javax.resource.cci.Connection

Connections are the basis for interacting with existing systems. The `Connection` interface provides the definition for the client handle to an EIS connection. These connections are stateless with respect to the physical resource and act as proxies to the physical connection (which implements `javax.resource.spi.ManagedConnection` that we describe below). Connections also provide an interface for managing local transactions. The JDBC analogue to a CCI Connection is the `java.sql.Connection` class. The `Connection` interface is defined below:

```
public interface Connection {
    public Interaction createInteraction();
    public LocalTransaction getLocalTransaction();
    public ConnectionMetaData getMetaData();
    public ResultSetInfo getResultSetInfo();
    public void close();
}
```

All of the methods in the Connection class throw the exception javax.resource.ResourceException, which we have omitted for clarity.

javax.resource.cci.ConnectionFactory

ConnectionFactory implementations provide a mechanism for acquiring javax.resource.cci.Connection instances. These connections are often pooled and managed by the application server. The ConnectionFactory defers instantiation of the Connection instance to the application server, which allows the application server to intercede for the purposes of connection pooling and transaction management.

Thus, the connection handle returned to the client program during the invocation of ConnectionFactory.getConnection()may not correspond to a newly instantiated physical connection but rather to a connection which has already been established; in fact, it is also possible for the application server to delay binding to any physical connection at all. The ConnectionFactory is akin to the javax.sql.Datasource interface introduced in JDBC 2.0.

javax.resource.cci.Record

The Record interface encapsulates the data or data structures that are used for interacting with the EIS system. Interactions with the connection take Record objects as inputs and outputs. A JDBC ResultSet may be considered a type of Record. (As a matter of fact, CCI defines a javax.resource.cci.ResultSet interface that extends both the Record interface as well as the java.sql.ResultSet interface.)

javax.resource.cci.Interaction

Interactions are acquired through the Connection.createInteraction() method. Interactions are the fundamental gateway to the EIS system for the application developer. The Interaction interface has two forms of an execute() method. The execute() method takes an input Record object and returns or modifies an output Record. The Interaction interface looks like this:

```
public interface Interaction {
    public void close();
    public Connection getConnection();
    public boolean execute( InteractionSpec, Record, Record);
```

```
public Record execute( InteractionSpec, Record);
public ResourceWarning getWarnings();
public void clearWarnings();
}
```

javax.resource.cci.InteractionSpec

All access to an EIS occurs through the same `Interaction` implementation class. However, it may be necessary to specify the execution of different business methods on the resource manager. The `InteractionSpec` provides a mechanism for doing so; in effect, it provides the command portion of the interaction with the EIS, while the `Record` encapsulates the data.

As you may have noticed, CCI is generic and provides a model that may be driven by metadata to specialize the client view to a particular EIS system. As it turns out, this is also a useful model for building integration tools and frameworks.

CCI Example

As we indicated earlier, relational databases are themselves a kind of EIS that is queried and updated with information based on well-established standards and APIs. In most instances a Java client application would utilize the JDBC API to perform these operations. However, it is illustrative to examine the way in which a resource adapter would be utilized in a relational database scenario in order to understand the similarities and differences between the JDBC and J2C and thus gain a better understanding of the J2C programming model.

A client application only utilizes the interfaces defined for CCI or subclasses of those interfaces provided as part of the resource adapter. In a typical scenario a `Connection` is acquired from a `ConnectionFactory` registered in a JNDI context, an `InteractionSpec` and input `Record` are initialized, and a command is issued to the server through an `Interaction` acquired from the `Connection`. In this programming model we find that it is helpful to keep in mind that `Interactions` represent the command channel, while `Records` encapsulate the data associated with a request. The following code sample illustrates these steps:

```
// Obtain the connection factory
Context nc = new InitialContext();
ConnectionFactory cf = (ConnectionFactory)nc.lookup(
"java:comp/env/eis/ConnectionFactory");
Connection connection = cf.getConnection();
// Initialize the record
QueryRecord record = new QueryRecord( );
QueryRecord.setQuery( "DELETE FROM CUSTOMER_TABLE;" );
// Create and initialize an InteractionSpec representing
// the command
QueryInteractionSpec spec = new QueryInteractionSpec();
spec.setQueryType( QueryInteractionSpec.QUERY_NOREPLY );
```

```
// Obtain an interaction object
Interaction interaction = connection.getInteraction();  \
// execute the interaction and get the result set
ResultSet rs = (ResultSet)interaction.execute(spec, record);
```

Note that the `ResultSet` returned by the execution of the query is an implementation of the `javax.resource.cci.ResultSet` interface that is an extension of both the `java.sql.ResultSet` interface as well as the `javax.resource.cci.Record` interface. Therefore, the client code from this point on would follow a path analogous to the JDBC scenario.

It is interesting to note that if a distributed transaction were in place and the backend resource manager supported XA transactions, the client code would be unchanged. This is due to the fact that distributed transactions are supported by the SPI implementation classes of the resource adapter working in conjunction with the J2EE application component support of the given application server. We discuss this in detail below.

However, a client can use the CCI `Connection` interface to control local transactional behavior by obtaining a `LocalTransaction` interface via the `getLocalTransaction()` method. In this case the client code above would be augmented with the method invocations required to begin, commit, or possibly rollback the local transaction. We examine all of the transactional modes supported by J2C in the SPI discussion below.

Now that we have an understanding of the client-programming model provided by CCI we can examine the underlying infrastructure support provided by implementing the interfaces of the Service Provider Interface (SPI).

SPI

The CCI is the preferred implementation strategy for resource adapters because it provides a normalized client programming model and lends itself well to use by tool developers. However, just understanding CCI gives an incomplete view of resource adapters and how they work.

If you plan to implement a resource adapter, you'll need an extensive understanding of the Service Provider Interface (SPI) package. However, even as a client application developer interested in transactions it is invaluable to have an understanding of the SPI XA interfaces in order to understand how J2C supports interactions with distributed transactions.

In the coming sections we look at the key SPI classes that are necessary for understanding the use of transactions with J2C. Adding XA support to resource adapters is almost certainly the most complicated part of connector implementation work. Although implementing the transactional interfaces of the SPI is generally the purview of resource adapter vendors you may encounter situations that demand a thorough knowledge of the transaction underpinning of J2C. For example, integration server vendors may include toolkits to assist application developers in building resource adapters that support XA transactions for existing EIS systems.

javax.resource.spi.ManagedConnection

ManagedConnection objects represent the underlying physical resource and are generally pooled by the application server. The ManagedConnection is responsible for maintaining the connection state with the backend EIS system. If you are familiar with JDBC, the ManagedConnnection in the J2C SPI package is analogous to the javax.sql.Pooled-Connection class defined for relational databases.

There are two important methods on the ManagedConnection class that are leveraged by the application server to support transaction management: getXAResource() and getLocalTransaction(). Depending on the level of transactional support provided by the resource adapter these methods either return the requested interface implementation or raise a javax.resource.NotSupportedException (e.g., if a resource adapter has no transactional support is will raise the exception for either invocation).

The getXAResource() method accesses the J2C resource adapter providers' XAResource implementations to allow an external transaction manager to coordinate the two-phase commit process using the XA protocol. Writing the XAResource is the most arduous part of providing a resource adapter, since it requires a deep understanding of both XA and how the underlying EIS system supports the two-phase commit protocol. If you are going down this implementation path, you may find it helpful to examine an XAResource implementation for an existing system. You will find useful information in Chapter 2, which covers the Java mapping of XA and an example of an XAResource implementation. We recommend that you have a copy of the XA specification itself on hand as well.

The getLocalTransaction() method returns an implementation of the javax.resource.spi.LocalTransaction interface. The LocalTransaction interface is defined by J2C to allow the application server to coordinate local transactions. A transaction coordinator running in a process external to the application server does not utilize the SPI LocalTransaction interface. Rather, the container utilizes it to manage local transactions. (It is not utilized by client components; they utilize the CCI LocalTransaction interface.) Local transaction behavior is analogous to the JDBC local transaction capabilities that are enabled by invoking the setAutoCommit(false) method on a java.sql.Connection implementation.

javax.resource.spi.ManagedConnectionFactory

The ManagedConnectionFactory implementation is responsible for creating ManagedConnections. As such, it is the primary interface used by the javax.resource.ConnectionManager implementation provided by the application server. ConnectionManagers control the lifecycle of ManagedConnections and represent the connection pooling facilities of application servers.

Now that we've examined some of the key SPI interfaces let's take a look at the services they enable.

Connection Management

Connection management of J2C connections deals with the lifecycle and state transitions for a connection. The J2C specification lays out rules for how J2EE containers may deal with the connection, especially for connection establishment, pooling and termination. Much of the connection management is handled via callback listeners that the containers can use to coordinate state changes with lifecycle management and policy enforcement.

Transactional participation has important implications for resource adapter implementations. Before we explain the series of interactions between the application server, the resource adapter, and an external transaction coordinator, it's important to establish the following aspects of J2C associated with connection lifecycle management (see Figure 7-1):

1. The application server is required to implement a `javax.resource.Connec-tionManager` class. This class is responsible for either creating new instances of `ManagedConnections` or handing out a `ManagedConnection` instance from a pool. Therefore, a `ConnectionFactory` defers the retrieval of connections to the application server via the `ConnectionManager` interface. Typically, the `ConnectionFactory` will implement the `getConnection()` method in a manner similar to the following code snippet:

```
Connection getConnection( ) {
return (Connection)
connectionManagerInstance.allocateConnection (   );
}
```

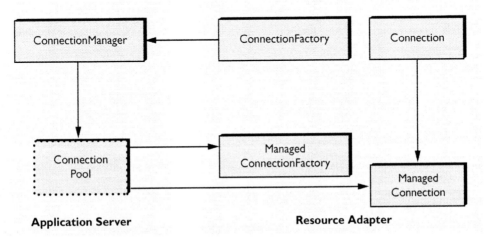

Application Server   **Resource Adapter**

Figure 7-1 Connection Management.

2. As you can see, the application server is able to intervene and supply a handle to a pooled physical connection.

3. Since resource adapters can be used in a non-managed environment (one that is not associated with an application server infrastructure), a resource adapter will typically provide a default implementation of a `ConnectionManager` in order to deal with the case where an external connection management infrastructure is not present. A common implementation for `allocateConnection()` is:

```
public Object allocateConnection( ManagedConnectionFactory
mcf, ConnectionRequestInfo info ) {
ManagedConnection mc =   mcf.createManagedConnection( null,
info );
   return mc.getConnection( null, info );
}
```

4. If the default, non-managed `ConnectionManager` is used, the connection will not be able to participate in distributed transactions or the two-phase commit protocol, even if the resource adapter and the resource manager both support the `XAResource` interface and the `ra.xml` declares that the resource adapter supports distributed transactions. This is due to the fact that the application server is no longer able to intervene in the distribution of connections and subsequently register resources with the coordinator.

5. Connection handles do not have a one-to-one relationship with `ManagedConnection` instances. However, the application server should only allow a single instance of a `Connection` for a given `ManagedConnection` to be in use at any given time. This is an important requirement for maintaining isolation of the resource in transactional scenarios. The application server can rely on this feature of the specification to return the underlying managed connection to the pool when a component such as session bean holds a connection for more than the duration of the execution of a business method. The application server may have to transparently reassociate `Connection` handles with `ManagedConnections` to support sharing of physical connections across threads. Resource adapter providers should also ensure that `Connection` implementations do not contain state associated with the underlying connection.

6. Connection events allow the resource adapter to notify the application server of state changes initiated by the client that have management implications. These include closing a connection, generating an error condition that invalidates a managed connection, and starting and terminating a local transaction. Note that events are not generated by a distributed transaction; they are already managed by the application server either through the EJB container or by interaction with the `UserTransaction` proxy to the transaction coordinator. However, the application server requires notification of other connection-related events to effectively manage distributed transactions. For example, the closing of a connection may cause the application server to delist an `XAResource` from a transaction and to re-pool the associated `ManagedConnection`.

7. Connection sharing is supported by the J2C specification. This allows multiple components to use the same connection within the context of a transaction. For example, two EJBs may be invoked serially in the course of a transaction, assuming the container has not intervened to suspend the transaction at any point. If both EJBs are accessing the same resource manager, the application may share the same connection between both EJBs as a way to utilize system resources more efficiently. If an EJB application has been designed such that connection sharing is inappropriate, the EJB should indicate that the by setting the `<res-sharing-scope>` element in the deployment descriptor within the EJB jar.

This should sound familiar if you've read Chapter 4. As you will notice, the Connector model generalizes the connection management that was defined for JDBC. Beyond the connection management facilities, a resource adapter defines via its implementation of the SPI interfaces the degree to which transactions are supported for a given EIS system.

Transaction Management

There are three levels of transactional support in the connector architecture: none, local and distributed. The transactional support is determined by the resource adapter vendor and can be declared within the deployment descriptor of the resource adapter archive:

```
<transaction-support>XATransaction</transaction-support>
```

NoTransaction

If the resource adapter is declared to have no support for transactions, it may neither participate in distributed transactions nor support local transactions. This is the basic case for transactions and the simplest for the resource adapter provider to support. Many EIS systems support atomic interactions only, for which the `NoTransaction` support option is appropriate. It is entirely possible for a resource adapter not to support transactional capabilities provided by the EIS.

Local Transactions

Local transactions are specific to a particular EIS, do not support the two-phase commit protocol, and are not managed by an external transaction coordinator. Local transactions are the simplest transactional case and familiar to programmers who have worked with JDBC.

SPI *LocalTransaction Interface*

Local transactions are represented by implementations of the `javax.resource.spi.LocalTransaction` interface:

```
public interface LocalTransaction {
    public void begin( ) throws ResourceException;
    public void commit( ) throws ResourceException;
    public void rollback( ) throws ResourceException;
}
```

The SPI `LocalTransaction` implementation defines the contract between the application server and the resource adapter for local transactions. A resource adapter may use an SPI `LocalTransaction` implementation class to manage the demarcation of local transactions.

The use of the SPI `LocalTransaction` is permitted by the specification for cases where "one-phase commit" is used. Typically, this is the case when the resource adapter only supports local transactions. However, this interface may also be used to avoid the overhead associated with an external transaction manager and the full two-phase commit protocol if the application server determines that only one resource manager is accessed during the transaction. This is referred to as the "local transaction optimization."

Generally an application server will utilize a vendor-specific mechanism to implement the local transaction optimization. The server may, for example, start a local transaction when a resource manager is accessed and lazily initiate a distributed transaction if other resource managers are included. The most likely implementation strategy for the application server is to utilize the last resource commit optimization.

N O T E   Chapter 2 discusses last resource commit in detail.

As we noted above, the application server is generally registered as a `Connection-EventListener` with the `ManagedConnection`. The `ConnectionEventListener` interface contains three methods related to local transaction management:

```
public void localTransactionStarted();
public void localTransactionCommitted();
public void localTransactionRolledBack();
```

These methods allow the application server to manage the transactional association of connections when multiple components participate in a local transaction by providing the application server with enough information about transaction boundaries to implement connection sharing.

CCI LocalTransaction Interface

As noted earlier, client applications do not directly leverage the SPI `LocalTransaction` interface. Rather, clients using CCI coordinate local transactions using the `javax.resource.cci.LocalTransaction` interface. An object implementing this interface is obtained by invoking the CCI `Connection` interface's `getLocalTransaction()` method.

Since the CCI `LocalTransaction` implementation class is entirely associated with a connection and not a two-phase commit coordinator, it is not exactly analogous to the `javax.transaction.UserTransaction` implementation available to J2EE components. However, the interface itself contains the same methods:

```
public interface LocalTransaction
{
public void begin( ) throws ResourceException
    public void commit( ) throws ResourceException
    public void rollback( ) throws ResourceException
}
```

The methods have similar semantics to the `UserTransaction`'s methods with respect to the transactional resource manager, but only apply to the resource manager to which the `Connection` provides a proxy. The `begin()` method initiates a local transaction and the `commit()` and `rollback()` methods terminate the transaction. Keep in mind that the CCI `LocalTransaction` interface is actually unrelated to the SPI `LocalTransaction` interface. CCI differs from JDBC in that local transaction management is explicit rather than being the byproduct of setting an autocommit rule to true or false.

> **N O T E** In the Connector Architecture, local transactions can be used to scope work performed across multiple EJBs, independent of whether the EJB was accessed through its remote or local interfaces as long as the EJBs are deployed in the same application server process. Since EJBs referenced by their remote interfaces may be deployed in different address spaces, it is impossible to reason about the correctness of the interactions based solely on the relationship between the EJBs; if the EJBs are not deployed in the same container the local transaction will not scope the work. Beware of this trap: behavior and outcomes will vary depending on the deployment topology of the application. This is a fundamental hole in the J2EE platform.
>
> Local EJB interfaces were introduced as a way to relax the location transparency requirements of the platform—they offer a way to provide semantic context to the caller with respect to the distribution of the component. Though they were developed to allow for relatively efficient use of EJBs for object persistence, local interfaces could allow the notion of transitive local transactions to be supported in a meaningful way. This problem may be taken up by a future revision of the J2C and EJB specifications. It may be possible to eliminate this issue by careful restrictive use of the `<res-sharing-scope>` element in EJB deployment descriptors. But this approach can also lead to deadlock: the underlying EIS has no way to know that the independent transactions created due to restrictions on connection sharing belong to the same client.

Let's take a look at an example that will help illustrate the use of local transactions.

Sample Scenario

Consider a Web application that allows human resources administrators to manage employee records maintained in a legacy EIS system. Once logged in, the administrators may create, update, or delete records in the system. Since all updates execute against a single EIS system there is no need to create a distributed transaction and incur the overhead associated with the full two-phase commit protocol. Rather, the web components of the application can lookup the connection factory provided by the EIS system's resource adapter, obtain a reference to a connection, request a local transaction handle from the connection, and manage all interactions with the EIS as a single unit of work.

The following code sample and interaction diagram (see Figure 7-2) illustrate these steps:

```
// create the JNDI initial context
Context ctx = new javax.naming.InitialContext();
// obtain the connection factory
ConnectionFactory cf = (ConnectionFactory) ctx.lookup ("java:comp/env/
eis/ConnectionFactory");
// create a connection
Connection conn = cf.getConnection();
// get the local transaction
LocalTransaction ltx = conn.getLocalTransaction();
// mark the beginning of the transaction
ltx.begin();
// create a CCI interaction
Interaction itx = conn.createInteraction();
.  .  .
// perform some work
.  .  .
// commit the transaction
ltx.commit();
// close the interaction
itx.close();
```

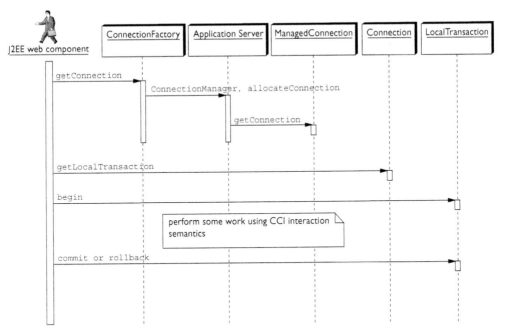

Figure 7-2 Local Transaction Interaction Diagram.

Distributed Transactions

Resource adapters can support global transactions. We delve into this scenario in some detail: it's important to know something about how the resource adapter interacts with the application server, particularly if you need to write a resource adapter.

The following interactions are involved in creating and managing a distributed transaction (see Figure 7-3):

1. A distributed transaction is initiated either by an application component using the `UserTransaction` object in its managed environment or by an EJB container if declarative container managed transactions are used.

2. When an application component calls `getConnection()` on the `Connection-Factory` for the resource adapter, the `ConnectionFactory` delegates the responsibility for acquiring a `Connection` to the `ConnectionManager` by calling `allocateConnection()`. The application server will acquire a `ManagedConnection`. If the transaction had previously been in place, the `ManagedConnection` is likely to be the same `ManagedConnection` already associated with the transaction. However, this is not required and the `XAResource` may be independently

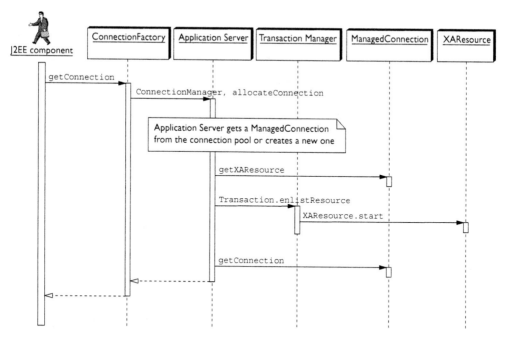

Figure 7-3 Distributed Transaction Interaction Diagram.

enlisted repeatedly for a resource manager within a given transaction. It is the responsibility of the transaction manager to handle this scenario.

3. The application server will acquire an XAResource from the ManagedConnection.
4. The application server will enlist the XAResource with the transaction.
5. The TransactionManager implementation will tell the resource manager to start a branch of the distributed transaction.
6. The application server will then retrieve a Connection handle from the Managed-Connection.
7. The application server will return the Connection to the ConnectionFactory.
8. The ConnectionFactory will return the Connection the application component that originally requested it.
9. The association between the transaction and ManagedConnection may be terminated in one of three ways: the connection may be closed, in which case the XARe-source is delisted from the transaction and the transaction branch associated with the ManagedConnection is ended, the transaction may be suspended and the XARe-source may be explicitly delisted from the transaction, or the transaction may be terminated by either a rollback or commit.

This example is illustrative, rather than prescriptive, for transaction enlistment. It is entirely acceptable to acquire the `Connection` before beginning a global transaction. The application server can use several strategies to ensure that enlistment occurs in the transaction after it is started, but the requirement to manage enlistment doesn't require any special action from the application.

It is possible to build a resource adapter that supports participation in a global transaction even though the EIS supports only local transactions. In the early days of JDBC, before XA compliant drivers were available, this was a common implementation strategy for application server vendors. In this case, the `XAResource` implementation would always return true from the prepare phase of the two-phase commit. This guarantees that the adapter will instruct the coordinator to proceed during the prepare phase—even if the EIS system cannot successfully commit the transaction. Outside of the last resource commit scenario we discussed in Chapter 2, this breaks the ACID constraints for the global transaction, and is not recommended as a practice in systems where data consistency is required. But it raises an interesting question: what happens if you mix local and distributed transactions during the same request?

Unfortunately, there is no clear answer to this question. The J2C specification leaves this behavior undefined and allows the application server vendor to handle this in a vendor-dependent manner. That's further complicated by the fact that the resource adapter may be built with a different set of assumptions about how to handle this scenario.

Our advice to application assemblers and developers is to avoid the mixing of transactions altogether if possible. If you are implementing resource adapters for your own application, it may be possible to handle this reasonably assuming a thorough understanding of the application server. This will most likely result in sacrificing portability across application servers; we suspect that relatively few enterprise applications are actually ported across multiple J2EE servers, but you'll have to make the appropriate decision for your environment.

Note that there should be no problem mixing the use of non-transactional resource adapters with resource adapters that support either distributed or local transactions within an interaction.

J2C Futures

As of this writing, the Java Connector Architecture 1.5 is being defined. One of the fundamental goals of the new iteration of the specification is to support asynchronous resource managers. This means that J2C will augment the JMS specification by providing the definition for interactions between asynchronous resource managers, XA transaction coordinators, and the application server. In addition, J2C 1.5 will support bi-directional communication between an EIS and an application server environment. This is very much like using JMS `MessageListeners` in a transacted environment. As a practical benefit, it means that JMS providers will have a contract through which they will be able to plug in to application servers portably, a serious problem we examined in our chapters on JMS and EJB.

One of the most interesting aspects of J2C 1.5 is the introduction of a work management contract that allows the resource adapter to submit work to the application server for it to perform. A part of this work management contract, J2C 1.5 supports the inflow of transactions initiated by the external EIS system with which the resource adapter is associated, as shown in Figure 7-4. This has a number of implications for application servers.

Resource adapters must be able to mediate external transaction contexts into a transaction that is understood by the application server natively; in practice, this means that the resource adapter will have to represent the transaction branch to the application server as an `Xid`. The application server may support distributed transaction processing between other nodes, in which case the EIS system is always the root coordinator in the tree of process model.

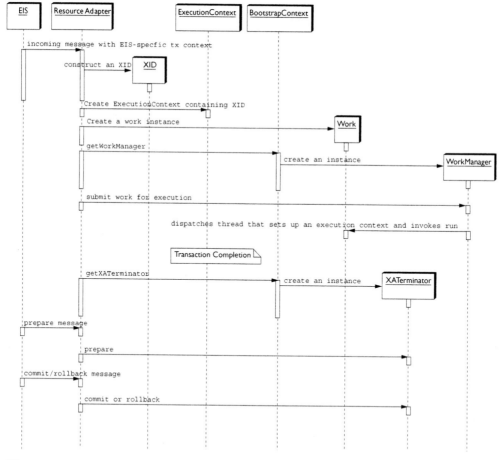

Figure 7-4 Transaction Inflow Sequence Diagram.

Application servers must support interposition to move from the EIS transaction domain into a localized global transaction in which XAResources may be enlisted.

Both termination and failure recovery is driven by EIS systems. The new specification provides an interface for the resource adapter to use (and for the application server to implement) named XATerminator. This interface contains the termination protocol and recovery methods from the XAResource interface. Since interposed coordinators are dependent on external management by an EIS coordinator; the application server itself may be in doubt for long periods of time. Therefore, make sure the application server has tools to detect and resolve in-doubt transactions.

The XATerminator interface looks like this:

```
interface XATerminator {
    void commit(Xid xid, boolean onePhase);
    void forget(Xid xid);
    int prepare(Xid xid);
    Xid[] recover(int flag);
    void rollback(Xid xid);
}
```

The completion and recovery semantics are identical to those we have discussed for the Java Transaction API and the DTP model.

Since this specification is not finalized, these features will require some time until they are released in products and proven by vendors and beta testers. However, they promise to open up the J2EE platform as a new execution context for functional extensions to transactional EISs.

Summary

Enterprise Information Systems include ERP, CRM, databases, and mainframe applications that are critical to run a business; these systems form the basis of modern IT infrastructures. The Java Connector Architecture provides a model for developing and deploying resource adapters to arbitrary EIS systems. As integration projects and solutions increase in importance, the connector architecture is becoming an increasingly important technology.

The Connector specification provides APIs and SPIs to expose transactional functionality supported by EISs. It includes the ability to support both local and global transactions. This allows developers to create new, reliable applications that integrate EIS systems with each other and with Internet technologies. In addition, the forthcoming version of J2C will support bi-directional communication with EISs, including the ability to import transactions from other systems. Traditional EIS systems will be able to be functionally extended to integrate with application servers and other transactional systems.

PART 3

The Future of Transactions in J2EE and Web Services

As we've seen throughout this book, the concepts of atomic transactions have played a cornerstone role in creating today's enterprise application environments. They provide guaranteed consistent outcome in complex multi-party business operations and a useful separation of concerns in applications. However, almost since the first time ACID transactions were used in industry and academia it was realized that they weren't a global panacea. This is especially true for long-duration transactional activities, where the strict ACID properties are often too restrictive.

For example, an online bookshop may well reserve books for shoppers for a specific period of time, but if an individual does not purchase the books within that time period they will be "put back onto the shelf" for others to purchase; to do otherwise could result in the shop never selling a single book. Furthermore, because it is not possible for anyone to have an infinite supply of stock, some examples of online shops may appear to users to reserve items for them but, in fact, if other users want to purchase them first they may well be allowed to (i.e., the same book may be "reserved" for multiple users concurrently); a user may subsequently find that the item is no longer available, or may have to be ordered specially for them.

If these example applications were modeled using atomic transactions, the reservation process would require the book to be locked for the duration of the atomic transaction and, hence, it would have to be available and could not be acquired by (sold to) another user. When the atomic transaction commits, the book will be removed from stock and mailed to the user. However, if a failure occurs during the commitment protocol, the book may remain locked for an indeterminate amount of time (or until manual intervention occurs).

It's difficult, if not impossible, to incorporate traditional transaction architectures within such environments. Furthermore, most collaborative business process management systems support complex, long-running processes where undoing tasks that have already completed may be necessary in order to affect recovery, or to choose another acceptable execution path in the process.

Therefore, it probably doesn't come as a surprise to learn that there has been much research work done in industry and academia on developing specific transaction models that allow ACID properties to be relaxed in a controlled manner. Such models are typically referred to as *extended transaction models*. Nevertheless, most of the proposed techniques have not found any widespread usage. Indeed, as we saw in Chapter 1, "Transaction Fundamentals," most commercial transaction processing systems do not even support nesting of transactions. One reason cited is lack of flexibility, in that the wide range of extended transaction models is indicative that a single model is not sufficient for all applications, so it would be inappropriate to "hard-wire" a specific extension mechanism.

However, in recent years this has started to change and interestingly (and importantly) this change has been driven by industry. The use of transactions has been popularized by object orientation, Java and the rise of the Internet. The types of application that want transaction-like semantics (reliability and fault-tolerance) but aren't suited for ACID transactions have also grown. Because people (application developers and companies) have tried to shoehorn ACID transactions into these applications it's become obvious that other solutions are required. This has driven extended transactions out of the research arena and into product development.

There are two areas where providing extended transaction functionality is extremely important to users and the industry: J2EE, which is the standard environment for developing enterprise-level applications, and Web services, which is fast becoming the enterprise-integration platform of choice. In both of these environments, transactions either already are, or are fast becoming, important and users are finding problems with the traditional functionality they provide. In the following chapters we look at how J2EE is approaching the concepts of extended transactions.

Advanced Transaction Concepts

So far we have looked at transaction fundamentals, the core specifications on which the J2EE transaction offerings are based (the OMG's Object Transaction Service and the X/Open XA specification), how transactions are used in the J2EE architecture, and some of the evolving transactional standards. However, though most of the issues involved in using transactions in Java and J2EE have been addressed in one way or another, there are still some issues that require consideration. In this chapter we look at and address some of the more advanced Java transaction concepts.

We take a look at what's known as *end-to-end transactions*, which can be used to provide much needed transaction guarantees between clients and servers. As we see, unlike the kinds of transactional applications we've previously observed, there are applications where the distinction between transactional object/server and client is blurred, requiring the client (or entities residing in the client's address space) to participate in the transaction.

We've discussed the idea of interposition several times already in this book, but in this chapter we look at how it can be an important design feature when building transactional applications that span different enterprise domains. We then give you some tips for structuring transactional applications to improve performance and throughput by reducing contention on important transactional objects or resources.

Is Java Suitable for High Performance Transaction Systems?

Since the advent of commercial transaction processing systems, one of the main aims has been to achieve greater and greater performance. Transaction systems have evolved from processing tens or hundreds of transactions per second to thousands of transactions per second and beyond. As transaction systems achieved these goals, even higher rates were set as a way of illustrating improvements and trying to obtain a competitive advantage. Although some of this increase in performance has been due to the improvements in physical hardware speed, others have come from changes in programming languages.

As transaction systems have evolved, so have programming languages, moving from raw machine code, through COBOL and C, to C++ and beyond. As a new language appears and becomes accepted by the general community, transaction processor providers assess its uses in their domain. Prior to Java, the languages used were compiled and transaction systems benefited from the improvements in compiler technology. However, acceptance of Java was at first limited since it is both compiled and interpreted. Few (if any) commercial transaction systems have ever appeared using interpreted languages, since they generally do not perform as well as natively compiled languages.

It is for this reason that many commercial J2EE offerings leverage existing transaction systems written in non-Java languages, such as IBM's CICS or BEA's Tuxedo. However, there are a number of pure Java transaction services available now that some vendors would have you believe are inferior to their C/C++ cousins (e.g., the Sun Reference Implementation or the Hewlett-Packard/Arjuna Technologies Transaction Service). However, is it necessarily the case that in order to get a transaction system that performs you must look beyond Java? Having implemented transaction systems in both C/C++ and Java, we believe the experiences we have gained can help answer this important question.

Compiled versus Interpreted

If performance is important, why are high-level languages such as Java or C++ used for implementing most applications rather than coding directly in assembler? The answer is fairly simple: the majority of programmers can write more lines of Java than machine code, it's easier to debug and understand Java, and technology has advanced to such a point that compilers can generate machine code that is as efficient as the code produced by native machine code programmers.

In addition, there are a large number of library routines available for Java in a range of areas, such as graphical user interfaces, management tools, logging utilities, and so on. These libraries can often be used wholesale in other applications, simplifying the development of those applications and, hence, reducing the amount of development time. In terms of distributed computing, existing client/server libraries can often be implemented in much shorter periods of time than was previously possible in other compiled languages.

Applications written in interpreted languages such as Basic or Lisp are, by their very nature, slower than their compiled counterparts. However, unlike a compiled application, which by necessity is hardware-specific, the interpreted application code can be moved from machine to machine without requiring modification: the interpreter, which is part of the language runtime, is responsible for generating hardware specific instructions from the application code.

Therefore, there's a trade-off between speed and portability that must be considered when deciding whether to use an interpreted or compiled language.

Moreover, continuous advances in the Java runtime environment and the libraries supplied by the JDK have significantly narrowed the gap between the performance of compiled code and interpreted code. Marked improvements have been made in the performance of garbage collection, a noted performance bottleneck, with each successive release of the JDK. The Hotspot Just In Time (JIT) compiler, along with other commercial JIT compilers, has produced dynamically optimized code that rivals similarly written C/C++ code in performance. As a matter of fact, the JIT compilers can make on-the-fly optimizations that simply cannot be performed by static C/C++ compilers. Finally, the JDK libraries themselves have been optimized and expanded to achieve better code performance; a significant improvement in I/O performance has been achieved with the release of the New I/O APIs of JDK 1.4.

The Java runtime environment is also inherently secure. Java security is imposed by a `SecurityManager` object, which defines what a program can and cannot do. To provide improved flexibility in security management policies, digital signatures were introduced into Java. Prior to being downloaded, programs can be signed with a unique signature for each provider. Users can associate a digital signature with a set of capabilities, e.g., being able to read from the user's home directory. Whenever a signed program attempts to perform an operation that would normally result in a security violation, the `SecurityManager` inspects the capabilities assigned to it. If the capability exists that allows the program to perform the operation, then it is carried out; otherwise a security violation exception is raised.

For transaction vendors, having to ensure that their systems can compile and run on a variety of different hardware and operating system combinations can be a major headache. The build-once, run-anywhere model that Java offers allows a systems programmer (or transaction system vendor in our case) to concentrate on developing the system rather than having to spend time and effort on the subtle and intricate differences between deployment platforms: these have (hopefully) been taken care of by the Java runtime.

Whether you're contemplating implementing a Java transaction service or buying one, what this means for you is that performance is not everything: Java has been successful despite the fact that in many cases it is slower than other languages. Having a reliable transaction service that can be executed on any operating system/hardware combination can be extremely beneficial, allowing you to deploy faster to fit a customer's requirements than a solution that requires compilation. In our experience being able to offer a reliable solution first is very important.

The Web-Effect on Transaction Systems

The Web and e-commerce in general promise a lot in terms of revenue for vendors and convenience for users. However, the Web frequently suffers from failures that can affect both the performance and consistency of applications. For commercial services, such failures can result in loss of revenue, credibility, and dissuade users from becoming involved in commercial ventures where their own money may be at stake. Therefore, there is a need for techniques that will allow applications to tolerate such failures and to continue to provide the service.

Transactions are an obvious solution to this problem. As we've already seen, the use of transactions to ensure the all-or-nothing effect is very important both for users and service providers. As a result, the next generation of transaction systems is being developed for use leveraging the Web. Several vendors see the use of Java as the right direction to take for a number of reasons, including its cross-platform capabilities and the high-level programming abstractions it offers.

However, there are two questions that need to be asked: (1) Is Java the right language for e-commerce applications, and (2) Is it possible to implement a high-throughput transaction system entirely in Java? In the following sections we shall attempt to answer these questions.

Java and E-commerce

Is Java the right language for e-commerce applications? The answer to this question is undoubtedly yes, simply because there is nothing currently better. The majority of vendors in the e-commerce arena agree that the ability to rapidly prototype and develop applications is critically important to their success. In addition, the portability of Java applications means that vendors are no longer required to have access to the myriad of hardware and operating system variations available to their customers. Subsequent programming languages and infrastructures (possibly C#, for example, and Web services) will learn from Java, just as Java learned from predecessor languages such as C++ and APL.

The 100% Solution

Is it possible to write a 100% pure Java high-throughput transaction system? Unfortunately, the answer to this question is much less straightforward. The efficiency of Java byte-code compilers and interpreters has improved over the years, and the advent of just-in-time compiler technology means that applications can typically run much faster than they did when Java first appeared. However, without leveraging some native code libraries (via the Java Native Interface), it is unlikely that Java applications will ever consistently reach the same performance figures as natively compiled languages such as C or C++. But as we asked earlier, does that really matter when a programmer can produce more (and possibly better) code in less time? Probably not in the Web domain, where *Web-years* dominate the schedules of developers and hardware performance is still increasing. Being able to get an application to market quicker than a competitor is an important factor.

It is our belief that its interpreted nature is not the obstacle to Java being accepted into the exclusive circle of languages suitable for transaction systems. As we've already mentioned, hardware improvements mean that faster processors can be thrown at slower Java applications in order to achieve better performance. In addition, the impediments to achieving better performance inherent in Java's goal of achieving platform neutrality (the virtual machine) are being addressed with newer releases of the Java runtime environment.

Historically, in order to make the virtual machine architecturally neutral, certain restrictions were placed on the APIs: the lowest common denominator approach had been taken. Some of these restrictions affected the implementation of a transaction processing system versus traditionally compiled counterparts. However, some (not all) of these have been addressed with the release of the new I/O APIs and Java runtime improvements:

- *File-level locking*: Prior to the advent of JDK 1.4 I/O extensions it was difficult for either a thread or JVM to lock a file from another thread or JVM. It was possible to emulate file-level locking programmatically, but in a much less efficient manner than that provided by the operating system. Unfortunately, the file locking mechanism available in JDK 1.4 does not work reliably. Once corrected, this ability potentially allows for an efficient implementation of certain types of transaction logs.
- *File-segment locking*: Previously, it was not possible to easily lock sections within a file. This feature is now available and can also improve the efficiency and performance of certain transaction log implementations.
- *Thread synchronization*: The Java language does not provide mutual exclusion and semaphore primitives as in advanced threading APIs, such as Posix Threads. The single `synchronized` keyword is often too coarse for efficient multi-threaded programming, requiring extra work to achieve more powerful primitives such as `trylock`, where a lock is obtained only if it is not already held by another thread, thus preventing blocking of the calling thread. Unfortunately, as a result the `synchronized` keyword is often overused, with resultant degradation of system performance. This deficiency is being addressed in the release of JDK 1.5 by inclusion of the constructs that were defined by the `util.concurrent` library that provides these required concepts as well as many others.
- *Memory mapped files*: In some transaction systems it is often more efficient to map log files directly into memory rather than use the raw file system APIs. This is now possible in Java since memory-mapped operations are enabled via NIO.
- *Shared memory*: It is not possible for one JVM to communicate with another residing on the same machine through shared memory. Although it can be argued that this is the result of security concerns, it could be solved with suitable access permissions. This may affect the performance of, for example, shared lock stores and non-volatile RAM (NVRAM) object stores or transaction logs.
- *Garbage collection*: Straddling the JVM and language divide, the garbage collection aspect of Java often proves a problem as much as it simplifies programming. Although significant improvements have been made in successive release of the Java runtime, the fact that it is not possible to delete objects when an application knows they are no longer required means that the size of the JVM is sometimes larger than it needs to be. Despite the fact that machines are now available with more and more physical memory, it is possible that the size of a JVM may become too large for it to reside entirely in this memory, requiring access to slower virtual memory subsystems.

Obviously, once the garbage collector runs the size reduces, but this may be some time later. Unfortunately, calling the garbage collector directly is still only interpreted as a "hint" that it should run and cannot be a guarantee that it will run at the desired time.

As you can tell, with the advent version 1.4 of Java, there has been an important extension to the set of input/output functionality that addresses some of the issues that existed in previous versions of Java. For example, when writing transaction logs it is often the case that the information to be written is split across many different objects, as shown in Figure 8-1.

In this example, there are three participants registered with the transaction and information about them will need to be recorded in the transaction log (assuming the coordinator decides to commit), as we discussed in Chapter 1, Transaction Fundamentals. Of course, there's also the coordinator's decision to record.

All of this information may be stored in many separate objects within the transaction service, but it needs to be written to some contiguous representation on the durable storage used by the transaction log. Prior to some of the changes in JDK 1.4, this would typically involve copying the state of these objects into a contiguous representation within the transaction service (e.g., a byte stream) and then writing this out to disk. In reality this involves at least two copy operations: one from the objects to the byte stream and then one from the byte stream to disk. Regardless of the size of the object state, this is obviously inefficient.

One of the new I/O routines introduced by JDK 1.4 is that of *scatter-gather buffers*: in essence, a scatter-gather buffer allows a contiguous data stream to be constructed from multiple disparate data sources. What this means is that the first copy in Figure 8-1 can be removed entirely. In its place a *reference* to the data to be copied is stored and only at the time when the

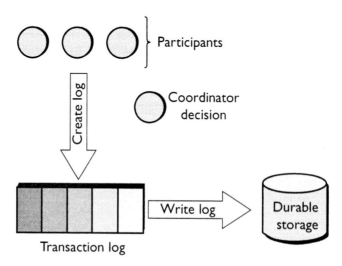

Figure 8-1 Example transaction log formation.

contiguous data is actually required (in our example, when the log is written to disk) is the data actually used. As you can probably imagine, this reduction in copying data can improve performance, sometimes quite significantly.

> **N O T E** Scatter-gather buffers have been around for a long time. One of the first appearances of this technique was in TCP/IP and UDP/IP, where network messages could be assembled from disparate data sources.

Implementations of the JDK 1.4 file-level locking are not well supported and memory mapped I/O. Unfortunately, the improved I/O routines provided by JDK 1.4 don't go as far as they might. Another example, which is related to the transaction log again, might help to illustrate at least one place where further improvements could be made. In some log implementations, there is often a single log on disk per process (JVM) or even per machine. This log is only ever appended to and never truncated by the transaction service directly. Typically a separate thread or process periodically scans the log and removes items from it that are no longer required.

This offers a number of performance benefits, including the removal of overhead incurred when deleting the transaction log and having to scan through the log for the correct place to write. However, it does require sophisticated I/O capabilities, because the file may contain "holes"—areas of the file that no longer contain data and can be released to the operating system to use for other files. Most operating systems support the notion of *sparse files*—files that have holes in them and may not therefore span contiguous blocks on the disk. Unfortunately at the moment, Java does not support this type of file system and if you were to try to implement this type of log in pure Java, then the result would be a file that simply grows and grows.

Conclusion

So, is it possible to implement an efficient 100% pure Java transaction system? Yes, in our opinion, but it requires more effort in some areas than should be necessary at the moment. Given that transactions and enterprise-level systems are becoming more and more important in the Java world, performance and efficiency requirements will certainly be addressed. The language must continue to evolve in order to match the continually evolving requirements placed on it.

End-to-End Transactional Guarantees

In this section we use the Web as an example area where *end-to-end transactionality integrity* is required. However, there are other areas (e.g., mobile) that are equally valid. Transposing the issues mentioned here to these other areas should be relatively straightforward.

We've already seen several times how the "all-or-nothing" property of transactions can be important and useful for application consistency and fault tolerance. We've concentrated up until this point on Java and the J2EE environment, but obviously transactions transcend any one specific deployment environment. They are useful in any environment where data consistency in the presence of failures or concurrent access is needed, particularly in coordination across multiple participants.

As you probably know, the Web often suffers from network or machine failures that can potentially affect the consistency of applications running on it. Fortunately, transactions have been used in Web applications for many years. Unfortunately, transactional guarantees only extend to resources used at Web servers, or between servers; clients (browsers) are not included.

For example, if a user purchases a cookie (a token) granting access to a newspaper site, it is obviously important that the cookie is delivered and stored if the user's account is debited; a failure could prevent either from occurring and leave the system in an inconsistent state. For resources such as documents, failures may simply be annoying to users; for commercial services, they can result in loss of revenue and credibility. The entities involved in an example newspaper application are:

- The user's online bank, from which funds will be debited. We shall assume that the newspaper's account is also located here.
- The newspaper site where the user's details will be added upon successfully completing the transaction.
- The user's browser site, where a cookie authenticating the user must be delivered and stored.

Each of the entities is represented as a separate transactional object (see Figure 8-2). A transaction will begin when the user downloads the Java application and types in the bank

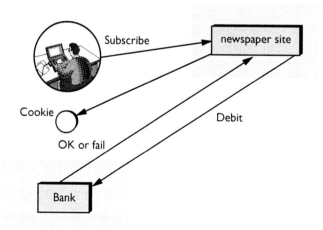

Figure 8-2 Transactional newspaper.

account details. The application will then attempt to debit the account and, if successful, send a cookie to the browser. It will then commit the transaction. If a failure occurs, the transaction and all of its work will be aborted.

Providing end-to-end transactional integrity between the browser and the application (server) is important, as it allows work involving *both* the browser and the server to be atomic. However, traditional techniques based on CGI scripts cannot provide end-to-end guarantees. As illustrated in Figure 8-3 the user selects a URL which references a CGI script on a Web server (message 1), which then performs the transaction and returns a response to the browser (message 2) *after* the transaction has completed. Returning the message during the transaction is incorrect since it may not be able to commit the changes.

In a failure-free environment, this mechanism works well. However, in the presence of failures it is possible for message 2 to be lost between the server and the browser, resulting in work at the server not being atomic with respect to any browser-related work. Thus, there is no end-to-end transactional guarantee.

Before moving on, let's consider what type of application might benefit from end-to-end transactions. Consider the case of an online bank that allows users to inspect, remove and insert money from their accounts. When money is removed it is converted into *digital cash tokens* (*e-cash*) which are stored and manipulated by the browser and contain the token's current "cash" balance; we shall assume that these tokens can be presented to other Web commerce applications as payment for services. Insertion of money to an account is simply the reverse, whereby a token is consumed and the user's account is credited by the amount left within the token. The bank requires making the delivery of the cash token to the user's browser *and* the debiting of the user's account atomic. Failures must not result in inconsistencies at the browser or the bank.

Although the user may be quite happy for failures to result in delivery of services but without losing e-cash, the bank and service providers won't be. Likewise, the user won't be happy if the e-cash tokens are debited and no services are provided. So, end-to-end transaction semantics are useful for both sides of the relationship. Imagine trying to do this without transactions. This

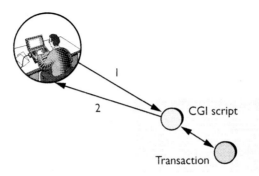

Figure 8-3 Transactions through CGI scripts.

must be done in a reliable, fault-tolerant manner and hopefully automatically. It's not an easy undertaking.

End-to-End Transactions and the New Generation of Transaction Systems

The question is often asked about whether or not the models on which current transaction systems are based (e.g., J2EE/JTA and OTS) are powerful enough to support end-to-end transactional guarantees for applications. In addition, it has been suggested that traditional Online Transaction Processing systems (OLTP) do not suffer from such limitations, rendering them more suitable vehicles for the emerging e-commerce applications that may require such guarantees.

In the following sections we consider this question and show that there is nothing inherent with these new models that would prevent applications using them to obtain end-to-end transactionality. However, before addressing the question of whether or not any specific transaction system can be used to provide end-to-end transactional guarantees, it is important to realize that end-to-end transactionality is not some Holy Grail of transactioning. It's a solution to one specific problem area and is in no way a global panacea to all transaction issues. The ability, or lack thereof, to provide end-to-end transaction integrity guarantees does not in and of itself prevent a specific transaction system from tackling many other equally important issues in today's evolving world of e-commerce and mobile applications.

So, unless end-to-end transactions are a necessity for you now, don't ignore the use of a specific transaction system implementation just because it may not provide them. But as with anything, if you are likely to require end-to-end transactions in the future then you'd either better ensure that your chosen system can support them now (or eventually), or that there is a suitable migration path from it to another transaction system.

Is End-to-End Transactionality Possible at All?

There is nothing inherent in *any* transaction protocol (two-phase, three-phase, presumed abort, presumed nothing, and so on) that prevents end-to-end transactionality. The transaction engine implementation (the coordinator) has very little effect on this, whether or not it is embedded in a proprietary service or within an industry standard application server. What does make end-to-end transactionality difficult is that it requires a transactional participant to reside at each "end."

> **N O T E** Importantly, end-to-end transactionality does not require a transaction coordinator and its associated baggage to reside at each "end," although failure recovery mechanisms may be necessary. Some transaction systems do require a component footprint to reside at each end, but this is an implementation choice and not required by the general concept of end-to-end transactionality.

As we saw in Chapter 1, "Transaction Fundamentals," there is a contract that exists between the transaction coordinator and its participants. To briefly reiterate (and with many simplifications, e.g., we ignore heuristic outcomes), this contract states:

- Once the transaction coordinator has decided whether to commit or roll back the transaction, it guarantees to deliver this information to every participant, regardless of failures of the coordinator or its participants. As we saw, there are various optimizations to this, such as the presumed abort protocol, but in essence the contract remains the same.
- Once told to prepare, a participant must make durable, sufficient information for it to either commit or roll back the work that it controls, even if failures of machines or the network occur. Until it determines the final outcome, a participant should neither commit nor roll back the work itself (here's where we carefully ignore heuristics). If a failure occurs or the final outcome of the transaction is slow in arriving, the resource can typically communicate with the coordinator to determine the current progress of the transaction.

In most transaction systems the majority of the effort goes into designing and developing the transaction coordinator engine, making it perform and be as reliable as possible. We've discussed many of the issues involved, such as failure recovery, interposition, and so on, and some of the important standards, so hopefully you'll understand why this is often the case. Then there's the other reason: you have to start somewhere and the coordinator is the obvious choice. Without a coordinator, you can't have any kind of transactions, end-to-end or not.

However, as we've already seen, by itself the coordinator is insufficient to provide a useable system: participants are obviously required. Although the two-phase protocol allows for any contract-conformant participant implementation to be registered with the coordinator, typically the only ones that the majority of people use are those that control work performed on databases; e.g., the aforementioned `XAResource`. This tends to result in the fact that many people equate transactions with databases only and, hence, the significant amount of resources required for these participant implementations. This is not the case: a participant can consume as many or as few resources as it needs to in order to fulfill the coordinator-to-participant contract. For example, a participant could use a local file-system in order to make state information durable, or it could use non-volatile RAM storage. It really depends upon what the implementer deems necessary for it in the environment in which it is to be deployed.

Prior to the advent of Java, resource-scare systems such as Web browsers had limited functionality that was defined when the system was originally created. When Java came along, these thin client environments could be enhanced dynamically with new functionality. What this means for us is that these clients can now potentially fully participate within transactional applications. Transaction participants tailored to the application and environment in which they are to work can be downloaded on-demand to the client to ensure that it can participate within the two-phase commit protocol.

N O T E   There is nothing special about specific transaction system implementations that makes them more easily adapted to this kind of environment. The specialization comes from the client-side participant.

Online Transaction Processing versus Object-Oriented Transaction Processing

So, is a "traditional" online transaction processing (OLTP) engine more suited to end-to-end transactionality guarantees than "newer" object-oriented transaction systems (OO-TP)? The quick answer is: no. Why should they be? We discussed the transaction fundamentals in Chapter 1 and you should be able to see that it doesn't matter whether a transaction system is supported by proprietary remote procedure call (RPC) and stub generation techniques or by an open-standard remote object invocation mechanism such as a CORBA ORB (Object Request Broker). Once the distributed layers are removed, they all share the same core—a two-phase commit protocol engine that supports durable storage (so that it can guarantee to complete any "in flight" transactions upon recovery) and failure recovery. How applications interact with that transaction engine and how it interacts with its participants is immaterial to the overall working of the transaction system.

The real benefit of OO-TP over OLTP is openness. Over the past 10 years there has been a significant move away from proprietary transaction processing systems and their support infrastructure to open standards. This move has been driven by developers and end-users who have traditionally found it extremely difficult to move applications from one vendor's product to another, or even between different versions of a product from the same vendor. As we saw in Chapter 3, the OMG pioneered this approach with the Object Transaction Service (OTS) in 1995, when IBM, HP, Digital, and others got together to provide a means whereby their existing products could essentially be wrapped in a standard veneer and interact with each other (something else which up until then was extremely difficult to do reliably).

It is, therefore, inaccurate to conclude that OLTP systems are inherently superior to OO-TP equivalents because of their architecture, support environment, or distribution paradigm. OLTP systems are typically monolithic closed systems, tying users to vendor specific choices for implementations, languages, and so on. If the experiences gained by the developers of efficient and reliable implementations of OLTP are transposed to OO-TP, then there is nothing to prevent such an OO-TP system from competing well.

The advantages should be obvious: open systems allow customers to pick and choose the components that they require to develop their applications, without having to worry about vendor lock-in. Such systems are also more readily ported to new hardware and operating systems, allowing customers even more choice for deployment.

N O T E We're not trying to give the impression that OLTP is inferior in any way to OO-TP. There are advantages and disadvantages to both approaches and for many applications either approach is equally valid. You should also remember that many OLTP implementations have been around for several years, giving them a measure of pedigree and inherent trust that only a few OO-TP systems can match. In addition, an OO-TP embedded in a J2EE application server looks quite similar to an OLTP.

The OTS and End-to-End Transactionality

Is the OTS a good basis for end-to-end transactionality? As we've already seen in Chapter 3, the OTS architecture provides standard interfaces to components that all transaction engines possess, such as the coordinator, the participant and the terminator. It does not modify the model underlying all of the existing different transaction monitor implementations: it mandates a two-phase commit protocol with presumed abort and *all* implementations of the OTS must comply with this. The majority of the issues we discussed in Chapter 1, "Transaction Fundamentals," have corresponding features or functionality in the OTS specification.

The OTS was never intended to replace existing transaction processing systems, but to be an adjunct to them. Transaction processing is at the core of commerce and enterprise systems. All businesses have the concept of a transaction, but they realize the concept using various architectures. Some transactions are very simple, such as purchasing a book or transferring funds, and can be processed immediately. Other transactions are more complex, such as fulfilling a purchase order or completing an insurance claim, and may take days or even years to process. Transaction processing forms the core of enterprise information systems and often drives the business. Once developed and proven, successful TP systems stay in place for decades.

Therefore, no company that has spent many years building up reliability in such a critical piece of software as transactions would be prepared to start from scratch and implement again. In addition, no users of such reliable transaction software would be prepared to take the risk of transitioning to this new software, even if it were "open." In the area of transactions, which are a critical fault-tolerance component, it takes time to convince customers that new technology performs and is stable enough to replace what they have been using for many years.

Although the CORBA model is typically discussed in terms of client-server architecture, from the outset its designers did not want to impose any restrictions on the types of environment in which it could run. There is no assumption about how "thin" a client is or how "fat" a server must be in order to execute a CORBA application. Many programmers these days simply use the client-server model as a convenient way in which to reason about distributed applications, but at their core these applications never have what would traditionally be considered a thin client: services that a user requires may well be co-located with that user (i.e., within the same process or JVM). CORBA was the first open architecture to support configurable deployment of services in this way, correctly seeing this separation of client and service as just that: a deployment issue.

There is nothing in the CORBA architecture that requires a client to be thin and functionally deficient.

N O T E   The OTS is a comparable model to the likes of CICS, Tuxedo and DEC ACMS. It differs only in that it is a standard and is intended to allow interoperation between different implementations. There is nothing fundamentally wrong with the OTS architecture that prevents it from being used in an end-to-end manner. The OTS supports end-to-end transactionality in exactly the same way CICS, or any other "traditional" OLTP would—through its resources.

The CORBA Effect

So, if the OTS architecture is up to the task of end-to-end transactions, are the CORBA implementations (ORBs) on which OTS implementations execute sufficient for mission-critical applications? It is true that back in the mid-1990s when CORBA implementations first appeared on the market their performance was not as good as hand-crafted solutions. However, that has changed over the latter few years. The footprint of some ORBs is certainly large, but likewise there are other ORBs that have been tailored specifically for real-time or embedded use. Companies such as IBM, IONA and BEA have seen ORBs develop over the years to become a critical part of the infrastructure that they have to control and therefore they have their own implementations. Other companies have licensed ORB implementations from elsewhere.

The crash failure of an ORB does not typically mean that it can recover automatically and continue applications from where they left off. This is because the ORB does not have necessary semantic and syntactic information to automatically checkpoint state for recovery purposes. However, by making use of suitably defined services such as the OTS and the persistence service, it is possible for *applications* to recover themselves or for vendors to use these services to perform this operation for applications.

It is true that OLTP systems provide this kind of feature out-of-the-box. However, it is an unfair comparison: an OLTP system does just one thing and does it well—it manages transactions. A CORBA ORB is meant to provide support for arbitrary distributed applications, the majority of which will probably not even need fault-tolerance let alone transactions. However, for those applications that do need these capabilities, it is entirely possible to provide *exactly* the same recovery functionality using OMG open standards.

The J2EE Effect

Although the J2EE model is client-server based, as with CORBA there is nothing to prevent a client being rich in functionality. It is a deployment choice that is made at design time and runtime. (Obviously, the capability for being so rich is required to be built into the client, and even if it were present, it would be up to the user to determine whether or not such functionality was required or was possible.)

> **N O T E**   As we described in Chapter 3, "The Object Transaction Service," although J2EE did not start out as an infrastructure that used CORBA, it quickly became evident that the experiences the OMG companies had obtained over the years in developing CORBA were extremely important to any distributed system. As a result, over the past few years J2EE got closer and closer to the CORBA world, and now requires some critical ORB components in order to run.

As we saw in Chapter 2, "Open Group Distributed Transaction Processing and Java," the typical way in which J2EE programmers use transactions is through the Java Transaction API (JTA), which is a *mandated* part of the specification. The JTA is intended as a higher-level API for programmers, to try to isolate them from some of the more complex aspects of constructing transactional applications. Although the JTA does not mandate a specific underlying transaction system implementation, the OTS is the transaction standard for many companies and it allows interoperation between different implementations.

Therefore, it was decided by the J2EE developers that the preferred implementation choice for interoperability would be based on the OTS. As we saw in Chapter 3, "The Object Transaction Service," this does not mean that an OTS implementation is required, only that the on-the-wire message formats used by a specific implementation are OTS compliant if interoperability with other OTS compliant implementations is required.

Application Servers and Thin Clients

Does the use of an application server require the use of thin clients? As we've already seen, this is a deployment issue. It is certainly correct to say that most J2EE programmers currently use a thin client approach, with most of the business logic residing within the server; however, this is simply because this is the solution that matches 90% of the existing requirements. Closer examination of all J2EE applications would certainly reveal that although thin clients are the norm, they are by no means the complete picture.

There is *nothing* to say that the client-side of J2EE application has to be wafer-thin. If the client wants to embed functionality such as a two-phase aware transactional resource within itself, then that is entirely possible. In fact, a client could just as easily be embedded within an application server itself, if the footprint allowed. The reasons for not doing this are more to do with the footprint size than any architectural issue.

Conclusions

We have shown there is nothing inherent in the JTA or OTS models that prevent them from providing end-to-end transactional guarantees. The two-phase commit protocol knows nothing about clients or servers, makes no assumptions about locality of coordinator or participants and requires no semantic knowledge of the applications. End-to-end transactional guarantees are simply a deployment view on the relative locality of different participants.

Are OLTP systems more suited to end-to-end guarantees than modern OO-TP systems? As we have shown, since they are both based on two-phase commit protocols there is nothing in either model that would mean they are any more or less ideal for any specific problem domain. However, there are obvious design and implementation decisions that can be made when building a transaction system using either model that may mean that specific instances are not best suited for end-to-end transactional solutions. It is important to realize that this is an implementation choice only.

The Usefulness of Interposition

As we've seen, transaction forms the core of enterprise information systems and often drives the business. Once developed and proven, successful TP systems stay in place for decades. All businesses have the concept of a transaction, but they realize the concept using various architectures, such as JTA or OTS. Some transactions are simple and can be processed immediately, such as purchasing a book or transferring funds. Other transactions are more complex and may take days or even years to process, such as fulfilling a purchase order or completing an insurance claim.

Business-to-business interactions occur between loosely coupled business domains that do not share data, location, or administration and have their own internal infrastructures, such as corporate workflow systems, asynchronous messaging, or a variety of transaction processing approaches. However, the overall business interactions (business process) will require some level of transactional support in order to guarantee consistent outcome and correct execution.

With the advent of Web services, these business domains are typically exposed to the world as individual services. Multiple Web services typically cooperate to perform a shared function, such as multiple related operations on a shared resource, or processing different portions of a purchase order using a predefined sequence.

A business process is typically split into business tasks and each task executes within a specific business domain. A business domain may itself be subdivided into other business domains in a recursive manner. Business transactions are responsible for managing interactions between these domains. All of these domains are coordinated to perform the overall business process.

This is an extremely important and evolving area of the software industry. How should these domains be tied together, when each domain may use a completely different internal protocol? Is there a Universal Adapter that converts from one domain-specific protocol to another and coordinates interactions across domains to ensure consistency? What software should be at the heart of the "engine" that directs the flow of execution of tasks?

The Universal Adapter

The transaction coordinator implementations at the heart of most industrial-strength transaction systems have been developed over many years and optimized for performance and reliability. Because of the places where transactions systems are used and the reliance companies place on them, the coordinator can be trusted to work correctly despite failures such as machine or network crashes. This level of trust is one that does not typically extend to other types of software components.

As we see in Chapter 9, there has been much discussion of the fact that ACID transactions are not suitable for most Web services transactions. While that is probably true, many people read that as "current transaction infrastructures are not suitable for most Web services transactions." This is a different statement entirely and overlooks the important aspects of what constitutes a transaction processing system.

Luckily for those companies that have invested large sums of money in transactional infrastructures, existing transaction systems can form the heart of Web services coordination and management. Although existing ACID transaction systems may be unsuited in their entirety for Web services transactions, the coordinator can often be used in isolation. What this means is that the development of Web services transactions protocols cannot occur in isolation from existing infrastructures.

Chapter 1, "Transaction Fundamentals," showed that one of the main benefits of a coordinator is that it can take the responsibility for notifying the participants of the outcome, making the outcomes of the participants persistent and managing the context. We also discussed interposition: a coordinator becomes a participant when it registers itself with another coordinator for the purpose of representing a set of other, typically local participants.

Interposition assists in achieving interoperability because the interposed coordinator can also translate a neutral outcome protocol into a platform-specific protocol. As far as the parent coordinator is concerned, the interposed (child) coordinator is a participant that obeys the parent's transaction protocol (typically two-phase). However, each child coordinator can be tailored to the domain in which it operates and the protocol(s) that domain uses. So, as far as the child's participants (and services) are concerned, it is a coordinator that executes its protocol (e.g., three-phase).

Prior to the arrival of Web services, we have seen transaction processing systems successfully used for coordination of inter-organizational work in precisely this manner. Consider the purchase of a home entertainment system, an example shown in Figure 8-4. The on-line shop interacts with its specific suppliers, each of which resides in its own business domain. The work necessary to obtain each component is modeled as a separate task. In this example, the HiFi task is actually composed of two subtasks.

In this example, the user may interact synchronously with the shop to build up the entertainment system. Alternately, the user may submit an order (possibly with a list of alternate requirements) to the shop that will eventually call back when it has been filled; likewise, the shop then submits orders to each supplier, requiring them to call back when each component is available (or is known to be unavailable).

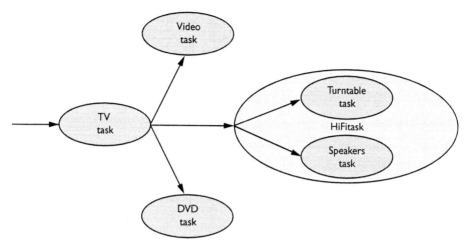

Figure 8-4 Business processes and tasks.

For example, Figure 8-5 shows how the home entertainment system would be federated into interposed coordinator domains. Each domain is represented by a subordinate coordinator that masks the internal business process infrastructure from its parent (e.g., workflow system). Not only does the interposed domain require the use of a different context when communicating with services within the domain (the coordinator endpoint is different), but each domain may use different protocols to those outside of the domain: the subordinate coordinator may then act as a translator from protocols outside the domain to protocols used within the domain.

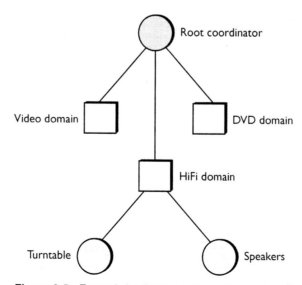

Figure 8-5 Example business process interposition.

Web services make the coupling of disparate business domains easier by breaking down interoperability barriers. However, they also bring to the foreground the coordination of inter-organizational transactions and how this can be achieved when each organization has previously invested in non-interoperable infrastructures. As you can see, the solution to this is not to reinvent reliable coordination but to use what already exists. It has taken decades to evolve transaction processing systems to their current levels of reliability, efficiency and performance. Even with the benefits of 20-20 hindsight, it is likely to take many years of effort to reinvent the wheel and assure users that what they are being asked to rely upon has the same level of pedigree as something they know they can rely on because of past experience.

Object Decomposition to Improve Throughput

The structuring mechanisms available within transaction systems are sequential and concurrent composition of (sub-) transactions. These are sufficient if an application function can be represented as a single top-level transaction. Frequently, this is not the case. Top-level transactions are most suitably viewed as "short-lived" entities; they are less well suited for structuring "long-lived" application functions (e.g., running for days). Long-lived, top-level transactions may reduce the concurrency in the system by holding on to locks for a long time; further, if such a transaction aborts, work already performed could be undone.

One approach to this problem is through the provision of relaxed ACID semantics, allowing locks to be released before the transaction terminates. In Chapter 9 we look at how this is currently being formalized in J2EE through the *Activity Service*. However, little attention has been paid to which applications have a need for such functionality and why. The applications cited tend to be "monolithic" with coarse locking granularity, such that locking one item prevents users from inspecting/modifying other, non-conflicting items.

We contend that object-orientation and application decomposition into objects offers another solution to some of the problems that can arise when using transactions over a long duration. The object is the natural unit of concurrency and persistence, and objects can obviously contain other objects. Therefore, the amount of resource contention can be reduced by restructuring an application into objects, with the benefit that no changes to the transaction model are required. Unfortunately, tools to assist programmers in this area are lacking.

To illustrate what we mean, let's take the example of a cinema booking system shown in Figure 8-6. Let's assume the cinema has `reserveSeat`, `unreserveSeat` and `seatStatus` methods that reserve a specific seat, unreserve a seat and return whether or not the specified seat is currently reserved, respectively.

A fairly basic implementation of this would have the theatre as an object (e.g., EJB) with its state being the current states of all of the seats (i.e., reserved or unreserved). In this case, because the state of the cinema is an amalgamation of all of the individual seat states, if one user makes a transactional enquiry on the state of a specific seat (say, 2B in the figure), the `seatStatus` operation will acquire a read lock on the cinema, which is implicitly a read lock on all

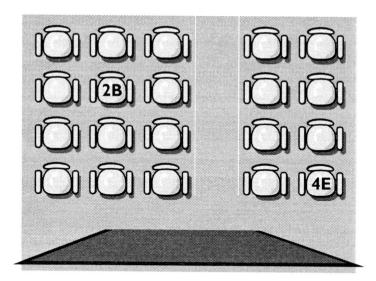

Figure 8-6   Implementing a cinema booking system as a composite object.

of the seats (this is a read lock because we're not modifying the state of the cinema by making an inquiry.) The result of this is that if another user attempts to invoke a reserveSeat operation on, say, seat 4E while the original seatStatus transaction is still active, the second user will be blocked, despite the fact that the operations don't conflict—operating on seat 4E doesn't affect seat 2B. Not a good situation to be in for the cinema, especially if the first user takes a while to terminate the transaction within which seatStatus was performed.

A more sensible implementation would structure the cinema as one transactional object, with each seat as separate transactional objects responsible for its own state and concurrency control. The cinema state will be referenced to the individual seats and may in fact be static, unless we want to add more complex operations such as addSeat and removeSeat. The seat objects would then have operations for reserve, unreserve and status.

In this implementation, when the status enquiry for 2B is received by the seat, a read lock is obtained only on that specific seat. As such, when the subsequent reserve operation for 4B is received by that seat object, it can be performed, even if the first status transaction is still active. This has obvious benefits on throughput for the cinema: multiple users can make reservations concurrently and will only be blocked if their requests really do conflict.

You could structure the cinema and seats as individual EJBs. However, if your back-end data store is a database, then you will need to ensure that their states reside in separate data structures, e.g., tables. This is because database locks, which will be acquired when accessing and manipulating state, occur on entire tables and not individual entries. Therefore, if all seats were in a single table, obtaining a write lock on one such seat would implicitly cause a write lock to be obtained on all seats, thus reducing throughput again.

Knowing how your object states are laid out in the data store is, therefore, extremely important. Getting the right data structuring layout for your application isn't easy, especially as the number of objects in your application and dependencies between those objects grow. Tools to assist in this approach are few and far between. For example, the Arjuna Technologies Transaction Service (formerly known as the Hewlett-Packard Transaction Service) provides Transactional Objects for Java (TOJ), a toolkit for constructing transactional Java objects (the current popular phrase is Plain Old Java Objects or POJOS) of arbitrary size such that each object has the ACID properties.

However, for certain applications object decomposition may not provide the entire solution, and some ACID relaxation may be necessary. Importantly, the required functionality may be achieved through higher-level APIs, e.g., nested top-level transactions that we saw in Chapter 1, "Transaction Fundamentals." The types of performance improvements currently required are achievable through a combination of object decomposition and these extended transaction APIs.

Summary

In this chapter we've looked at some of the more advanced transaction concepts and techniques. Some knowledge of them is important to understand how transactions can be used in an environment like J2EE. An important point that is always asked is whether or not Java is up to the demanding task of a transaction system. After all, Java is an interpreted language and interpreted languages can never perform as well as their compiled cousins. However, as we saw, performance and the interpreted nature of Java is not necessarily the issue, especially when compared to the ability to produce a reliable system that can run on all deployment platforms. And it is always possible to create poor transaction service implementations in a compiled language.

We then looked at the concept of end-to-end transactions. The all-or-nothing property that transactions provide can be made to extend across your entire application, encompassing clients as well as servers; this can be extremely useful as you might well imagine. We looked at whether or not this capability is possible at all and showed that as far as transaction principles are concerned, there is nothing special about end-to-end transactionality. Any limitations are placed by transaction service implementations. Hopefully, we also managed to destroy the myth that traditional transaction processing monitors (OLTP) are needed to provide this capability: the current generation of object-based specifications and their implementations are more than a match for their OLTP equivalents.

If you need end-to-end transaction support, then you shouldn't be swayed by OLTP versus OO-TP arguments. Both types of transaction service implementations are equally well suited for this job. However, where you need to look is at the participant and failure-recovery support provided to you as a developer. Having to write participants for both ends of the interaction is often a difficult and time-consuming task, especially when they have to tolerate failures and recovery. Any implementation that provides you with support for this kind of development (and even testing) can save a lot of time, effort and money. Likewise, if your transaction service implementation doesn't support failure recovery, then you'd better make sure failures don't happen! Meanwhile, back in the real world, we'd recommend you look for an implementation that does support failure recovery.

> **N O T E** Hopefully you have noticed by now that failure recovery is an extremely important aspect of distributed transaction systems. It crops up over and over again.

Although we looked at interposition in Chapter 1, "Transaction Fundamentals," in terms of improving performance, in this chapter we examined how it can be used to provide protocol-bridging when tying together disparate enterprise domains. Coordinating these domains to ensure consistent outcomes across them all is a critically evolving area and one where existing transaction infrastructures should be involved, rather than starting from scratch.

In Chapter 1, "Transaction Fundamentals," we looked at two-phase locking and how locks on resources must be held for the duration of the transaction in order to ensure ACID semantics. This can obviously have a detrimental affect on an application if a resource remains locked for a long duration. Although extended transaction models can help in this, where ACID semantics are relaxed, a more straightforward approach is through the use of object-orientation. Many problems occur because many resources are governed by the same lock (e.g., a single database table that contains numerous different and unrelated data elements). Objects naturally become the granularity of transactional resources and by using fine-grained objects; locks can be obtained on only those data structures that are really required.

CHAPTER 9

The J2EE Activity
Service

As we've seen throughout this book, distributed objects plus ACID transactions provide a good foundation for building high integrity business applications. The ACID properties of transactions ensure that even in complex business applications the consistency of the application's state is preserved, despite concurrent accesses and failures.

However, as we see in this section, ACID transactions are only part of the story: traditional transaction processing systems are sufficient if an application function can be represented as a single top-level transaction. Frequently, this is not the case. In this chapter we first examine why traditional transaction systems are insufficient for all type of applications that require "transaction-like" semantics. We then look at what the industry is doing to try to address these problems. There are two specific areas of interest where these new transaction models are being used: J2EE enhancements, which we discuss in this chapter, and the evolving world of Web services, which we cover in the next chapter. We then conclude with an indication of where we believe these standards belong in the developers' arsenal of transactional tools.

When ACID Is Too Strong

Top-level transactions are most suitably viewed as "short-lived" entities, performing stable state changes to the system; they are less well suited for structuring "long-lived" application functions (e.g., running for minutes, hours, days, or longer). Long-lived top-level transactions may reduce the concurrency in the system to an unacceptable level by holding on to resources (e.g., locks) for a long time. Further, if such a transaction aborts, much valuable work already performed could be undone.

The reasons for this should be understandable given what we saw in Chapter 1. Transactional services or objects are responsible for the *Isolation* aspect of ACID and do this using locks or timestamps. In order to make sure that concurrent users don't see intermediate results and potentially violate application consistency, locking rules require two-phase concurrency control: any locks obtained during the transaction must be retained until the transaction has completed.

What this means ultimately is that structuring certain applications from long-duration (*long-running*) transactions can reduce the amount of concurrency within an application or (in the event of failures) require work to be performed again. In the types of applications we've considered so far in the book, this hasn't been an issue: transactions are typically of short duration or conflicts between users are minimal. However, there are certain classes of application where it is known that resources acquired within a transaction can be released early, rather than having to wait until the transaction terminates. In the event of the transaction rolling back, compensation activities may be necessary to restore the system to a consistent state. Such compensation activities (which may perform forward or backward recovery) will typically be application specific, may not be necessary at all, or may be more efficiently dealt with by the application itself.

For example, let's take the relatively simple scenario of arranging travel and accommodation for a conference, as illustrated in Figure 9-1. In particular, the attendee will require a flight to the city where the conference is being held, a room reservation at a hotel and possibly a rental car for the duration of the conference.

While locating flight, hotel and car rental options, we need to ensure likely options can be reserved as we assemble the set of reservations required for the trip as a whole. As well as considering the needs of the conference attendee, service providers also need to have some autonomy and maintain control of their own resources (flight, room, and car rental reservations).

The elements required for the booking are interrelated within this domain and yet they are not necessarily predetermined. Obviously without a flight, it makes no sense to book the hotel or to rent a car unless the conference is local, but in other circumstances it may make sense to book the flight and hotel, but if the hotel booking we make is at the same hotel as the conference it may be possible to do without the car rental.

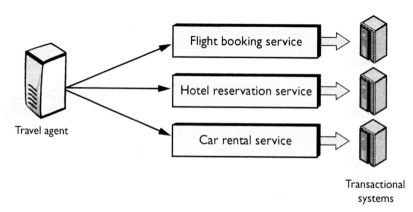

Figure 9-1 Travel agent scenario.

We may also want to keep our options open by reserving a number of flights while looking for other more direct travel options or other convenient hotels. The customer solicits multiple quotes to determine the lowest-cost supplier. Therefore, conducting the entire travel arrangements within a single ACID transaction is inappropriate: this type of flexibility is unavailable since either all of the work performed within the transaction will succeed or none will. It would not be possible to have the partial outcomes (relaxed atomicity) we might require if visiting multiple flight booking services, for example.

Before we look at how this type of problem can be solved by what are termed *extended transaction models*, let's look at examples of other scenarios where traditional transaction semantics are inappropriate.

- *Bulletin board*: Posting and retrieving information from bulletin boards can be performed using transactions. While it is desirable for bulletin board operations to be structured as transactions, if these transactions are nested within other application transactions then bulletin information can remain inaccessible for long periods of time. Releasing of bulletin board resources early would therefore be desirable. Of course, if the application transaction aborts, it may be necessary to invoke compensating activities; this is consistent with the manner in which bulletin boards are used.
- *Name server access*: For the sake of availability and consistency, it may be desirable to replicate name services and structure operations on them as transactions. Application transactions, upon finding out that certain objects are unavailable due to a machine crash, for example, can invoke operations to update the name server replicas accordingly, while carrying on with the main computation. There is no reason to undo these name server updates should the application transaction subsequently abort.
- *Billing and accounting resource usage*: If a service is accessed by a transaction and the user of the service is to be charged, then the charging information should not be recovered if the transaction rolls back. Telecommunications companies use precisely this arrangement so that you'll always be billed for trying to call your friends or family, even if the call doesn't actually succeed!
- *Arranging a meeting*: The requirement is to arrange a date for a meeting between groups of people; it is assumed that each user has a *personal diary object* which records the dates of meetings and so on, and each diary entry (slot) can be locked separately. The application starts by informing people of a forthcoming meeting and then receiving from each a set of preferred dates. Once this information has been gathered, it will be analyzed to find the set of acceptable dates for the meeting. This set is then broadcast to the users to get a more definitive idea of the preferred date(s). This process is repeated until a single date is determined. To reduce the amount of work that must be re-performed in the event of failures, and to increase the concurrency within the application, it is desirable to execute each "round" of this protocol as a separate top-level transaction. However, to prevent concurrent arrangement activities from

conflicting with each other, it is beneficial to allow locks acquired on preferred diary entries to be passed from one transaction to another, i.e., the locks remain acquired on only those entries that are required for the next "round."

These applications share a common feature: as viewed by external users, in the event of successful execution, the work performed appears to possess ACID features of traditional transactional applications. If failures occur, however, non-ACID behavior is possible, typically resulting in non-serializability. For some applications, e.g., the name service example above, this does not result in application-level inconsistency and no form of compensation for the failure is required. However, for other applications, e.g., the bulletin board, some form of compensation may be required to restore the system to a consistent state from which it can then continue to operate.

Fortunately, long-running activities can be structured as many independent, short-duration, top-level transactions to form a "logical" long-running transaction. This structuring allows an activity to acquire and use resources for only the required duration of this long-running transactional activity. This is illustrated in Figure 9-2, where an application activity (shown by the dotted ellipse) has been split into many different, coordinated, and short-duration top-level transactions.

Let's look at a variant of our travel agent scenario again and assume that the application activity is concerned with booking a taxi (t1), reserving a table at a restaurant (t2), reserving a seat at the theater (t3), then booking a room at a hotel (t4), reserving a taxi home the following day (t5), and delivery of a bouquet of flowers (t6). If all of these operations were performed as a single transaction, then resources acquired during t1 would not be released until the top-level transaction has terminated. If subsequent activities t2, t3, and so on do not require those resources, then they will be needlessly unavailable to other clients.

However, if failures and concurrent access occur during the lifetime of these individual transactional activities, then the behavior of the entire "logical long-running transaction" may not possess ACID properties. Therefore, some form of compensation may be required to attempt

Application activity

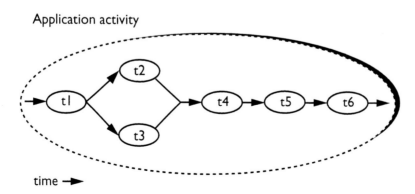

time ➤

Figure 9-2 An example of a logical long-running "transaction" without failure.

to return the state of the system to consistency. For example, if you look at Figure 9-3, let's assume that *t4* rolls back and that the application can continue to make forward progress, but in order to do so must now undo some state changes made prior to the start of *t4* (by *t1, t2* or *t3*). In addition, because the original flow of control didn't happen, the work that was to be performed by transactions *t5* and *t6* can't happen.

Therefore, new activities are started; *tc1*, which is a compensation activity that will attempt to undo state changes performed by, say, *t2*, and *t3* that will continue the application once *tc1* has completed. *t5'* and *t6'* are new activities that continue after compensation, e.g., since it was not possible to reserve the theatre, restaurant and hotel, it is decided to book tickets at the cinema (*tc5'*) and a limousine home with the bouquet delivered by the driver (*t6'*).

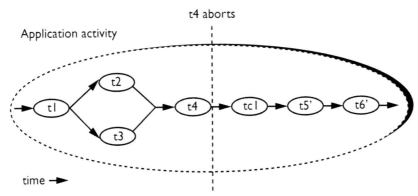

Figure 9-3 An example of a logical long-running "transaction" with failure.

The Proposed J2EE Solution

The approach suggested for J2EE to address extended transactions is called the *J2EE Activity Service*. At the time of writing, it's important to know that this work has still yet to be adopted by J2EE, although it has successful negotiated the Java Community Process. As with the JTS, the basis of the J2EE Activity Service is cutting edge work that occurred within the Object Management Group (OMG); as we see in Chapter 10, the original OMG work has also heavily influenced two of the main suites of specifications in the evolving area of Web services transactions. So, the J2EE Activity Service shares a lot of similarities with the OMG work.

N O T E   As we saw in Chapter 3, "The Object Transaction Service," the JTA requires the on-the-wire message format to be the same as the OTS for interoperability; the J2EE Activity Service places a similar requirement on implementations—if you want interoperability, then your on-the-wire implementation had better be conformant with the OMG specification. This doesn't mean that you require a CORBA-based implementation though.

The architecture of this service is based on the concept that "one-size doesn't fit all" in the world of extended transactions. By examining the range of extended transaction models that currently exists, it is possible to see that they have several things in common:

- A notion of coordinator and participants.
- Coordination events that, depending upon the model, may occur at arbitrary points during the extended transaction.
- The coordinator sends specific messages to the participants and expects specific responses, though the coordination protocol differs between each model and may change depending upon when the coordination event occurs.

The Activity Service architecture uses these observations as the basis for a low-level framework capable of supporting the construction of arbitrary coordination protocols. The design is based on the insight that the various extended transaction models can be supported by providing a general purpose event signaling mechanism that can be programmed to enable activities—application specific units of computations—to coordinate each other in a manner prescribed by the extended transaction model under consideration. The designers of the Activity Service framework believe that it is sufficient to allow middleware to manage complex business protocols that extend the concept of transaction from the well-understood, short-duration atomic transaction. The different extended transaction models can be mapped onto specific implementations of this framework permitting such transactions to span a network of systems connected indirectly by some distribution mechanism.

As we've mentioned, the approach taken in the Activity Service is to provide a low-level infrastructure capable of supporting the coordination and control of abstract, application-specific entities to enable construction of various forms of extended transaction models as desired by workflow engines, component management middleware and other systems. These entities (which are termed *activities*) may be transactional, they may use weaker forms of serializability, or they may not be transactional at all. The important point is that a computation is viewed as composed of one or more activities and the activity service is only concerned with their control and coordination, leaving the semantics of such activities to the application programmer.

In the following sections we look at the core concepts involved in the J2EE Activity Service. Many of these concepts will be familiar to you from previous chapters; where concepts are truly new, we cover them in more depth. A tip we'd recommend when reading this chapter is to try to map the abstractions to the traditional ACID transaction model we've already described. This shouldn't be too difficult because the Activity Service must be able to support that model as well. At the end of this chapter we describe how ACID transactions are supported, as an example.

Activities, Participants and Coordination

The concept of an *activity* is central to the Activity Service. An activity is a unit of work (potentially distributed) that may or may not be transactional. During its lifetime an activity may have transactional and non-transactional periods. An activity is allowed to contain other activities, which allows an application to better delineate the application work.

Within the Activity Service model an activity is *created*, made to *run*, and then *completed*. The result of a completed activity is its *outcome*, which can be used to determine subsequent flow of control to other activities. Activities can run over long periods of time and can thus be *suspended* and then *resumed* later, in the same way that transactions can be suspended and resumed in the JTA or OTS.

Although transactions may not be suitable for everything, it is reasonable to assume that applications will want to use transactions at some point. As we saw in Figure 9-4, this may not be for the duration of the entire application but may just be for certain short-duration units of work (the aforementioned activities). Therefore, a core component of the Activity Service architecture is how activities and transactions are related. Being designed to integrate with J2EE, the Activity Service integrates well with both JTA and OTS transactions.

An activity may run for an arbitrary length of time, and may use atomic transactions at any point(s) during its lifetime. For example, consider Figure 9-4, which shows a series of connected activities cooperating during the lifetime of an application. The solid ellipses represent transaction boundaries, whereas the dotted ellipses are activity boundaries. Activity *A1* uses two top-level transactions during its execution, whereas *A2* uses none. Additionally, transactional activity *A3* has another transactional activity, *A3'* nested within it.

One thing that all extended transaction protocols have in common is coordination. We've already seen how a traditional transaction coordinator uses the two-phase commit protocol when

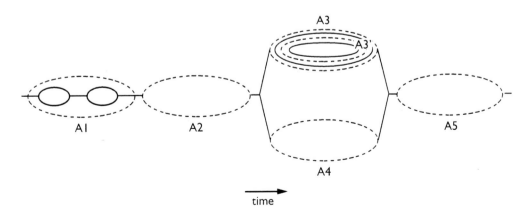

Figure 9-4   The relationship between transactions and activities.

it terminates. Other transaction models use different protocols (e.g., three-phase commit) and may allow coordination to happen at points other than when the transaction terminates.

The activity service provides coordination and control in a simple manner. Basically, associated with each activity is an *activity coordinator* that can coordinate the execution of constituent activities or participants. In general, the coordination required can vary depending upon the phase of the execution of the entity (e.g., starting or terminating), so associated with a coordinator is one or more *protocol managers*, each manager implementing a specific coordination protocol. For example, a manager could implement a two-phase commit protocol.

The Activity Service allows demarcation signals of any kind to be communicated to registered entities (*actions*) through *signals*. For example, the termination of one activity may initiate the start/restart of other activities in a workflow-like environment. Signals can be used to infer a flow of control during the execution of an application. Actions are the participants in all transaction models and signals are the messages that are used to carry the protocol information necessary for coordination. The behavior of an action will be peculiar to the extended transaction model of which it is a part.

One of the keys to the extensibility of this framework is the *signal set* whose behavior is peculiar to the kind of extended transaction—the protocol manager we mentioned previously. The signal set is the entity that generates signals that are sent to actions by the coordinator and processes the results returned to determine which signal to send next. Think of the signal set as the intelligence necessary for driving the specific coordination protocol and the Activity Service as providing a basic (intelligence-free) coordinator that the signal set plugs into.

As new types of extended transaction models emerge, so will new signal set instances and associated actions. This allows a single implementation of the Activity Service framework to serve a large variety of extended transaction models, each with its own idea of extended transactions, each with its own action and signal set implementations. The *Activity Service implementation* will not need to know the behavior that is encapsulated in the actions and signal sets it is given, merely interacting with their interfaces in an entirely uniform and transparent way.

Relationship to the J2EE Architecture

A high-level view of the role of the Activity Service within the J2EE architecture is shown in Figure 9-5. As with traditional transaction systems such as the OTS or JTA, it's not expected that the operations in the Activity Services will be used directly by end-user application programmers. As with OTS, the interfaces provided by the Activity Service are really too low-level to use directly in most applications. That's why it is envisioned that higher-level services (termed *HLS* in the specification) are provided to isolate the user from the underlying Activity Service This is similar to the way in which the *JTA* can be used to isolate you from the OTS.

We saw in Chapter 1, "Transaction Fundamentals," how failure recovery is an important part of implementing a transaction processing system. Obviously, failure recovery is important for any transaction protocol, and the Activity Service spends considerable effort in this area.

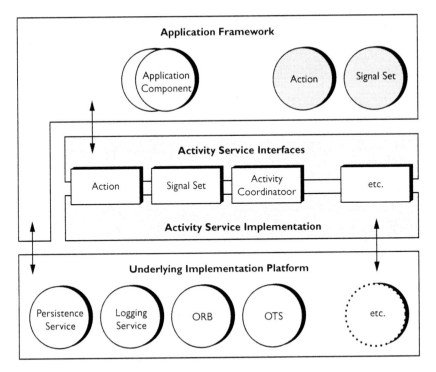

Figure 9-5 The role of the Activity Service.

However, without covering the entire specification in a lot more detail than we have space for here, it's impossible for us cover it in this chapter. So, although we won't mention failure recovery, you should remember that it is there.

Coordinating Activities

If you look back at our example scenario from Figure 9-3, each transaction would be modeled as an activity. In this case, what is required is a way for activity termination (either successfully or as a result of a failure) to affect the flow of other activities. This knowledge then needs to be related to the eventual outcome of enclosing (child) activities or sibling activities. Returning to our example scenario, knowing whether *t4* has failed (rolls back in our case) is important so that the enclosing activity can then schedule other activities to compensate for it and then make forward progress.

An activity that contains other activities may impose a requirement on the Activity Service for managing these component activities. If the flow of work depends upon the outcomes of specific activities, then it must be determined whether these component activities worked as specified, or failed, or terminated exceptionally and then how to map this to the enclosing activity's outcome. This is true whether the activities are strictly parallel, strictly sequential or some combination of the two. In general, an activity (or some entity acting on its behalf) that needs to coordinate the outcomes of component activities has to know what state each component activity is in:

- Which are active?
- Which have completed and what were their outcomes? An activity is allowed to complete in either a success or fail state (roughly corresponding to a transaction commit and transaction roll back).
- Which activities failed to complete?

Constituent activities are required to register themselves with a given signal set of the enclosing activity; this is done by an activity registering an action with the signal set. At an appropriate time, the coordinating activity triggers the execution protocol implemented by one of its signal set by invoking a standard operation; this leads to the set signaling each registered activity by invoking an operation on the registered action. The signaled activity can now perform some specific computation and return results (e.g., flush the data on to stable store and return "done"), and this way the protocol advances. Don't worry if this still seems a little confusing. We'll cover these aspects of activity coordination in more detail in the subsequent sections.

The High-Level Service (HLS)

The HLS is the embodiment of an extended transaction service in the Activity Service architecture. It's a service-provider component that plugs into the application server and offers to applications service-specific interfaces that are mediated by the application server through interactions between the HLS and the Activity Service. An HLS implements the interfaces of the `javax.activity.coordination` package. As you might imagine, there's a lot involved in the Activity Service and hence the HLS, so we are just able to give a flavor of the more pertinent interfaces.

Actions, SignalSets and Signals

The most important components in the HLS are the `Action`, `Signal` and `SignalSet`. As we see in this section, it's these interfaces and classes that are at the heart of the pluggable coordination nature of the Activity Service.

An activity may decide to transmit coordinator protocol specific messages (`Signals`) to any number of other activities at specific times during its lifetime, e.g., when it terminates. The transmission of these messages actually happens through the activity coordinator, in a similar manner to the way in which the traditional ACID transaction coordinator sends two-phase commit messages to its participants when it terminates. The receiving entities (the coordinator's participants) may either have been running and are waiting for a specific `Signal`, or may be started by the receipt of the `Signals`. The information encoded within a `javax.activity.Signal` depends upon the implementation of the extended transaction model and, therefore, the class is designed to accommodate this as shown in Code Listing 9-1:

Code Listing 9-1 The `Signal` class

```
public class Signal
{
    public org.omg.CORBA.Any getExtendedAny ();
    public java.io.Serializable getExtendedValue ();
    public java.lang.String getName ();
    public java.lang.String getSignalSetName ();
};
```

You might look at this class and wonder about the `org.omg.CORBA.Any`: this is the legacy of the original OMG specification on which the J2EE Activity Service is based. It's basically CORBA's way of allowing arbitrary object types to be communicated between clients and services. If you look closely at the other methods in the `Signal` class you'll see that it's basically a template that can encapsulate any data. Essentially `Signals` are used to encode the protocol messages that flow between the coordinator and its participants.

Obviously, in order for this to work, the sender and receiver need to agree on the format of that information and how to interpret it. That's what the `getName` operation is for—because all messages a participant receives will be `Signals`, the participant needs to be able to differentiate one message from another (e.g., prepare from commit or rollback).

A participant may actually need to receive lots of different protocol messages from the coordinator and as we've mentioned already, these messages are grouped into `SignalSets`. As such, a participant needs to know what `SignalSet` the message it has received is associated with—hence the `getSignalSetName` operation.

`Signals` are sent to `Actions`, which represent the participants in all activities. An `Action` can then use the `Signal` in an application specific manner and return an indication of it having done so. As we've seen with traditional transaction participants, an `Action` can encapsulate arbitrary implementations. So, for example, when an `Action` receives a message from the coordinator (is signaled), it could start an entire workflow system. In order to support this powerful notion, the `Action` interface is abstract, as shown in Code Listing 9-2:

Code Listing 9-2 The `Action` interface (representing participants)

```
public interface Action
{
    public javax.activity.Outcome processSignal(Signal sig)
throws ActionErrorException;
};
```

We've seen that the `Signal` is the message that the coordinator sends to the participant (`Action`) and obviously the `Action` will then need to communicate a response back to the coordinator. However, because of subtleties in the Activity Service architecture, the `Signal` isn't the way in which an `Action` returns a response. An `Action`'s response (the `Outcome`) doesn't need to be associated explicitly with a `SignalSet`. So, the `Outcome` is:

Code Listing 9-3 The Outcome class for returning results.

```
public class Outcome
{
    public org.omg.CORBA.Any getExtendedAny ();
    public java.io.Serializable getExtendedValue ();
    public java.lang.String getName ();
};
```

As you can see, there is a similarity between the `Outcome` and the `Signal`, which makes sense given that they are both used for essentially the same thing: communicating arbitrary information between two abstract end-points.

SignalSets

As we've mentioned, to drive the `Signal` and `Action` interactions an *activity coordinator* is associated with each activity. Participants (which could represent other activities) that are required to be informed when another activity sends a specific `Signal` can register an appropriate `Action` with that activity's coordinator. When the activity sends a `Signal` (e.g., at termination time), the coordinator's role is to forward this signal to all registered `Actions` and to deal with the outcomes generated by the `Actions`.

The implementation of the coordinator will depend upon the type of extended transaction model being used. For example, the model we described and illustrated in Figure 9-6 is similar to what is known as the Sagas model and can be mapped to the Activity Service where a compensating `Signal` may be required to be sent to `Actions` if a failure has happened.

However, if you had to implement the coordinator each time you wanted to have a new extended transaction model then you're back to square one, which wasn't the point of the Activity Service. What's required is pluggability at the level of the coordinator, allowing the coordinator to be implemented once irrespective of the extended transaction model. How this is accomplished in the Activity Service model is through the realization that at its core, a coordinator simply sends messages to participants and gets responses; the coordinator's "intelligence," or its protocol-specific nature comes in the interpretation of those responses. Therefore, the Activity Service provides a means to define a single coordinator with pluggable intelligence.

To enable the coordinator to be configurable for different transaction models, the coordinator delegates all `Signal` control to the `SignalSet`. `Signals` are associated with `SignalSets` and it is the `SignalSet` that generates the `Signals` the coordinator passes to each `Action`. The set of `Signals` that a given `SignalSet` can generate may change from one use to another, for example, based upon the current status of the Activity or the responses from `Actions`. The intelligence concerning which `Signal` to send to an `Action` is hidden within a `SignalSet` and may be as complex or as simple as is required.

It's important to know that a `SignalSet` is dynamically associated with an activity (actually the coordinator), and each activity can have a different `SignalSet` controlling it. In addition, the `SignalSet` associated with a given activity coordinator can change during the lifetime of the activity. For example, if the extended transaction model allows coordination "events" to happen at multiple times during an activity, then the `SignalSet` may change many times.

Since it may not be possible to determine beforehand the set of `Signals` that will be generated by a `SignalSet`, `Actions` register interest in `SignalSets` rather than specific `Signals`. Whenever a `SignalSet` generates any `Signal`, those `Actions` which have registered interest in that `SignalSet` will be sent the `Signal` via the coordinator. An `Action` may register interest in more than one `SignalSet` and as we've already mentioned, an activity may use more than one `SignalSet` during its lifetime, as shown in Figure 9-6.

In the rest of this section we look at how the activity coordinator uses the `SignalSet`. So, let's first look at the `SignalSet` interface, as shown in Code Listing 9-4:

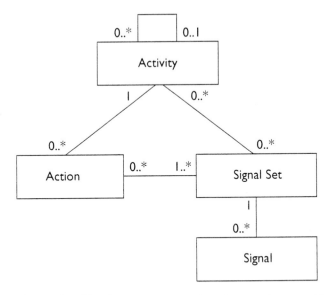

Figure 9-6 UML relationship of `SignalSets`, `Signals`, `Actions` and `Activities`.

Code Listing 9-4 The SignalSet interface used to provide intelligence to the activity coordinator.

```
public interface SignalSet
{
    public java.lang.String getSignalSetName ();

    public Signal getSignal ();
    public Outcome getOutcome () throws SignalSetActiveException;

  public CoordinationInformation setResponse (Outcome response)
                                   throws SignalSetInactiveException;

    public void setCompletionStatus (int completionStatus, int status);
    public int getCompletionStatus () throws SignalSetActiveException;
};
```

As we see in Code Listing 9-5, the `CoordinationInformation` interface is used by the coordinator to determine how to use the `SignalSet`:

Code Listing 9-5 The CoordinationInformation interface.

```
        public interface CoordinationInformation
        {
            public boolean isActionInterested ();
            public boolean useNextSignal ();
        };
```

As shown in Figure 9-7, a given `SignalSet` is assumed to implement a state machine, whereby it starts off in the *Waiting state* until it is required by the Activity Coordinator to send its first `Signal`. It then either enters the *Get Signal state* or the *End state* if it has no `Signals` to send. Once in the *End state*, the `SignalSet` cannot provide any further `Signals` and will not be reused. Once in the *Get Signal* state, the `SignalSet` will be asked for a new `Signal` until it enters the *End state*. A new `Signal` is only requested from the `SignalSet` when all registered `Actions` have been sent the current `Signal`.

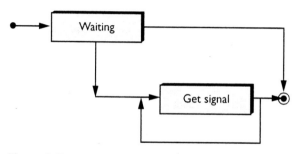

Figure 9-7 SignalSet state transition diagram.

The activity coordinator interacts with the `SignalSet` to obtain the `Signal` to send to registered `Actions`. Because a `SignalSet` may generate a different sequence of `Signals` depending upon the state of the activity (e.g., rollback versus commit), the coordinator must first tell the `SignalSet` what state the activity it is in. It does this via the `SignalSet`'s `setCompletionStatus` method. The coordinator can then start calling the `getSignal` method to get the `Signal` to send to each participant.

As shown in Figure 9-8, the coordinator passes every `Signal` to each participant that was registered with the `SignalSet` it is using. It passes the results (the `Outcomes`) back to the `SignalSet`, which can collate them into a single result

When a `Signal` is sent to an `Action`, the `SignalSet` is informed of the `Outcome` through its `setResponse` method. This method returns a `CoordinationInformation` instance that the coordinator uses to determine the flow of the `Signals`. As we saw in Chapter 1, "Transaction Fundamentals," a two-phase participant could return a read-only response during the prepare phase, which would mean that it doesn't need to be informed of any second-phase messages. So obviously the Activity Service needs to be able to support this (there are other transaction models where there is a similar requirement). The coordinator uses the returned `CoordinationInformation` to determine whether or not the participant (`Action`) that was associated with the `Outcome` wants any more `Signals`; it does this through the `isActionInterested` method (which returns true if the `Action` should continue to receive `Signals`).

We also saw in Chapter 1, "Transaction Fundamentals," that in a two-phase protocol even if the transaction is asked to commit it may eventually rollback. For example, if a participant fails during the first phase, then the second phase message will be to rollback. Once again, the coordinator uses the `CoordinationInformation` returned by `setResponse` to determine whether it should continue using the existing `Signal` (e.g., prepare) for any remaining participants or whether it should ask the `SignalSet` for a new `Signal` (e.g., rollback).

When a given `Signal` has been sent to all registered `Actions`, or the coordinator needs to get a new `Signal`, the `SignalSet` will be asked by the coordinator for the next `Signal` to send (`getSignal` again).

With the exception of some predefined `Signals` and `SignalSets`, the majority of `Signals` and `SignalSets` will be defined and provided by the higher-level applications that make use of this Activity Service framework. Predefined `SignalSets` include a *Synchronization* protocol (similar to the one we discussed in Chapter 1, "Transaction Fundamentals") and a *Lifetime* protocol that allows activities to be informed when other activities start or end.

Hopefully by now you can see that the Activity Service accomplished its goal: a pluggable framework for extended transactions. The coordinator only needs to be implemented once, with the actual protocol intelligence encapsulated in the `Signal`, `SignalSet` and `Action`. This allows transaction model designers to concentrate on the core aspects of the protocol. It should also facilitate reuse of components from one protocol to another.

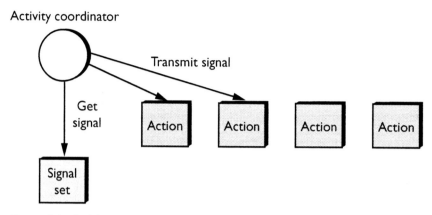

Figure 9-8 Activity coordinator signaling actions.

Example Extended Transaction Models

We've looked at the core elements of the J2EE Activity Service framework, but you may have difficulty tying these abstract concepts together into how an implementation could actually be used. In this section we describe how the Activity Service can be used to support a variety of coordination protocols, ranging from two-phase commit to workflow coordination.

Two-Phase Commit

Let's begin with a simple example illustrating how the Activity Service can be used to implement the two-phase commit protocol we saw in Chapter 1, "Transaction Fundamentals." Hopefully by now you're familiar with the concepts of traditional ACID transactions and this will allow us to concentrate on the Activity Service, rather than having to also describe an extended transaction model. We then build on these ideas in subsequent examples.

Figure 9-9 shows the exchanges involved when the transaction commits. We assume that the two-phase protocol logic is embedded within a 2PCSignalSet. The activity coordinator initiates commit by invoking the getSignal operation of the 2PCSignalSet. The SignalSet returns a "prepare" Signal that is sent to the first registered Action, whose response—done, rather than abort in this case—is communicated to the SignalSet (operation setResponse); the SignalSet returns the "prepare" Signal again that is then sent to the next registered Action and so forth.

Once the last Action has received the "prepare" Signal, the Activity Coordinator will ask the 2PCSignalSet whether or not there is another Signal to send (via the useNextSignal method of the CoordinationInformation instance). In this case getSignal will return the "commit" Signal which the coordinator then sends to the registered participants.

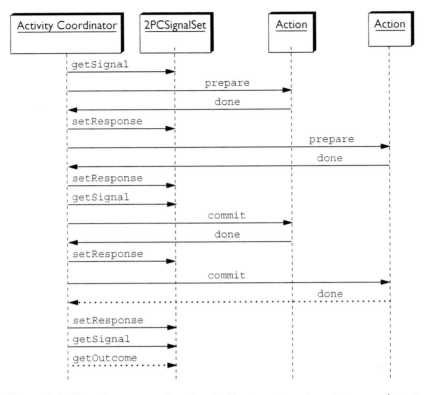

Figure 9-9 Two-phase commit protocol with `Signals`, `SignalSets` and `Actions`.

In reality the coordinator will be invoking the `useNextSignal` method after every `setResponse` call, but only once the prepare phase is complete will `useNextSignal` return true.

In the example, all participants are assumed to return a successful response to the "commit" `Signal` and the two-phase protocol ends cleanly; this means that when the coordinator asks the 2PCSignalSet for another `Signal` after the "commit" `Signal` has been sent to all `Actions`, it will indicate that there are no more `Signals` to send (it returns null). The coordinator then obtains the final result of the two-phase protocol via the `getOutcome` method and can return that response to the application.

Nested Top-Level Transactions with Compensations

In Chapter 1, "Transaction Fundamentals," we described nested top-level transactions as one means whereby serializability may be relaxed. As we mentioned then, any work performed by a committed, nested, top-level transaction will not be undone should the enclosing transaction rollback. If it's important for this to happen, then some form of compensation will be required.

We now illustrate how a nested, top-level transaction with compensation for failures can be provided using the Activity Service framework: this is a transaction model that is more suited to long duration interactions where traditional transaction semantics are unsuitable, as we saw earlier.

Consider the sequence of transactions shown in Figure 9-10, and assume that solid ellipses represent transaction boundaries and dotted ellipses represent an enclosing activity. What we want to provide is the situation where within a top-level transaction (A), the application can start a new top-level transaction (B) that can commit or rollback independently of A. This scheme can be useful if resources are required for only a short duration of the transaction A (as in the bulletin board example we discussed at the start of this chapter). If A subsequently commits, then there is no problem with application consistency. However, if A rolls back, then it is possible that the work performed by B may be required to be undone (represented by transaction !B).

To make this example simpler to understand (and describe), we make the following assumptions:

1. Each enclosing activity has a single `SignalSet` that is used when the activity completes (the CompletionSignalSet), and this `SignalSet` has *Success*, *Failure* and *Propagate* `Signals`, depending upon whether it completes successfully (and has no dependencies on other activities), completes abnormally (rolls back), or completes successfully but has other activity dependencies, respectively.
2. There is an `Action` that is responsible for starting !B if it receives the Failure `Signal` from an enclosing activity (the CompensationAction).

The state transitions for the `Action` are:

- If it receives the Success `Signal` then it can remove itself from the system.
- If it receives the Propagate `Signal`, then encoded within this `Signal` will be the identity of an Activity it should register itself with. It must also remember that it has been propagated.

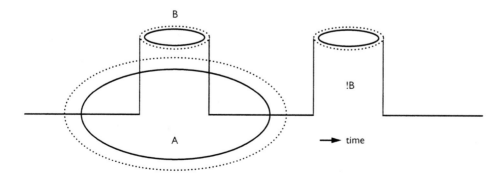

Figure 9-10 Nested top-level transactions.

- If it receives the Failure `Signal` and it has never been propagated then it can remove itself from the system. If the `Action` has been propagated then it should start !B running, before removing itself.

Then the above structure can be obtained in the following manner:

- When transaction A's enclosing activity is begun, it registers the `CompletionSignalSet` as the one to use when the activity terminates. At this point no `Actions` are registered with that activity and hence with the `SignalSet`.
- When B is begun (and hence it's enclosing activity is also started), the activity registers the `CompensationAction` with B's activity, i.e., its `CompletionSignalSet`.
- If B commits, the enclosing activity will terminate in the successful state, and the `CompletionSignalSet` will have the coordinator send the Propagate `Signal` to the registered `CompensationAction`. Encoded within this `Signal` will be the identity of the activity to propagate to, i.e., A. The `CompensationAction` can then enlist itself with A.
- If B rolls back, the enclosing activity will terminate in the failure state, and the CompensationAction will do nothing when it receives the Failure `Signal`.
- If A subsequently commits, its enclosing activity's `CompletionSignalSet` will generate the Success `Signal` (since it has no dependencies on other activities), which will be delivered to the `CompensationAction`. In this case, no compensation is required, so the `Action` does nothing.
- On the other hand, if A subsequently rolls back, its enclosing activity's `CompletionSignalSet` will generate the Failure `Signal`, and the `CompensationAction` will start !B to undo B.

Workflow Coordination

Transactional workflow systems with scripting facilities for expressing the composition of an activity (a business process) offer a flexible way of building application specific extended transactions. In this section we describe how the Activity Service Framework can be utilized for coordinating workflow activities, similar to those we mentioned in Chapter 1, "Transaction Fundamentals." The `SignalSet` required to coordinate a business activity contains four `Signals`, *start*, *start_ack*, *outcome* and *outcome_ack*.

- *start*: This `Signal` is sent from a "parent" activity to a "child" activity, to indicate that the "child" activity should start. Encoded within the `Signal` is any additional information required to parameterize the starting of the activity. Remember what we discussed earlier: the `Signal` interface is defined to be extensible in this manner in order to allow arbitrary information to be encoded.

- *start_ack*: This `Signal` is sent from a "child" activity to a "parent" activity, as the return part of a "start" `Signal`, to acknowledge that the "child" activity has started.
- *outcome*: This `Signal` is sent from a "child" activity to a "parent" activity, to indicate that the "child" activity has completed. The `Signal` contains the information about the outcome of the activity, e.g., whether or not it completed successfully.
- outcome_ack: This `Signal` is sent from a "parent" activity to a "child" activity, as the return part of an "outcome" `Signal`, to acknowledge that the "parent" activity has completed.

The interaction depicted in Figure 9-11 is activity a coordinating the parallel execution of *b* and *c* followed by *d*.

Referring to Figure 9-10, we can tie an activity to a single top-level transaction, such that when an activity begins (e.g., *t1*) it immediately starts a new transaction. A coordinating activity (implied by the dotted ellipse in Figure 9-10) would send appropriate *start* `Signals` and wait for the *outcome* `Signals` to occur. To do this, each potential activity registers an `Action` with a specific `SignalSet` at the coordinating activity (the parent); each activity that needs to be started for a specific event would register an `Action` with a specific `SignalSet`, e.g., *t2* and *t3* would register with the same `SignalSet` since they need to be started together, whereas *t4* would be registered with a separate `SignalSet`.

Whenever a child activity is started, the parent activity registers an `Action` with it that is used to deliver the *outcome* `Signal` to the parent. Let's assume that each child activity has a Completed `SignalSet` to facilitate this. When a child activity terminates, it uses the Completed `SignalSet` to send a `Signal` to the parent's registered `Action`. The content of this `Signal` will contain sufficient information for the parent to determine the outcome of the activity and use this to control the flow of activities appropriately.

For example, in Figure 9-10, the parent activity would receive a successful termination outcome from *t1*, which would cause it to send *start* Signals to *t2* and *t3* via their registered `Actions`. When they both complete successfully (i.e., sent *outcome* `Signals`), it can then start *t4*. However, if *t4* sends a failure outcome, or simply fails to send any outcome (e.g., it crashes), the parent activity can use this information to start *tc1* in order to do the compensation.

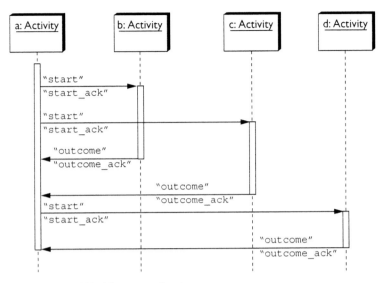

Figure 9-11   Workflow coordination.

Where Do I Get an Activity Service?

As you might imagine, since the J2EE Activity Service is fairly new, finding implementations of it can be difficult. At the moment we know of only two implementations and these come from the main developers of the specification: IBM and Arjuna Technologies Limited. Some of the main advocates of the Activity Service believe that as J2EE (and CORBA) continues to evolve and experiences with extended transaction models improve, the use of the Activity Service will increase and it is likely that more vendors will support this, especially if this becomes a mandatory part of J2EE.

> **N O T E**   This notion is not necessarily shared by all J2EE vendors. Only time will tell who is right, but we know that a few vendors, including IBM, have had success with the Activity Service.

A word of warning though: if you think implementing traditional ACID transaction systems is complex, imagine the complexity involved in implementing an Activity Service. Throughout this book, we attempted to give advice on things to watch out for when choosing an implementation of a transaction processing system and probably the most important piece of advice is: understand who implemented it and what their background is in the area. That advice goes double for something as inherently complex and advanced as the Activity Service.

Summary

Although it has long been realized that ACID transactions by themselves are not adequate for structuring long-lived applications and much research work has been done on developing specific extended transaction models, no middleware support for building extended transactions is currently available and the situation remains that a programmer often has to develop application-specific mechanisms. The J2EE Activity Service Framework is a way out of this situation. It provides a general purpose event-signaling mechanism that can be programmed to enable activities to coordinate each other in a manner prescribed by the model under consideration. Using a few examples, we've shown that the framework has the flexibility to support a wide variety of extended transaction models.

So, where does all of this work get placed in relation to traditional transaction systems? Will the Activity Service, for example, replace ACID transactions? Should you be writing systems based on the J2EE Activity Service? Where does this leave traditional transaction processing systems?

In order to answer these questions and others, it is first necessary to remember that none of the work on extended transactions starts from the premise that the ACID transactions model is broken or not useful. Quite the contrary. In fact, ACID transactions are perfect for many (though not all) problem domains in which they are used. For the past few decades, a range of transaction service products have proven their value to businesses time and again and these products have raised a level of confidence in the reliability and performance of ACID transactions in general and the individual products in particular. To believe that industry users will immediately replace these systems with new, potentially untried products is unrealistic.

However, that is not what the extended transaction models, as exemplified by the Activity Service, are trying to do. In the case of the Activity Service, it considers the ACID model to be simply another extended transaction model on a sliding spectrum of models, as shown in Figure 9-12. Where current transaction products work well they will, in all likelihood, continue to be used.

What these new industry supported standards do is change the story for *future* development projects. In the past there was only a single model supported by the industry and it was forced into areas for which it simply wasn't appropriate. There are some existing situations where transaction products based on the ACID model are used despite the fact that ACID trans-

Extended transactions

Figure 9-12   The spectrum of extended transactions.

actions do not best suit the problem domain: users often prefer to use any kind of transactioning technology, even if it is not completely appropriate. However, other developers have taken to not using ACID transactions at all, despite the fact that to not do so leaves them vulnerable to certain types of failures and consistency issues.

The advent of the J2EE Activity Service gives developers in the J2EE space new tools with which to address their transactioning problems. Rather than having to consider only ACID transactions with their associated pros and cons, a developer can now work out precisely what their requirements are and, if there is not an existing extended transaction model that solves the problem exactly, they can either develop a new model and associated implementation themselves or work with transaction vendors to do likewise.

ACID is no longer the only game in town and before rushing in to purchase a transaction system that may not suit your needs now or in the future, it would be better to determine precisely what those needs are first and foremost. Does the product you are purchasing allow for upgrades to the transaction model should ACID no longer become appropriate for some (or all) of the applications which use transactions?

Finally, it should be pointed out that one of the other benefits of using ACID transactions is that a lot of hard work has gone into this area over the years to make their use relatively straightforward. For example, interfacing to the most popular databases typically requires just binding to the right JDBC driver. Obviously, the same cannot be said of all extended transactions technologies and some additional development effort may be necessary. However, the end result may be a much closer fit with your original requirements than simply continuing to use traditional transaction technologies.

CHAPTER 10

Transactions and
Web Services

Most business-to-business applications require transactional support in order to guarantee consistent outcome and correct execution. These applications often involve long-running computations, loosely coupled systems and components that do not share data, location, or administration. It is difficult to incorporate traditional ACID transactions within such architectures. For example, an airline reservation system may reserve a seat on a flight for an individual for a specific period of time, but if the individual does not confirm the seat within that period it will be unreserved.

Business-to-business (B2B) interactions using Web services may be complex, involving many parties, spanning many different organizations, and potentially lasting for hours or days, e.g., the process of ordering and delivering parts for a computer which may involve different suppliers, and may only be considered to have completed once the parts are delivered to their final destination. Unfortunately, for a number of reasons, B2B participants simply cannot afford to lock their resources exclusively on behalf of an individual indefinitely. This rules out the use of atomic transactions. Thus, there's a requirement for extended transaction models in the Web services domain.

So far there have been three efforts to incorporate transactions into Web services and in the following sections we examine them all. You may wonder why you need to know about them all and the answer to that question is straightforward: at this moment it's not possible to say which of these attempts (if any) will become the standard for Web services transactions. It's even possible that a completely new effort will be the standard. However, knowing where the industry is at the moment is important, as it gives you an indication of where it is likely to head in the future.

In this chapter we look at how the concepts of traditional transactions and extended transactions are merging with those of Web services. Because Java and J2EE are the de facto standard for implementing Web services, we'll probably see implementations of these new protocols appearing here first. Since most Web service applications will typically involve existing back-end infrastructures such as J2EE, you'll also want to see how you can tie Web service transactions into the more traditional transactional systems.

> **N O T E**   We're going to look at these Web services transaction protocols in some detail because this is an extremely important area for transaction processing and J2EE in particular. It's important to see how these protocols leverage many of the principles we've discussed elsewhere in this book. There are very few sources of literature other than the (rather dry) specifications. Therefore, it's also one of the aims of this chapter to try to make these protocols more approachable.

Some Common Features of Web Services Transactions

Before examining the different Web services protocols, in this section we look at some of the things they have in common.

> **N O T E**   Web services offer the possibility of a straightforward solution to a very important transaction problem: interoperability. Ever since transaction processing began, there have been a variety of transaction protocol standards, as we saw in Chapter 1, "Transaction Fundamentals," with many corresponding implementations. Interoperability between these various protocols has always proved problematical and there has been limited success.

Obtaining Consensus

In general, a business transaction requires the capability for certain participants to be structured into a *consensus group*, such that all of the members have the same result. Importantly, different participants within the same business transaction may belong to different consensus groups. The business logic then controls how each group completes. In this way, a business transaction may cause a subset of the groups it naturally creates to perform the work it asks, while asking the other groups to undo the work.

For example, let's return to the travel agent scenario described in Chapter 9 and extend it to also cover the purchase of travel insurance. We assume that the user has provisionally reserved a flight and car to the airport and is now looking for travel insurance. The first consensus group holds the flight and car, since neither of these can occur independently. The user may then decide to visit multiple insurance sites (called A and B, in this example), and as he goes may reserve the quotes he likes. So, for example, A may quote $50, which is just within budget, but the user may want to try B in case he can find a cheaper price, but without losing the initial quote. If the quote from B is less than that from A, the user may cancel A, while confirming both the flights and the insurance from B. Each insurance site may, therefore, occur within its own consensus group. This is not something that is possible when using ACID transactions.

Consensus groups achieve consistent outcomes among participants, but are only part of the picture. Often in business-to-business relationships there are hierarchies of these groups (*scopes of work*), with parent and child relationships existing between them. Typically, the work performed by a child is provisional on the successful completion of the parent, i.e., the parent scope can perform a counter-effect for the completed child.

It is important to realize that parent-child (activity-task) scopes are *not* equivalent to inter-position. In an interposed hierarchy, subnodes complete only when instructed to by the comple-tion of their superior nodes. In a nested scope relationship (e.g., nested transactions), the sub-scopes can complete independently of their parents and may then impose compensation require-ments on the parent.

In addition to understanding the outcomes, a participant within a business transaction may need to support provisional or tentative state changes during the course of the transaction. Such parties must also support the completion of a business transaction either through confirmation (final effect) or cancellation (counter-effect). In general, what it means to confirm or cancel work done within a business transaction will be for the participant to determine.

For example, an application may choose to perform changes as provisional effect and make them visible to other business transactions. It may store necessary information to undo these changes at the same time. On confirmation, it may simply discard these undo changes or on cancellation, it may apply these undo changes. An application can employ such a compensa-tion-based approach or take a conventional "rollback" approach, for example.

Finally, it's also important for any Web services transactions protocol to have interopera-bility with existing transaction processing systems: such systems already form the backbone of enterprise level applications and will continue to do so for the Web services equivalent.

General Architecture

All Web services transactions protocols share the common notion of a transaction coordi-nator, participants and a transaction context, as shown in Figure 10-1. We briefly describe how this architecture works, although it should seem familiar to you by now. There's also a familiar split between transactional service and participant as we encountered in Chapter 1, "Transaction Fundamentals," in traditional transaction processing systems.

As Figure 10-1 shows, the application client interacts with the Web service transaction coordinator in a similar manner to traditional transaction systems (after all, a coordinator is a coordinator, whether it exists in a J2EE or Web services environment). The specifics of the cli-ent and coordinator interactions will depend upon the transaction protocol; however the end result will be a context (although what information is in the context will depend upon the type of protocol).

The type of information encoded within the context and the requirement for it is identical to what we saw in Chapter 1, "Transaction Fundamentals." The context information is propagated between clients and services to provide a flow of context information between distributed execution environments, for example using SOAP header information. This may occur transparently to the client and application services.

Whenever a user contacts a service whose work it wishes to be under the control of a transaction, components of the transaction system are responsible for propagating the context to that service. When the service receives an application invocation that also carries a transaction context, it will probably have to register a participant with the transaction referenced in the context. The service is responsible for ensuring that concurrent accesses by different applications are managed in a way that guarantees some internal consistency criteria for that service.

Once registered, the work controlled by the participant will ultimately be controlled by the transaction coordinator. A participant in Web services transactions is similar to the participant we saw in traditional transaction systems: it's the entity that actually does the real transaction work. The Web service (e.g., a theater booking system) contains some business logic for reserving a seat, enquiring availability, and so on, but it will need to be back-ended by something that maintains information in a durable manner. The transaction coordinator and participant interactions occur according to the specifics of the transaction protocol.

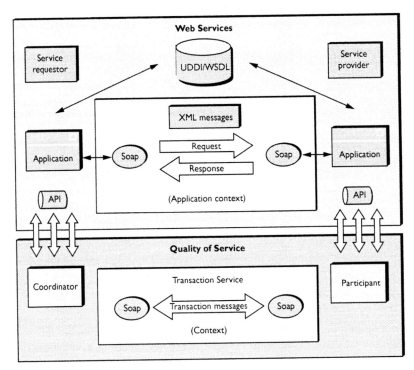

Figure 10-1 Web services, transactions and contexts.

In the following sections we examine the current state of play for Web services transactions. At present there have been three significant attempts at integrating some kind of transaction semantic within Web services and there may well be others to come. We can't say which, if any, of the currently available specifications will become the standard, so we try to take an objective approach and examine each of them in chronological order, going from oldest to newest.

The OASIS Business Transactions Protocol

In 2001, a consortium of companies including Hewlett-Packard, Oracle and BEA began work on the OASIS Business Transaction Protocol (BTP), which was aimed at business-to-business transactions in loosely coupled domains such as Web Services. The specification developed two new models for "transactions," requiring business-level decisions to be incorporated within the transaction infrastructure. By April 2002, it had reached the point of a committee specification. Hewlett-Packard quickly followed this with the first commercial product based on this specification and there are versions from BEA and Choreology.

> **N O T E** Unlike the next two specifications we look at, OASIS BTP was not designed specifically for Web services. It is intended to be useable in other environments.

Open-Top Coordination

BTP's approach to providing consensus group functionality is to use a *two-phase completion* protocol to guarantee atomicity of decisions. However, there are two important differences between the BTP two-phase completion protocol and the two-phase commit protocol used in a traditional transaction processing system:

- The implementation of consensus, especially in the case of failures, is not imposed on the participants. In a traditional transaction processing environment the participants use backward failure recovery. To enforce this distinction, rather than call the second phases of the termination protocol "commit" and "rollback," they are termed "confirm" and "cancel," respectively, with the intention of decoupling the phases from any preconceptions of specific backward compensation implementations. The first phase is still called prepare, though.
- Although BTP uses a two-phase protocol, it does not imply ACID transactions. How implementations of prepare, confirm and cancel are provided is a back-end implementation decision. Issues to do with consistency and isolation of data are also back-end choices and not imposed or assumed by BTP. A BTP implementation is primarily concerned with two-phase coordination of participants.

As we saw in Chapter 1, "Transaction Fundamentals," in a traditional transaction system the application or user has few verbs with which to control the transaction. Typically, these are "begin," "commit" and "rollback." When an application asks for a transaction to commit, the coordinator will execute the entire two-phase commit protocol before returning the result to the application. The elapsed time between the execution of the first phase and the second phase is typically milliseconds to seconds, but is entirely under the control of the coordinator. This is what BTP terms a *closed-top commit protocol.*

However, the actual two-phase protocol does not impose any restrictions on the time between executing the first and second phases. By now you should realize that the longer this period, the more chance there is for a failure to occur and the longer (critical) resources remain locked or isolated from other users.

BTP on the other hand, took the approach of allowing the time between these phases to be set by the application by expanding the verbs available to include explicit control over both phases of the term, i.e., "prepare," "confirm" and "cancel," what BTP terms an *open-top commit protocol.* The application has complete control over when it can tell a transaction(s) to prepare and using whatever business logic is required, later determine which transaction(s) to confirm or cancel.

Initially, it may seem like a good idea to let business logic directly affect the flow of a transaction from within the "commit" protocol, but in practice it doesn't really work. It blurs the distinction between what you would expect from a transaction protocol (guarantees of consistency, isolation, and so on) which are essentially non-functional aspects of a business "transaction," with the functional aspects (reserve my flight, book me a taxi, and so on) In BTP, because business logic is encoded within the transaction protocol, it essentially means that a user has to be closely tied to (or perhaps even be) the coordinator. In addition, business information, such as the ability for a participant to remain "prepared" (e.g., hold onto a hotel room) for a specific period of time is propagated from the participant to the coordinator, but there is nothing within the protocol to allow this information to filter up to the application/client where it really belongs.

Furthermore, the BTP specification expends great efforts to ensure that two-phase completion does not imply ACID semantics. This is good in so far that traditional ACID transactions are not suitable for all types of Web services interactions, as we've already seen. However, everything is left up to back-end implementation choices and there is nothing in the protocol to allow a user to determine what choices have been made by a service. What this means is that it's impossible to reason about the ultimate correctness of a distributed application. For example, if you wanted to use BTP for ACID transactions, then of course services could use traditional XA resource managers wrapped by BTP participants. Unfortunately, there's no way within the BTP for those services to inform external users that this is what they have done so that they can safely be used within the scope of a BTP "ACID" transaction.

Atoms and Cohesions

To address the specific requirements of business transactions, BTP introduced two types of *extended transactions,* both using the open-top completion protocol:

- *Atom*: An atom is the typical way in which "transactional" work performed on Web services is scoped. The outcome of an atom is guaranteed to be consistent, such that, all enlisted *participants* will see the same outcome, which will either be to accept (*confirm*) the work or reject (*cancel*) it.

- *Cohesion*: This type of transaction was introduced in order to relax atomicity and allow for the selection of work to be confirmed or cancelled based on higher-level business rules. Atoms are the typical participants within a cohesion but, unlike an atom, a cohesion may give different outcomes to its participants such that some of them may confirm while the remainder cancel. In essence, the two-phase protocol for a cohesion is parameterized to allow a user to specify precisely which participants to prepare and which to cancel. Cohesions are meant to model long-running business activities, where services enroll in atoms (which are enrolled in the cohesion) that represent specific units of work and as the business activity progresses, it may encounter conditions that allow it to cancel or prepare these units, with the caveat that it may be many hours or days before the cohesion arrives at its *confirm-set*: the set of participants that it requires to confirm in order for it to successfully terminate the business activity. Once the confirm-set has been determined, the cohesion collapses down to being an atom: all members of the confirm-set see the same outcome.

In fact, BTP really only has a single transaction model, since the atom model is a subset of the cohesion model, but where prepare, confirm and cancel parameterization isn't used (e.g., an atom prepares all participants). What this means is that the single BTP model must be suitably generic enough to support a wide variety of applications. This is almost the opposite approach to the J2EE Activity Service we described in Chapter 9, where it is envisioned that specific extended transaction models will be developed to best suit each problem domain.

So let's recap: Web services do work within the scope of *atoms*, which are created by the initiator of the business transaction. Multiple atoms are composed into a business transaction (e.g., arranging a holiday) by a *cohesion composer* such that different atoms may possess different outcomes, as directed by the business logic, e.g., cancel one insurance quote and confirm another. Businesses take part in atomic or cohesive transactions via *participants*, and both cohesions and atoms use *coordination* to ensure that participants see the desired outcome.

This may seem fairly straightforward at first, but as we shall see in the following sections, there is a lot more going on under the covers.

XML Message Sets and Carrier Bindings

Within the Web services world information is communicated in XML documents, but how those documents are exchanged may be a function of the environment, business relationship, and so on. Therefore, although BTP mandates that its own information (context and protocol messages) must be carried in XML payloads, it does not specify how these payloads are transmitted: it does not mandate a specific carrier protocol.

> **N O T E** BTP is not programming-language specific and as
> such, it does not specify an API for users. As we shall see, this is
> one of the areas where JAXTX should provide some help.

Obviously, without a carrier protocol, BTP is of very limited use. The technical committee did define a binding to SOAP 1.1 over HTTP 1.1 as part of the BTP 1.0 specification. But the intention has always been that other specific carrier protocol bindings to the BTP XML schema would be provided on a needs-basis. So, if for example a group of companies sees merit in defining a binding using pigeons (!), they could so define it and submit it as an appendix on optional bindings to the BTP specification.

As with traditional transaction processing systems, the BTP message set is concerned with messages for driving the protocol and messages containing information for participating within the protocol. The former are typically of interest only to implementers of either BTP or participants, whereas the latter are of interest to service providers and their associated participants.

Typically a BTP message is propagated within the *body* of the SOAP envelope. For example, a typical *begin* message is represented in Code Listing 10-1:

Code Listing 10-1 An example of a BTP `begin` message

```
<?xml version="1.0" encoding="UTF-8" ?>
<SOAP:Envelope
  SOAP:encodingStyle=http://schemas.xmlsoap.org/soap/encoding/
  xmlns:SOAP="http://schemas.xmlsoap.org/soap/envelope/">
  <SOAP:Body>
    <btp:begin transaction-type="atom"
      xmlns:btp="urn:oasis:names:tc:BTP:1.0:core" />
  </SOAP:Body>
</SOAP:Envelope>
```

For application messages that also carry BTP content, the situation is different. In this situation he BTP messages are typically located within the *header* of the SOAP envelope, as can be seen in the example in Code Listing 10-2, where a BTP context is propagated with an application-specific method call:

Code Listing 10-2 An application message with a BTP context

```
<?xml version="1.0" encoding="UTF-8" ?>
<SOAP:Envelope
  SOAP:encodingStyle=http://schemas.xmlsoap.org/soap/encoding/
  xmlns:SOAP="http://schemas.xmlsoap.org/soap/envelope/">
  <SOAP:Header>
    <btp:messages xmlns:btp="urn:oasis:names:tc:BTP:1.0:core">
      <btp:context>
        <btp:superior-address>
          <btp:binding-name>soap-http-1</btp:binding-name>
```

```
                    <btp:binding-address>
                        http://mybusiness.com/btpservice
                    </btp:binding-address>
                </btp:superior-address>
                <btp:superior-identifier>
                    12fa6de4ea3ec
                </btp:superior-identifier>
                <btp:superior-type>atom</btp:superior-type>
            </btp:context>
        </btp:messages>
    </SOAP:Header>
    <SOAP:Body>
        <ns:myMethod xmlns:ns="http://tempuri.org/">
            <arg1 xsi:type="xsd:int">99</arg1>
            <arg2 xsi:type="xsd:int">101</arg2>
        </ns:myMethod>
    </SOAP:Body>
</SOAP:Envelope>
```

Participants

We've already mentioned that each BTP participant supports a two-phase termination protocol via *prepare*, *confirm* and *cancel* operations. What the participant does when asked to *prepare* is implementation-dependent (e.g., reserve the theater ticket); it then returns an indication of whether or not it succeeded. However, unlike in an atomic transaction, the participant does not have to guarantee that it can remain in this *prepared state*; it may indicate that it can only do so for a specified period of time, and also indicate what action it will take (confirm or undo) if it has not been told how to finish before this period elapses. In addition, no indication of how *prepare* is implemented is implied in the protocol, such that resource reservation (locking) as happens in an ACID transaction system, need not occur.

Unfortunately, in order to use cohesions it is necessary for Web services to expose back-end implementation choices about participants: to parameterize the two-phase completion protocol, the terminator of the cohesion obviously needs to be able to say "prepare A and B and cancel C and D", where A, B, C and D are *participants* that have been enrolled in the cohesion by services (such as a flight reservation system). In a traditional transaction system, users don't see the participants (imagine if you had to explicitly tell all of your XA resource managers to prepare and commit). Naturally, this is something that programmers don't feel comfortable with and it goes against the Web services orthodoxy.

The Composer

Associated with every transaction type (atom or cohesion) is a *coordinator*, which is responsible for governing the outcome of the transaction. The coordinator may be implemented as a separate service or may be co-located with the user for improved performance. As with any coordinator technology, such as that in traditional ACID transaction systems, the BTP coordinator communicates with enlisted participants to inform them of the desired termination requirements, i.e., whether they should accept (*confirm*) or reject (*cancel*) the work done within the scope of the given transaction. For example, it informs them whether to purchase the (provisionally reserved) flight tickets for the user or to release them.

Most transaction systems support the notion of a transaction factory (the transaction manager) and BTP is no different: a transaction factory is responsible for managing coordinators for many transactions. The initiator of the transaction (e.g., the client) communicates with a transaction manager and asks it to start a new transaction and associate a coordinator with the transaction. Once the transaction coordinator has been created, the context may be propagated to Web services.

Although both atoms and cohesions require coordination, BTP gives a different name to the cohesion coordinator: the *cohesion composer*. But don't worry—whatever it's called, it is still a coordinator at heart. However, there is a good reason for the difference in terms: the atom coordinator is used to scope work performed on Web services in a similar way to traditional ACID transactions, but the cohesion composer is used directly by the *business logic* for gluing together the flow of the application into one or more atoms.

Although Web services do work within the scope of a specific atom, it is the composer that ultimately determines which atoms to confirm and which to undo. The composer may prepare and cancel atoms at arbitrary points during the lifetime of the business transaction, e.g., preparing the flight reservation early in the transaction and preparing the insurance quote much later after canceling a prior quote.

Roles in BTP

Although for simplicity we have talked about services, coordinators and participants, within BTP all end-points are either *Superiors*, *Inferiors* or both. An entity within the coordinating entity's system plays the role of Superior (e.g., the Atom Coordinator) and an entity within the service plays the role of an Inferior (e.g., the participant). Each Inferior has only one Superior. However, a single Superior may have multiple Inferiors within each or multiple parties. A tree of such relationships may be wide, deep or both, as shown in Figure 10-2. This is essentially the same idea we saw in Chapter 1, "Transaction Fundamentals," for interposition where the root of the tree is the coordinator (the Superior in BTP parlance) and the subnodes are the subordinate coordinators or participants (the Inferiors).

A Superior receives reports from its Inferiors as to whether they are "prepared." It gathers these reports in order to determine which Inferiors should be cancelled and which confirmed. The Superior does this either by itself or with the cooperation of the application element responsible for its creation and control, depending upon whether the transaction is an atom or a cohesion, as we shall see later.

The *initiator* of a transaction communicates with an *atom/cohesion coordinator* (factory) and asks it to start a new atom or cohesion. Once created, information about the atom or cohe-

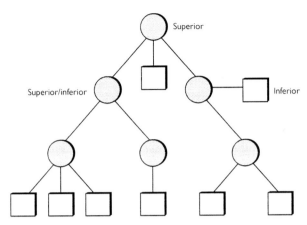

Figure 10-2 Superior and Inferior relationships.

sion (the *context*) can be propagated to Web services in order for them to associate their work with it. Although work is typically conducted within the scope of an atom, it is entirely possible for services to register participants directly with cohesions.

The *terminator* of the atom or cohesion will typically be the same entity as the initiator, but need not be, e.g., a long running stock purchase transaction that may be started by the company that requires the stock, and finished by the company that delivers it. Although an atom can be instructed to confirm all participants immediately, it is more typically instructed to *prepare* them first, and later (hours, days or longer) to either confirm or cancel them.

We've seen some of the BTP roles and relationships and we've also seen that there are a lot of similarities within traditional transaction processing systems. Now let's look at some of the optimizations that BTP defines, some of which are different from what we've already encountered.

Optimizations

We have described how BTP can be used to conduct typical business-to-business interactions in a reliable manner. In order to do this, many protocol specific messages need to be exchanged between entities and this will have an adverse affect on the time taken to complete a business transaction. This is a necessary side effect of achieving reliability and consensus and is not specific to BTP.

Since BTP is intended for long running transactions, you might assume that performance has not been a prime factor in its development. However, this is not the case and in fact BTP contains a number of optimizations not usually found in traditional transaction processing systems.

One-shot

Typically a participant is enlisted with a BTP transaction when a service invocation occurs (e.g., "book flight"). When the service request completes, the response is sent back to the initiator of the request. As described earlier, during transaction termination the coordinator will interact with the participant to ensure completion.

In some circumstances, it may be possible to compound many of the above messages into a "one-shot" message. For example, the service invocation may cause a state change to occur that means the participant can prepare immediately after the invocation completes. Rather than having to wait for an explicit coordinator message, BTP allows the enroll request and statement of preparation to be compounded within the service response. The receiver is then responsible for ensuring that this additional information is forwarded to the responsible entities.

Resignation by a Participant

As we saw in Chapter 1, "Transaction Fundamentals," in a two-phase commit protocol, in addition to indicating success or failure during the preparation phase, a participant can also return a "read-only" response; this indicates that it does not control any work that has been modified during the course of the transaction and therefore does not need to be informed of the transaction outcome. In some situations this allows the two-phase protocol to complete quickly since a second round of messages is not required.

The equivalent of this in BTP is for a participant to resign from the transaction it was enrolled in. Resignation can occur at any time up to the point where the participant has prepared and is used by the participant to indicate that it no longer has an interest in the outcome of the transaction.

Spontaneous Prepare

In some situations, rather than preparing when instructed to by the coordinator, a participant may be able to prepare spontaneously. For example, consider a service invocation which occurs and moves that service into an idempotent state such that further invocations have no effect on it; in this case, an associated participant may prepare that service immediately, rather than wait for the instruction to do so. In BTP, a participant is allowed to attempt to prepare at any point and inform the coordinator of the result.

Autonomous decision by a participant

In a traditional two-phase protocol a participant enrolls with a transaction and waits for the termination protocol before it either confirms or cancels. We've already seen that to achieve consensus, two-phase commit is a blocking protocol, meaning that if a coordinator fails before delivering the final phase messages, prepared participants must remain blocked, holding onto resources. Modern transaction-processing systems augmented two-phase commit with *heuristics*, allowing such participants to make unilateral decisions about whether they will commit or rollback. Obviously if a participant makes a choice that turns out to be different to that taken by other participants, non-atomic behaviors occur.

BTP has its equivalent of heuristics, allowing participants to make unilateral decisions as well. However, unlike in other transaction implementations, the protocol allows a participant to give the coordinator prior knowledge of what that decision will be and when it will be taken. A participant may prepare and present the coordinator with some caveats as to how long it will remain in this state and into what state it will then migrate (e.g., "will remain prepared for 10 days and then will cancel the flight reservation"). This information may then be used by the coordinator to optimize message exchange.

Qualifiers

An interesting approach taken by BTP to that of loosely coupled domains and long-running interactions was of introducing the notion of *Qualifiers* to the protocol. A Qualifier can be thought of as a caveat to that aspect of the protocol on which it is associated. Essentially, a Qualifier is a way of providing additional extended information within the protocol.

Although the BTP specification provided some standard Qualifier types (such as timeouts for how long a participant is willing to remain in a prepared state), it is possible to extend them and provide new implementations that are better suited to the application or participant. Obviously, any use or reliance on non-standard Qualifiers will reduce application portability.

Unfortunately, although the concept underlying Qualifiers is sound, their implementation with BTP is flawed. The main reason for this is that in some cases the information contained within Qualifiers is not made available to the entity that can best make use of it. For example, one of the standard Qualifiers in BTP is used during the prepare phase and allows a participant to specify how long it is willing (or able) to remain in a prepared state (and possibly what state it will then transit to). This information is passed to the coordinator, but in reality it is the application that requires it.

Using BTP

Consider the flight booking example presented earlier. How could we use BTP in order to coordinate this application in a reliable manner? The problem is that we wish to obtain the cheapest insurance quote as we go along and without losing prior quotes until we know that they are no longer the cheapest; at that point we will be able to release those quotes while maintaining the others. In a traditional transaction system, all of the work performed within a transaction must either be accepted (committed) or declined (rolled back); the required loosening of atomicity is not supported.

In BTP, however, we can use atoms and cohesions. A cohesion is first created to manage the overall business interactions. The business logic (application, client, and so on) creates an atom (ReserveAtom, say) and enrolls it with the cohesion, as shown in Figure 10-3.

Once the client has obtained the context from the factory, it can invoke the airline and taxi reservation services within the scope of the atom, such that their work is then ultimately controlled by its outcome. When a suitable flight and taxi can be obtained, ReserveAtom is prepared to reserve the bookings for some service specific time, as illustrated in Figure 10-4.

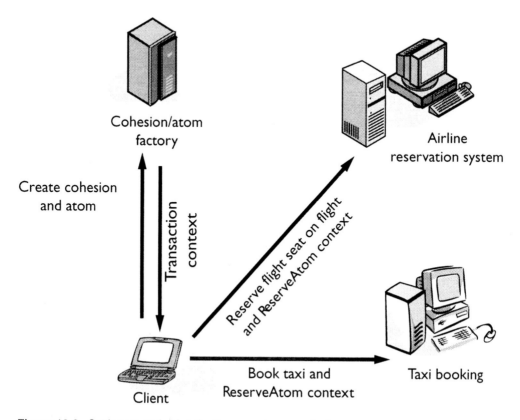

Figure 10-3 Setting up and using the `ReserveAtom` context.

Then two new atoms (`AtomQuote1` and `AtomQuote2`) are created and enrolled with the cohesion, before being used to obtain two different quotes from the respective insurance services (Figure 10-5).

When the quote from the first insurance site is obtained it is obviously not known whether it is the best quote, so the business logic can prepare `AtomQuote1` to maintain the quote, while it then communicates with the second insurance site. If that site does not offer a better quote, the application can cancel `AtomQuote2` and it now has its final confirmation set of atoms (`ReserveAtom` and `AtomQuote1`), which it can confirm, as shown in Figure 10-6.

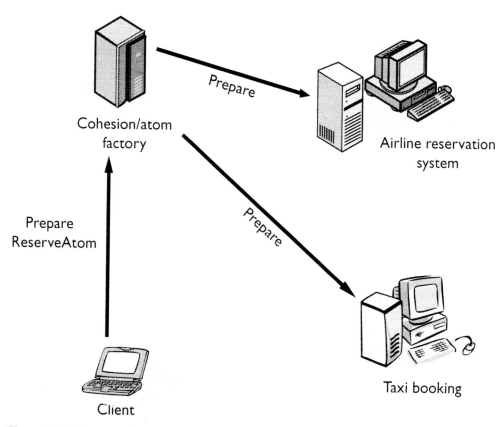

Figure 10-4 Prepare of `ReserveAtom` and associated services.

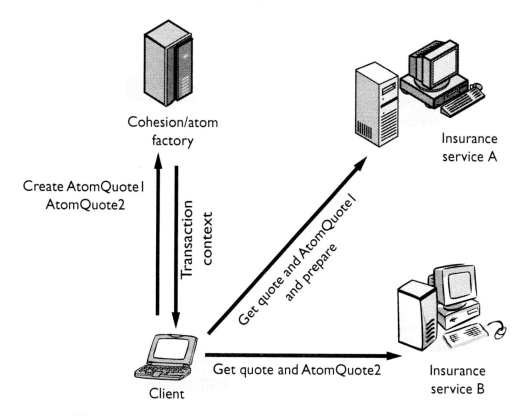

Figure 10-5   Obtaining insurance quotes.

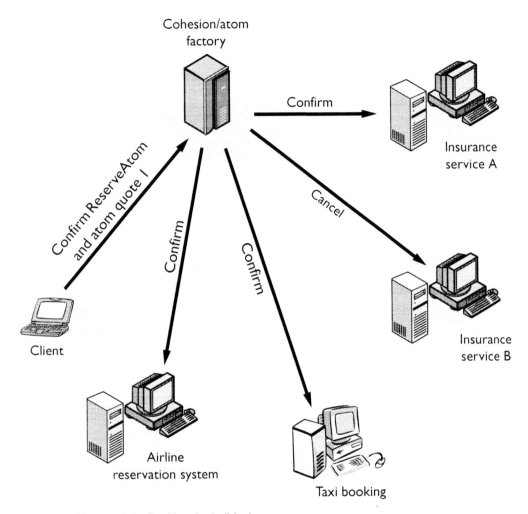

Figure 10-6 Booking the holiday!

Web Services Coordination and Transactions

In August 2002, IBM, Microsoft and BEA released the Web Services Coordination (WS-C) and Web Services Transactions (WS-Tx) specifications. During 2003 and 2004, these specifications were updated and WS-Tx was split into two: WS-AtomicTransaction and WS-BusinessActivity. However, most reference articles and implementations are currently based on the original WS-C/WS-Tx specifications, so we concentrate on those and try to indicate where changes have occurred in the revised versions of the specifications. Hopefully, this should make it easier for you to find additional collateral on these specifications in the short term and do a mapping to the updated drafts.

The fundamental idea underpinning WS-C is that there is a generic need for a coordination infrastructure in a Web services environment. The WS-C specification defines a framework that allows different coordination protocols to be plugged-in to coordinate work between clients, services and participants. WS-T provides specific plug-ins for transactions. This should be familiar, given what we saw in Chapter 9 when we discussed the J2EE Activity Service. It should also come as no surprise that both specifications have some common authors.

In the rest of this section we give an overview of what WS-T offers. Although WS-T plays in the same arena as BTP, you'll see that there are many subtle and not-so-subtle differences between these specifications.

We won't say much about the Web Services Coordination specification since it's not specific to transactions. Whatever coordination protocol is used and in whatever domain it is deployed, the same generic requirements are present:

- Instantiation (or activation) of a new coordinator for the specific coordination protocol, for a particular application instance.
- Registration of participants with the coordinator.
- Propagation of context.

The main components involved in using and defining the WS-C are:

1. The *Activation Service*: on behalf of a specific coordination protocol, this service creates a new coordinator and its associated context. It also implicitly creates an associated *Registration Service* instance. The type of protocol support required is identified at creation time by a Universal Resource Identifier (URI) provided by the initiator of the transaction.

2. The *Registration Service*: again, acting on behalf of a specific coordination protocol (and specific instance of a coordinator), an instance of this service is used by specific participants to enroll with the coordinator.

3. The *context*: this contains information necessary for WS-C to perform coordination as well as information specific to the protocol implementation.

This is shown Code Listing 10-3 where the schema states that a context consists of a URI that uniquely identifies the type of coordination that is required (`xs:anyURI`), an endpoint where participants to be coordinated can be registered (`wsu:PortReferenceType`), and an extensibility element designed to carry specific coordination protocol context payload (`xs:any`), which can carry arbitrary XML payload.

Code Listing 10-3 WS-Coordination Context Schema Fragment

```
<xs:complexType name="CoordinationContextType"
abstract="false">
  <xs:complexContent>
    <xs:extension base="wsu:ContextType">
      <xs:sequence>
        <xs:element name="CoordinationType"
            type="xs:anyURI" />
        <xs:element name="RegistrationService"
                                type="wsu:PortReferenceType"
/>
        <xs:any namespace="##any" processContents="lax"
            minOccurs="0" maxOccurs="unbounded" />
      </xs:sequence>
    </xs:extension>
  </xs:complexContent>
</xs:complexType>
```

We saw earlier how the OASIS BTP coordinates participants in either atomic or cohesive transactions in order to achieve consensus. The protocol defined in the BTP specification is an open-top two-phase completion protocol. However, there is no separation between transactions and coordination in BTP and all of the protocol assumes two-phase. Attempting to change the type of coordination protocol (e.g., to a three-phase protocol) would require significant modifications to the specification and affect all aspects of coordination and transactions.

An important aspect of WS-Transaction that differentiates it from traditional transaction protocols is that a synchronous request/response model is not assumed. This model derives from the fact that WS-Transaction is, as we see in Figure 10-7, layered upon the WS-Coordination protocol, whose own communication patterns are asynchronous by default.

WS-Transaction leverages the context management framework provided by WS-Coordination in two ways. First, it extends the WS-Coordination context to create a transaction context. Second, it augments the Activation and Registration services to support two transaction models with associated protocols, as we describe in the following sections.

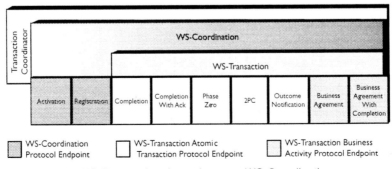

Figure 10-7 WS-Transaction dependency on WS-Coordination.

WS-Transaction Models

Given that we have already seen that traditional transaction models are not appropriate for Web services, let's pose the question, "What type of model or protocol *is* appropriate?" The answer to that question is that no one specific protocol is likely to be sufficient, given the wide range of situations within which Web services transactions are likely to be deployed. Hence, the WS-Transaction specification proposes two distinct models, where each supports the semantics of a particular kind of business-to-business interaction. Again, these are similar to the concepts to those underlying the J2EE Activity Service that we saw in Chapter 9.

Atomic Transaction

You should find the atomic transaction model easy to understand (it was revised into the WS-AtomicTransaction specification). An atomic transaction (AT) is similar to traditional ACID transactions and intended to support short-duration interactions where ACID semantics are appropriate. Within the scope of an AT, services typically enroll transaction-aware resources, such as databases and message queues, as participants under the control of the transaction. When the transaction terminates, the outcome decision of the AT is then propagated to each enlisted resource via the participant and the appropriate commit or rollback actions are taken by each.

It is assumed that all services (and associated participants) provide ACID semantics and that any use of atomic transactions occurs in environments and situations where this is appropriate: in a trusted domain, over short durations. In fact, the AT model can be used within J2EE as a replacement for the OTS to provide interoperability between different transaction service implementations. The JTA would continue to isolate the EJB from the underlying transaction service, which in this case would be Web services-based.

To begin an atomic transaction, the client application firstly locates the right type of transaction coordinator. Once located, the client sends a WS-Coordination `CreateCoordinationContext` message to the Activation Service specifying the type of transaction required as `http://schemas.xmlsoap.org/ws/2002/08/wstx` and it will get back an appropriate transaction context. The returned context has its `CoordinationType` element set to the AT namespace, `http://schemas.xmlsoap.org/ws/2002/08/wstx` and also contains a reference to the atomic transaction coordinator endpoint (the Registration Service) where participants can be enlisted, as shown in Code Listing 10-4.

Code Listing 10-4 Atomic transaction context

```
<!-- Create atomic transaction context message -->
<CreateCoordinationContext>
  <ActivationService>
    <wsu:Address>
      http://example.org/ws-transaction/activation
    </wsu:Address>
  </ActivationService>
```

```
    <RequesterReference>
      <wsu:Address>
        http://example.org/ws-transaction/client-app
      </wsu:Address>
    </RequesterReference>
    <CoordinationType>
      http://schemas.xmlsoap.org/ws/2002/08/wstx
    </CoordinationType>
  </CreateCoordinationContext>

  <!-- Atomic transaction context -->
  <wscoor:CoordinationContext
    xmlns:wscoor="http://schemas.xmlsoap.org/ws/2002/08/wscoor"
    xmlns:wsu="http://schemas.xmlsoap.org/ws/2002/07/utility">
    <wsu:Identifier>
      http://example.org/tx-id/aabb-1122-ddee-3344-ff00
    </wsu:Identifier>
    <wsu:Expires>2003-06-30T00:00:00-08:00</wsu:Expires>
    <wscoor:CoordinationType>
      http://schemas.xmlsoap.org/ws/2002/08/wstx
    </wscoor:CoordinationType>
    <wscoor:RegistrationService>
      <wsu:Address>
        http://example.org/ws-transaction/registration
      </wsu:Address>
    </wscoor:RegistrationService>
  </wscoor:CoordinationContext>
```

After obtaining a transaction context from the coordinator, the client application then proceeds to interact with Web services to accomplish its business-level work. With each invocation on a business service, the client propagates the context, such that the each invocation is implicitly scoped by the transaction. As you can see, this is identical to the way in which traditional transaction systems operate.

Once all the necessary application level work has been completed, the client can terminate the transaction. To do this, the client application registers its own participant for the `Completion` or `CompletionWithAck` protocol (this protocol was actually removed in WS-Atomic-Transaction). Once registered, the participant can instruct the coordinator either to try to commit or roll back the transaction.

Transaction termination normally uses the two-phase commit protocol (2PC in WS-Tx, or Durable Two-Phase Commit in the revised specification). If a transaction involves only a single participant, the protocol supports a one-phase commit optimization similar to that in traditional transaction systems. Figure 10-8 shows the state transitions of an atomic transaction and the message exchanges between coordinator and participant; the coordinator-generated messages are shown in the solid line, whereas the participant messages are shown by dashed lines.

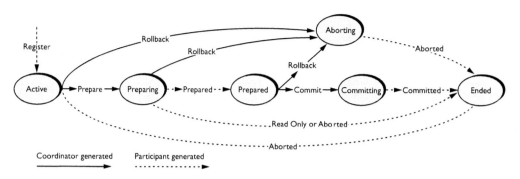

Figure 10-8 Two-phase commit state transitions.

Once the coordinator has finished with the transaction, the protocol that originally began the termination of the transaction can complete, and inform the client application whether the transaction was committed or rolled back.

> **N O T E**   Note: The `CompletionWithAck` protocol insists that the coordinator must remember the outcome until it has received acknowledgment of the notification from the terminator of the transaction.

Given the lack of reliable message delivery in Web services, this protocol represented a problem to implementations because a client that sent such an acknowledgement should wait for a reciprocal acknowledgement from the coordinator in order to know that the message was safely delivered. Likewise for the coordinator's acknowledgement message to the original acknowledgement so that it can forget about the transaction. Loss of any of these messages could result in the accumulation of garbage.

In addition to the 2PC protocol, the AT model also provides two other protocols, `PhaseZero` and `OutcomeNotification`. Once again these have their basis in traditional transaction processing systems: they are the equivalent of the `Synchronization` protocol we saw in Chapter 1, "Transaction Fundamentals." In fact, when the authors were working on the revised WS-AtomicTransaction specification, they decided to collapse these two protocols into one, called the Volatile Two-Phase Commit protocol. However, the intent is the same: the prepare phase of all participants for this protocol executes before the prepare phase of the Durable Two-Phase Commit, and the commit or rollback phases may execute afterwards.

If we return to the original AT model, then when an atomic transaction is terminating, the associated coordinator first executes the `PhaseZero` protocol if any participants registered for it. All `PhaseZero` participants are told that the transaction is about to complete and they can respond with either the `PhaseZeroCompleted` or `Error` message; any failures at this stage will cause the transaction to rollback. (In WS-AtomicTransaction, the message would be `Pre-pare`, to which the responses would be the usual `ReadOnly`, `Aborted` or `Prepared`).

Additionally, some services may have registered an interest in the completion of a transaction and they will be informed via the `OutcomeNotificaton` protocol after 2PC has completed. Any registered `OutcomeNotification` participants are invoked after the transaction has terminated and are told the state in which the transaction completed (the coordinator sends either the `Committed` or `Aborted` message). Since the transaction has terminated, any failures of participants at this stage are ignored – `OutcomeNotification` is essentially a courtesy, and has no bearing on the outcome of the transaction.

The fact that there are distinct protocols for synchronization and two-phase commit is important in AT as it is in traditional transaction systems. Being able to rely upon the order in which certain types of participants will be invoked allows performance optimizations such as caching to be supported. As we saw earlier, BTP has only one type of participant that can be enlisted in an atom or cohesion, and neither protocol supports any kind of relative ordering. Hence, providing an equivalent to synchronizations is not possible within the scope of vanilla BTP.

Figure 10-9 illustrates the various AT protocols and how they work together.

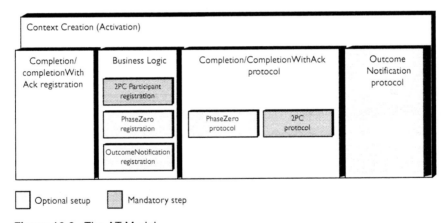

Figure 10-9 The AT Model.

There is another fundamental difference between the AT model and the BTP atom model to which it is often compared: the termination protocol is not open-top and hence the distinction between participants and services is well defined. The termination protocol does not mix business level decisions into the commit protocol, overloading what it may mean for a participant to receive a prepare request, for example.

The reason for this is that Web services are typically written to operate in the following way:

- A service receives a document requesting it to perform some work (e.g., reserve a seat on a specific flight).

- Later that service may be sent another document requesting it to either undo the work or accept it.

If the work is being performed within the scope of a transaction, then the interaction between the application and the transaction service should be minimal—the transaction coordinator only requires access to the participants and they should not require strong interactions with the services on whose behalf they operate. That's not the way participants and services work in traditional transaction systems and that separation of concerns has worked well for many decades. So it seems reasonable to assume that it's a good starting point for Web services transactions.

In the scenario of a flight reservation service, the business-level (service) methods such as booking a seat have already performed the necessary work (e.g., provisionally reserving the seat). The explicit prepare operation of the open-top protocol is simply not required to have business semantics. The assumed advantages of an open-top approach (allowing decision time between the two-phases) are not required: when the application decides to terminate the business transaction it wants the work to happen (or not) immediately, and all that is required is to guarantee consensus between the participants.

Business Activity

Most business-to-business applications require transactional support in order to guarantee consistent outcome and correct execution. These applications often involve long-running computations, loosely coupled systems and components that do not share data, location, or administration and it is difficult to incorporate atomic transactions within such architectures. For example, an online bookshop may reserve books for an individual for a specific period of time, but if the individual does not purchase the books within that period they will be "put back onto the shelf" for others to buy. Furthermore, because it is not possible for anyone to have an infinite supply of stock, some online shops may appear to users to reserve items for them, but in fact may allow others to pre-empt that reservation (i.e., the same book may be "reserved" for multiple users concurrently); a user may subsequently find that the item is no longer available, or may have to be reordered specially for them.

A business activity (BA) is designed specifically for these kinds of long-duration interactions, where exclusively locking resources is impossible or impractical. In this model (revised into the WS-BusinessActivity specification) services are requested to do work, and where those services have the ability to undo any work, they inform the BA so that if the BA later decides to cancel the work, it can instruct the service to execute its undo behavior.

While the full ACID semantics are not maintained by a BA, consistency can still be maintained through compensation, though the task of writing correct compensating actions (and thus overall system consistency) is delegated to the developers of the services under control of the BA. Such compensations may use backward error recovery, but will typically employ forward recovery.

Central to business activities is the notion of *scopes* and defining activity-to-task relationships. A business activity may be partitioned into scopes, where a scope is a business task or unit of work using a collection of Web services. Such scopes can be nested to arbitrary levels, forming parent and child relationships. A parent scope has the ability to select which child tasks are to be included in the overall outcome protocol for a specific business activity, and so clearly non-atomic outcomes are possible. A Business Activity defines a consensus group that allows the relaxation of atomicity based on business level decisions. In a similar manner to traditional nested transactions, if a child task experiences an error, it can be caught by the parent who may be able to compensate and continue processing.

As we saw earlier, although BTP supports interposition, it does not support nesting of scopes. This is an important difference between Business Activities and BTP. Nested scopes are important for a number of reasons, including:

- *Fault-isolation*: If subscope fails (e.g., because a service it was using fails) then this does not require the enclosing scope to fail, thus undoing all of the work performed so far.
- *Modularity*: If there is already a scope associated with a call when a new scope is begun, then the scope will be nested within it. Therefore, a programmer who knows that a service requires scopes can use them within the service: if the service's methods are invoked without a parent scope, then the service's scopes will simply be top-level; otherwise, they will be nested within the scope of the client.

When a child task completes, it can either leave the business activity or signal to the parent that the work it has done can be compensated later. In the latter case, the compensation task may be called by the parent should it ultimately need to undo the work performed by the child.

Unlike the AT protocol, where participants inform the coordinator of their state only when asked, a task within a business activity can specify its outcome to the parent directly without waiting for a request; similar to BTP participants. This feature is useful when tasks fail so that the notification can be used by business activity exception handler to modify the goals and drive processing forward without having to wait until the end of the transaction to fail.

Underpinning all of this are three fundamental assumptions:

- All state transitions are reliably recorded, including application state and coordination metadata (the record of sent and received messages).
- All request messages are acknowledged, so that problems are detected as early as possible. This avoids executing unnecessary tasks and can also detect a problem earlier when rectifying it is simpler and less expensive.
- As with atomic transactions, a response is defined as a separate operation and not as the output of the request. Message input-output implementations will typically have timeouts that are too short for some business activity responses. If the response is not received after a timeout, it is re-sent. This is repeated until a response is received. The request receiver discards all but one identical request received.

As with atomic transactions, the business activity model has multiple protocols: `BusinessAgreement` (renamed `BusinessAgreementWithParticipantCompletion` in the WS-BusinessActivity specification) and BusinessAgreementWithComplete (renamed BusinessAgreementWithCoordinatorCompletion). However, unlike the AT protocol, which is driven from the coordinator down to participants, this protocol is driven much more from the participants upwards.

Under the BusinessAgreement protocol, a child activity is initially created in the active state; if it finishes the work it was created to do and no more participation is required within the scope of the BA (such as when the activity operates on immutable data), then the child can unilaterally send an *exited* message to the parent; this is equivalent to the BTP capability of a participant resigning from the business transaction. However, if the child task finishes and wishes to continue in the BA, it must be able to compensate for the work it has performed (e.g., cancel the seat on the flight). In this case it sends a *completed* message to the parent and waits to receive the final outcome of the BA from the parent. This outcome will either be a *close* message, meaning the BA has completed successfully or a *compensate* message indicating that the parent activity requires that the child task reverse its work.

The BusinessAgreementWithComplete protocol is identical to the BusinessAgreement protocol with the exception that the child cannot autonomously decide to end its participation in the business activity, even if it can be compensated. Rather the child task relies upon the parent to inform it when the child has received all requests for it to perform work, which the parent does by sending the *complete* message to the child. The child then acts as it does in the BusinessAgreement protocol.

> **N O T E**   A fundamental difference between the BA model and the BTP cohesion model is that it does not mix business-level semantics with the transaction protocol. The reason for the BA approach is that it's similar to what traditional workflow systems do and how most Web services are being written today: the compensation work is simply considered as another activity. The work required to compensate is already available from the service (e.g., cancel the seat reservation), and obviously book seat does the work somehow (and this may well be provisional until the application confirms the seat reservation).

Most workflow systems don't distinguish compensate activities from forward progress activities: an activity is an activity and it just does some work. If that work happens to compensate for some previous work then so be it. In addition, most services you'll find already have compensate operations written into their definitions, like "cancel seat reservation" or "cancel holiday" and they don't need to be driven by some other transaction/coordination engine that then sends "prepare" or "commit" or "rollback" to a participant which then has to figure out how to talk to the service to accomplish the same goal.

Example of Using Business Activities

We've already seen how the travel agent scenario could be modeled using BTP. So the obvious question is: Can the same scenario be supported by Atomic Transactions and Business Activities? Obviously the AT model is inappropriate for this because it essentially uses an ACID transaction protocol. Therefore, we're really looking at the appropriateness of the BA model.

For simplicity, let's concentrate just on the purchasing of the cheapest travel insurance, and we now add a third insurance service, as shown in Figure 10-10. In this example, the travel agent must now obtain three quotes before choosing the cheapest for the customer.

In this case a BA is used and so quotes are committed immediately as per the BA model. In the non-failure case, things are straightforward and each Child BA reports back to the coordinator that it has performed the work (obtained a quote) via a *completed* message. Remember though that this implicitly means that the work can be compensated for later. Once the travel agent has received all of the quotes, it can choose the cheapest and send it a *close* message; all other insurance sites receive a *compensate* message. Fairly straightforward.

The failure case, however, is a little more interesting. Let's assume that Insurance B could not get a quote so its corresponding BA fails. It reports that it has failed back to the coordinator through a *faulted* message. Upon receiving this message, the logic driving the BA may uses forward error recovery to try to obtain a quote from an alternate site as shown in Figure 10-11. (Obviously what the travel agent does in the event of a quote will be implementation dependent, but if it did nothing then this example would be boring.)

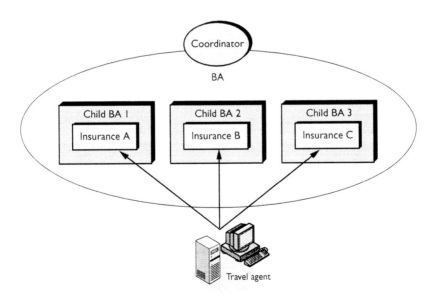

Figure 10-10 Using Business Activities to choose the cheapest insurance quote.

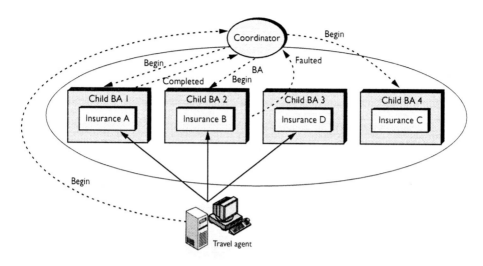

Figure 10-11   Handling errors and making forward progress.

If the forward error recovery works and the alternate quote is obtained, the BA proceeds as before. However, if the forward error recovery fails, the BA finds itself in a situation where it cannot make forward progress (remember, the agent must obtain three quotes before being able to choose the cheapest). Therefore, there is no choice but to cancel and compensate for all of the previous successfully completed activities. The BA coordinator does this by sending *compensate* messages to all of these activities. Once the compensation has successfully taken place (and bear in mind that an added complexity here is that compensations can themselves fail), the system should be in a state that is equivalent to the state before the purchase operations were carried out.

The API

It shouldn't come as a surprise to learn that, as with BTP, neither the WS-C nor WS-T specifications define an API. After all, they are specifications defined for Web services, which can be translated into a variety of different programming languages. However, without an API they aren't of much use. Thankfully, JAXTX once again comes to the rescue for J2EE. As we see later, this specification is defining all of the APIs for the translation of these various standards into Java.

The Web Services Composite Application Framework

In July 2003, Arjuna Technologies, Fujitsu, IONA Technologies, Oracle and Sun released the Web Services Composite Application Framework. The Web Services Composite Application Framework (WS-CAF) is divided into three parts:

- Web Services Context (WS-Context), a lightweight framework for simple context management.

- Web Services Coordination Framework (WS-CF), a sharable mechanism to manage context augmentation and lifecycle, and guarantee message delivery. The overall concept here is similar to the J2EE Activity Service and the WS-C specification we discussed earlier. The fact that several of the authors of WS-CAF worked on the J2EE Activity Service shouldn't come as a surprise.
- Web Services Transaction Management (WS-TXM), comprising three distinct protocols for interoperability across multiple transaction managers and supporting multiple transaction models (two phase commit, long running actions, and business process flows).

> **N O T E**   It may come as a surprise to note that several of the authors of the WS-C/WS-T and WS-CAF specifications began working on these ideas together, before splitting them into separate Web services specifications.

The overall aim of the combination of the parts of WS-CAF is to support various transaction processing models and architectures. The individual parts of WS-CAF are designed to complement Web services orchestration and choreography technologies such as BPEL, WSCI and WS-Choreography and to work with existing Web services specifications such as WS-Security and WS-Reliability. The parts define incremental layers of functionality that can be implemented and used separately by these and other specifications separately or together.

The parts of WS-CAF comprise a stack, starting from WS-Context, adding WS-CF, and finally WS-TXM to deliver the complete features and functionality required by composite applications. An implementation of WS-CAF can start with WS-Context for simple context management, and later add WS-CF for its additional context management features and message delivery guarantees, and finally add WS-TXM for managing a variety of recovery protocols. Similarly, a composite application can use the level of support required, from simple context management through to transactional recovery mechanisms.

Before we look at the various transaction models that WS-TXM defines, it's worth examining the context and coordination frameworks. It's also worth noting that WS-CAF supports both synchronous and asynchronous invocation patterns for these services.

The Context Service

We've discussed context several times in the book so you are probably familiar with the overall aims it attempts to address. In WS-CAF, the purpose of a context is to allow multiple individual Web services to enter a relationship by sharing certain common attributes as an externally modeled entity. Typical reasons for Web services to share context include:

- Common security environment—multiple Web services execute within a single authentication session or authorization check.
- Participation in an automated business process execution, or choreography.

The definition of a context is application-specific, but contains at a minimum a unique ID in the form of a namespace URI. The namespace URI qualifies the elements in context, which can include any or all of the following:

- Security tokens or attributes
- Transaction IDs
- File ID
- Database session ID

The ability to scope arbitrary units of distributed work by sharing common context is a requirement in a variety of distributed applications, such as choreography and business-to-business interactions (and transactions, as we've seen). Scoping makes it possible for Web services participants to be able to determine unambiguously whether or not they are in the same composite application, and what it means to share context. Scopes can be nested to arbitrary levels to better delineate application work.

The context contains information, including a unique context identifier (URI) and optionally the URIs of each additional Web service within the scope of the composite application. WS-CAF defines a composite application to be a collection of Web services that executes in a specified sequence for the purpose of carrying out multiple operations on a shared resource, such as a database, display, or XML document, in which the unresolved failure of an individual Web service execution causes the failure of the entire application. Any Web service execution that fails has the responsibility to notify any previously successful Web services of the failure, and terminate the application. A failure can be resolved if the service requester includes sufficient failure recovery logic.

A Web service is identified as belonging to a composite application by the inclusion of the context URI in the header and optionally a namespace URI identifying the list of Web services participating in the application. The namespace URI can be translated in a variety of ways, including referencing an XML document containing the list or a WSDL providing the interface to the list of participants. In the case where Web services register themselves with a coordinator, the coordinator maintains the list and the namespace URI is interpreted as referencing the coordinator location.

An example is shown in Code Listing 10-5.

Code Listing 10-5   Identifying the participants in a composite application

```
<env:Envelope xmlns:env="http://www.w3.org/2002/12/soap-
envelope">
 <env:Header>
 <n:Composite xmlns:n="http://example.org/
CompositeApplication">
   <n:Context>
     http://example.org/contextURI
```

```
    </n:Context>
    <n:ApplicationList>
      http://example.org/ListLocation
    </n:ApplicationList>
  </n:Composite>
  </env:Header>
  <env:Body>
  <m:Message xmlns:m="http://example.org/MessageSchema"
    <m:...
  </m:Message>
  </env:Body>
</env:Envelope>
```

The Coordination Framework

We won't say too much about WS-CF, since its overall aims are similar to the J2EE Activity Service and the WS-C specification. Individual Web services as well as composite applications can register as participants with a coordinator, which takes over responsibility for context management and notifying them of the outcome of a series of related Web services executions. The executions are defined as related when they share a common context. A coordinator can register itself with another coordinator and become a participant, thereby improving interoperability (yes, this is interposition again).

As shown Code Listing 10-6, including a coordinator URI in a SOAP header identifies to the SOAP processor that the Web service is registering with the coordinator defined by the WSDL interface returned by dereferencing the URI.

Code Listing 10-6   Adding the coordinator URI reference to the message

```
<env:Envelope xmlns:env="http://www.w3.org/2002/12/soap-
envelope">
 <env:Header>
 <n:Composite xmlns:n="http://example.org/
CompositeApplication">
  <n:Context>
    http://example.org/contextURI
  </n:Context>
  <n:Coordinator>
    http://example.org/coordinatorURI
  </n:Coordinator>
  </n:Composite>
  </env:Header>
  <env:Body>
  <m:Message xmlns:m="http://example.org/MessageSchema"
    <m:...
  </m:Message>
  </env:Body>
</env:Envelope>
```

The Transaction Models

WS-TXM defines a set of pluggable transaction protocols that can be used with the coordinator to negotiate a set of actions for all participants to execute based on the outcome of a series of related Web services executions. The executions are related through the use of shared context (scopes). As mentioned previously, scopes can be nested (parent-child relationships) and concurrent, representing application tasks. Counter-effects for completed scopes may then become the responsibility for the enclosing scope. Examples of coordinated outcomes include the classic two-phase commit protocol, long running outcomes, open nested transaction protocol, asynchronous messaging protocol, or business process automation protocol.

There are three transaction protocols defined by WS-TXM:

1. *ACID transaction*: A traditional ACID transaction (AT) designed for interoperability across existing transaction infrastructures. It supports two-phase commit and synchronizations. This should be familiar to you already, so we won't spend any time on this protocol. As with the WS-Tx Atomic Transaction model, ACID transactions are intended to be used in environments where transaction service interoperability is a requirement (e.g., J2EE-to-J2EE).

2. *Long running action*: An activity, or a group of activities, which does not necessarily possess the guaranteed ACID properties. A long-running action (LRA) still has the "all or nothing" atomic effect, i.e., failure should not result in partial work. Participants within an LRA may use forward (compensation) or backward error recovery to ensure atomicity. Isolation is also considered a back-end implementation responsibility.

3. *Business process transaction*: An activity, or a group of activities, that is responsible for performing some application specific work. A business process (BP) may be structured as a collection of atomic transactions or long running actions depending upon the application requirements.

Long-Running Activities

The long-running action model (LRA) is designed specifically for those business interactions that occur over a long duration. Within this model, an activity reflects business interactions: all work performed within the scope of an application is required to be compensatable. Therefore, an application's work is either performed successfully or undone. How individual Web services perform their work and ensure it can be undone if compensation is required are implementation choices and not exposed to the LRA model. The LRA model simply defines the triggers for compensation actions and the conditions under which those triggers are executed.

In the LRA model, each application is bound to the scope of a compensation interaction. For example, when a user reserves a seat on a flight, the airline reservation center may take an optimistic approach and actually book the seat and debit the user's account, relying on the fact that most of their customers who reserve seats later book them; the compensation action for this activity would obviously be to cancel the seat and credit the user's account. Work performed within the scope of a nested LRA must remain compensatable until an enclosing service informs the individual service(s) that it is no longer required.

Let's consider the original travel agent example we saw in Chapter 9. To remind you, the application is concerned with booking a taxi, reserving a table at a restaurant, reserving a seat at the theater, and then booking a room at a hotel. If all of these operations were performed as a single transaction then resources acquired during booking the taxi (for example) would not be released until the top-level transaction has terminated. If subsequent activities do not require those resources, then they will be needlessly unavailable to other clients.

Figure 10-12 shows how part of the night out may be mapped into LRAs. All of the individual activities are compensatable. For example, this means that if LRA1 fails or the user decides to not accept the booked taxi, the work will be undone automatically. Because LRA1 is nested within another LRA, once LRA1 completes successfully any compensation mechanisms for its work may be passed to LRA5: this is an implementation choice for the Compensator. In the event that LRA5 completes successfully, no work is required to be compensated, otherwise all work performed within the scope of LRA5 (LRA1 to LRA4) will be compensated.

As in any business interaction, application services may or may not be compensatable. Even the ability to compensate may be a transient capability of a service. The LRA model allows applications to combine services that can be compensated with those that cannot be compensated (in the WS-T Business Activity model this would be equivalent to having services that always respond with an *exit* message to the coordinator.) Obviously, by mixing the two service types the user may end up with a business activity that will ultimately not be undone by the LRA model, but which may require outside (application-specific) compensation.

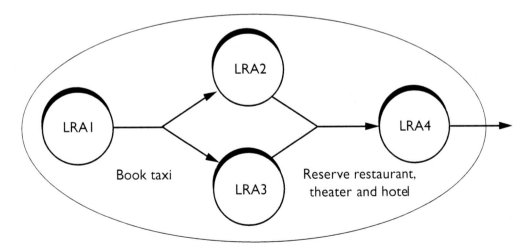

Figure 10-12   LRA example.

A *Compensator* is the LRA participant that operates on behalf of a service to undo the work it performs within the scope of an LRA. How compensation is carried out will obviously be dependent upon the service; compensation work may be carried out by other LRAs which themselves have Compensators.

For example, consider the travel example illustrated in Figure 10-13, where normal (non-failure) activities are connected by solid lines while compensation activities are connected by dashed lines. In this case the user first attempts to book a first-class seat on an airline; the Compensator for this (which is executed in the event of a crash or failure to complete the booking, for example) starts another LRA that tries to cancel the booking. If the cancellation LRA fails, then its Compensator e-mails the system administrator for the airline reservation site; if the cancellation succeeds, however, it tries to book an economy seat on the same flight (which for simplicity does not have a Compensator task).

When a service performs work that may have to be later compensated within the scope of an LRA, it enlists a Compensator participant with the LRA coordinator. The coordinator will send the Compensator one of the following messages (illustrated in Figure 10-14) when the activity terminates:

- *Success*: The activity has completed successfully. If the activity is nested then Compensators may propagate themselves (or new Compensators) to the enclosing LRA. Otherwise the Compensators are informed that the activity has terminated and they can perform any necessary cleanups.

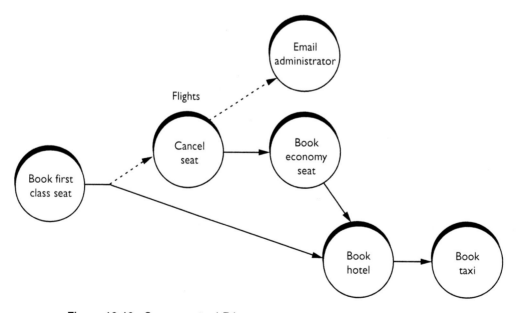

Figure 10-13 Compensator LRAs.

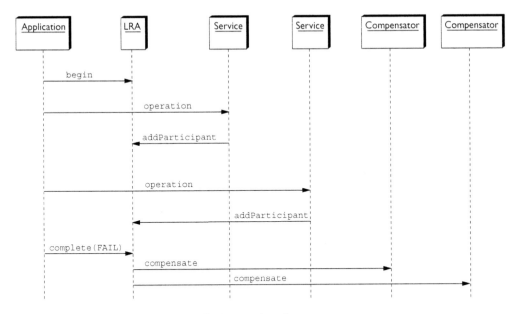

Figure 10-14   Example LRA interaction diagram.

- *Fail*: The activity has completed unsuccessfully. All Compensators that are registered with the LRA will be invoked to perform compensation in the reverse order. The coordinator forgets about all Compensators that indicated they operated correctly. Otherwise, compensation may be attempted again (possibly after a period of time) or alternatively a compensation violation has occurred and must be logged.

Each service is required to log sufficient information in order to ensure (with best effort) that compensation is possible.

So far we have not really considered the relationship between LRAs in an application. Obviously, LRAs may be used sequentially and concurrently, where the termination of an LRA signals the start of some other unit of work within an application. However, LRAs are units of compensatable work and an application may have as many such units of work operating simultaneously as it needs to accomplish its tasks. Furthermore, the outcome of work within LRAs may determine how other LRAs are terminated.

An application can be structured to so that LRAs are used to assemble units of compensatable work and then held in the active state while the application performs other work in the scope of different (concurrent or sequential) LRAs. Only when the right subset of work (LRAs) is arrived at by the application will that subset be confirmed; all other LRAs will be told to cancel (complete in a failure state).

For example, Figure 10-15 illustrates how our travel agent scenario may be structured using this technique. LRA1 is used to obtain the taxi to the airport. The user then wishes to get the cheapest flight from three different airlines. Therefore, the agency structures each seat reservation as a separate LRA. In this example, the airline represented by LRA2 gives a cost of $150 for the flight; while LRA2 is still active, the application starts LRA3, a new independent-level LRA to ask the next airline for a costing: LRA3 gives a value of $160 and so it is cancelled. Finally, the travel agency starts LRA4 to check the other airline, which gives a value of $120 for the seat. Thus, LRA2 is cancelled and LRA4 is confirmed, with the result that the seat is bought. The travel agency then uses the same technique to select the cheapest travel insurance between two options (using LRA5 and LRA6).

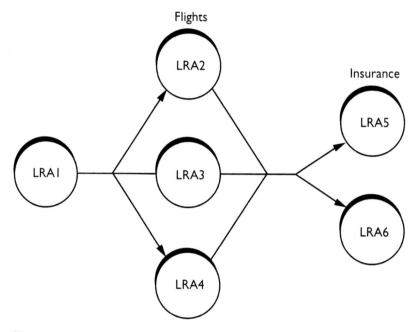

Figure 10-15   Using LRAs to select units of work.

Business Process Model

The business process (BP) model is significantly different from any of the other transaction models we've looked at so far. This model is specifically aimed at tying together heterogeneous transaction domains into a single business-to-business transaction. So, for example, with the BP model it's possible to have a long-running business transaction span messaging, workflow and traditional ACID transactions. The reason for this is to allow business to leverage their existing corporate IT investment, which is an important consideration.

In the business process transaction model all parties involved in a business process reside within *business domains*, which may themselves use business processes to perform work. Business process transactions are responsible for managing interactions *between* these domains. A business process (business-to-business interaction) is split into *business tasks* and each task executes within a specific business domain. A business domain may itself be subdivided into other business domains (business processes) in a recursive manner.

Each domain may represent a different transaction model if such a federation of models is more appropriate to the activity. Each business task (which may be modeled as a scope) may provide implementation-specific counter-effects in the event that the enclosing scope must cancel. In addition, periodically the controlling application may request that all business domains checkpoint their state such that they can either be consistently rolled back to that checkpoint by the application or restarted from the checkpoint in the event of a failure.

An individual task may require multiple services to work. Each task is assumed to be a compensatable unit of work. However, as with the LRA model, how compensation is provided is an implementation choice for the task.

For example, let's return to our travel agent and see how it might be mapped into the BP model. If you look at Figure 10-16, you can see that the online travel agent interacts with its specific suppliers, each of which resides in its own business domain. The work necessary to obtain each component is modeled as a separate task, or Web service. In this example, the Flight Reservation task is actually composed of two subtasks: one that gets the flight and the other that gets the necessary travel insurance. This example and some of the concepts we're about to mention may seem familiar: we briefly touched on the concept of interposition as the universal adapter in Chapter 8, "Advanced Transaction Concepts," and WS-CAF builds upon the same ideas.

In this example, the user may interact synchronously with the travel agent to build up the details of the holiday required. Alternately, the user may submit an order (possibly with a list of

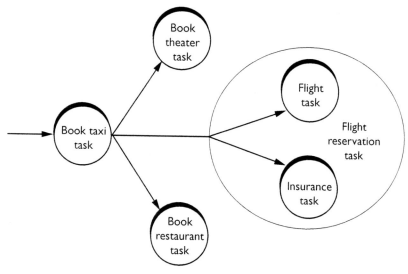

Figure 10-16 Business processes and tasks for a travel agent.

alternate requirements, such as destinations, dates, and so on) to the agent who will eventually call back when it has been filled; likewise, the travel agent then submits orders to each supplier, requiring them to call back when each component is available (or is known to be unavailable).

The business process transaction model supports this synchronous and asynchronous interaction pattern. Business domains are instructed to perform work within the scope of a global business process. The business process has an overall manager that may be informed by individual tasks when they have completed their work (either successfully or unsuccessfully), or it may periodically communicate with each task to determine its current status. In addition, each task may make period checkpoints of its progress such that if a failure occurs, it may be restarted from that point rather than having to start from the beginning. A business process can either terminate in a confirmed (successful) manner, in which case *all* of the work requested will have been performed, or it will terminate in a cancelled (unsuccessful) manner, in which case all of the work will be undone.

If it cannot be undone, then this fact must be logged. One key difference between the business process transaction model and that of traditional 2PC is that it assumes success: the BP model is optimistic and assumes the failure case is the minority and can be handled or resolved offline if necessary, or through replay/void/compensation, but not always automatically, often requiring human interaction.

Logging is essential in the BP model for replay, void, and compensation. However, recovery may ultimately be the responsibility of a manual operator if automatic recovery/compensation is not possible. As we shall see, interposition plays a major role in the BP model to improve performance or to federate a distributed environment into separate domains. In fact user intervention is likely to be an important part of business process management, as is monitoring of every step. As such, although the protocols are described in terms of participant services, it is expected that in some cases implementations of participants will interact directly with operators.

Figure 10-17 illustrates the state transitions for a business process (and business task). Once created, the business process (which is structured as an activity) is in the *Active* state. From here it may transit to the *Cancelled* state and in which case no further work is performed. More typical is that it moves to the *Working* state where it may remain for as long as is necessary to perform the work necessary.

How the business process moves from this state will depend upon the application and the structure of any individual business tasks. If there are no failures (e.g., all work requested can be performed), then the process moves to the *Confirmed* state and all work is completed. However, if there are failures (e.g., a machine crash or the fact that a requested item cannot be found to fulfill an order) then the process may either move to the *Cancelled* state (signifying that all work performed has been undone) or it moves to the *Failure* state where business-level compensation (or other recovery mechanisms such as void and replay) may occur.

This compensation is different from that which occurs to undo the entire business process: it is an attempt by each task/process to compensate for the inability to fulfill a specific business requirement. If it is possible to compensate then the task moves back to the *Working* state; other-

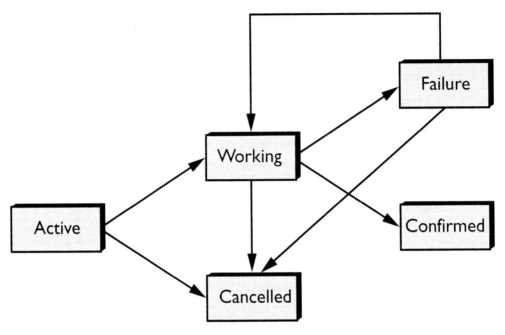

Figure 10-17   Business process state transitions.

wise it moves to the *Cancelled* state. Because compensation may occur in an application/domain specific manner it may include manual (operator) involvement. As such, compensation can take arbitrary amounts of time.

In order to participant within a business process transaction (BP model), each business domain is exposed as a single subordinate (interposed) coordinator, forming a parent-child relationship; the business domain is identified by the coordinator URI. The interposed coordinator is responsible for managing the domain's participation within the overall business transaction. The internal implementation of a domain is not the responsibility of this specification. In order to perform work necessary for a business task a domain may use its own business process transaction, ACID transactions, or some other infrastructure.

For example, Figure 10-18 shows how the home entertainment system would be federated into interposed coordinator domains. Each domain is represented by a subordinate coordinator that masks the internal business process infrastructure from its parent. Not only does the interposed domain require the use of a different context when communicating with services within the domain (the coordinator endpoint is different), but each domain may use different protocols to those outside of the domain: the subordinate coordinator may then act as a translator from protocols outside the domain to protocols used within the domain.

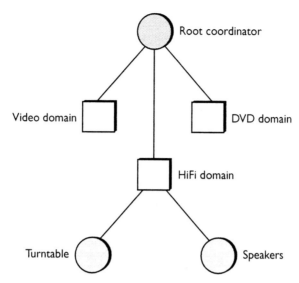

Figure 10-18   Example business process interposition.

For example, a domain may be implemented entirely using the OASIS BTP with the interposed coordinator responsible for mapping BP protocol messages into BTP's atom or cohesion messages and vice versa. Another domain (possibly in the same overall business process) may use the Object Transaction Service and therefore provide an interposed coordinator to translate between the BP model and the OTS. The important point is that as far as a parent coordinator in the BP hierarchy is concerned it interacts with participants and as long as those participants obey the BP protocol, it cannot determine the implementation.

The API

Guess what? Once again in the J2EE world JAXTX will define the API for the various WS-CAF transaction related models. However, before we look at JAXTX, we use the following section trying to give an indication of where we think the standardization efforts will go in this evolving area.

Which Specification?

So, will BTP become the transaction protocol of choice for businesses, or will it be WS-T or WS-TXM? What should your transactional Web services applications be written against when all of these protocols seem subtly different?

You should remember something that we discussed in relation to the J2EE Activity Service: just as with that framework, Web services transactions are not meant to replace your current transactional infrastructures and investments, but rather are designed to work with them. It is extremely unlikely that transactional Web Services will be developed from the bottom up, re-implementing all functionality and especially not transactions. As we've seen throughout this book, there's a lot of effort involved in providing a reliable ACID transaction system that performs well, so just imagine the kinds of effort required when you start relaxing the various ACID properties.

If you're choosing a Web services transaction product or looking to implement one, you need to consider what it'll interface with. As we mentioned at the start of this chapter, Web services are about interoperability as much as they are about the Web (or the Internet). Most of the applications that run in this environment are going to use Web services to glue together islands of strongly coupled domains, such as J2EE or CORBA. Therefore, you'll probably want to look at an implementation (and hence protocol) that allows you to plug in your existing infrastructure investment.

Web services transactions is a new area and BTP is still not a ratified standard. Since many of the key players have moved on to WS-T or WS-CAF, it is now uncertain as to whether BTP will ever be an adopted OASIS specification. Therefore, there aren't many commercial implementations available at the moment. However, if you believe that BTP is the right protocol for your applications, there are a couple of compliant implementations available from the definers of the specification (e.g., Arjuna Technologies Limited, a spin-off from Hewlett-Packard). There are also public domain offerings, but at present none of those are fully compliant with the BTP specification (typically they ignore the cohesion transaction type).

As you might expect, both IBM and Microsoft are in the process of offering commercial implementations of these specifications. There are also offerings from some of the usual transaction vendor suspects, e.g., Arjuna Technologies. However, because these specifications are not yet complete, it is likely that they (and hence products based on them) will continue to evolve. In addition, WS-C/T are not currently in a recognized standards body such as OASIS and the licensing rules attached to them are not royalty free. This may change in the future, but until it does it is likely to affect the take-up of these specifications outside of the original author companies.

Because WS-CAF is relatively new to this arena, there are fewer implementations. Several of the specification's supporter companies have stated that they either have or are working on implementations, so the current state of affairs is unlikely to last long. WS-CAF has also been submitted to OASIS for standardization so the original five supported companies are likely to be joined by many more. As with the OASIS BTP specification, OASIS WS-CAF will be royalty free so you're likely to see a quicker up-take into the wider market than the IBM and Microsoft specifications.

Java API for XML Transactions (JAXTX)

What does it mean to a client to begin a BTP transaction, a JTA transaction, or a glued transaction, for example? In many cases the answer is very little, since much of the transactionality guarantees and semantic knowledge reside within and between the services and the coordinator with which the client interacts. Therefore, conceptually a single client implementation could interact with several different transaction services according to requirements placed on the application by: the services, the environment, the business needs, and so on. In a Web services environment, the services used by a client may be dynamically selected based upon the transaction model(s) they support (e.g., specified in UDDI) by a layer between the client and the actual service, explicitly by the business logic, and so on. At the level of the client/user all they are typically interested in is starting a transaction and performing work within its scope, leaving the actual transactional specific aspects to the services and the coordinator.

The J2EE XML API for Java Transactions (JAXTX) specification (one of the so-called JAX Pack specifications), aims to provide an interface to different transaction protocols that allows different implementations to be plugged in. The currently supported transaction protocols are JTA (using SOAP and XML), the J2EE Activity Service, BTP, WS-T and WS-TXM. If necessary, the user introspects over the underlying implementation to determine specific attributes and properties. In addition, if specific models require enhanced interfaces in order to operate, these can be obtained in a structured and well-defined manner.

> **N O T E** At the time of writing this book, JAXTX is still going through the Java Community Process, so some of the things we're going to discuss may change by the timethe process is finalized.

Container-driven APIs for the different Web services transactions protocols will also be defined, though obviously these are not generic: the server-side user (e.g., the container or EJB) must know the type of transaction it is operating within, for example in order to leverage the correct type of participant.

The JAXTX components allow the management in a Web services interaction of a number of *activities* or *tasks* related to an overall application. In particular JAXTX allows a user to:

- Define demarcation points which specify the start and end points of transactional activities.
- Register participants for the activities that are associated with the application.
- Propagate transaction-specific information across the network.

Because JAXTX is concerned with Web services and transactions, it assumes an overall architecture similar to what we saw illustrated in Figure 10-1. We now briefly describe the JAXTX definition of some of these architectural components, but most of this should be familiar to you by now:

1. A *Transaction Service*: Defines the behavior for a specific transaction model. The Transaction Service provides a processing pattern (implemented by the *transaction coordinator*) that is used for outcome processing. For example, an ACID transaction service is one implementation of a Transaction Service that provides a two-phase protocol definition whose coordination sequence processing includes Prepare, Commit and Rollback. Other examples of Transaction Service implementations include patterns such as Sagas, Collaborations, Nested or Real-Time transactions and non-transactional patterns such as Cohesions and Correlations [14]. Multiple Transaction Service implementations may co-exist within the same application and processing domain. JAXTX does not specify how a Transaction Service is implemented.

2. A *Transaction API*: Provides an interface for transaction demarcation and the registration of participants.

3. A *Participant*: The operation or operations that are performed as part of the transaction coordination sequence.

4. The *Context*: This contains information necessary for services to use the transaction, e.g., enlist participants and scope work.

JAXTX does not provide a means whereby existing transaction service implementations can be provided to Web services and their users, since it assumes that this has been done elsewhere in other specifications. Neither is it meant to place additional requirements on such implementations (e.g., BTP, WS-T or WS-CAF). What JAXTX does accomplish is to allow these implementations to be plugged into a common architecture.

JAXTX Architecture

In keeping with the J2EE model, JAXTX divides responsibilities between application component providers who focus on writing the business logic, and product providers, who focus on providing a managed system infrastructure in which the application components are deployed.

The transaction coordination service is responsible for managing transactions created by the client. Work performed by the client may be executed under the scope of a transaction such that the coordinator will ensure that the work performed in some manner consistent with the underlying transaction model (e.g., that it either happens or does not despite failures).

Because of where JAXTX plays in the Web services stack, all of the concepts it defines should be familiar by now: JAXTX does not define any new protocols or place new twists on a theme—it has to work with existing specifications and protocol and is therefore constrained in what it can do.

When a client performs an invocation on a service such that the work is required to be transactional, the client (or the infrastructure in which it is located) must flow information about the transaction (the context) to the service. The service is then responsible for ensuring that the work is performed in such a way that any final outcome is controlled by the transaction coordinator. This normally occurs by enlisting a participant in the transaction that has control over the work, e.g., a XAResource that can issue *prepare*, *commit* or *rollback* on a database when instructed to by the coordinator.

The JAXTX designers believe that in most situations the client/service protocol implementation (essentially the interactions shown) and context manipulation are already provided by existing standards and systems. For example, we've already seen that BTP, WS-T and WS-CAF define precisely how the transaction context appears in transmitted XML documents, how coordinator-specific messages are formatted, how participants behave under certain failure circumstances, and so on. However, the language interfaces to these components (e.g., the coordinator interface) may not be defined in their specifications at all (and in fact none of the specifications we've discussed define an API). JAXTX provides a uniform set of interfaces for Java that are intended to isolate users from the underlying implementations.

The Components

The various components defined by JAXTX are illustrated in Figure 10-19. All of the API components are defined by JAXTX, but only the client API is mandated. This is because it is only the client API that can truly be generic, whereas the specific transaction model used will

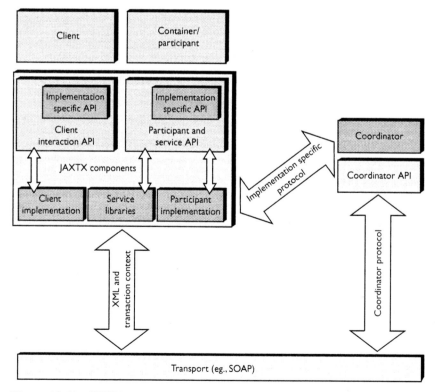

Figure 10-19   JAXTX components.

essentially impose the service APIs. The context and coordinator-to-participant protocol are specific to the type of transaction model provided by the implementation.

JAXTX defines both mandatory and optional interfaces. The *mandatory* interfaces can be categorized as follows:

- *Client*: These interfaces provide clients with a uniform means by which they may access and use client-specific functionality from different transaction implementations. Typically these interfaces will be concerned with demarcating transactions.
- *Implementation*: The interfaces are for client-side extensions required for specific transaction models that may not be covered by the more generic client interfaces. For example, as we've already seen, when using the OASIS Business Transactions Protocol, it is often preferable to drive both phases of the two-phase completion protocol explicitly, whereas in a traditional transaction model the individual phases are hidden from users.

The *optional* interfaces are:

- *Container*: These interfaces provide containers with a means by which they may access service-specific functionality from different transaction implementations. For example, a service provider may be able to support multiple transaction protocols and use different participants for each; when the transaction is imported by the container, the enterprise bean may determine the type of the transaction and enlist the right type of participant.

XML Configuration

In order to select a specific transaction implementation, it is necessary to be able to define precisely the type of transaction service that is required. This must occur in an extensible manner that does not require changes to application code should the requirements or transaction definition change. As such, the use of XML is appropriate and JAXTX provides a *transaction-definition schema*.

Each protocol type (e.g., WS-T-based) is required to be uniquely identified by a URI. In addition, each implementation of a specific transaction service may also be uniquely identified. This allows a user to select an implementation based purely on the transaction model it defines or to select on the specific implementation.

The configuration portion of the transaction schema is shown in Code Listing 10-7.

Code Listing 10-7   The JAXTX configuration schema

```xml
<?xml version="1.0" encoding="UTF-8"?>
<xsd:schema xmlns:xsd="http://www.w3.org/2001/XMLSchema"
elementFormDefault="qualified">


  <xsd:element name="transaction-config">
    <xsd:complexType>
      <xsd:sequence>
        <xsd:element name="transaction-protocol"
type="xsd:anyURI" minOccurs="1" maxOccurs="1"/>
        <xsd:element name="transaction-implementation"
type="xsd:anyURI" minOccurs="0" maxOccurs="1"/>
      </xsd:sequence>
    </xsd:complexType>
  </xsd:element>
</xsd:schema>
```

JAXTX differentiates between transaction protocols (such as WS-T or WS-TXM) and their specific implementations (such as may be provided by an application server vendor). When an application selects the type of transaction system to use, it must at least specify the protocol type, but may also request a specific implementation. All protocols that are available to JAXTX must be uniquely identified using a URI. Likewise, all implementations are identified by a URI.

The API

As we mentioned at the start of this section, JAXTX is still going through the Java Community Process (JCP), so some things may change before it is finally adopted. However, we can still take a look at a representative set of the interfaces it will probably be defining.

> **NOTE**   Every interface and class defined by JAXTX occurs within the `javax.jaxtx` package, or one of its subpackages.

Transaction Termination State

As we've seen many times over the course of this book, transactions (including extended transactions) typically end in one of two states: successfully (e.g., commit) where all of the work is done, or unsuccessfully (e.g., rollback) where the work is undone or compensated for. So it shouldn't come as a surprise that JAXTX has a similar notion of how its transactions can terminate. Because different underlying implementations are expected to be plugged into JAXTX, the concept of how a JAXTX transaction can end is deliberately abstract, allowing it to be mapped down accordingly.

The `javax.jaxtx.completionstatus.CompletionSatus` interface and associated classes define the basic modes in which a transaction can terminate. Users may instruct the transaction to complete in one of these states or may set the completion status so that it will take effect when the transaction is eventually told to complete; this is like forcing a traditional ACID transaction into a rollback-only state.

As shown in Figure 10-20, at any time in its life a transaction will typically be in one of three *completion states*, such that if it is asked to complete it will do so in a manner prescribed by that state:

- ConfirmCompletionStatus: The transaction should complete in a successful state, i.e., all work performed within its scope should be accepted. If the transaction cannot complete in this state then it will transition to the CancelCompletionStatus state.
- CancelCompletionStatus: The transaction should complete in a failure state, i.e., all work performed within its scope should be undone in an implementation-specific manner. When in this state, the transaction may be transitioned into any other state. This is the default completion state in which all transactions begin.
- CancelOnlyCompletionStatus: The transaction should complete in a failure state, i.e., all work performed within its scope should be undone in an implementation-specific manner. Once in this state, the transaction state cannot transition any further.

The transaction implementation will map these statuses in a model-specific manner. For example, an implementation based on JTA would interpret ConfirmCompletionStatus as commit the transaction, whereas one based on BTP would interpret it as confirm the transaction.

N O T E It is possible that a specific transaction model may have additional states in which is can complete, and these states may need to be available to JAXTX users. Therefore, in order to ensure extensibility and that required state transitions do not conflict, state types are required to be extensions (classes or interfaces) of the CompletionStatus interface.

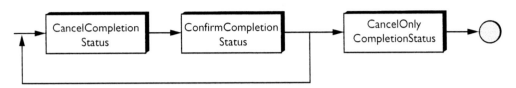

Figure 10-20 CompletionStatus state diagram.

Current Transaction Status

The state of a transaction at any point in its life is determined by the `javax.jaxtx.Status` class and its associated implementations, as illustrated in Figure 10-21.

- `ActiveStatus`: the transaction initially starts in this state. An implementation returns this value prior to the coordinator entering a termination protocol or being marked as `CancelOnlyCompletionStaus`.
- `MarkedCancelOnlyStatus`: The transaction has been forced into a state whereby its eventual completion must be to cancel, i.e., `CancelOnlyCompletionStaus`.
- `CompletingConfirmStatus`: The transaction transitions to this state when told to complete and the completion status is `ConfirmCompletionStatus`. The transaction will remain in this state until it has completed in one termination outcome or another. If it cannot complete in the `ConfirmCompletionStatus` state, the transaction will transition to the `CancelCompletionStatus` state and complete. For example, in a two-phase completion protocol if the first phase (prepare) succeeds, then the coordinator will commit (confirm) all state changes; if it fails, then the coordinator will roll back (cancel) all state changes. If there are no failures, the transaction will typically remain in this state until it has received all responses to its termination protocol.
- `CompletedConfirmStatus`: The transaction has terminated successfully in the `ConfirmCompletionStatus` completion status. If this status is returned from a call to `UserXMLTransaction.status`, it is likely that errors specific to the protocol exist (e.g., heuristics); otherwise the transaction would have been destroyed and `NoTransactionStatus` returned.
- `CompletingCancelStatus`: The transaction transitions to this state when told to complete and the completion status is `CancelCompletionStatus`. The transaction will remain in this state until it has completed.
- `CompletedCancelStatus`: The transaction has terminated successfully in the `CancelCompletionStatus` completion status.
- `NoTransactionStatus`: There is no transaction associated with the invoking thread.

The `CompletionStatus` and `Status` are closely related. Figure 10-21 essentially illustrates the lifecycle of a transaction, where Figure 10-20 indicates how users affect the lifecycle and force the transaction status down a specific path.

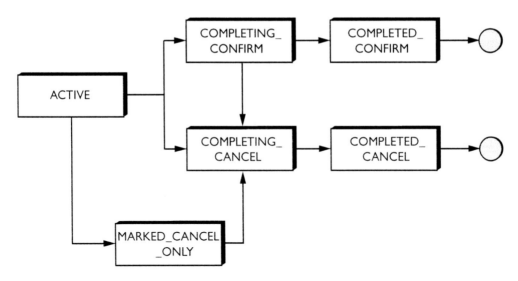

Figure 10-21   Transaction status transitions.

The Result of a Transaction

When a user informs a transaction to terminate, the act of termination will usually return information about how the transaction completed. This information may be present both for successful and unsuccessful termination of a transaction. For example, in an implementation of the JTA protocol for Web services, the `ConfirmCompletionStatus` state for a transaction would correspond to committing the transaction; a successful outcome would result in no exceptions being generated. However, an unsuccessful termination, for example because of participant failures, could return a specific heuristic exception.

In order to support the different transaction model requirements for return types, the `Outcome` interface is used, as shown in Code Listing 10-8. The types of `Outcome` and their internal encodings are required to be specified by the definer/implementer of the transaction implementation.

Code Listing 10-8   The JAXTX Outcome interface

```
public interface Outcome
{
    public Status completedStatus () throws SystemException;
    public Object data () throws SystemException;
    public String name () throws SystemException;
}
```

You may think this is similar to what we saw with the J2EE Activity Service, and you'd be right. Both specifications share several authors in common.

Demarcating Client-Side Transactions

The UserXMLTransaction, shown in Code Listing 10-9, is the interface that most users (e.g., clients and J2EE containers) will see and is obtained via a JNDI lookup of java:comp/UserXMLTransactionFactory. This isolates them from underlying protocol-specific aspects of the transaction implementation. If required, an underlying implementation may provide additional methods to users, who may cast or reflect to the underlying implementation if necessary. Importantly, a UserXMLTransaction does not represent a specific transaction, but rather is responsible for providing access to an implicit per-thread transaction context. Therefore, all of the UserXMLTransaction methods implicitly act on the current thread of control in the same was as the equivalents in OTS (Current) and JTA (UserTransaction) that we've seen already.

Code Listing 10-9   The user's interface to a JAXTX transaction

```
public interface UserXMLTransaction
{
        public org.w3c.dom.Document configuration () throws
                                               SystemException;

        public void start (int timeout) throws WrongStateException,
                        NestingNotAllowedException, InvalidTimeoutException,
                        SystemException;

        public Outcome end () throws NoTransactionException,
                        InvalidTransactionException, WrongStateException,
                        NoPermissionException, ProtocolViolationException,
                        SystemException;

        public Outcome end (CompletionStatus endStatus) throws
                        NoTransactionException, InvalidTransactionException,
                        WrongStateException, ProtocolViolationException,
                        NoPermissionException, SystemException;

        public void setTimeout (int timeout) throws
                                InvalidTimeoutException, SystemException;

        public int getTimeout () throws SystemException;

        public void setCompletionStatus (CompletionStatus endStatus)
                        throws NoTransactionException, WrongStateException,
                        SystemException;
```

```
public CompletionStatus getCompletionStatus () throws
                         NoTransactionException, SystemException;

public Status status () throws SystemException;

public String globalIdentity () throws SystemException;
}
```

The type of transaction service implementation can be obtained via the `configuration` method.

A new transaction is begun and associated with the invoking thread by using the `start` method. If nested transactions are supported by the transaction service implementation, then a transaction that is already associated with the invoking thread will become the *parent* of this newly created transaction. If nesting is not supported, then the `javax.jaxtx.exceptions.NestingNotAllowedException` is thrown.

The `setTimeout` method modifies a state variable associated with the `UserXMLTransaction` that affects the time-out period in *seconds* associated with the transaction created by subsequent invocations of the `start` method. This is equivalent to the OTS and JTA functionality. The `getTimeout` method returns the timeout value.

The state in which the current transaction should be completed is set using the `setCompletionStatus` method. If the completion state is invalid given the state of the transaction (e.g., it has already begun to complete) then the `javax.jaxtx.exceptions.InvalidStateException` will be thrown. The completion status of the transaction currently associated with the invoking thread can be obtained from the `getCompletionStatus` method.

A transaction can be told to complete using the `end` method; this will also disassociate the thread from the transaction before it returns. The completion status the transaction implementation uses will either have been set by a previous call to `setCompletionStatus`, may be provided as a parameter to end, or will be the default of `CancelCompletionStatus`. If this is a top-level transaction, upon completion the thread will have no transaction associated with it. Alternately, it will be set to the parent of the just completed transaction. If no transaction is associated with the current thread, the `javax.jaxtx.exceptions.NoTransactionException` is thrown.

Some transaction models may restrict the ability for threads to end transactions, e.g., such that only the transaction creator may terminate the transaction. If this is the case, the implementation must throw the `javax.jaxtx.exceptions.NoPermissionException`. If the specified completion state of the transaction is not compatible with the transaction's state (for example, its completion state is `CancelOnlyCompletionStatus` and the user has asked the transaction to terminate with a status of `ConfirmCompletionStatus`), or the state of the transaction does not allow it to be terminated, then the `javax.jaxtx.exceptions.InvalidStateException` will be thrown.

Obviously, a transaction may not be able to complete in the state originally requested by the user (equivalent to a user wanting to commit a transaction, but the coordinator ultimately having to rollback because of participant failure, as we saw in Chapter 1, "Transaction Fundamentals"). When the transaction terminates it may return an `Outcome` to indicate how it did complete.

The current status of the transaction is returned by the `status` method. If there is no transaction associated with the thread, `NoTransactionStatus` is returned. If the exact determination of a transaction's status is not possible when `status` is invoked, `Unknown-Status` is returned. This is a transient value and calling `status` again will eventually return a definitive answer.

Every transaction is required to have a unique identity, which can be obtained from the `globalIdentity` method.

Controlling Server-Side Transactions

The `XMLTransactionManager`, shown in Code Listing 10-10, is the basic container/bean programming interface; it's obtained via a JNDI lookup of `java:comp/UserXML-TransactionFactory`. As with `UserXMLTransaction`, this interface isolates services from underlying protocol specific aspects of the transaction implementation they are using. `XMLTransactionManager` does not represent a specific transaction, but rather is responsible for providing access to an implicit per-thread transaction context. Therefore, all of the `XML-TransactionManager` methods implicitly act on the current thread of control.

Code Listing 10-10 The container's interface to the transaction

```
public interface XMLTransactionManager
{

    public TxContext suspend () throws SystemException;

    public void resume (TxContext tx) throws
                        InvalidTransactionException, SystemException;

    public TxContext getTransactionContext () throws SystemException;
}
```

A thread of control may require periods of non-transactionality in order for it to perform work that is not associated with a specific transaction. In order to do this, it is necessary to disassociate the thread from any transactions. The `suspend` method accomplishes this, returning a `TxContext` instance, which is a handle on the transaction context. If the current transaction is nested, then the `TxContext` will implicitly represent the stack of transactions up to and including the root transaction. The thread then becomes associated with no transaction.

TxContext is essentially a black-box interface, betraying little about the format of the underlying context. The reason for this is that each transaction model has its own version of a context, but at the application level (client or server) you don't really need to know what that format is. All you require is the ability to reference the context.

The resume method can be used to (re-) associate a thread with a transaction(s) via its TxContext. Prior to association, the thread is disassociated from any transaction(s) with which it may be currently associated; this is very much like the JTA and dissimilar to the OTS. If the TxContext is *null*, then the thread is associated with no transaction. The javax.jaxtx.exceptionsInvalidTransactionException is thrown if the transaction that the TxContext refers to is invalid in the scope of the invoking thread. It is up to the underlying transaction implementation to determine the validity of a specific context.

The getTransactionContext method returns the TxContext for the current transaction, or *null* if there is none associated with the invoking thread. Unlike suspend, this method does not disassociate the current thread from the transaction(s). This can be used to enable multiple threads to execute within the scope of the same transaction.

Transaction Model-Specific APIs

Most of what we've seen so far is intended to allow the majority of applications to be written without having to consider the type of transaction model being used (e.g., whether it's WS-TXM or BTP). However, there are areas where these generic APIs simply aren't enough. For example, when registering a participant with a transaction, the type of participant is closely tied to the transaction model, as are the parameters (if any) that can be supplied.

So, as we've mentioned, JAXTX supports specific interfaces through inheritance of reflection: the container-side of an application is expected to take the basic XMLTransactionManager interface and narrow it to an interface closely tied to the specific transaction model. At the moment JAXTX provides specific server-side APIs for BTP, WS-T and WS-TXM.

There obviously isn't enough space to describe all of the mappings JAXTX supports. However, to conclude we try to give you a flavor of what to expect from JAXTX by taking a brief look at the interfaces defined for the Atomic Transaction model of WS-T.

The basic client and server interfaces are sufficient to demarcate the WS-T transaction. However, they're not sufficient for enlisting participants, as we mentioned earlier. Therefore, JAXTX provides additional interfaces and classes in the javax.jaxtx.model.wst.opt package. As you might imagine, there are interfaces for each of the different types of participant: PhaseZeroParticipant, TwoPCParticipant and OutcomeNotificationParticipant.

Let's take a look at the TwoPCParticipant, as illustrated in Code Listing 10-11:

Code Listing 10-11 The WS-T two-phase commit participant

```
public interface TwoPCParticipant
{

    public Vote prepare () throws WrongStateException,
                                  SystemException;

    public void commit () throws WrongStateException,
                                 SystemException;

    public void rollback () throws WrongStateException,
                                   SystemException;

    public void commitOnePhase () throws WrongStateException,
                                         SystemException;

}
```

You should be familiar with this type of interface by now; nothing should really surprise you as this is a traditional, two-phase commit participant. Vote is an empty interface and is subclassed by ReadOnly, Prepared and Aborted classes.

The javax.jaxtx.model.wst.opt.TransactionManager class is the specific container-side interface for demarcating transactions. It derives from UserXMLTransaction and XMLTransactionManager, and provides a single method getTransaction that returns an instance of a class derives from the javax.jaxtx.model.wst.opt.Transaction interface, which represents the current transaction. This is illustrated in Code Listing 10-12.

Code Listing 10-12 The WS-T container transaction interface

```
public interface Transaction
{

    public void enlistForPhaseZero (PhaseZeroParticipant pzp) throws
                WrongStateException, InvalidTransactionException,
                AlreadyRegisteredException, SystemException;

    public void enlistForTwoPhase (TwoPCParticipant tpp) throws
                WrongStateException, InvalidTransactionException,
                AlreadyRegisteredException, SystemException;

    public void enlistForOutcomeNotification
                                (OutcomeNotificationParticipant onp)
            throws WrongStateException, InvalidTransactionException,
                AlreadyRegisteredException, SystemException;

    public Status replay () throws SystemException;

}
```

As you can see, there are operations for enlisting each of the different types of participant, one for each subprotocol. In addition, the `replay` method is used for supporting failure recovery.

Summary

We've looked at the current candidates for the title of "Web services transactions standard." Although other protocols may well evolve over the coming years, it's likely that some combination of WS-C/T and WS-CAF will become the standard, since these specifications are specifically about fostering interoperability with existing infrastructures and have the backing of the heavyweights in the area of Web services. Whether a single standard will ever evolve is unknown and is probably more in the realm of politics than technology. However, as we've seen, in the world of J2EE the JAXTX specification will probably be your interface to the underlying Web services transactions implementation.

It's popular for individuals in the Web services arena to make statements like "ACID transactions aren't for Web services" and quote some of the issues we've discussed in earlier chapters, such as the blocking nature of the two-phase commit protocol. However, this is an unsafe argument on at least two counts:

1. As we've just said, interoperability is an important feature offered by Web services. Interoperability of heterogeneous ACID transaction systems is now possible and has been an often unfulfilled requirement for many enterprises for a long time.
2. Very little attention has been paid to the fact that these loosely coupled environments tend to have large strongly coupled corporate infrastructures behind them.

The question that was asked when Web services transaction protocols such as BTP were first designed was essentially, "What can replace ACID transactions?" However, it should have been, "How can we leverage what already exists?" because that existing investment in tried and tested products and technology is not going away. The investment in transaction processing systems over the past few decades has cost billions of dollars and any scheme to leverage that investment rather than replace it is the way forward.

Although Web services represent a new arena of distributed system that is loosely coupled, potentially large scale and heterogeneous, they are for interoperability as much as for the Internet. As such, interoperability of existing transaction processing systems will be an important part of Web services transactions: such systems already form the backbone of enterprise level applications and will continue to do so for the Web services equivalent.

Business-to-business activities will involve back-end transaction processing systems either directly or indirectly and being able to tie together these environments will be the key to the successful take-up of Web Services transactions. Web services will operate as the glue between different environments (e.g., corporate domains) and application components will be implemented using tried and tested technologies such as J2EE, CORBA and .NET. We've examined the existing transaction story for J2EE throughout this book, from JMS through JTS to JCA and all of these technologies remain important in the development of current and future applications and their components, even if Web services aren't important to you.

Since their inception, ACID transactions have proven useful in a wide range of applications, particularly when used in distributed environments and they will continue to do so. This is irrespective of whether distribution occurs via CORBA IIOP, JMS messages or SOAP. Compensation transactions such as the WS-TXM Long-Running Action model or other extended transaction models (perhaps epitomized by the J2EE Activity Service) will be important in areas where ACID transactions are inappropriate.

As we've seen, there are more transaction models than pure ACID and when considering using transactions in your application you should look carefully at your requirements: don't just rush into the ACID camp but also don't ignore it. Whatever transaction model you settle for, an implementation that is reliable, supports failure recovery and performs is obviously important. We've tried to show throughout this book that providing such an implementation is not trivial and so you should also be cautious when choosing a transaction service, especially if it's required to support some of the new transaction models such as those in Web services.

It's also not easy to create applications that use transactions efficiently, particularly if you're mixing them across subsystems like JMS and JTS. One of our intentions in writing this book was to try to assist application programmers in the creation of applications and their components that can use transactions more efficiently by leveraging our combined experiences in this area. Hopefully, we've given you some help with the various hints and tips you've found throughout the various chapters.

Resources

T he following is a listing of resources we feel are valuable to gain a better understanding of transactioning and Java.

Transactional J2EE/J2SE Specifications

The key transactional J2EE API specifications are as follows:

Java 2 Plaform, Enterprise Edition (J2EE) Specification 1.4

Defines an enterprise platform enabling the development of robust, secure, transactional, and interoperable business applications.

- URL: http://java.sun.com/j2ee/download.html#platformspec

The Java Transaction API (JTA) Specification 1.0.1B

Specifies standard Java interfaces defining the contracts between a transaction manager and the other elements involved in a distributed transaction system (see Chapter 2).

- URL: http://java.sun.com/products/jta/index.html

The Java Transaction Service (JTS) Specification 1.0

Defines the Java mapping of the OMG Object Transaction Service (OTS) 1.1 Specification (see Chapter 1).

- URL: http://java.sun.com/products/jts/index.html

The JDBC Specifications, 3.0, 2.1, and Optional Package API 2.0

Defines an API for accessing DBMS systems as well as other tabular data sources (see Chapter 4).

- URL: http://java.sun.com/products/jdbc/download.html

Java Message Service (JMS) Specification 1.1

Defines a common set of programming concepts and models for interacting with enterprise messaging systems (see Chapter 5).

- URL: http://java.sun.com/products/jms/docs.html

Enterprise JavaBeans (EJB) Specification 2.1

Defines a component model for assembling secure, transactional, and concurrent enterprise applications (see Chapter 6).

- URL: http://java.sun.com/products/ejb/docs.html#specs

J2EE Connector (JCA) Specification 1.5

Provides a standard architecture for integrating heterogeneous EIS systems (see Chapter 7).

- URL: http://java.sun.com/j2ee/connector/download.html

Java API for XML Transactions

This specification aims to provide an API for packaging and transporting ACID transactions (as in JTA) and extended transactions.

- URL: http://www.jcp.org/en/jsr/detail?id=156

J2EE Activity Service for Extended Transactions

This specification provides methods for composing an application using transactions, thus enabling the application to possess some or all ACID properties.

- URL: http://www.jcp.org/en/jsr/detail?id=95

Transactional Web Services Specifications

There are a number of transaction-related specifications emerging in the Web services domain. Some of the more promising specifications are listed here.

Web Services Composite Application Framework (WS-CAF) 1.0

This specification is actually composed of three parts (see Chapter 9):

1. Web Services Context (WS-CTX) specifies a lightweight framework for simple context management.
2. Web Services Coordination Framework (WS-CF) defines a mechanism to manage context augmentation and lifecycle, and guarantee message delivery.
3. Web Services Transaction Management (WS-TXM) provides for interoperability across multiple transaction managers and transaction models (e.g. two-phase commit, long-running actions, and business process flows).

- URL: http://developer.sun.com/techtopics/webservices/wscaf/primer.pdf

Web Services Transaction (WS-Transaction)

This specification defines atomic and business activity coordination types for enabling distributed applications with consistent outcomes (see Chapter 9).

- URL: http://www-106.ibm.com/developerworks/library/ws-transpec/

Web Services Coordination (WS-Coordination)

This specification describes a framework for providing protocols that coordinate the actions of distributed applications.

- URL: http://msdn.microsoft.com/library/default.asp?url=/library/en-us/dnglobspec/html/ws-coordination.asp

Web Services Choreography (WS-C)

This specification describes how to compose and describe the relationships between lower-level services.

- URL: http://www.w3.org/2002/ws/chor/

Business Process Execution Language for Web Services Version 1.1

- URL: http://www-106.ibm.com/developerworks/webservices/library/ws-bpel/

BTP Committee Specification

This specification aims to define how interdependent workflows among multiple trading partners can be coordinated to achieve reliable outcomes.

- URL: http://www.oasis-open.org/committees/business-transactions/

Other Transaction-Related Specifications

Key transaction-related specifications:

Object Transaction Service (OTS) Specification 1.3

- URL: http://www.omg.org/technology/documents/formal/transaction_service.htm

Additional Structuring Mechanisms for the OTS, version 1.0

- URL: http://www.omg.org/technology/documents/formal/add_struct.htm

Distributed TP: The XA Specification

- http://www.opengroup.org/public/pubs/catalog/c193.htm

Distributed TP: The TX (Transaction Demarcation) Specification

- URL: http://www.opengroup.org/public/pubs/catalog/c504.htm

Distributed TP: Reference Model, Version 3

- URL: http://www.opengroup.org/public/pubs/catalog/g504.htm

Books

- Bernstein, Philip A. and Eric Newcomer. *Principles of Transaction Processing.* Morgan Kaufmann, 1997.
- Gray, Jim and Andreas Reuter. *Transaction Processing: Concepts and Techniques.* Morgan Kaufman, 1993.
- Lewis, Philip M., Michael Kifer and Arthur J. Bernstein. *Database and Transaction Processing.* Pearson Addison Wesley, 2001.
- Weikum, Gerhard and Gottfried Vossen. *Transactional Information Systems: Theory, Algorithms, and the Practice of Concurrency Control.* Morgan Kaufman, 2001.

Articles

- Little, M. C. and S. K. Shrivastava. "Distributed Transactions in Java." *Proceedings of the 7th International Workshop on High Performance Transaction Systems.* September 1997, 151-155.
- —. "Java Transactions for the Internet." *Special Issue of the Distributed Systems Engineering Journal,* 1998.
- Parrington, G. D. et al "The Design and Implementation of Arjuna." *USENIX Computing Systems Journal,* Vol. 8., No. 3, Summer 1995, 253-306.
- Various articles on replication and transactions can be found at http://arjuna.ncl.ac.uk/publications/.

Experiences Gained and Lessons Learned

Over our careers we've had the good fortune to work on the development of several transaction service implementations and integrate them and others into a variety of application servers. In this appendix we attempt to give an objective discussion about what to take into account when choosing a transaction solution.

Commercial Implementations versus Open-Source

So, you've decided you need transactions in your environment and now you begin to look at where you can get them. There are many different implementations of the JTS/OTS, JTA and proprietary transaction protocols and sometimes it can be a bit daunting to decide among them. In this section we are not going to recommend a specific product or implementation, but give some hard-earned advice that may help you make that choice.

So, obviously the first question is, why pay for transactions in the first place? There are a number of free, open-source or public domain implementations, both in pure Java and other languages like C++ that have Java support through the Java Native Interface. So why not use one of them? Unfortunately, writing a reliable transaction service that performs and scales under load is not rocket science, but it comes close. Many of the large transaction service vendors have been in the business of writing and tuning their implementations for decades. We have implemented several transaction services in different languages, some of which are available as commercial products, and we also have experience working with others: all of these systems took years and considerable experience to develop.

There are several successful open source projects available in areas as diverse as operating systems to simulation engines. However, even the most successful of these take years to develop, test and make inroads to established areas. Hopefully by this point in the book you've begun to appreciate the intricacies of distributed transaction processing and the many pitfalls that can happen when using them, let alone implementing such a system. We're certainly not saying that it's impossible to do from scratch in the open-source arena, only that it is often a lot more difficult than people expect. In addition, because you typically only see the benefit of transactions when there are failures, it's often not seen as an area where developers can really make their mark; hence, to date it has often been difficult for open source projects to get the necessary resources to do the subject justice.

Questions to Consider

Now, this is not to say that all commercial transaction systems are well implemented and offer value for the money, or that a public domain version cannot compete with a commercial equivalent. However, before assigning the consistency of your data or application to *any* transaction implementation, you need to assess the risks involved, and we hope the following will help you formulate the right questions to ask and the types of answers you should (we hope) get back. You may also find these questions useful in evaluating your current transaction system implementation.

W A R N I N G Buying a transaction system is like buying insurance: if failures never happen you don't see the benefit and may begin to think about buying cheaper insurance. But when a failure does happen, with good implementations (and insurance packages) you will reap the benefits.

Development Background

What is the development background of the people or company involved in the implementation? For example, simply being experienced programmers in specific languages is not sufficient. Implementing a transaction processing system is much more than just a programming exercise. Unfortunately, we have come across a number of implementations where the well-meaning developers have had little or no experience in transaction processing and have based their entire systems on the contents of specifications. As we saw in Chapter 3, "The Object Transaction Service," this is a good starting point, but much more extensive research and experience is required in order to adequately understand the various issues involved.

Performance

What are the performance characteristics of the transaction service? When transaction implementations were first developed, the goal was to try to achieve 10 transactions per second, then 100 and so on. Now with the advances in hardware and operating system performance, achieving thousands of transactions per second is not uncommon. However, what you'll probably find is that some vendors (commercial and open source) will quote transactions per second figures for "empty" transactions—transactions that have no participants. As we saw in Chapter 1, "Transaction Fundamentals," if a transaction has no participants, the coordinator does no work. So, when timing an empty transaction, what you're really seeing is how fast the system can create and destroy a coordinator. This does not necessarily give you any indication of how the system will perform when it has one, two or more participants, and especially not how it scales as the number of concurrent users increases. Try to obtain performance figures for realistic tests when choosing an implementation. You should take this into account if you're considering implementing.

N O T E   Current transaction performance metrics aren't part of J2EE. A future version may address this shortcoming.

Fault Tolerance

Does the implementation tolerate failures (e.g., machine crashes) and still guarantee that transactions will be completed upon recovery? You may think that this is a little pointless, because how can you have a transaction implementation if it does not guarantee all ACID properties? However, there are many open-source implementations and even some commercial implementations that do not save transaction states after the prepare phase, for example, and cannot tolerate a crash at this point. Unfortunately in our experience, although the developers of these deficient systems know the limitation exists, they rarely publicize it, for obvious reasons! In our opinion, if there is only one question you ever ask when choosing an implementation, this should be it: How does the system function in the presence of failures, especially in a distribute environment?

Two-Phase Commit

Does the implementation support the two-phase protocol? If you are using more than one transactional resource in a transaction, then you *must* use a two-phase commit protocol to ensure atomicity. Some transaction service implementations do not support two-phase commit and as such should only be used with a single resource. Unfortunately, for whatever reason, the providers of some of these restricted implementations do not ensure that it is impossible to enlist more than one resource with a transaction. What you then end up with is a coordinator that runs a termination protocol using a single-phase commit across multiple participants; as you can probably guess by now, a failure can easily result in non-atomic behavior.

Reliability Characteristics

How reliable is the transaction service? It is one thing having an ultra-fast implementation, but if it fails every hour, what use is it? Although performance figures are usually available for most commercial implementations and some open-source implementations, reliability figures are extremely difficult to obtain. If none exist for the system you are considering, then you should consider evaluating the system carefully before purchasing; most vendors support the notion of free evaluation periods and this can be invaluable for a lot of different reasons.

Support for Nested Transactions

As we indicated in Chapter 1, "Transaction Fundamentals," nested transactions are a useful structuring and fault-tolerance mechanism. Do you need them and if so, does the implementation support them?

Support for Arbitrary Participants

Although it is likely that most of the transactional resources you will use initially will be XA compliant (and probably hidden by suitable JDBC drivers), is this always going to be the case? If you wanted to use a file system for durability, for example, then interfacing it with a transaction service that only supports XA resources will be difficult. The two-phase protocol isn't XA-specific so a transaction implementation need not be specific either. There are several implementations that allow arbitrary two-phase aware participants to be enrolled in a transaction, thus giving you the capability to tie in disparate participant implementations. This may not be a necessity for you in the short term, but perhaps it will be later.

Quality Assurance

What kind of testing do the developers have for the implementation? In general software development testing is divided into unit tests and quality assurance (QA) testing. The former is typically used for testing specific aspects of the software (e.g., does the transaction service write the log correctly), where the latter is involved with stress-testing the software in all kinds of environments and loads.

We know of several open-source transaction services that have no QA tests and very few unit tests and yet are used in products. This is roughly equivalent to flying an airplane that has never been tested! There is an old software adage that says you should have four times the amount of source code for tests than exists in the software being tested. And comments don't count. You should be extremely wary of any transaction service that has very few or no tests to back it up. If at all possible, ask to see the latest QA record for the system.

> **NOTE** Many commercial vendors won't release their QA reports. However, these companies are more used to providing good support for their products with well-defined Service Level Agreements (SLAs). In many ways, a good SLA is worth more than QA reports because it is a contract between you and the vendor for a guaranteed level of support. So, don't be put off if you can't get a QA report but can get an SLA.

Distributed Transactions

If your application is distributed, distributed transactions may be important as well. Once again, some transaction service implementations do not allow transactions to span more than one process (JVM). They may also restrict the ability for clients to start transactions or for the locality of the transaction coordinator to be positioned where it makes sense; for example, if a client really does want to start a transaction it may be appropriate for the coordinator to reside with the client. Some implementations will not allow this to happen.

Management Support

Managing a transaction system is often a complex task, particularly if that system supports distributed transactions. Imagine having to track down which participants have yet to be resolved in the event of a failure when those participants may reside on machines on the other side of the world. Most of the good commercial transaction service implementations have a range of administration tools, some of which are graphical in nature to help present information in a more natural way. In our experience, this is another area often overlooked by open-source implementations, making management a nightmare. If no tools (graphical or not) exist, then you *will* pay the penalty sooner or later.

Pedigree

As with many things, pedigree is important. If the implementation has been around and used for many years, it has an implicit level of trust that is difficult for a new implementation to obtain, no matter who it is from. If it's been around for a while, then it has probably been deployed before. You should ask for reference sites if at all possible and follow these up. Don't reject implementations just because they haven't been deployed, but do spend more time evaluating them. It will pay dividends in the long run.

However, once again a good SLA is worth a lot. Several commercial J2EE vendors are rolling out new transaction service implementations that may have been completely written from scratch. Given that these implementations will be accompanied by an SLA, this is an implicit level of trust (almost a guarantee) from the vendor and makes up for the relative newness.

Support for Web Services Transactions

We mentioned earlier that it is likely for the core of Web services transactions to be formed around existing transactional infrastructures. This should come as good news if you've already invested a lot of time and money in a favorite transaction system. Alternately, if you don't have a need for Web services at the moment, but may have in the future, perhaps you should check to see whether the transaction system you use or are evaluating has such an upgrade path. It could save you a lot of time and effort in the long run. Having to manage a separate Web services transaction implementation alongside your existing "traditional" implementation will cost you in more ways than simply monetary.

Cost

Cost will always be a factor and may be a good reason to consider an open-source implementation. The cost of commercial implementations can range from the low thousands of dollars to the high tens of thousands of dollars. However, you should always read the fine print. Some vendors charge per processor/machine, others per developer, and for some it's a one-off charge. And there may be a difference between a developer license and a deployment (runtime) license. You obviously need to take all of this into consideration when choosing the system for you. However, remember that there's no such thing as a free lunch and sometimes you do need to pay for something that's worth having.

Openness

How open or standards-compliant is the implementation? Although you may wonder why this is important, consider that the system you buy today may not be the one you need in a few years' time. If the implementation you are about to buy is not standards-compliant, then you may find it extremely difficult to move from one system to another later. Vendor lock-in is a powerful tool and never usually operates in favor of the end user. So you'd be advised to ask the vendor how easy it would be to migrate to another implementation later; they obviously won't like the question and its implications, but remember that you've got the money they want.

Support for Multi-Threading

Although threading is an integral part of the Java language, it is surprising to note that some transaction service implementations are not multi-threading aware. For example, we know of at least one implementation that imposes the restriction that only one thread within the JVM may be running a transaction at a time.

Summary

Although this list is by no means complete, we hope it gives you some indication that one transaction service implementation is not necessarily the same as another. There may well be a trade-off that you have to make between how good an implementation is and how much it will cost (to buy, to deploy and to maintain). But you should always remember that at the end of the day, it is your data and application integrity that is at stake and how much is that worth to you?

Catalog of Transaction System Implementations

In this section we list a few of the transaction systems that you may have (or will) come across and whether they are commercial or open-source implementations. Although many of these systems have deficiencies, it would be inappropriate for us to list them here. However, if you use the questions we outlined above in any dealings with these systems, you should be able to come to your own conclusions.

We break down the implementations into those that are available in a stand-alone configuration and those that are available in conjunction with a J2EE application server; if a transaction service is available in both categories then we indicate this, too. Your individual needs will obviously dictate which implementation type is applicable to you.

> **N O T E** As with most things, there are trade-offs to be made between the stand-alone transaction service and embedded application server approach and which you require will depend heavily upon your application requirements. Don't immediately dismiss a transaction service simply because it comes tightly coupled to an application server. The added functionality such as the transactional application development environment (e.g., EJBs, container-managed transactions, close coupling between JDBC and the transaction service, etc.) may well be an advantage for you. Likewise, don't dismiss a stand-alone implementation. Most commercial implementations can offer similar development tools that have evolved over many years of use.

Commercial Implementations

There are many commercial implementations available, *most* of which have been around for quite a few years. As such, they have typically been deployed on many different occasions and have a good pedigree. You probably won't go wrong with any of these implementations in terms of reliability and performance. Some of the things you really need to consider are openness, standards compliance and cost.

Stand-Alone Implementations

- *CICS*: Probably the best known transaction system from IBM, it has been around for many decades and has proven itself time and again. However, it isn't a Java implementation (mixing C and assembler), tends to run only on mainframes, and is usually expensive to deploy. CICS is also available as the transaction service implementation in some versions of WebSphere, IBM's application server.
- *Encina*: Developed in C (and later C++) by Transarc Corporation in the early 1990s, this transaction system was first intended for use on the Distributed Computing Environment (DCE), a precursor to CORBA. When CORBA grew in popularity, Encina became one of the first OTS implementations. Transarc was acquired by IBM, who continued to market Encina. It is now used almost solely by IONA Technologies in both a stand-alone configuration and embedded in their application server.
- *Hewlett-Packard/Arjuna Technologies Transaction Service*: As we saw in Chapter 1, "Transaction Fundamentals," Arjuna has been around since the mid-1980s, where it first began life in C++. It was the first fully compliant OTS (and later JTS) implementation and is a highly flexible and configurable implementation; power and

performance are key factors in its design. It is deployable on a wide range of environments, from mainframes to servers to hand-held devices, and had been deployed in a number of environments. The Arjuna Transaction Service has also been embedded in several application servers, including JBoss, to provide a more resilient, enterprise-ready application server.

- *Hitachi Transaction Service*: This system is another non-Java-based implementation. It was marketed by Hitachi but also licensed to other vendors to embed in their own products. For example, one version of the Inprise transaction service was Hitachi (Inprise was later acquired by Borland).

- *Tuxedo*: Another implementation that isn't Java-based, but has been around for quite a while (developed by AT&T back in the mid-1980s and now marketed by BEA). Although it has been deployed widely, there are a number of well-publicized "quirks" with the implementation, such as its single-threaded model.

Application Server Embedded Implementations

- *J2EE Reference Implementation from Sun Microsystems*: Originally developed by IBM, this Java transaction service is now maintained and marketed by Sun Microsystems. It's not exactly the most flexible commercial implementation around, and it does suffer from a number of problems. However, it's not the worst and does have fairly good performance characteristics.

- *Oracle Transaction Service, embedded in the Oracle Application Server*: This is a relatively new pure Java transaction service, based originally on the implementation from the Orion application server. However, coordination and recovery can be configured to utilize the robust transaction engine in the Oracle database.

- *WebSphere Transaction Service*: This is the transaction service utilized in most versions of the IBM application server. As we mentioned earlier, some versions of WebSphere can use CICS, but there is a cost to this type of configuration.

- *WebLogic Ttransaction Service*: Originally the transaction service used by BEAs application server was Tuxedo. However, over the last few years a new implementation has been developed and is now the mainstay of their application server product.

Open-Source Implementations

Surprisingly, there aren't as many open-source transaction services around as you might imagine. Most of them haven't been around for that long, nor do they have the transaction expertise behind them of companies such as IBM, BEA or Arjuna Technologies. As a result of their relative newness, deployments for these implementations may be hard to find. Probably as a result of the fact that they can't compete purely on pedigree, performance and reliability, most of the open-source implementations strive to be standards compliant and open. However, as we've mentioned many times already, you shouldn't be swayed by the fact that these systems may be free and forget to ask important questions like their record on distributed failure recovery, and so on.

Stand-alone Implementations

- *JOTM*: This transaction service is used within the ObjectWeb application server, but is also available in a stand-alone configuration. It currently is JTA-compliant, but does not support distributed transactions in a standard manner. An important omission is that the coordinator does not do logging, which as we saw in Chapter 1, "Transaction Fundamentals," affects recovery capabilities.
- *Tyrex*: Developed by Intalio, this is a widely embedded transaction service implementation. For example, Apple Corporation uses this system in their WebObjects application server. However, to the best of our knowledge, this project has finished and Tyrex is no longer being supported by the original developers. As with JOTM, it has poor fault tolerance and recovery capabilities.

Application Server Embedded Implementations

- *JBoss Transaction Manager*: This implementation is used by the open-source JBoss application server. It suffers from several limitations; for example, the current implementation does not support distributed transactions (although it is JTA compliant) and does not do logging.

Experiences of Choosing a Transaction Service

Over the years, we've been involved with transaction systems from the perspectives of both developing and deploying them. Through our professional careers we've also been closely involved with the experiences of other companies in this area. What we're going to attempt to do in this section is to condense many years of experience for you. However, for legal reasons we have to change the names of one or two companies.

Build versus Buy

Over the years, we have worked for companies that possessed transaction service implementations and were willing to license those implementations to others. As a result, we have been involved with trying to persuade other companies (ranging from pre-eminent ORB vendors and application server providers to end users) that did not have transaction services to license such implementations. On several occasions these have proven successful, but on others it hasn't and the reasons for the failures have never come down to being out-maneuvered by a competitor, but what is known as *build versus buy*: should the company build its own transaction service or buy one elsewhere. In the case of the failures, the reason has always been that the company has determined that building is in their best interests and how difficult can it be to implement a transaction service anyway?

On one occasion the company was a major ORB vendor (let's call them company XYZZY) that had licensed a transaction service written in C from another large software provider. Unfortunately, that transaction service under performed and was monolithic, making tailoring it to XYZZY's changing requirements more and more difficult. So the decision had been made to get another transaction service and that's where we came along. The transaction service implementation we had to offer was mature, reliable, performed well, and matched all of their requirements. XYZZY correctly identified the transaction service as being critical to their software offering and believed that as a result its development should be kept in-house. Their engineers had no real background in transactioning but believed that they could implement a system in approximately six months, despite the fact that the transaction system under offer to them had taken years to develop, debug and tune.

Unfortunately for XYZZY, despite having a lot of people and resources, they found throwing more engineers (who also didn't have a background in transaction system development) at the problem simply did not help. Over two years later they still did not have a new transaction service to offer their customers and they eventually terminated the project.

As we mentioned earlier, this isn't the only situation where developers underestimate the amount of effort required to build a good transaction service. For example, a marginal application server provider (let's call them GoldWater) had no transaction service and very little experience in the area. Furthermore, they had very few people to commit to the development. And yet their lead engineer still believed that implementing something comparable to that on offer would be possible in a matter of months. It took them nearly three years and the end result was still not perfect.

Unfortunately, simply being good developers is not sufficient. As you will hopefully be able to appreciate by now, there is a lot more to a transaction service than "just" a two-phase protocol. This isn't to say that if you are considering build versus buy you should always look at buying, but you should definitely not underestimate the amount of time and money it will take to implement your own. There are good reasons why the best transaction services have been around for many years and continue to be used in new applications and environments—providing something equivalent doesn't happen over night (and certainly takes more than six months).

Underestimating Your Requirements

There are several examples of companies that did not do their homework when choosing a transaction service and ultimately fell afoul of the smallprint. For example, on one occasion a national telecommunications company (we'll call them FP Telcom) purchased a transaction service that appeared to offer them everything they needed *at that time*. In fact, the implementation they purchased (let's call it Vulcan) was one of the most popular systems around and in many ways their choice made sense. Unfortunately, they didn't look closely enough at their own rapidly evolving requirements for transactions and the limitations that Vulcan had.

The first problem that FP Telcom ran into was cost. When they first started using transactions, they projected deployments of a transaction service on a few machines. The fact that Vulcan's vendor charged over $10,000 per CPU didn't really affect them. However, within a few years the initial projections proved inadequate and they were looking at hundreds and possibly thousands of deployments.

It was at this point that FP Telcom ran into their next hurdle: Vulcan was not open or standards-compliant and therefore FP Telecom's applications were closely tied to it. In order to swap out Vulcan, it was going to take a lot of time and effort to re-implement those applications.

Choosing the Right Implementation

For every company that makes the wrong choice of transaction service implementation, there are many more that do the necessary background work and get the right system for their immediate and future needs. For example, there was a large hospital chain in Asia that wanted to centralize all patient records in a series of databases and network all of their hospitals (over 2,000) so that they could share the records, as illustrated in Figure B-1.

All operations on the patient records had to be transactional, and it had to be possible to access a patient's record from anywhere in the country (and this is a large country). Although the basic architecture of the hospital system appears to be straightforward and any transaction service might do, the developers looked at the possibilities and the future requirements. They found that there was an eventual need to support nested transactions, e.g., there were long-running management routines that worked on multiple patient records that could be restructured as nested transactions, so that the failure of a nested transaction (operations on a patient's record) would not necessarily cause the entire top-level transaction to roll back.

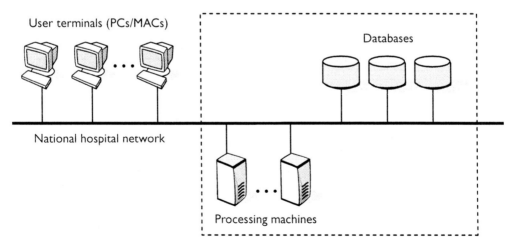

Figure B-1 The transactional hospital network.

With their current and future requirements in mind, the hospital chain eventually settled on the right transaction service implementation for them. In this case it was the Hewlett-Packard Transaction Service.

Down and Out

Although at the extreme, there is at least one example we know of where a company chose a transaction service implementation that eventually contributed to its downfall. This company was an emerging application server vendor who required a transaction service in order for them to be J2EE compliant. Because they had little money, they decided to look at the open-source offerings. Unfortunately for the company, their engineers had no transactions experience and believed the publicity for the open-source system they eventually chose (which, by the way, was not standards compliant). What they failed to realize was that the implementation had no QA, didn't support failure recovery, and had many more fundamental problems that resulted from the naivety of its original developers.

By the time these failings became apparent, the company had closely tied their application server to the transaction system, meaning they couldn't swap it out. They were also unable to provide the necessary support to new customers to try to rectify these problems—after all, their engineers' expertise lay elsewhere. Unfortunately, the end result was a lack of trust in the application server and the company, which eventually led to the loss of existing customers and, obviously, no new customers.

Summary

We've looked at the differences between commercial and open-source implementations and tried to give an objective analysis of what to look for when choosing a transaction service, or even implementing one. It's certainly not clear-cut that all commercial implementations are good and open-source implementations are bad. In both categories important features such as failure recovery are overlooked, and poorly performing implementations are quite common. It's at least as important to understand the background of the transaction service (its developers, whether it has been deployed before, any success stories, and so on) as it is to understand its capabilities. We hope we've given you enough information to help you choose (or implement) the right insurance policy for your applications. If you always think of a transaction service as an insurance policy, then it may help you to determine just how important it is to you. For example, how often do you go on vacation without suitable insurance protection? The temptation is always there to try to save some money by not getting insurance because "I've never claimed on it before." But you only have to be caught once to regret it and wonder whether the perceived savings was really worth it. Transactions and the integrity of your application data shouldn't be overlooked either.

A Brief History of Transaction Systems

n this appendix we briefly describe some of the more important transaction systems that exist and are relevant to J2EE. This is in no way meant to be a complete or in-depth list.

CICS

The CICS system from IBM is one of the first TP monitors and is still probably the most popular and widely used transaction implementation. It was developed in the mid-1960s for mainframe environments and is now at the heart of most of IBM's transactional offerings, including WebSphere. These days CICS systems run on most operating systems including Sun's Solaris, HP-UX, IBM's AIX and AS/400.

Tuxedo

AT&T Bell Laboratories originally developed the Tuxedo system in 1984, and it is BEA Systems' main transaction offering. The Tuxedo design is based on the Informational Management System (IMS) from IBM (which was originally developed in the late 1960s) and was originally intended to replace IMS. It was also heavily influential in the development of the X/Open DTP standards such as XA, TX and XATMI. It is heavily queue-oriented, with the notion of a distributed shared bulletin board where clients post transactional requests for services and the system maps (and routes) these requests and responses.

The Hewlett-Packard Transaction Service (HP-TS)

One of the first object-oriented transaction systems was Arjuna, originally developed in 1987 using C++ by the Arjuna Group within the University of Newcastle upon Tyne, England. It later became the basis of the HP-Transaction Service, the world's first 100% pure Java transaction service implementation. The HP-TS supports nested transactions, runs on a number of different ORBs and includes an integrated toolkit for the construction of transactional applications (*Transactional Objects for Java*) that is essentially a superset of the EJB functionality.

Encina

Encina began life in the early 1990s, when researchers at Carnegie Mellon University who had worked on the Camelot/Avalon project decided to commercialize their ideas and set up Transaction Corporation. It is a multi-platform transaction system that was originally implemented to use the Distributed Computing Environment (DCE) to provide scalability and high performance. However, when CORBA became the dominant technology in the area of distributed object systems, Encina was quickly moved to also support it. Encina has been licensed to IONA Technologies for use in their OrbixOTM product. Transarc was eventually acquired by IBM.

X/Open

X/Open is part of The Open Group Incorporated, whose goals are to promote application portability through the development of API standards. In 1991, it developed a distributed transaction processing model, which includes many of the features offered by traditional TP monitors. The model divides a transaction processing system into components: the transaction manager, the database or other resource manager, and the transactional communications manager, with interfaces between them all as shown in Figure C-1. It is of particular importance to us as it forms the basis of the JTA. We covered this in more detail in Chapter 2, but briefly the main actors are:

- *Transaction manager*: The TM is what you would expect—the transaction coordinator and its associated systems. The X/Open specification does not support nested transactions.
- *Communications resource manager*: The CRM provides an API to a communications system that can be used for distributed transactional systems (essentially a means of performing transactional RPCs).
- *Resource manager*: The RM represents the transactional participants, including databases, messaging queues, file systems, and so on.
- *XA*: This defines the interface between the RM and the TM. Most transaction processing systems and major databases support XA.
- *XA+*: This is a superset of XA and allows the CRM to inform the TM when new machines join a distributed transaction.
- *TX*: This defines a transaction demarcation API and allows applications to inquire as to the status of transactions.

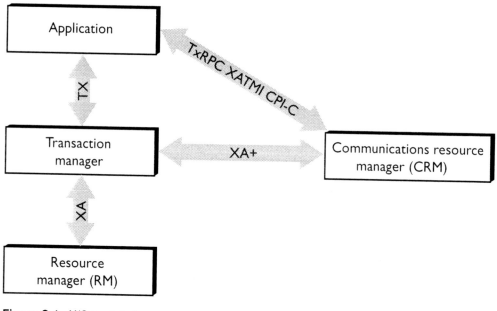

Figure C-1 X/Open interfaces.

The Object Transaction Service (OTS)

The most widely accepted standard for distributed objects is the Common Object Request Broker Architecture (CORBA) from the Object Management Group (OMG). It consists of the Object Request Broker (ORB) that enables distributed objects to interact with each other, and a number of services have also been specified, which include persistence, concurrency control and the Object Transaction Service, which was released in 1992.

The OTS does not require all objects to have transactional behavior. Instead objects can choose not to support transactional operations at all, or to support it for some requests but not others. The transaction service specification distinguishes between *recoverable objects* and *transactional objects*. Recoverable objects are those that contain the actual state that may be changed by a transaction and must, therefore, be informed when the transaction commits or aborts to ensure the consistency of the state changes. In contrast, a simple transactional object need not necessarily be a recoverable object if its state is actually implemented using other recoverable objects. The major difference is that a simple transactional object need not take part in the commit protocol used to determine the outcome of the transaction since it does not maintain any state itself, having delegated that responsibility to other recoverable objects that will take part in the commit process.

Glossary of Terms

The following is a list of definitions that will prove helpful during the reading of this book.

A

ACID: acronym describing the properties of top-level transactions: Atomicity, Consistency, Isolation, Durability.

Active replication: replication protocol in which all replicas receive the same set of invocations, perform the work and return the same result.

Activity Service: a CORBA-based framework for supporting extended transaction models defined by the Object Management Group.

Application program: computer instructions that manage the demarcation of transactions and actually specify the operations within the scope of the transaction.

Atom: one of the extended transaction models supported by OASIS Business Transactions Protocol—allows atomic outcomes.

Atomicity: transaction property that dictates that a given transaction completes successfully (commits) or if it fails (aborts) all of its effects are undone (rolled back).

B

Business activity: the extended transaction model defined by Web Services Transaction (WS-T) allowing long-running transactions with compensations.

Business Process Transaction: one of the extended transaction models defined by the OASIS Web Services Transaction Management (WS-TXM) specification for combining multiple transaction protocols in a single business process flow.

Business Transaction Protocol (BTP): an XML-based transaction protocol from OASIS; not Web services-specific.

C

Checked transactions: process whereby the transaction system ensures all outstanding work occurring within a transaction has completed prior to its termination.

Closed-top commit: Business Transactions Protocol (BTP) term for traditional transaction system approach to two-phase commit where applications only call commit or rollback and only the coordinator sees the actual phases of the termination protocol.

Cohesion: one of the extended transaction models supported by OASIS Business Transactions Protocol—allows non-atomic outcomes across participants.

Commit: successful completion of the transaction.

Common Object Request Broker Architecture (CORBA): an Object Management Group (OMG) specification that provides interface definitions for application interoperability independent of platforms, operating systems, programming languages, and network protocols.

Consistency: transaction property indicating a valid state. In general, it is the responsibility of the application to respect application-specific invariants.

Context: used in a distributed transaction to represent the transaction (hierarchy) when flowing information between remote entities.

Coordinator: in traditional transaction systems, the component responsible for driving the completion protocol.

D

Direct transaction management: the user takes all responsibility for creating transactions and managing the thread-to-transaction association.

Distributed transaction: transaction that spans multiple address-space boundaries.

Durability: transaction property that guarantees the effects of a committed transaction are never lost (except by a catastrophic failure).

E

Enterprise Information Systems (EIS): provide an information infrastructure for an enterprise and are accessed via local or remote client interfaces. Examples are ERP or database systems.

Enterprise JavaBeans (EJB): transactional component framework for the Java 2, Enterprise Edition (J2EE) platform.

Explicit context propagation: transaction context is transmitted as an extra parameter on remote calls.

Extended transaction: transaction that relaxes the traditional ACID properties.

F

Failure recovery: component responsible for driving transaction completion in the event of a failure.

H

Heuristic outcome: non-atomic outcome, generally the result of administrative intervention to resolve a transaction branch that has been in doubt for an extended period.

I

Implicit context propagation: transaction context is transmitted on remote calls transparently.

Indirect transaction management: transaction system takes responsibility for managing the thread-to-transaction association. This is the model used in J2EE.

Interposition: process whereby a remote transaction is imported to a domain and a proxy (subordinate) coordinator is created locally to that domain to represent the remote transaction. All transaction use within the importing domain occurs on the subordinate coordinator.

Isolation: transaction property indicating that intermediate states produced while a transaction is executing are not visible to others. Furthermore, transactions appear to execute *serially*, even if they are actually executed concurrently.

J

Java 2, Enterprise Edition (J2EE): de facto standard platform for the creation of distributed, transactional, and secure enterprise applications. J2EE is based on the Java programming language.

Java API for XML Transactions (JAXTX): defines the J2EE APIs for Web services transactions.

Java Message Service (JMS): specification that defines APIs for the Java programming language to access message-oriented middleware systems.

Java Transaction API (JTA): Maps the Open Group TX and XA specifications to the Java programming environment. JTA is the foundation for transactions in J2EE.

Java Transaction Service (JTS): provides the Java language mapping of the OMG Object Transaction Service.

JDBC: API for accessing tabular data sources from the Java programming language. Most often this API is used to access relational databases.

L

Last resource commit: optimization in which a resource manager that supports only local transactions can be included in a global transaction.

Local transaction: transaction that is created and committed against a single resource manager.

Long Running Actions: one of the extended transaction models defined by the OASIS Web Services Transaction Management (WS-TXM) specification for long-running transactions with compensations.

M

Message-oriented middleware (MOM): system software that supports non-blocking message exchange between applications.

N

Nested transaction: transaction that is a child of another transaction (forming a hierarchy). Does not possess all ACID properties. Permanence of effect occurs only when all enclosing transactions commit.

O

Object Management Group (OMG): organization responsible for establishing guidelines and specifications for a common object-based application development framework.

Object Transaction Service (OTS): OMG transaction protocol used to achieve interoperability across transaction service implementations and languages.

One-phase commit: optimization to the two-phase commit protocol when there is only one participant. The prepare phase is skipped.

Organization for the Advancement of Structured Information Standards (OASIS): global consortium that drives the development and adoption of e-business standards.

Open Nested Transactions: an extended transaction model that relaxes the isolation property. The model allows changes made in committed, nested transactions to be visible to other transactions. The model requires compensators.

Open-top commit: Business Transactions Protocol (BTP) term for protocols that allow applications to drive both phases of a two-phase protocol explicitly.

Optimistic concurrency control: locking strategy that assumes data collisions occur infrequently.

P

Participant: software entity enrolled within a transaction in order to receive coordination signals.

Passive replication: replication strategy in which only one replica performs work and checkpoints its state to the other replicas.

Pessimistic concurrency control: locking strategy that assumes data collisions are common.

Presumed abort: optimization to the two-phase commit protocol that allows the coordinator to save information to the log only if it decides to commit.

Q

Qualifier: used by Web Services Composite Application Framework (WS-CAF) and Business Transactions Protocol (BTP) specifications to allow extra information to be communicated in the protocol at runtime.

R

Read-only: optimization to the two-phase commit protocol that allows the coordinator to ignore a participant that has not done work in the scope of the transaction—typically this is communicated to the coordinator during the prepare phase.

Remote Procedure Call (RPC): a protocol that allows a program running on one host to execute code running on another host by executing synchronous operations on a local proxy.

Resource Manager (RM): provides client applications with access to shared resources A database server is a familiar example of a resource manager.

Rollback: termination of the transaction such that all work is undone.

S

Sagas: a pioneering extended transaction model that relied on compensating transactions to undo completed work.

Serializability: condition in which the effect of interleaving the work of two transactions is equivalent to the serial execution of the same transactions.

Synchronization: protocol used on to signal a participant before and after the two-phase commit process. Typically used to flush cached data to disc prior to the commit phase.

T

Top-level transaction: traditional ACID transaction, which does not have a parent transaction.

Transactional object: business logic that does work for the application required to be under the control of a transaction.

Transaction log: store used to durably record the decisions of a coordinator.

Transaction manager (TM): service that provides functions required to identify, monitor, and complete.

Two-phase commit: protocol used by the coordinator to obtain consensus between multiple participants. It consists of two phases, a voting phase and a commit phase.

W

Web Service Composite Application Framework (WS-CAF): umbrella term used to group the three OASIS specifications related to transactions: WS-Context, WS-Coordination Framework, and WS-Transaction Management.

Web Service Coordination (WS-C): vendor proprietary Web services-based specification defining service enlistment for coordination events and a coordination context.

Web Service Coordination Framework (WS-CF): OASIS specification based on WS-Context for enlisting services for coordination events and recovery.

Web Service Context (WS-Context): OASIS specification defining a generic model for sessions and contexts.

Web Service Transaction (WS-T): vendor proprietary Web services-based transaction specification based on WS-C. WS-T defines atomic and long running transaction models.

Web Service Transaction Management (WS-TXM): OASIS specification defining three transaction protocols: ACID, Long-Running action, and Business Process Management. WS-TXM is based on WS-Context and WS-CF.

Workflow: automation of business processes that involve jobs or messages being passed from one system to another based on predefined rules.

X

X/Open: an important transaction standard from the Open Group, implemented by most transactional resource managers. This standard forms the basis of the Java Transaction API.

INDEX